BARRON'S
BUSINESS
REVIEW
SERIES

International Marketing

Richard L. Sandhusen

Barron's Educational Series, Inc.

All inquiries should be addressed to:
Barron's Educational Series, Inc.
250 Wireless Boulevard
Hauppauge, New York 11788

Library of Congress Catalog Card No. 97-1489

International Standard Book No. 0-8120-9432-8

Library of Congress Cataloging-in-Publication Data

Sandhusen, Richard.
    International marketing / Richard L. Sandhusen.
        p.   cm. — (Barron's business review series)
    Includes index.
    ISBN 0-8120-9432-8
    1. Export marketing.   I. Title   II. Series.
HF1416.S263   1997
658.8′48—dc21   97-1489
                                                                   CIP

PRINTED IN THE UNITED STATES OF AMERICA

9 8 7 6 5 4 3 2

CONTENTS

7 ECONOMIC INFLUENCES ON INTERNATIONAL MARKETS

8 CULTURAL INFLUENCES ON INTERNATIONAL MARKETS

9 PROSPECTS AND OPPORTUNITIES IN INTERNATIONAL MARKETS

12 MEASURING INTERNATIONAL MARKET AND SALES POTENTIAL

13 INTERNATIONAL PRODUCT PLANNING I: PRODUCT/MARKET GROWTH STRATEGIES

14 INTERNATIONAL PRODUCT PLANNING II: PRODUCT DESIGN AND DEVELOPMENT STRATEGIES

17 INTERNATIONAL PROMOTION PLANNING

18 INTERNATIONAL DISTRIBUTION PLANNING I: DISTRIBUTION CHANNEL STRATEGY

PREFACE

As the world spins into the first decade of the twenty-first century, dramatic changes continue to create unprecedented opportunities and incentives for global trade. Highlights include the renewal of fallen communist command economies, the continuing spread of competitive free markets, technological breakthroughs that create better ways to make and market new products and services, and a growing global commitment to the importance of free trade in generating the productivity and purchasing power that drive global prosperity.

Developing and developed nations are responding to these changes in manifold ways, by privatizing state industries, slashing deficits and inflation rates, adopting diverse economic reforms, and merging into regional and global communities designed to grow markets by expanding productivity and toppling restrictive trade barriers.

Ironically, the United States, the prime mover in creating the technological, economic, political, and competitive conditions for expanding world trade, has hardly been an aggressive player in this game. Some statistics tell the story: fewer than 500 companies (the Fords, Boeings and Coca-Colas) are responsible for more than 85 percent of our exports, and even among major brands, more than 85 percent of revenues are generated in the domestic or Canadian market. Among small- and medium-sized companies, only one in five in a position to profitably export products actually does so.

One upshot of this sluggish participation in the trade game is the loss of our competitive advantage in world markets to countries like Germany and Japan that export a much larger proportion of their gross domestic product than we do. Another consequence is a monstrous annual trade deficit sufficient to transform history's largest creditor nation into its largest debtor nation in less than a decade.

Reasons for this lack of robust participation by U.S. firms in international markets—in addition to the size, safety and stability of the home market—pertain to concerns among U.S. firms over ways to successfully identify foreign market opportunities, and over risks implicit in attempting to exploit these opportunities.

This book is designed to address these concerns by providing students in international marketing courses and managers of companies surveying global opportunities with conceptual and analytical tools needed to successfully market goods and services in the international marketplace.

• *UNDERSTANDING MARKETING CONCEPTS IN GLOBAL MARKETS*

In content, style, and structure, the goal of this book is to create a stimulating learning environment and provide a concise, clear, comprehensive understanding of marketing concepts, problems, practices, and applications in global markets. For these reasons, it embodies the following characteristics:

1. **It is comprehensive.** A content analysis of international marketing texts confirms that there is little in these texts not found in this book. Beyond this core content, the book also covers the following areas of special importance:

   • How basic concepts pertaining to marketing mixes, functions, and philosophies; target marketing; and strategic marketing planning are modified to conform to the nature and needs of global markets.

   • How integrated systems for organizing, planning, implementing and controlling strategic marketing initiatives apply in global markets.

   • How political, economic, technological, cultural, and competitive climates in global markets create threats or opportunities for strategic marketing initiatives.

   • How modern marketing research tools and techniques help identify and solve marketing problems, segment markets, and measure potential in the international marketplace.

   • How global logistics concepts pertaining to total costs and total systems help optimize efficiencies and economies of order processing, inventory management, storage and transportation functions.

2. **It is concise.** Style, format, and structure combine to create an extremely efficient vehicle for quickly and clearly conveying information. As to style *International Marketing* is written in a tight, active journalistic style, not labored academese. As to format, each chapter focuses on aspects of a single master case (Merton Electronics) specifically designed to illustrate the application of marketing concepts in global markets. Supplementing this master case are cases involving product/service challenges in global markets contained in "Global Focus" chapter features, and cases in end-of-chapter exercises that challenge the student's ability to apply marketing concepts in analyzing and solving global marketing problems.

Each chapter begins with an overview summary of chapter content, and concludes with a chapter perspective summary of key concepts covered.

3. **It is current.** Although footnote references are kept to a minimum, most of them are recent, reflecting the contemporary orientation of text content.

• *CHAPTER CONTENT AND SEQUENCE*

As to structure, chapter content is sequenced in terms of the logic of the strategic marketing planning process as follows:

- The first two chapters lay a foundation for what is to come by discussing the nature and dynamics of global trade (Chapter 1), defining basic marketing concepts as they apply in international markets, and examining the role of the international marketing manager in formulating and implementing strategic marketing plans (Chapter 2).

- The next three chapters focus on integrated company systems through which marketing plans and programs are carried out, including systems for organizing, planning, and controlling marketing programs (Chapter 3), and the marketing information system, with its marketing research input, that underpins the entire strategic marketing planning process in international markets (Chapters 4 and 5).

- The next four chapters focus on the nature and scope of environmental influences affecting global marketing planning, and tools and techniques for identifying and measuring the impact of these influences. Chapter 6 focuses on major areas of concern in assessing political/legal climates that define welcoming or hostile political environments; Chapter 7 covers economic criteria that define the likelihood of successfully entering and growing in international markets; and Chapter 8 discusses significant cultural characteristics that predispose people and groups to purchase products and services. Chapter 9 integrates key concepts from the 3 previous chapters with an examination of how they combine to define threats and opportunities in key global markets in Asia, Europe, and the Americas.

- Chapters 10 through 12 focus on another important stage of the strategic marketing planning process: identifying and defining targeted global behaviors that help define international consumer and organizational markets. Chapter 10 defines these markets; Chapter 11 covers approaches for segmenting them and formulating strategies for favorably positioning competitive offerings; and Chapter 12 discusses approaches for measuring market and sales potential in international markets.

- Chapters 13 through 19 focus on components of the global marketing mix designed to meet target market needs and achieve company business and marketing objectives. Chapters 13 and 14 examine product management decisions, including branding, packaging, labeling, developing new products and services, and using the product-services spectrum and product life cycles to formulate global products/market strategies.

- Chapters 15 and 16 focus on pricing problems, objectives, strategies, and tactics characterizing international markets. Chapter 17 focuses on direct and indirect promotional activities, and how they are affected by unique needs and constraints in global markets. Chapters 18 and 19 focus on the "place" element of the international marketing mix, including channel types, functions and flows in global markets, and global logistics concepts pertaining to transporting, storing, and distributing products in international markets.

Richard Sandhusen
January, 1997

1

THE INTERNATIONAL MARKET: FORCES AND STRATEGIES

OVERVIEW

This chapter examines reasons for the burgeoning growth of world trade and the general lack of U.S. participation in this growth; benefits and difficulties, for countries and companies, from participating in world trade; international entry/growth strategies appropriate to different situations; and trends that will shape global market threats and opportunities.

WHY INTERNATIONAL TRADE GROWS

Beginning in the second half of the twentieth century, international trade—the exchange of goods and services among countries—became the fastest growing sector of the world economy, increasing from less than $200 billion to more than $4 trillion between 1975 and 1995.

The following interrelated conditions facilitated this growth.

• *LONG PERIODS OF GLOBAL PEACE*

In contrast to the first half of the twentieth century, when much of the substance of advanced countries was diverted toward military adventures, the second half was largely characterized by localized conflicts among less developed countries, leaving a stable foundation for healthy, rapid growth of the global economy. Global economic growth, in turn, is a potent imperative to peace, as countries, through open trading relationships, create the wealth, productivity, and living standards that substitute for the goals of aggression.

• *TECHNOLOGICAL BREAKTHROUGHS*

Ironically, the wars that diverted resources from peaceful trading pursuits before midcentury were largely responsible for technological breakthroughs that fueled trade after midcentury. Particularly in the fields of power, communication, and transportation (e.g., jet aircraft, electronic data transmission, television), these breakthroughs created products to trade, processes to make them, and the means to market them in geographically dispersed areas. To quote Levitt:

> Technology has created a new commercial reality . . . the emergence of global markets for standardized consumer products on a previously unimagined scale . . . Almost everyone, everywhere, wants all the things they've heard about, seen, or experienced via the new technology.[1]

• *INTERNATIONAL TRADING AGREEMENTS*

If peace and technology were largely responsible for creating an environment in which international trade could flourish, a common commitment among nations to avoid restrictive trade practices and foster global economic growth was largely responsible for creating agreements to enhance the free flow of goods and services among nations. Examples of these agreements include the General Agreement on Tariffs and Trade (GATT), the International Monetary Fund (IMF), and the World Bank. GATT provides principles and procedures for reducing tariffs and liberalizing trade, such as the most-favored nation principle whereby each signatory country extends to all countries its most favorable trade terms.

The IMF creates multinational reserve assets that member nations can draw upon for financial support. These assets are usually drawn upon by developing countries with severe balance-of-payments problems, in return for which they are usually expected to make politically unpopular concessions. For example, when the exchange value of the Mexican peso fell by almost half in 1995—reducing living standards and leaving many businesses near ruin—the price of a new line of credit from the United States Treasury and the IMF was a draconian economic program guaranteed to ensure recessive conditions.

The World Bank, initially formed in 1944 to aid countries suffering from the destruction of war, tends to take a more active role than the IMF in helping countries modify basic economic policies in return for aid. This aid usually focuses on infrastructure development such as transportation, communication, and power. More recently, the bank has worked with the IMF to resolve debt problems in the developing world, including playing an active role in bringing market economies to former communist bloc countries.

---

[1] Theodore Levitt, "The Globalization of Markets," *Harvard Business Review* (May–June 1983), p. 92.

THE ROLE OF THE UNITED STATES IN INTERNATIONAL TRADE

As the main initiator of technological innovation and agreements to enhance free trade among nations, the role of the United States as a player in international markets hardly seems to have approached its potential.

Figure 1-1 and Tables 1-1, 1-2, and 1-3 focus on the U.S. role in international markets in the context of past trends and future prospects.

Figure 1-1 compares relative share of world exports and imports of key trading countries. Note that, among these countries, the United States imported about 16 percent of all the world's goods and services, while exporting about 12 percent, leaving a trade deficit—the amount by which imports exceed exports—of about $130 billion. At the other extreme, Japan, which exported about 10 percent of the world's goods and services while importing only about 7 percent, generated a trade surplus of about $100 billion. The United States has the lowest exports per capita ($1,816) among major industrialized nations, amounting to about one third of Germany's per capita figure ($5,334) and considerably less than figures for Canada ($4,898), France ($4,111), the United Kingdom ($3,284), and Japan ($2,734). Although U.S. imports per capita ($2,270) were also relatively low, they exceed exports, thus creating the trade deficit.

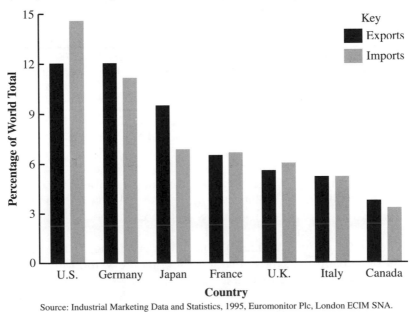

Source: Industrial Marketing Data and Statistics, 1995, Euromonitor Plc, London ECIM SNA.

Figure 1-1. Merchandise Exports and Imports as a Percentage of World Total

Measured as a share of its Gross Domestic Product (GDP), U.S. exports, at 7.3 percent (Table 1-1) pale in comparison to countries like Canada (26 percent), Germany (20 percent), the United Kingdom (19 percent), and France (17 percent). Japan, often maligned as the problem child of international trade, exported only 8.3 percent of its GDP in 1994.

Table 1–1. Merchandise Exports as a Percentage of Gross National Product

Period	United States	France	Germany	Italy	Nether-lands	United Kingdom	Japan	Canada
1980	8.1	17.5	23.6	17.1	43.7	20.5	12.2	24.6
1981	7.7	18.2	25.7	18.4	48.5	19.8	13.0	23.5
1982	6.7	17.5	26.8	18.2	48.0	20.0	12.8	22.6
1983	5.9	18.0	25.7	17.5	48.3	19.9	12.4	22.3
1984	5.8	19.5	27.6	17.7	52.4	21.6	13.5	27.1
1985	5.3	19.3	29.1	18.4	53.7	22.0	13.2	26.5
1986	5.1	17.2	27.1	16.1	45.4	18.8	10.7	25.7
1987	5.4	16.8	26.3	15.4	43.7	18.8	9.5	24.3
1988	6.6	17.4	26.9	15.3	45.6	17.3	9.1	24.5
1989	7.0	18.6	28.6	16.3	48.0	18.2	9.5	22.7
1990	7.2	18.2	27.2	15.8	47.0	18.8	9.7	22.8
1991	7.4	18.1	23.6	14.7	45.6	18.3	9.3	21.5
1992	7.4	17.8	22.2	14.5	43.7	18.2	9.2	23.6
1993	7.2	16.4	19.9	16.4	n.a.	19.4	8.6	25.9
1994	7.3	17.0	20.0	16.4	n.a.	19.0	8.3	26.0

Sources: Various 1994 editions of OECD Main Economic Indicators, January 1994; Deutsche Bundesbank; Wirtschaft und Statistik; Information Rapides; U.S. Bureau of the Census; and London Telegram.

HOW WE GROW OUR DEFICITS

Table 1-2 depicts trade patterns among the United States and its major trading partners in 1994. Note Japan's contribution to the total U.S. trade deficit of $104 billion: $60 billion, or more than half, on imports to us of $112 billion versus exports from us of only $52 billion. Other countries contributing to this out-sized deficit include China ($21 billion), Canada ($11 billion), Germany ($9 billion), and newly emerging East Asian countries ($8 billion). Among these major trading partners, the only countries with which the United States had a trade surplus in 1994 were the United Kingdom and Mexico. (In 1995, the surplus with Mexico became another deficit as the peso plummeted.)

**Table 1–2. Trade Patterns Among the United States
and Major Trading Partners**

	Exports to			Imports From			Balance		
	1992	1993	1994	1992	1993	1994	1992	1993	1994
Canada	91	100	104	98	111	115	–7	–11	–11
Japan	48	48	52	97	107	112	–49	–59	–60
European Union	103	97	103	94	98	101	9	–1	2
Germany	21	19	19	29	29	28	–8	–10	–9
United Kingdom	23	26	30	20	22	22	3	4	8
Mexico	41	42	47	35	40	45	6	2	2
East Asia	49	53	55	62	65	63	–13	–12	–8
Taiwan	15	16	17	25	25	24	–10	–9	–7
China	7	9	9	26	32	30	–19	–23	–21

Source: U.S. Bureau of the Census, *Statistical Abstract of the United States: 1995* (115th edition) Washington, DC, 1995.

Table 1-3 examines the 1994 U.S. trade deficit in terms of major end-use categories. Note that three of these categories—consumer goods, automotive, and industrial materials—generated a $168 billion deficit, a deficit one-and-a-half times as large as the actual deficit. Major categories counterbalancing this deficit included capital goods, with a $24 billion surplus; foods and beverages, producing a $10 billion surplus; and, largest of all, services, which generated a surplus of exports over imports of $55 billion.

Table 1–3. Trade Balances by End-Use Category

	Exports			Imports			Balance		
	1992	1993	1994	1992	1993	1994	1992	1993	1994
Foods and beverages	40	40	40	28	28	30	12	12	10
Industrial materials	109	112	113	138	145	146	–29	–33	–33
Capital goods	177	183	195	134	153	171	43	30	24
Automotive	47	52	55	92	102	108	–45	–51	–53
Consumer goods	50	53	55	123	134	138	–73	–81	–82
Services	180	187	191	123	131	136	56	56	55

Source: U.S. Bureau of the Census, *Statistical Abstract of the United States: 1995* (115th edition) Washington, DC, 1995.

HOW WE LOSE COMPETITIVE EDGE

Viewing the current U.S. role in world trade in its historical context, we see a country that is losing its competitive edge to most of our developed nation trading partners, who import much less from us than we import from them. This loss is the culmination of a long-time trend, which saw the U.S. share of world exports decline from 25 percent in the mid-fifties to 12 percent today. During the last decade, the U.S. trade deficit passed the trillion dollar mark, transforming history's largest creditor nation into its largest debtor nation. This shift in financial flows, and the subsequent buildup of U.S. debt, has had a diversity of adverse effects, such as weakening the international value of the dollar and triggering many foreign direct investment activities. For example, currently, more than one third of U.S. employees in the chemical industry work for foreign owners, many of the office buildings Americans work in are owned by foreign landlords, and countries like Japan and Germany now hold a sufficient amount of our debt to influence both debt structure and American firms' capability to expand.

Reducing the U.S. trade deficit through increased participation in export markets can have a direct, positive influence on the U.S. economy. In 1994 merchandise exports accounted for more than seven million jobs in the United States, and every billion dollar increase in exports creates about 20,000 new jobs, which, on average, pay more than domestic jobs.

That the United States is capable of greater participation in international markets is documented by Commerce Department figures showing that, while more than 100,000 U.S. firms were engaged in some level of exporting in 1994, fewer than 300 of them—led by global giants like General Motors, IBM, Ford, Boeing, and General Electric—accounted for about 85 percent of U.S. exports.

Statistics from the General Accounting Office further document the comparative lack of participation by U.S. firms in international markets. During the entire decade of the 1980s, for example, while foreign direct investment in the United States soared 616 percent, U.S. outbound investment rose just 9.9 percent; only one in five U.S. companies positioned to export actually did so.

One reason for this dramatic imbalance in international investment derives from differences in opportunities among nations. For example, the United States, with its relative affluence, stable political climate, and strong commitment to free trade, represents a much more attractive opportunity for foreign investment than many other countries represent for us. Many third world nations, with more than half the world's population, simply don't have the capacity to absorb enough of our output to qualify as profitable markets. Also, entry barriers effectively close many foreign markets to U.S. exports. (Barriers to entry and export are covered in Chapter 6.)

Other reasons for the comparative lack of U.S. participation in international markets include high labor costs, which often make U.S. products less competitive; the decision of U.S. firms to virtually abdicate such markets as televisions and VCRs; and an overall mindset among American policymakers that the United States, as the leading country in world power and world trade, should assist other countries with their trade performance, with less attention paid to cultivating export markets for U.S. firms. For example, the U.S. budget for nonagricultural export assistance, at 0.03 per $1,000 of GDP, is exceeded by all of its major trading partners.

Perhaps the main reason, however, derives from a complacent satisfaction with the depth and size of the domestic market, which is capable of satisfying consumer wants and national needs with a minimum of reliance on foreign trade. This perception keeps many U.S. managers blissfully ignorant of foreign markets, while the U.S. education establishment generally assigns low priority to knowledge of global environments, languages, and cultures or of approaches for exploiting international business opportunities.

BENEFITS OF ENTERING FOREIGN MARKETS

Conditions favoring growth of world trade have combined to reinforce among nations the realization that trade holds the promise of better societies, improved living standards, and even a more peaceful world.

These conditions also help individual companies realize the following more focused benefits of participation in international markets.

• *EXPLOIT COMPARATIVE ADVANTAGE*

One reason why companies—and countries—frequently gain from trade in foreign markets has to do with the theory of comparative advantage, meaning that they exchange goods and services in which they have a relative advantage (e.g., better resources, specialization, mechanization, or climate) for those in which they are at a relative disadvantage. For example, some foreign producers have a comparative advantage vis-à-vis U.S. firms in producing footwear, which involves labor-intensive processes that favor low-wage countries. The United States, on the other hand, has a comparative advantage in the production of goods that have a high ratio of capital to labor, such as jet airliners, healthcare services, communication satellites, and power generation equipment. The availability of inexpensive imports (e.g., shoes and clothing), the theory states, enhances living standards of U.S. citizens and shifts capital and labor used in these labor-intensive industries to produce products (e.g., cars, computers, housing) we are good at producing.

On the basis of the preceding example, one might expect that greater dissimilarities among countries would lead to more trade among them (e.g., capital-intensive producers exchanging products with labor-intensive producers). In actual fact, most world trade occurs among similar countries, that is, industrialized nations with highly educated populations located in temperate zones. The theory of acquired advantage helps explain this phenomenon. Specifically, having developed a product in response to observed needs in its domestic market, a producer will turn to foreign markets perceived to be most similar to these markets. However, while countries that trade most with each other tend to be similar in terms of economic, political, and technological sophistication, they differ in how they specialize to gain acquired advantage. As examples, the British have an advantage in biochemistry, the French in pharmacology, and the Germans in synthetics, all acquired through technology rather than natural resources.

• *INCREASE SALES*

Since there are more people with greater total purchasing power in the world as a whole than in a single domestic market, companies can increase sales by successfully penetrating international markets. Often, these markets are more receptive to the product than the domestic market. For example, during downturns in the domestic business cycle, foreign markets are often unaffected because of time lags, offering excellent outlets for excess inventories and opportunities to utilize productive capacity fully. Global Focus 1-1 shows how global entry initiatives helped pull three U.S. firms out of the domestic doldrums.

GLOBAL FOCUS 1-1

Exports as a Hedge Against Flat U.S. Market

Exports enable many U.S. firms to maintain and increase their overall sales when the American market is flat.

- "In the late 1980s, we made a decision to expand into the international marketplace as a hedge against the domestic economic downturn," reported Harold Adams, president of RTKL Associates, Inc., of Baltimore. The architectural/engineering company cranked up to export its services six years ago. Since that time, it has performed work in more than 40 countries.

- Finding the U.S. domestic housing market slow, New England Homes, Inc., of Hamden, Conn., began exporting homes. Peter M. Hart, the company's senior vice president, said, "Home builders and manufacturers of home elements who want to break out of the housing doldrums should consider building and exporting residences to areas of the world experiencing a housing crisis." The firm is off to a good start in Israel and Japan and is exploring additional foreign markets.

- A company official of C.R. Onsrud, Inc., of Troutman, N.C., a manufacturer of woodworking machinery, told the Commerce Department, "One very important lesson we have learned; the broader your sales base the less a recession in the United States will affect you." In a recent year, increased exports enabled the firm to show a profit, even though U.S. sales volume was down one-third.

Source: *Business America*, U.S. Department of Commerce, Washington, DC, *World Trade Week*, Vol. 114, No. 9 (1993), p. 7.

Furthermore, the fact that most fixed costs can be captured in the domestic market often means that the firm can penetrate a foreign market with a competitive pricing policy that focuses mainly on variable costs. (The behavior of costs in formulating pricing strategies, as well as risks and opportunities implicit in these strategies, are covered in more detail in Chapter 15.)

• *LEVERAGE STRENGTHS*

As companies successfully enter foreign markets, "leverage" benefits accrue from company resources and market resources. Thus, larger international markets multiply the effectiveness of whatever company resources—a unique product, management expertise, access to natural resources, exclusive marketing information, etc.—helped the firm succeed in the domestic marketplace. After the company has successfully penetrated international markets, it can apply strategies, systems, sources of labor, materials, or funds that prove successful in one country's market to other countries. For example, a global manufacturer of consumer electronics planning the development of a new product line might find that low interest rates and a stable currency suggest the United States as the best source of financing, technological expertise suggests India as the best locale for engineering these products, and wage rates and worker skills suggest Mexico as the best site for assembling these products. Some indication of the extent to which expanded international operations can enhance a firm's competitive posture in all markets is offered in a study by the Boston Consulting Group, which found that economies of scale and shortened learning curves resulting when production is doubled through global expansion can reduce production costs up to 30 percent, creating cost and price reductions that can be passed on to customers in all markets.

• *ACHIEVE A COMPETITIVE EDGE*

A firm that successfully penetrates international markets poses two competitive threats to firms left behind: These stay-at-homes (1) will lose market share to leverage benefits generated by the firm's international marketing activities and (2) will lose a future opportunity to enter and grow in foreign markets now occupied by early-bird competitors. For example, in spite of its recognized technological expertise, the United States has become noncompetitive in its own domestic market against Pacific rim countries that got a head start in marketing video recorders, television sets, and other consumer electronics products in global markets.

• *ACHIEVE TAX ADVANTAGES*

Many countries entice businesses by offering incentives in the form of reduced property, import, and income taxes for an initial time period. Multinational firms may also adjust revenue reports, or operations, so the largest profits are recorded in countries with low tax rates (often a risky strategy, as discussed in Chapter 15).

In the United States, a tax mechanism called the Foreign Sales Corporation (FSC) has been set up, according to strict IRS guidelines and in conformity with international agreements, to make international marketing activities potentially more profitable by providing firms with certain tax deferrals. For example, if a firm's foreign subsidiary qualifies for an FSC, a portion of its income is exempt from U.S. corporate income tax.

• *PROLONG PRODUCT LIFE*

Often, exporting provides a second life to products and services that are no longer competitive in home markets; for example, Asia represents a booming market for vintage U.S. "B" motion pictures.

• *INCREASE PROFITS*

Through leverage, tax, and competitive advantages, overseas strategies of American companies can produce profits well in excess of domestic markets. For example, whereas American automobile firms suffered huge profit losses in the domestic market in the mid-1980s, their European operations remained largely profitable. In 1991 Coca-Cola's foreign profits, as a percent of total profits, was 56 percent, while its foreign revenues as a percent of total revenues was only 38 percent. Other large firms whose profits from overseas markets exceed those of domestic markets include Michelin from France, Sony from Japan, Philips from the Netherlands, and BASF from Germany.

DIFFICULTIES IN ENTERING FOREIGN MARKETS

Offsetting these prospective advantages, a company also faces a number of environmental hurdles in attempting to enter and grow in international markets. These hurdles, which are summarized below (and elaborated in Chapters 6–8), include the following.

• *POLITICAL AND LEGAL INFLUENCES*

Hostile attitudes by host country governments toward foreign firms that can stifle any chance of successful entry include confiscatory taxes and tariffs, quotas that limit the amount of imports accepted, and "local content" regulations requiring use of host country products, personnel, funds, and facilities.

• *ECONOMIC/DEMOGRAPHIC INFLUENCES*

Measures of economic viability—such as the population's standard of living and the country's stage of economic development and currency stability—are often insufficient to justify the expense and risk of attempting to enter a foreign market. Unfriendly demographic environments might include a lack of people in age, income, or occupational groups likely to buy the company's products.

• *SOCIO/CULTURAL FACTORS*

Personal beliefs, aspirations, languages, interpersonal relationships, and social structures differ among countries and can adversely affect the way a product offering is perceived and received, and the cost and risk associated with overcoming these negatives.

• *TECHNOLOGY*

Underdeveloped infrastructures to facilitate transportation and communication can make it prohibitively expensive to market product offerings in foreign countries.

• *CONTROL PROBLEMS*

Most firms that achieve multinational or global status find it considerably more difficult to coordinate and control manufacturing and marketing activities—and monitor competitors—in dispersed markets, with different customs, languages, transportation, and communication media.

OFFSHORE PLANS: INTERNATIONAL TO GLOBAL

Although there are many approaches—and combinations of approaches—for entry and growth in risky international markets, most firms generally follow a cautious, staged approach designed to minimize risk and cost, while maintaining control and flexibility. Such an approach typically encompasses the following stages.

• *INTERNATIONAL STATUS*

Initially, the firm achieves international status by entering one or two host country (foreign) markets that best match characteristics of home country (domestic) markets. Canada is overwhelmingly the country of choice. Firms that achieve international status mainly export or import products, or buy and sell products to capitalize on price differentials in different nations. Host country facilities are used initially to market the firm's products, later supported by home country personnel, supply sources, finances, and facilities.

• *MULTINATIONAL STATUS*

Then, learning from a hopefully successful experience, multinational status is achieved as additional foreign countries are entered, with greater use made of host country personnel, supply sources, finances, and facilities. Multinational does not simply imply doing business in many countries; rather, it refers to companies that produce products, or have subsidiaries add value in one or more foreign countries, as opposed to merely trading. This is what the Japanese, for example, did in transplanting automobile manufacturing to the United States after years of just marketing their automobiles here.

• *GLOBAL STATUS*

Conceivably, over time, a firm achieves global status, which refers to firms that take advantage of synergies between their various affiliates, planning strategies according to the comparative advantage of each country location, and utilizing the commonality of production and marketing into a coherent operation spanning several countries so as to derive economies of scale and scope. Global companies search for global synergies, as opposed to running several parallel but separate multinational operations.

STRATEGIES FOR SUCCESS IN THE GLOBAL MARKETPLACE

While passing through these stages, companies engage in one or more entry and growth strategies, depending on such considerations as the firm's strategic objectives, the product being marketed, and political, legal, economic, and competitive threats and opportunities in the host countries. Typically, a firm will begin with an exporting strategy during the first, international stage and then move to joint venture and direct ownership strategies during multinational and global stages. As shown in Figure 1-2, commitment, risk, resource needs, and degree of control all increase with joint venture and direct ownership strategies; flexibility, or the ability to change or terminate an entry strategy, is highest with joint ventures and lowest with direct ownership.

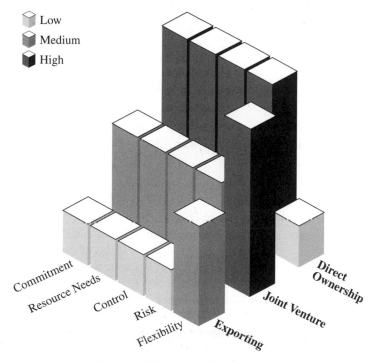

Figure 1–2. Dimensions Characterizing Alternative Global Market Entry Strategies

Following are characteristics, pros, and cons of these entry/growth strategies:

• *EXPORTING*

Using this strategy, the exporting firm markets products produced in the

United States to foreign customers either directly— through the firm's sales force located in the United States or the host country—or indirectly— through host country distributors. This low-risk, low-cost approach works best when customers are concentrated and easy to locate. A big drawback is that there is less control over host country distributors, who may not be knowledgable enough to market the firm's products.

• *JOINT VENTURES*

This strategy can assume a number of formats, all of which have in common a partnership arrangement between the exporting firm and a host country company to combine some aspects of manufacture or marketing in order to share expertise, costs, and/or connections. Potential advantages of joint ventures include lower costs and more favorable trading terms, because foreign ownership is established. (Some countries require joint ownership with a local company as an entry condition.)

Potential disadvantages include losing patents and profits to host country owners or, if the firm isn't wise enough to maintain a controlling interest in the jointly held company, complete control can be lost. Also, the possibility exists that a host country co-owner can become a competitor.

Joint ownership formats include:

- *Licensing*, under which, for a fee or royalty, a host country company is assigned some rights, such as the use of patents, trademarks, or marketing expertise. Licensing is often an effective way to establish foreign production with minimal capital outlays, prevent free use of assets by foreign firms, and generate income in markets where exportation or investment is not otherwise feasible.

- *Franchising* is a form of licensing whereby the exporter (i.e., the franchiser) grants an independent entity (the franchisee) the right to do business in a prescribed manner. This right can entail selling the firm's products and/or using its name, production, and marketing techniques. Although there are myriad problems involved in franchising foreign firms—securing good locations, finding franchisees and suppliers, maintaining standards and cost controls, agreeing on contract terms, etc.—the expansion of U.S. franchisers into global markets has been dramatic since the late 1960s. Reasons for this expansion include foreign market potential, financial gain, and saturated domestic markets.

- *Contract manufacturing* entails negotiating contracts under which host country companies manufacture the exporter's products, with the exporter keeping control of any patented processes. Like *management contracting*, under which the exporter only contracts to provide management expertise to a host country manufacturer or marketer, contract manufacturing represents an effective way to generate income through trade with little capital outlay. Both options are most frequently used in start-up operations, in the face of host country ownership restrictions and for facilities with operating problems. Although these options avoid most risks of global market participation, they also forfeit most of the benefits and are hence generally seen as a last line of defense.[2]

- *Turnkey operations* are specialized management contracts in which the exporting company provides complete operating facilities for a host country client, including all associated equipment, materials, programs, and expertise. This package arrangement assigns responsibility to one source, thereby easing negotiation, supervision, and accountability problems for the host country client. To the extent that turnkey operations are owned and controlled by the host country client, they are often perceived by foreign governments as acceptable alternatives to foreign direct investment.

- *Joint ownership arrangements,* whereby the exporter joins with foreign investors to create a local business in which they share ownership and control of manufacturing and marketing programs, is often the best way for a firm to spread geographically at a faster rate and help spread fixed costs over a larger sales base. Shared ownership also helps firms identify synergies among multiple partners in different countries and take on a local character that deflects host country criticism of foreign ownership.

- *Strategic alliances* are special forms of joint ventures designed to achieve competitive advantages by leveraging capabilities, increasing innovation, and improving flexibility in responding to market threats and opportunities. Firms comprising the alliance, at either the corporate or industry level, have common business objectives that focus on such areas as impoved profitability, new technologies, and better organization or management. Penetrating foreign markets, protecting domestic markets, co-opting competitors, and spreading cost and risk are all reasons for forming a strategic alliance, as illustrated by the following initiative:

The U.S. geothermal companies, California Energy Company, Inc., and Ormat, Inc., recently completed a financing package with the assistance of the Ex–Im Bank and OPIC to build and operate a geothermal energy power plant in the Upper Mahiao region of the Philippines.

---

[2] Lawrence Welch and Anubis Pacifico, "Management Contracts: A Role in Internationalization?" *International Marketing Review,* Vol. 7 (1990), pp. 64–74.

The project, valued at an estimated $225 million, will produce 120 megawatts of electricity and is expected to be in service by July 1996. Says the CEO of California Energy, David Sokol, "This project is a true example of public agencies assisting and supporting companies overseas to increase U.S. exports.[3]

• *FULL OWNERSHIP*

Under full-ownership arrangements, the exporter fully implements and controls global operations, with ownership of production, marketing, and other facilities. This control gives the exporter much greater freedom of action, without having to share profits or policies with local stockholders, who can be very vocal in global markets. Governments are growing increasingly hostile to full ownership, which they perceive as threatening to local ownership arrangements.

TRENDS THAT WILL INFLUENCE GLOBAL MARKETING

Following are major trends that will continue to create and shape threats and opportunities in global markets.

• *ECONOMIC COOPERATION AMONG NATIONS*

The European Union (EU), under which, in 1994, fourteen European nations became a single market, is perhaps the most visible manifestation of economic cooperation among groups of nations that will have significant ramifications for any country—or company—interested in succeeding in the global marketplace. These cooperating groups of nations represent, for marketers, prospectively much larger, more vibrant markets for products, with fewer tariffs, monetary differences, and local regulations to encumber trade. However, to the extent that these nation-groups are mandated to give preferences to each other (rather than to outsiders) and now have a home-sized market large enough to develop and test products with which they can go global (such as the European Airbus), they can also represent competitive threats. (The EU and other economic communities are covered in Chapters 7 and 9.)

• *A FREER FLOW OF TECHNOLOGY*

Dramatic breakthroughs in communication and transportation technology have combined to lower the cost and increase the speed and capacity of technology transfers, making it easier for firms in various countries to

---

[3] *Business America*, U.S. Department of Commerce, Washington, D.C., Vol. 115, No. 9 (October 1994), p. 21.

upgrade their products and production processes. As with the trend toward economic cooperation, this trend will create both customers and competitors for global marketers.

• *GROWTH OF EMERGING NATIONS*

As production and marketing of mature products move from more to less developed countries to take advantage of lower wages and other costs, countries such as India, the People's Republic of China, and practically all South American countries are achieving much higher growth rates than their more developed counterparts, becoming, in the process, more attractive customers as well as more threatening competitors. This dynamic process and its effects are illustrated in Global Focus 1-2.

GLOBAL FOCUS 1-2

The Free Market at Work: From Dirty Hands to Skilled Hands

With low wages and productive workers, South Korea snatched up the global athletic shoe market during the 1980s. The Kukje Corporation's factory in Pusan, South Korea, ran 24 lines and employed 20,000 workers at its peak, making it the largest shoe factory in the world. Korean conglomerate HS Corporation's shoe factory employed 9,000 people by the late 1980s and made hundreds of thousands of shoes for such giants as Nike, Inc., and Reebok International Ltd.

An interesting thing happened to the industry since reaching the top. Both of these huge shoe factories are now closed and are waiting to be converted into apartments. Factories like these are shutting down all over Korea, as well as economically similar Taiwan. The reason? As Taiwan and Korea, once low-wage countries themselves, open up trade and investment links to China, hundreds of thousands of jobs have vanished over the past three years in the shoe industry and others, including apparel and toys. Rising wages have simply priced the products out of much of the world market.

"This is the free market at work," proclaims a Hong Kong economist. "Labor is being released from low-wage, low-productivity industries . . . and it's moving into higher value-added, higher-productivity industries and into services." This transition is occurring so fast that those jobs lost in such industries as shoes barely show up in the unemployment statistics. "People are moving from dirty-hand work to skilled-hand work—this is what drives the region's growth."

Source: Paul Blustein, "Asia's Dragons Accept Trade's Pain and Gains," *The Washington Post*, November 7, 1993. © 1993, *The Washington Post*. Reprinted with permission.

• *REDUCTION IN DIFFERENCES AMONG COUNTRIES*

This trend is due, in considerable measure, to trends already discussed—communication and transportation advances, growth of emerging nations, and economic cooperation among nations. In addition, differences in such areas as income, energy costs, marketing practices, and needs for products and services seem to be narrowing among nations. For global marketers, these similarities suggest an opportunity to base marketing strategies, including identifying worthwhile customer groups and building attractive product/price/place/promotion marketing mixes, on broadly applicable criteria.

• *MORE AGGRESSIVE INDUSTRIAL POLICIES*

Such countries as Germany, Taiwan, and Japan have governments strongly oriented toward making the international business climate more competitive. For marketers, this could mean problems in penetrating these markets and more competition from them in marketing products in other countries.

CHAPTER PERSPECTIVE

Reasons why four of five U.S. firms in a position to do so don't enter foreign markets—including lack of potential in many markets, and barriers to entry in others—are becoming less valid in the upcoming century of all-out global competition. More and more, disadvantages of entering international markets are offset by profit-enhancing advantages, including tax savings, less competition, and opportunities to leverage global marketplace strengths. Typically, a firm entering the international marketplace achieves, sequentially, international, multinational, and global status. Status defines entry/growth strategies. For example, international status might be achieved with a flexible, low-risk, low-cost exporting arrangement; then, as multinational and global status are achieved, riskier, costlier, but potentially more rewarding joint venture and ownership strategies might be implemented. Underpinning these arrangements is a strategic marketing plan based on a researched understanding of marketplace threats and opportunities, the nature and needs of customers, and product/place/price/promotion marketing mixes best calculated to meet these needs. This strategic marketing planning process will be the focus of upcoming chapters.

KNOW THE CONCEPTS

TERMS FOR STUDY

acquired advantage
comparative advantage
contract manufacturing
currency stability
direct ownership
economic communities
entry strategies
exports
financial flows
Foreign Sales Corporation
full ownership
GATT
global firms
imports
International Monetary Fund

international firms
joint ownership
joint ventures
legal/political factors
leverage
licensing
monetary systems
most-favored nation principle
multinational firms
strategic alliances
tax advantage
trade deficit
trade surplus
turnkey operations
World Bank

MATCHUP EXERCISES

1. Match the organization in the first column with the descriptor in the second column.

   1. IMF
   2. GATT
   3. World Bank
   4. FSC

   a. Provides tax deferrals for qualified firms
   b. Most-favored nation principle
   c. Assists growth of fledgling economies
   d. Member nations draw upon reserve assets

2. Match the country in the first column with the descriptor in the second column.

   1. Canada
   2. United States

   3. Germany
   4. Japan

   a. Largest contributor to U.S. trade deficit
   b. Lowest exports per capita among industrialized countries
   c. Largest exporter in absolute terms
   d. Largest exporter as a share of GDP

3. Match the global trading stage in the first column with the characteristic listed in the second column.

   1. International

   2. Multinational

   a. Achieves major synergies based largely on exploitation of comparative advantage. Integrated, interactive management.
   b. Focuses on the domestic market while

pursuing international objectives. Top-down management.

3. Global   c. Recognizes differences in global markets that require adaptation of the marketing mix (product, price, place, promotion) in order to succeed. Bottom-up management.

QUESTIONS FOR REVIEW AND DISCUSSION

1. France and Germany, traditional enemies during previous centuries, are now each others' largest trading partners. Discuss the role of trading agreements, peace, and technological breakthroughs in bringing about this situation.

2. Give examples of natural advantage and acquired advantage that illustrate the differences between these concepts and explain why most world trade takes place among developed countries.

3. In terms of demographic, economic, legal/political, and technological factors that can work for or against successful entry into the global market, speculate on why a company might decide to reject a country for consideration as an entry market.

4. What is a trade deficit? List three reasons why it would be advantageous for the United States to transform its trade deficit into a trade surplus.

5. Assume that the United States implements a policy of reducing its trade deficit by increasing sales in categories where we have acquired advantages to countries with which we presently have our largest balance of payment deficits. Does this policy make sense? If so, which product groups would be promoted to which countries?

6. What is the difference between export, joint venture, and direct partnership stages in terms of commitment, risk, resource needs, flexibility, and degree of control?

7. How will economic cooperation among nations, reduction in differences among nations, and competition from newly emerging nations help a company engaged in the manufacture of consumer electronics products compete more effectively in the global market?

ANSWERS

MATCHUP EXERCISES

1. 1d, 2b, 3c, 4a
2. 1d, 2b, 3c, 4a
3. 1b, 2c, 3a

QUESTIONS FOR REVIEW AND DISCUSSION

1. Both France and Germany are strong, supportive members of the European Union (EU), which facilitates trade among its 14 member countries by prohibiting import/export duties and by improving the mobility of labor, capital, and technology among member states. The absence of half a century of large-scale wars on the European continent encouraged trade between France and Germany by diverting resources away from military adventures toward healthy, rapid economic growth that was fueled by, and helped to fuel, global trade. Particularly in the fields of communication and transportation, technological breakthroughs created products to trade, processes to make them, and the means to market them more efficiently and economically.

2. The term "natural advantage" implies an endowment based on climatic conditions or access to certain natural resources that give a country or region an advantage to the extent that other countries desire this endowment but don't have it. For example, climatic conditions give some countries the wherewithal to produce fruits (pineapples, bananas) demanded, but not produced, elsewhere. By trading these fruits to these other countries, the naturally endowed country creates a larger market for its products and income to purchase products that it needs but doesn't produce. The term "acquired advantage" generally implies a product or process resource, also in great demand, that a country has created through technological sophistication and specialization (e.g., computers). Since most acquired advantage resources are produced and purchased by developed countries and cost more than natural advantage commodities, the percentage of total global trade is much greater among developed countries than among less-developed countries or among developed and less-developed countries.

3. A company might decide to reject a country for consideration as an entry market for the following reasons: *demographic*—an insufficient number of people in various age and occupational groups attracted to the offering to justify the risk and expense of an entry strategy; *economic*—the stage of development of the country, as reflected in indices like corporate and per-capita income, is not sufficiently advanced to generate profits for the firm's product line; *legal/ political*—high tariff barriers and "local protection" laws designed to help domestic companies might make it prohibitively expensive for the firm's products to compete in the entry market, regardless of other favorable factors; *technological*—insufficiently developed infrastructures, particularly in the areas of transportation and communication, might make it prohibitively expensive for the firm to produce, distribute and promote its product line even in a country that might otherwise represent an excellent market.

4. A trade deficit is the amount by which a country's imports exceed its exports. In June 1995, for example, U.S. imports—of oil, automobiles, coffee, etc.—exceeded its exports—of services, grains, computers etc.—by $12 billion. Such deficit levels are unsustainable in the long run. They indicate that a country, in its international activities, is consuming more than it is producing and affect domestic employment by transferring jobs to exporting countries. Conversely, a trade surplus generates jobs. According to Commerce Department figures, $1 billion worth of exports creates, on average, 22,000 jobs. (The levering influence of exports on economic growth was apparent during the economic slowdown of the early 1990s, when export growth accounted for practically all domestic growth and new employment.)

   From the perspective of individual firms, export, by broadening market reach, can achieve economies of scale that help achieve lower costs and higher profits both domestically and abroad. Exporting also helps firms gain stability by not being dependent on a single market and prove their ability to survive in less-familiar environments in spite of higher transaction costs and different demand structures and cultural dimensions.

5. This policy makes sense to the extent that countries with which the United States has the largest trade deficits—such as Japan, China, Germany, and Taiwan—are also our largest customers, particularly for products in which we have a comparative advantage (e.g., lumber products to Japan). These countries are also developed or fast-developing, and hence have a greater ability to consume and pay for these imports. Given this potential, such a strategy might focus on marketing services (the category in which we have our largest trade surplus), capital goods (such as turnkey processing plants), and foods and beverages to Japan, China, and Germany.

6. All increase with joint venture and direct ownership strategies as greater financial commitment, higher risk of failure, less ability to

change course, and more control over strategies and operations are incurred. Flexibility, or the ability to change or terminate strategies, is the highest with joint ventures and lowest with direct ownership.

7. Economic cooperation among nations, in the form of regional economic communities like NAFTA and the EU, effectively transform many smaller markets into single large markets, with many fewer trade constraints and the fast, flexible flow of human and financial resources. Together with the reduction of differences among nations, this means that the manufacturer, in dealing with these market aggregates, will be able to reach a much larger market with the same marketing mix. Much less will have to be done to adapt product features, price, distribution and promotion strategies to a diversity of individual countries. Competition from newly emerging nations implies that they are making the overall pie bigger—just as, for example, competition among many computer producers in the United States benefits all by vastly expanding the market—and that they, themselves, are developing to the point of being worthwhile customers for the firm's products.

2 INTERNATIONAL MARKETING PLANNING

OVERVIEW

In this chapter we examine the role of the global marketing manager in formulating strategic marketing plans that account for unique needs and constraints in international markets in bringing together target markets and marketing mixes. We also examine marketing concepts and philosophies that comprise and guide strategic marketing planning, with emphasis on how they differ in international and domestic markets.

INTRODUCING MERTON ELECTRONICS

In this and subsequent chapters, we focus on activities of international marketing managers in formulating strategic marketing plans that create fits among a firm's goals, resources, and changing opportunities in international markets. Throughout this text, we will use the following case, based on the fictitious Merton Electronics Company, to illustrate this strategic marketing planning process. This process involves identifying and defining worthwhile target markets, product/place/price/promotion marketing mixes attractive to these markets, and environmental threats and opportunities that must be accounted for in the marketing planning process.

The Merton Electronics Company is a large manufacturer of chip circuits and other electronic components, which it markets to firms in the consumer electronics segment of the organizational market. Recently, Merton's research and development department, working with its engineering and product design departments developed a line of lightweight computers, featuring the recently developed, new-generation Merton Moonchip and infrared ports that connect, remotely if necessary, to desktop computers, facsimilie, and telecommunication units. Called the Merton Mighty Mind (MM) line, these advanced computers perform admirably in a diversity of applications, including interpersonal conferencing, spreadsheets, electronic mail, and word processing. The fact that introducing the MM line of laptop and notebook computers into the consumer market means competing with their own best customers did not especially concern Merton's management; in the free-wheeling, highly competitive consumer electronics market, this was hardly unprecedented. What did concern them was the nature of this competition. With faster, smarter, smaller computers appearing practically overnight, Merton management realized it would take large, established competitors (like IBM and Apple) little time to catch up with, and rush past, Merton's MM line of notebook and laptop computers.

By way of insulating themselves against this likelihood, Merton did two things before launching the MM line into the domestic consumer market:

1. Entrenched the MM line in strong niches through selection of associated software. Specifically, members of various professions—doctors, lawyers, accountants etc.—could purchase with each MM purchased software packages that addressed problems and opportunities in each specialty. For example, the architect's software package accompanying each MM purchased included programs for keeping the professional abreast of new trends and developments in the field, designing structures, and profitably administering an architectural practice.

   Prominent in all these software packages (dubbed "Professional Information Systems") were training and development programs that created online environments for computer conferencing training sessions. In promoting its MM systems, Merton emphasized the quality and timeliness of the software as much as performance features of the MM computers.

2. Retained Lora Moore, a global marketing specialist, as Merton's international marketing manager. Moore's mandate was to develop profitable global markets for the MM line to absorb the shock of anticipated losses of market share in Merton's domestic market. In carrying out this mandate, Moore explored questions like: Did profitable markets exist in the international sphere for Merton's products and services? If so, could these markets be profitably reached with products, prices, promotion campaigns, and channels of distribution? How would differing cultural, demographic, technological, competitve, and economic conditions combine to support or thwart marketing plans designed to bring markets and products together? What would be the most effective strategy for entering and growing in the international marketplace?

WHAT GLOBAL MARKETING MANAGERS DO

In creating and implementing strategic marketing plans designed to harmonize a firm's objectives and resources with changing market opportunities, the global marketing manager analyzes, plans, organizes, implements, and controls.

For example, analysis of quantitative and qualitative research data might identify a potentially profitable target market for Merton MMs in a foreign country where language and life-style differences would create barriers to marketing these systems successfully. Based largely on this analysis, Lora Moore's strategic plan for successfully entering this market would specify how MM product, price, distribution, and promotional strategies would meet the defined needs of target market members while achieving company profit objectives. This plan would also specify any needed organizational changes needed to prepare for the plan's execution.

Implementation activities involved in the actual carrying out of the plan would be based on an assessment of Merton's "fit" in this new market, while accounting for unforeseen environmental changes and allowing for corresponding changes in the original plan. Concurrently with implementation activities, control mechanisms would lock into place, monitoring environmental forces, competitors, channel participants, and customer receptiveness, indicating areas where planned activities were not achieving desired goals, and providing input to ensure that future plans did achieve these goals.

MARKETING CONCEPTS THAT SUPPORT MARKETING PLANS

Underpinning Moore's planning activities are a number of marketing concepts, including marketing itself, marketing environments, marketing mixes, markets, needs, demands, exchanges, and competition, as well as marketing philosophies that guide these activities. In defining these concepts and philosophies, we will examine how each differs as applied in domestic and global markets and how all come together in the strategic marketing planning (SMP) process.

• _MARKETING_

The American Marketing Association (AMA) recently broadened its definition of marketing to stress what the process achieves as well as what it does:

> Marketing is the process of planning the conception, pricing, promotion, and distribution of ideas, goods and services to create exchanges that satisfy individual and organizational objectives.

Like most quick definitions of complex phenomena, this one leaves a lot of questions unanswered. For example, what is "planning" and "execution" in marketing terms? How are "ideas, goods, and services" conceived, priced, promoted, and distributed? What is an "exchange" and how do exchanges satisfy needs? How do these concepts differ in international and domestic markets?

These and related questions will be addressed in the rest of this chapter and book. For our present purposes, regarding marketing processes, we focus on the following assumptions that Lora Moore took into account in charting Merton's path from domestic to global status.

1. *Marketing processes are generally similar regardless of circumstances.* Whether a firm is large or small, markets a tangible or intangible product, aspires to profit or nonprofit objectives, or sells in domestic or international markets, the basic marketing process will be the same. Buyers must be found; products must be conceived, priced, promoted, and distributed; and uncontrollable factors, such as differing economic and competitive conditions, must be taken into account in bringing buyers and products together. These basics are called the technical universals of marketing.

Also similar in domestic and international markets are the basic functions performed by marketing processes, such as researching markets and planning, buying, pricing, promoting, transporting, storing, and selling products. Benefits created by marketing processes are also similar, including bringing together the right products at the right prices for the right people at the right time in the right place.

2. *International marketing is generally riskier than domestic marketing.* If activities, functions, and benefits characterizing domestic and international marketing are similar, the carrying-out of these activities is generally riskier and more difficult in the global marketplace, where the marketer is subject to a new set of constraints deriving from cultural, technological, economic, demographic, political, and competitive differences among nations that must be accounted for in the strategic planning effort. Another constraint is the frequent lack of information about markets in foreign countries and the difficulties encountered in getting this information.

3. *International marketing can be more profitable than domestic marketing.* Examples of firms whose profits from foreign operations exceed their domestic profits abound, including global companies like Coca-Cola, Exxon, Gillette, Dow Chemical, and Citicorp. What these firms generally have in common is the ability to account for threats and opportunities in diverse foreign markets and to leverage strengths presented by these markets.

• MARKETING ENVIRONMENTS

Marketing environments are forces that influence marketing managers' abilities to create and carry out plans that satisfy organizational objectives and target market needs. The marketing microenvironment comprises forces close to the company that affect its ability to serve customers, including company strengths and weaknesses and company suppliers, publics, and competitors. The macroenvironment comprises larger political, legal, economic, cultural, and technological forces that influence the microenvironment. These elements are often called uncontrollables in that the marketing manager must adjust to them, but has little, if any, control over them.

The global marketing environment has changed dramatically in the last decade, creating new threats and opportunities for marketing planners. As the world economy has globalized, world trade and investment have grown rapidly, with many attractive markets opening in South America, China, and Eastern Europe. Financial systems have become more complex and sophisticated, and the dominant position of the United States has declined in the face of the increased economic power of countries like Japan and Germany. The trend toward economic communities among groups of nations has also increased, raising tariff and non-tariff barriers in some situations and lowering them in others. Moore had to account for these and other microenvironmental and macroenvironmental considerations in seeking worthwhile entry markets for MM systems and formulating plans to enter and grow in these markets.

• MARKETING MIXES

Marketing mixes are combinations of marketing tools that marketing managers orchestrate to satisfy customers and company objectives. Called the offering from the customer's perspective, the marketing mix is usually associated with the four Ps: product, place, price, and promotion.

An important issue affecting all these Ps in the global marketplace is the extent to which each will have to be modified from country to country. Products, like Coca-Cola and Colgate toothpaste, that can adopt a "standardization" policy, whereby there is little change in marketing mix elements from country to country, will generally achieve more significant improvements in marketing performance and lower marketing costs than companies forced by competitive conditions to follow an adaptation policy of custom-tailoring marketing programs in each country.

- *Product*, in marketing terms, is defined as anything, tangible or intangible, offered for attention, acquisition, use, or consumption that is capable of satifying needs. Included can be objects, people, places, services, and ideas. The satisfaction people get from products can derive from any aspect of the product, such as its quality, brand name, service warranty, package, supplementary use, or symbolic value. Frequently, in global markets, various of these aspects can be standardized without standardizing the entire product. For example, the brand name IBM conjures up similar associations throughout the world, while actual product components and technology might differ from country to country (IBM produces 20 different keyboards for Europe alone).

- *Promotion programs*, designed to persuade customers to buy the product, include personal selling, advertising (paid messages carried by the media), publicity (unpaid messages carried by the media), and sales promotion (marketing activities, other than those already mentioned, designed to stimulate customer purchasing and dealer effectiveness).

    Among the factors that help define the nature, scope, and effectiveness of promotion programs in foreign markets are the cost and availability of media to reach target markets; consumer attitudes and governmental constraints, regarding information sources; and the ability of the distribution system to get promoted products to customers. Because these factors often differ appreciably among countries, it is usually more difficult to standardize a promotion program than a product in a given country, and economies achieved are not as great as those found in product standardization.

- *Place* refers to where the product is made available to market members and covers two areas: (1) channels of distribution, such as wholesalers or retailers handling products between producers and consumers, and (2) physical distribution, such as transportation, warehousing, and inventory control facilities designed to make products available at appropriate times and places in marketing channels. Of all the marketing mix elements, place is generally the most difficult to change. It is usually also the most difficult to standardize, since distribution channels tend to reflect economic, cultural, and legal characteristics of each country more than promotional channels do. For example, few U.S. wholesalers or retailers have expanded abroad, while most large advertising, public relations, and marketing research firms have.

- The *Price* that customers pay for products influences the product's image and likelihood of purchase. It is the only revenue-generating element of the marketing mix, and the easiest to change. Among global marketers, only product is placed above price when ranking the importance of marketing mix variables.[1]

Price is usually based on analyses of costs, customer needs, competitive prices, and government regulatory and political mandates. Because these factors are often more likely to intrude when pegging prices in global markets, price standardization across borders is usually difficult to achieve.

In building marketing mixes for MM systems sold in international markets, Moore realized that she would face problems not faced in the domestic marketplace. In the product area, for example, MM programs that accounted for differences in language and customs would have to be developed. With respect to place, means would have to be found to transport, store, and distribute MM systems to customers, possibly in countries where few such means presently existed. In pricing the systems, a whole spectrum of problems would arise, including the effect on MM prices of different exchange and inflation rates, differing dealer discount schedules, and escalating costs of exporting MM systems. Promotion problems would include translating appeals into different languages and the availability of media to carry these appeals.

Overarching all these problems was the big problem of developing information to solve them. For example, information was needed to determine the real product needs of prospective customers or the competitive environment in different markets or the relative effectiveness of different promotional appeals. This information would be critical in devising each marketing mix element and in determining the relative emphasis each should receive in Moore's strategic plan for global entry and growth. (Global Focus 2-1 illustrates how one company modified its marketing mix to meet the nature and needs of its Japanese target market.)

---

[1] Saeed Samiee, "Pricing in Marketing Strategies of U.S.- and Foreign-Based Companies," *Journal of Business Research*, Vol. 15, No. 1 (February 1987), pp. 17–30.

GLOBAL FOCUS 2-1

Domino's Pizza Changes Its Mix

When Ernest Higa, a Japanese-American, considered franchising Domino's, he found the history of pizza in Japan to be dismal. Faced with the research conclusion that pizza and Japan do not mix, Higa set out to prove otherwise. He believed that the key was to make alterations appropriate for the market.

In Japan, the changes began with the size of the pizza. In Higa's words, "The Japanese aren't big eaters, especially women." So he trimmed the product from 12 to 10 inches. In Japan food delivery, *demae*, is usually expected. Faced with such obstacles as crowded and limited parking, Higa provided his employees with newly designed scooters to help them deliver the pizzas. Higa discovered that the Japanese consumer associates delivery businesses with small-scale operations and limited service capacity. Therefore, he upgraded the marketing materials provided by U.S. headquarters by producing four-color advertisements and handbills. And, of course, new pizza flavors were introduced, so appealing that customers clamored for bowls of rice to go with them.

Today, Higa owns 98 franchises in Japan, runs the most successful Domino's operation abroad, and his franchises average more than double the volume of a typical American Domino's.

Source: Greg Matusky, "Going Global: Franchisors Crack New Overseas Markets," *Success* (April 1993), pp. 59–63. Reprinted with permission from *Success* Magazine, by *Success* Holding Company, L.L.C.

• *MARKETS*

Markets are groups of actual or potential buyers who can afford to buy the product, have the needed authority to buy the product, desire the product, and will respond similarly to a marketing mix appeal. The acronym MAD-R—for money, authority, desire, and response—will help you remember these characteristics. Groups of people who possess these MAD-R attributes in greater abundance are called target markets. For example, in Merton's domestic market, tax accountants represented an excellent target market for MM programs in that their firms could afford to invest heavily in their continued education, they had the "authority" (i.e., they were professionals) to use MM programs, they desired these programs to keep abreast of tax changes affecting client firms, and they generally responded similarly, and favorably, to appeals that stressed how MM programs would help accountants address client needs.

Markets are broadly categorized in terms of what they do and what they buy; the consumer market comprises people and groups who buy products for personal, family, or household use; the organizational market comprises people and groups who buy products for further production, use in operating the organization, or resale to consumers. Together with government and farm markets, these categories cover practically all the people and groups who buy products in international markets.

In these markets, however, Moore realized that target markets would be harder to identify, define, and relate to. Information needed would be harder to come by, over barriers that would be harder to surmount.

• *NEEDS*

Needs are states of physical or mental felt deprivation. In more advanced economies, needs become more numerous and arise on different levels. For example, needs satisfied by enrolling in a diet program in the United States might simultaneously be functional (to lose weight), psychological (to feel better about your appearance), and social (to attract a mate). In undeveloped countries, the single functional need a diet satisfies might be to ward off starvation.

An important job of marketing managers is to determine what product-related needs predominate among various customer groups, then turn these needs into wants by focusing on need-satisfying benefits of products they are marketing.

Moore recognized that this job of identifying needs satisfied by Merton MMs would be considerably more difficult in the diverse, different global marketplace, as would be the job of transforming these needs into wants.

• *DEMANDS*

Demands are wants backed by purchasing power. In Merton's domestic market, for example, all the money spent by, or for, managers in tax accounting firms who want MM systems to help them better serve clients comprises the demand for these programs in this single target market. Purchases by all groups comprising Merton's market represents total demand for MM systems.

Kotler[2] identifies eight demand states that marketing managers must recognize and respond to.

- *Negative demand* occurs when a significant segment of the market dislikes the product and may pay to avoid it. This was the situation facing the leisure/travel industry in 1990 when many Americans cancelled trips to Middle East countries over the prospect of terrorist incidents engendered by the Persian Gulf "Desert Storm" war. Here, the marketing manager's task is to define reasons for this demand state and take measures to counteract them. Discount fares, extra security measures, and advertised assurances of safety were examples of such measures.

- *No demand* occurs when target market customers are unmotivated or indifferent to the product, like a Broadway play that opens to lukewarm reviews. The job of the marketing manager, then, is to connect potential product benefits to the needs and interests of prospective customers.

---

[2] Philip Kotler, *Principles of Marketing*, 5th ed. Englewood Cliffs, N.J.: Prentice-Hall, 1991, p. 10.

- *Latent demand* occurs when many prospective customers share a strong desire for a satisfaction that can't be provided by existing products. Hair restoratives or painless diets are examples of such satisfactions. Here, the job of the marketing manager is to measure the size of potential demand and develop products to meet this demand.

- *Falling demand* is illustrated by problems facing Merton as competitive firms make inroads into its domestic market share. Here, the job of the marketing manager—Lora Moore in this case—is to analyze causes and plan marketing strategies to counter the trend.

- *Irregular demand* occurs when seasonal, daily, or even hourly demand fluctuations cause significant differences in product usage. This problem faces most mass transit systems, with rush hour peak demand occurring only a few hours each day. Here, the marketing manager attempts to alter demand patterns by altering marketing mix variables, such as flexible pricing or special off-season promotions.

- *Full demand* occurs when the firm has all the business it needs. It becomes the marketing manager's job to monitor changes in customer needs and in the competiton to maintain this desirable demand level.

- *Overfull demand* occurs when demand is higher than the organization can or wants to handle. Yellowstone Park, with its annual hordes of campers, is an example of overfull demand. Demand is discouraged by manipulating marketing mix variables, such as higher prices or fewer product features. Using marketing mix variables to decrease demand is called demarketing.

- *Unwholesome demand* for products like cigarettes, alcohol, and pornography challenges marketers of these products to devise marketing plans and mixes that take into account negative public attitudes to these products. In international markets this demand state can also be defined in terms of conditions in some global markets where satisfying demand would be conditioned by considerations not considered morally or legally acceptable in the U.S. market.

Moore realized that, while full and falling demand characterized sales of MM systems in the domestic market, no and latent demand patterns would probably characterize sales as Merton attempted to penetrate the international market. This difference in the nature of demand would influence all the elements of her strategic marketing plan, from defining markets to building marketing mixes. She also realized that reliable estimates of the extent of this demand—an important first step in the strategic planning process—would be much more difficult to come by in quixotic international markets.

• *EXCHANGE*

Exchange is the process by which two or more parties give something of value to one another to satisfy wants. As such, exchange is both the objective and common denominator of all marketing activity. It can take diverse forms in addition to the exchange of money for tangible products: exchange of tuition for an education, votes for political action, skills for a job, and so on. A tax accountant who pays $3,000 for a Merton MM system illustrates conditions required for a voluntary exchange to take place:

- At least two parties, each with something of value to the other party;
- Each party capable of communication and delivery;
- Each party free to accept or reject the other's offer;
- Each party believing it appropriate and desirable to deal with the other party;
- Legal authority, such as a law of contracts, to protect the agreement.

In domestic markets, all these conditions apply in most situations where things of value are exchanged: a price is agreed upon that represents appropriate value to both willing parties, and the product is purchased and delivered. If either party is later dissatisfied, legal agreements provide recourse, such as returning the product for a refund or suing for damages.

Moore realized, however, that the likelihood of these conditions prevailing in international markets would be considerably less than in the domestic marketplace. For example, the value of an MM system would be difficult to agree on in a country where exchange or inflation rates change the daily value of a local currency. Also, legal authority, as defined in U.S. courts, might have a completely different, and unacceptable, meaning in foreign courts. In newly freed-up Eastern Bloc countries, for example, concepts like personal property, ownership, and liability—all key in consummating and protecting exchanges—are still being interpreted.

In other situations, the desirability of dealing with other parties might not be clear, such as when it is mandated by government regulation or confused by a lack of information about the real needs or resources of market groups.

• *COMPETITION*

Competition is defined as other direct and indirect ways customers can satisfy needs other than making an exchange for a particular offering. For example, a prospective buyer might purchase an MM Professional Information system, or a competitive brand, directly from a distributor of these systems. Or, this prospect might spend the money, indirectly, on other ways to achieve the same educational objectives, such as through a correspondence course, or at a local college. Direct and indirect competition falls into four categories:

- *Brand competition* includes other brands of the product marketed e.g., among New York newspapers, *The Times*, the *Daily News*, and the *Post.*

- *Form competition* encompasses other forms of the product marketed (e.g., newspapers on microfilm).

- *Generic competition* encompasses products different from the marketed product that provide the same benefits as this product (e.g., a television news show instead of a newspaper).

- *Desire competition* encompasses other desires prospective customers might satisfy before satisfying the desire to buy the marketed product (e.g., spending a dollar for a lottery ticket instead of a newspaper at the local newsstand).

Products introduced into international markets, like MM systems, generally face a broader, more diverse range of competition than existed in their domestic market. Initially, the product usually faces a more indirect form of desire and generic competition than in its domestic market; then, as it gains market share, it faces more direct, brand competition, although not necessarily of the sort faced in its domestic market. For example, in the U.S. market, Gillette is the sales leader for disposable razors, with BIC a distant runner-up; in Europe, these roles are reversed.

Types of competition encountered in global markets are largely a function of political, economic, social/cultural, and technological influences and are an important consideration in identifying target markets and planning competitive strategies. Given the complexity of competitive environments and the dramatically quickening pace with which products are introduced, upgraded, and distributed in international markets, Moore recognized that an important part of any MM marketing program would be to monitor continually the nature and scope of competition in each entry market, track competitive initiatives, and assess and respond to these initiatives.

• *STRATEGIC MARKETING PLANNING*

Strategic marketing planning (SMP) is the managerial process of developing and maintaining a strategic fit among the organization's resources and objectives and its changing market opportunities. It relies on a clear company mission, supporting objectives and goals, a sound business port-folio, and coordinated functional strategies.

In Merton's domestic market, a number of strategic marketing plans are formulated each year for products in a variety of demand stages—some falling, some full, others irregular, and so on. Each plan began with Merton's mission statement from which objectives, market specifications, strategies, tactics, and controls emerged. (Global Focus 2-2 identifies and illustrates components of successful export marketing strategies.)

GLOBAL FOCUS 2-2

Formulating a Successful Export Strategy

In general, a successful export strategy identifies and correlates at least four factors that jointly determine the most suitable kind of export operation: (1) the firm's export objectives, both immediate and long range; (2) specific tactics the firm will use; (3) scheduling of activities, deadlines, etc., that reflect chosen objectives and tactics, and (4) allocation of resources among scheduled activities.

The marketing plan and schedule of activities should cover a 2- to 5-year period, depending on the kind of product exported, the strength of competitors, conditions in target markets, and other factors.

Following are three success stories of companies that follow the strategic planning approach for penetrating global markets.

- The SIT String Corp. of Akron, Ohio, emphasizes the high quality of its guitar strings and seeks to develop a reputation for reliability. Robert Hird, vice president, said, "We keep trying to develop better sounding strings. Foreign customers, in particular, want to know a U.S. supplier is dependable and has some longevity. It takes time to develop this kind of reputation, but we think we are doing it, because our exports are growing. SIT sells 40 percent of its products overseas, in 36 countries, and Hird says "We are just getting started!"

- A similar export strategy is used by Purafil, Inc., of Atlanta, Ga., to show that its air purification equipment is technologically superior. "To get the leading edge, American companies need to offer something that is technologically ahead of the others," says William Weiller, president and CEO. "We find that technology is the key ingredient in differentiating our product offering." For this reason, Purafil emphasizes quality and research and development. To get the word out, it takes part in scientific forums around

the world and publishes technical articles in international trade/
scientific journals.

- Until 1989, Metrologic Instruments of Blackwood, N.J., paid little
  attention to small countries and small customers. In that year, it
  made a strategic decision to concentrate on small opportunities
  and establish relationships with many new dealers and resellers.
  The refocusing was successful. Within 2 years, the company had
  added 70 new foreign customers, it was selling in 24 countries
  where it had not operated previously, and its international sales
  had increased 25 percent.

Source: *Business America*, Vol. 114, No. 9 (Spring, 1993).

Merton's marketing plan for MM Professional Information Systems in
domestic markets, for example, began with this statement:

> To help business executives and professionals become more produc-
> tive and efficient by providing the best information and training for
> learning to apply modern tools and techniques in areas of general and
> specialized expertise.

This mission statement then helped define Merton's business and
marketing objectives. For example, among mission-defined business
objectives, Merton would have to attract top-level software developers to
develop state-of-the-art reference materials and training courses for specific professional groups. Marketing objectives would entail identifying
and defining target market groups of professionals and preparing marketing mix offerings (e.g., designing, distributing, and promoting the MM systems) attractive to these groups. Also implicit in this mission statement
is the goal of earning a profit in meeting the needs of target market
members.

Then, having identified and defined target markets and devised marketing mixes attractive to these markets, the strategic marketing planning
process identified environmental threats and opportunities, their impact on
the success of the plan, and how they would be addressed through long-
term strategies and short-term tactical plans.

Missions, objectives, analyses of environmental opportunities and
threats, definitions of target markets, descriptions of marketing mixes,
strategies and tactics for bringing markets and products together, and controls to ensure that appropriate measures are taken, when necessary, to
get the plan back on track all were formalized in a written marketing plan.

In Merton's domestic market, Moore realized that components of strategic marketing plans such as target markets, marketing mixes, and envi-

ronmental threats and opportunities were relatively easy to identify. In international markets, however, they aren't, for all the reasons already discussed pertaining to environmental differences among nations and the general paucity of information about these differences.

MARKETING PHILOSOPHIES THAT GUIDE MARKETING PLANNING

Guiding Moore's efforts to meld marketing concepts into strategic marketing plans to enter and grow in global markets were a number of marketing philosophies, including production, sales, marketing concept, and societal marketing concept philosophies.

• *THE PRODUCTION PHILOSOPHY*

Dating back to the industrial revolution, when major manufacturing centers and distribution networks were established, this philosophy focuses on making and distributing products in sufficient quantities to meet burgeoning demand. The prevailing philosophy, "a good product will sell itself," implies emphasis on production rather than sales. In international markets, this philosophy supports sales of undifferentiated raw materials and agricultural commodities, and passive sales that arrive from abroad with no special promotional effort on the part of the seller.

• *THE SALES PHILOSOPHY*

The production philosophy was replaced by the sales philosophy in the early 1920s, when mass production technology, spawned by the industrial revolution, produced more products than markets could effectively absorb. This product glut, combined with dramatic increases in consumer discretionary income, led to an emphasis on sales forces and advertising campaigns to find new customers and persuade resistant customers to buy. As in the production philosophy era, however, there was rarely a unifying force within the organization to integrate these sales-oriented activities in terms of defining and satisfying customer needs. Communication with customers was unilateral, and the sales function was generally subordinate to finance, production, and engineering. In international markets, this philosophy is usually appropriate in organizational markets, or when initially seeking to penetrate global consumer markets, where primary emphasis is on the selling function to communicate product values quickly and efficiently.

• *THE MARKETING CONCEPT*

Defined as an integrated, customer- and profit-oriented philosophy of business, the marketing concept philosophy differs from predecessor philosophies that emphasized products ("a good product will sell itself") and selling ("don't sell the steak, sell the sizzle") in a number of significant ways:

- The marketing concept defines the firm's mission in terms of benefits and satisfactions it offers customers, rather than in terms of products it makes and sells.

- It emphasizes two-way communication to identify customer needs and then develops and markets products to satisfy these needs. Gone is the emphasis on one-way communication to persuade people to buy products already made.

- It emphasizes both long- and short-range planning to achieve profits by meeting customer needs; gone is an exclusive focus on short-range planning to achieve sales volume objectives.

- It emphasizes a total systems integration of all departments to achieve profit goals. Gone is the exclusive focus on the efforts of individual departments and sales forces.

In recent years, the marketing concept philosophy of working back from defined customer needs to marketing mix offerings calculated to profitably satisfy these needs has come under increasing attack from critics who claim that this "customer knows best" pandering to diverse needs is wasteful, inefficient, and inconsistent with an era of shortages and concerns for the environment. In international markets, where the rationale for this philosophy has generally not taken hold as in the domestic market, and where cost considerations often predominate, it is often replaced with a sales or production philosophy.

The societal marketing concept, which responds to these critics, doesn't oppose the free enterprise notion of determining needs of target market members and delivering desired satisfactions more efficiently and effectively than competitors. It does maintain, however, that these satisfactions should be delivered in a way that also addresses the needs of society. In short, marketing managers should balance three interests in setting policies and formulating marketing plans: the buyer, the seller, and society at large. Consider, for example, the bottle laws that mandate a concern for the environment in the supercompetitive wars among soft drink companies.

In its domestic market Merton, a good neighbor, had adopted the societal marketing philosophy as a guide to its strategic planning efforts. In other countries with different environments and outlooks, however, Moore recognized that different marketing philosophies might be more appropriate. Of particular interest was a piece she had just read concerning the approach a Merton competitor had taken to penetrate foreign markets successfully.

> The Dell Computer Company, which began European operations in 1987, had sales of $260 million in 1994, or 30 percent of total Dell sales, and 2 percent of all personal computer (PC) sales in the European market. (During the same period, IBM's European PC sales dropped from 21 to 17 percent of total sales.) Central to Dell's success was a direct mail discount campaign that observers said couldn't possibly work: Computer buyers never purchase big ticket items like PCs through the mail and tend to equate discounted prices with shoddy merchandise. Dell management disagreed. Research showed that PC prices in Europe, set by firms like Groupe Bull's Zenith Data Systems and Olivetti, were about twice that charged in the United States, and that European dealer networks were sluggish and expensive. Dell began its campaign with an intense education program, featuring a series of ads in computer magazines and direct mailings throughout Britain and the continent, stressing Dell's reputation for high quality, fast service, and lowest price. Future plans included instituting a single price throughout its Western European market, with a guarantee of 5-day delivery and 2-day service.

Thus, with a minimum of research and a sales-oriented approach more characteristic of an inexpensive consumer product than a high ticket business product, Dell had scored a quick, solid success in the foreign market.

CHAPTER PERSPECTIVE

Strategic marketing planning, the managerial process of developing and maintaining a strategic fit among the organization's resources and objectives and its changing market opportunities, relies on a clear company mission, supporting objectives, and coordinated strategies and tactics. It also relies on an understanding of supporting marketing concepts like needs, exchange, marketing mixes, and marketing environments, and how these basic concepts are reinterpreted in international markets.

In formulating strategic marketing plans, the marketing manager analyzes information to identify marketplace threats and opportunities, creates plans for bringing together marketing mixes and identifies target market needs, establishes controls to keep the plan aimed toward objectives, and organizes resources to ensure efficient, effective implementation of the plan.

In international markets, however, strategic marketing planning is considerably more difficult—though potentially much more rewarding—than in the domestic marketplace. Cultural, demographic, economic, political, and technological differences among nations contribute to this difficulty, as does lack of information on markets.

KNOW THE CONCEPTS

TERMS FOR STUDY

adaptation
competition
consumer market
demand states
exchanges
MAD-R
market
marketing
marketing concept
marketing management
marketing mixes
marketing philosophies
macroenvironment

microenvironment
mission statement
needs
objectives
organizational market
strategic marketing planning
strategies
tactics
target markets
technical universals
uncontrollables
wants

MATCHUP EXERCISES

1. Match the marketing mix element in the first column with the descriptor in the second column.

1. product
2. price
3. distribution
4. promotion

a. stimulates customer spending and dealer effectiveness
b. anything that satisfies needs
c. most difficult to standardize
d. easiest to change

2. Relate the demand state in the first column with the appropriate strategy in the second column.

1. latent
2. irregular
3. negative
4. overfull

a. alter marketing mix elements
b. develop new products
c. take counteractive measures
d. demarket

3. Match the concepts in the first column with the second column descriptors pertaining to various elements of an encyclopedia salesman's sales plan.

1. MAD-R
2. mission
3. generic competition

a. benefit-oriented reason for selling these encyclopedias
b. your long-term plan to increase encyclopedia sales by 50 percent
c. the reference desk at the library

4. needs
5. strategy

d. members of your target market
e. the feeling among members of your target market that their kids are too dumb

QUESTIONS FOR REVIEW AND DISCUSSION

1. Discuss similarities and differences between marketing processes carried out in domestic and international markets.

2. Discuss how three negative impacts on price could invalidate an otherwise successful entry for Merton's MM line in a foreign market.

3. Explain how two different market aggregates—consumer and organizational—could be customers for the same MM system. What are the marketing mix implications of the different natures and needs of these markets?

4. What is the relationship among needs, wants, and demand? How does this relationship differ between developed and less developed markets?

5. In terms of the definition of competition, explain why a company like Merton would probably face a different competitive environment in a foreign market than in its domestic market.

6. What is the relationship among the following elements of the strategic marketing planning process: environmental assessment, mission statement, business objectives, and marketing objectives. Why is this process generally more difficult to implement in foreign than in domestic markets?

7. How does the definition of target markets help define marketing mixes in the strategic marketing planning process?

8. What is the main difference between the marketing concept on the one hand and the sales and production philosophies on the other? Between the marketing philosopy and the societal marketing philosophy?

ANSWERS

MATCHUP EXERCISES

1. 1b, 2d, 3c, 4a
2. 1b, 2a, 3c, 4d
3. 1d, 2a, 3c, 4e, 5b

QUESTIONS FOR REVIEW AND DISCUSSION

1. Marketing processes carried out in domestic and international markets are similar as to specific activities encompassed (e.g., products and services must be developed, priced, distributed, and promoted to meet the needs of defined target markets and company objectives) and in accounting for marketplace threats and opportunities as well as company strengths and weaknesses. Differences among marketing processes in relatively homogeneous domestic and heterogeneous international markets derive mainly from environmental differences. For example, differences in language, cultural values, state of economic development, currency stability, infrastructure development, legal systems, and political orientation can combine to scuttle the most effective, aggressive market entry strategy. Well planned and implemented global marketing strategies that succeed, however, tend to generate more profits than their domestic counterparts.

2. Following are examples of negative impacts on price that could combine to scuttle a foreign market entry strategy for the MM line (1) government policies, such as price controls or mandates that profits or ownership be kept within the host country; (2) currency valuation differences, which could mean that products would be priced, in host country money, beyond the means of host country cutomers; (3) escalating costs for transporting and distributing MM systems to host country customers could also effectively price them out of the market.

3. In the organizational market, MM systems would most likely be purchased in quantities for training groups of associates (for example, in law firms, accounting firms, and medical centers), while, in the consumer market, individual professionals would purchase individual MM systems for home study purposes. Some possible marketing mix implications follow. In each market, MM systems would be priced differently, reflecting quantity and other discounts organizations get that individuals don't; they would also be distributed differently, through outlets peculiar to each market (e.g., wholesalers to the trade, retailers to consumers). Additionally, they would probably be promoted with different appeals and media; for example, in the organizational market, ads in professional journals might stress savings to companies using MM systems; in the consumer market, systems might be promoted through direct mail, stressing the career advancement benefits of using information and training provided through MM software.

4. Needs are defined as states of mental or physical felt deprivation; wants are needs focused toward specific products; and demand is wants backed by purchasing power. In developed countries, needs tend to arise on many levels; for example, a mode of transportation

(motorcycle, automobile, etc.) purchased in a developed country might be used for functional reasons (basic transportation), social reasons (to improve status with peers), and psychological reasons (ego enhancement), while in an undeveloped country the main motive might be purely functional. These "needs" differences determine what products people are going to want and the demand patterns that will prevail (e.g., latent, negative), and have to be taken into account in designing, positioning, pricing, and promoting products.

5. Competition is broadly defined as anything else a prospctive customer can purchase other than the product offered. In Merton's domestic market, its competition, like that of most other mature, successful companies, is primarily of the direct variety (i.e., other brand name producers of computer systems). However, in a foreign market, Merton's MM systems will more likely be perceived as new and relatively unfamiliar, with much, if not most, of its competition of the indirect variety (i.e., other ways that professionals can keep up with their fields such as college classrooms and library databases). These differences in the competitive environment have to be accounted for in strategic planning, especially in defining target market needs, and in positioning, pricing, and promoting products.

6. The environmental assessment of marketplace threats and opportunities, and a company's resources for profitably exploiting opportunities, helps shape the firm's mission, which in turn helps define overall company objectives (such as a desired return on investment), as well as marketing objectives that must be achieved so that the company's overall objectives can be achieved. In foreign markets, environments (i.e., culture, technological and economic development, and political and legal systems) are generally more complex and unfamiliar to home country marketers, and information about them more difficult to generate, with the result that missions, objectives, and the planning and implementation needed to achieve them are frequently much less certain to reflect reality.

7. Depending largely on the product/service being marketed, target markets can be defined along many different dimensions, including demographic (age, income, gender, etc.), psychographic (motives, attitudes, life-styles, etc.), and behavior (when and why they buy the product) criteria. This defining information, in turn, helps build marketing mixes that relate to these criteria, such as a product or service consistent with a customer's attitudes, age, and life-style that is distributed in the most convenient manner.

8. The most significant difference between the marketing concept philosophy and production/sales philosophies has to do with the customer orientation associated with the marketing concept philosophy. Unlike sales/production philosophies, which start with products and

focus on unilateral ways to get these products to customers the marketing concept starts with customers and focuses on multilateral ways to develop product/price/place/promotion offerings that will meet their identified needs. The societal marketing philosophy differs from the marketing philosophy in that it includes another partner in the exchange process—the welfare of the society in which the exchange takes place.

3

INTERNATIONAL MARKETING SYSTEMS

OVERVIEW

A marketing system consists of the organization itself, the marketing mix offering, the target market, and marketing intermediaries that facilitate exchange. Activating and directing the marketing system are interacting systems for organizing the enterprise, formulating strategic plans, controlling plan effectiveness, and generating, analyzing, and distributing information. All systems have inputs, flows, and outputs. If they work together efficiently to satisfy target market and company objectives, synergy is created whereby the total effect is greater than that of individual elements acting alone.

INTERNATIONAL MARKETING PROCESSES AND SYSTEMS

In Chapter 2 we viewed global marketing as a process culminating in the formulation of strategic marketing plans (SMP) designed to reconcile a firm's objectives and resources with changing marketplace opportunities. We also examined marketing concepts and philosophies that comprise and guide the SMP process in domestic and international markets.

In this chapter and Chapter 4, we view international marketing as a system comprising four major systems that facilitate the preparation, implementation, and control of strategic marketing plans in global markets. Lora Moore's efforts in planning for Merton's entry and growth in the global marketplace will continue to provide illustrative examples.

SYSTEMS THEORY EXPLAINS MARKETING PROCESSES

According to *Webster's New Collegiate Dictionary*, a system is "a regularly interacting or interdependent group of items forming a unified whole." Four concepts define a system: input, flows, output, and synergy. For example, a computer software program, designed to help integrate a multinational firm's international markets, would function as a system: Input on marketing performance in a specific country would flow into a database to be matched with similar data from other country markets. Analyses of all these data would then be summarized in a report noting areas of subpar performance and possible reasons for this result. This output information would then become input for better managerial decisions for bringing performance up to par in all markets.

This cooperative interaction among various agencies—the computer components, the software program, the decision makers—would help produce a total effect greater than the sum of effects taken separately. It is called synergy.

In an efficient marketing system, all functions—sales, marketing research, advertising, etc.—interact synergistically with other internal and external systems including other departments, customer groups, distributors, and outside agencies to achieve organizational goals by meeting the needs of target customers. In the process, one department's output becomes input for other departments: sales reports, for example, fuel activities in accounting, marketing research, and production departments.

SYSTEMS WITHIN THE MARKETING SYSTEM

The marketing system consists of the organization itself, the marketing mix offering, target markets, and marketing intermediaries, such as banks, retailers, and transport agencies that facilitate exchanges between the marketing organization and its markets.

In designing a marketing system to effectively and profitably market Merton products in international markets, Lora Moore focused on four major systems within this system:

- The *organizational system* holds together and harmonizes the interacting systems comprising the marketing system.

- The *marketing planning system* identifies marketing opportunities and helps generate customer-oriented strategic plans.

- The *marketing control system* monitors performance of strategic plans and activates necessary measures to keep performance pointed toward objectives.

- The *marketing information system* generates, analyzes, and disseminates decision information needed to fuel the other systems and the overall marketing system.

Working together synergistically, these four systems support each step of the SMP process, discussed in Chapter 2 (see Figure 3-1).

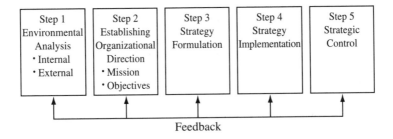

Figure 3–1. The Strategic Marketing Planning Process

THE ORGANIZATIONAL SYSTEM HARMONIZES MARKETING EFFORTS

In a modern marketing organization, the organizational system provides a structural framework within which marketing analysis, planning, implementation, and control activities are effectively coordinated and carried out. Formal organization charts, like those displayed in this chapter, supplemented by job descriptions, spell out duties of all line and staff personnel and establish lines of authority and communication through which managers on all levels accomplish their work.

Among firms committed to global marketing programs, the nature and shape of organizational structures and reporting systems change over time to reflect a company's increased involvement in foreign activities. Generally, they evolve from integrated to separated international structures and systems based on products, areas, functions, or combinations of these dimensions.

Figure 3-2 shows how these changes might occur over time as a firm evolves through domestic, international, and multinational stages to achieve global status. The firm begins this evolution with a simple export department, perhaps managed by a single individual, responsible for processing orders from abroad through a distributor who takes title to the merchandise and handles all export details. Because title changes hands in home country currency, the seller has little concern for things like cultural differences, currency valuations, tax and legal considerations, and promotion, price, and distribution strategies. This was Merton's situation when the firm hired Lora Moore to develop global markets for Merton products.

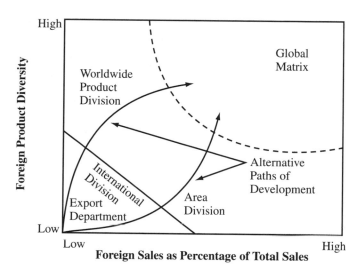

Figure 3–2. Evolution of International Organizational Structures

Moore's first initiative was to move Merton to the next organizational stage—an international division that centralizes international expertise, information flows, authority over international activities, and many other functions associated with global operations such as marketing research, sales, export documentation, and foreign government relations. Manufacturing and related functions remained with domestic divisions to achieve economies of scale.

Figure 3-3, a simplified version of the international division structure, suggests a major problem associated with this form: dependence on domestic divisions for needed product, personnel, technology, and other resources. Since domestic division managers are assessed against domestic performance, they may withhold resources from the international division to enhance this performance.

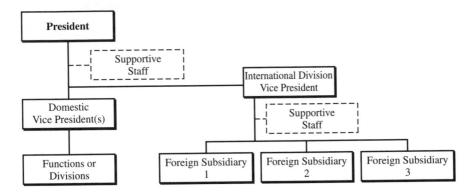

Figure 3–3. The International Division Structure

To avoid situations in which the international division was at a disadvantage in competing for corporate resources, Merton senior management agreed with Moore's recommendation to structure this division along the lines of the Strategic Business Unit (SBU) pioneered by the General Electric Company.

GE's SBUs: SMALL BUSINESSES WITHIN BIG BUSINESSES

Consistent with the SBU model, Merton's international division would be structured around a single business (MM systems) and would have outside competitors (other firms marketing computer systems in international markets) and a distinct mission. This SBU would have strategic and operational planning capabilities, with control over the production of MM units, and profit center responsibility for formulating, implementing, and controlling plans for marketing these units. Coordination between domestic and international operations would be achieved by a joint domestic-international staff that interacted in strategic planning, with plan approval required at senior management levels. Moore believed that this structure would facilitate decentralized, delegated authority and responsibility and encourage an entrepreneurial spirit, with less formalized roles and communication channels to encourage fast, flexible responses to marketplace threats and opportunities. (Global Focus 3-1 shows how the Ford Motor Company's reorganization along SBU lines decentralizes operational and strategic capabilities to more efficiently and economically serve international markets.)

GLOBAL FOCUS 3-1

Ford Reorganizes to Serve Global Markets
Better, Faster, and Cheaper

The Ford Motor Company today announced its most sweeping reorganization in more than 25 years in a bid to compete better in the coming decades not only in its established European and North American markets but also in the potentially huge car and truck markets developing in Asia.

At the end of the year, Ford's North American Operations and Ford of Europe will vanish, merging into a single operating unit, Ford Automotive Operations, with global reach. Ford's Asian-Pacific and Latin American operations will remain separate until the other, more extensive operations are merged.

Under its new organization plan, Ford plans to establish centers dedicated to developing specific types of vehicles that Ford will sell worldwide. For example, the new center in Europe . . . will develop Ford's small, front-wheel-drive cars, like the Escort, for sale in Europe, Asia, and America.

"We're going to combine the resources of a large and successful company with the speed and responsiveness of a small company," said Alexander Trotman, Ford's British-born chairman and chief executive. "This, of course, will assure a better return for our stockholders, a more certain future for all employees and, we believe, much better product, and a wider array of product, for all our customers around the world."

Source: James Bennet, "Ford Revamps With Eye on the Globe," *The New York Times*, April 22, 1994, p. D1.

PRODUCT, AREA, AND MATRIX STRUCTURES

An integrated international structure, while characteristic of firms committed to proactive development of a global market presence, does not necessarily suit the needs of firms that have achieved this presence. Typically, when a firm's international market approaches, or achieves, parity with its domestic market in sales and profits, the functions of the international department will be absorbed into structures in which international and domestic divisions have equal status. Now, with equal access to company resources and senior decision makers, the absorbed divisions will presumably be able to plan for and respond to market threats and opportunities more efficiently and effectively. Examples of these structures include product and area structures.

• *PRODUCT STRUCTURE*

The product structure, which is most used by multinational firms like Motorola that market highly diverse product groups, gives worldwide responsibility to strategic business units for marketing specific product lines. Moore envisioned this structure for Merton once its major product lines had achieved a substantial presence in international markets. As shown in Figure 3-4, this structure would create business teams with a global strategic focus for each of these product lines, with status equal to domestic market business teams. The central pool of specialized expertise characterizing the international division would now be fragmented among the divisions, placing a premium on managers with strong international experience. Also emphasized would be coordinating mechanisms to provide expertise in such areas as marketing research and international law and to settle resource allocation problems among the product divisions.

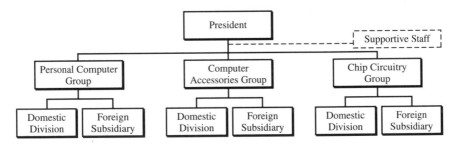

Figure 3-4. The International Product Structure

• *AREA STRUCTURE*

The area structure, illustrated in Figure 3-5, organizes the firm in terms of geographic areas served. This structure, the second most frequently used worldwide, characterizes large European multinationals like Nestle that have large foreign operations not dominated by a single area. It is also used where market conditions affecting product acceptance and operating conditions vary widely. As with product structures, central staffs are responsible for providing coordination support for worldwide planning, implementation, and control activities.

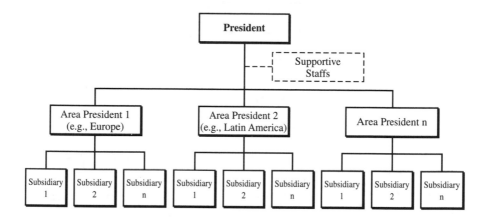

Figure 3–5. The International Area Structure

MATRIX STRUCTURES INTEGRATE OTHER STRUCTURES

The matrix organizational structure addresses problems implicit in integrated or separated structures by combining elements of both. For example, as illustrated in Figure 3-6, Merton's three major product divisions intersect with area divisions to provide much closer coordination among country managers and business managers. Conceivably, a three-dimensional matrix structure would include functional managers (e.g., marketing, manufacturing, and research) in this mix. The driving force within the matrix structure is the product manager, who builds a team with the other intersecting managers, exchanging information and resources and encouraging a strategic global focus. Competition among product, functional, and area managers to attract resources and build teams presumably creates more productive, creative responses to marketplace threats and opportunities.

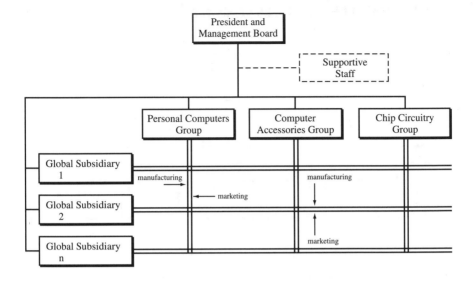

Figure 3-6. The International Matrix Structure

This very competition, however, is cited as a drawback to the matrix structure, often resulting in unproductive conflict and confusion. Another drawback is the complexity of the matrix model, which can cause problems in reporting relationships that can actually lower the company's reaction time. Among the alternatives for addressing these problems are rotating managers among the groups and reporting relationships with line and staff oversight groups.

THE PLANNING SYSTEM HELPS DEFINE AND EXPLOIT OPPORTUNITIES

The end product of the global planning system is a strategic marketing plan that adopts the firm's objectives and resources to its changing foreign situations. In formulating marketing plans for Merton's entry into international markets, Moore followed a four-stage process involving:

- An environmental assessment;
- A SWOT analysis matching Merton strengths and weaknesses to market opportunities and threats;
- A statement of strategic intent and corporate objectives;
- Preparation of a formal marketing plan.

• *ENVIRONMENTAL ASSESSMENT*

This assessment aimed to identify and define elements in Merton's internal and external environments that justified, and helped shape, a strategic planning initiative. Internally, this assessment focused on Merton's resources and constraints, such as product, people, and financial capabilities required for global entry/growth initiatives. Externally, the focus was on market conditions in prospective host countries that would help determine components of these initiatives, for example, competitive, cultural, logistical, and political climates that a marketing mix strategy would have to address.

• *SWOT ANALYSIS*

SWOT analyses of company strengths and weaknesses matched to opportunities and threats were made using planning models integrated into the marketing information system. In Merton's international operations, Moore relied on three models in particular: the General Electric (GE) strategic planning grid, the Boston Consulting Group (BCG) growth share matrix, and Porter's competitive analysis model.

THE GE STRATEGIC PLANNING GRID

The General Electric strategic planning grid (Figure 3-7) provides a framework for analyzing a prospective new product or business opportunity in terms of the attractiveness of a prospective market and the business strengths of the firm assessing the opportunity. The more attractive the market and the stronger the business strengths of the company, the better the prospects of success in entering this market. As such, the grid helps facilitate SWOT analyses that balance a firm's internal strengths and weaknesses with external opportunities and threats.

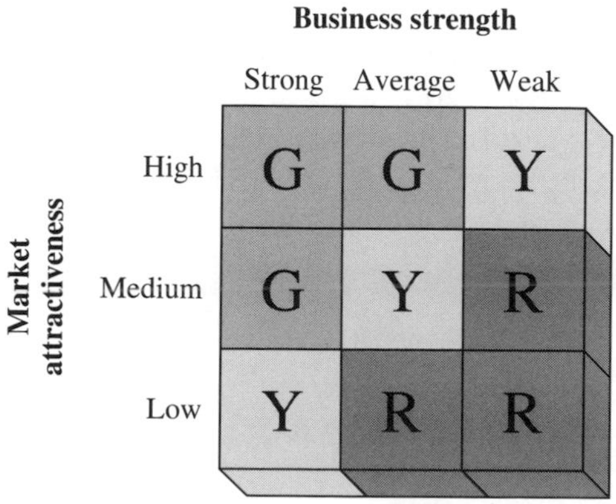

Figure 3–7. The Strategic Planning Grid

Green light opportunities, in the G boxes in the grid, indicate an invest and grow planning strategy; full marketing resources are appropriate, and profitability is expected to be high. Yellow light opportunities, in the Y boxes, indicate a cautious planning strategy; a product might have a strong position in a weak industry, a moderate position in an attractive industry, or a weak position in an attractive industry. Weaknesses should be strengthened before the new product is launched; otherwise, with an existing product, no additional resources should be committed. Red light opportunities (R boxes) signal no-go strategies and no new product launches; they indicate the need to harvest or divest existing products.

In using the GE grid to select worthwhile international markets for MM systems and to formulate entry and growth strategies in these markets, Moore used these criteria to determine industry attractiveness: market size, market growth rate, competitive intensity, need for product adaptation, need for communication adaptation, distribution economies of scale, macroenvironmental constraints, and profit margin potential. A country or region with favorable scores in these criteria areas would score "high" on the "market attractiveness" dimension of the grid.

Criteria used to assess Merton's resources for entering attractive foreign markets included financial resources (e.g., capital availability and ability to transfer funds), product resources (e.g., quality, ability to accept adaptations, transport practicality, production capacity, and monopolistic characteristics), price competitiveness (e.g., ability to profitably price product under competition), human resources (e.g., knowledge of foreign markets and marketing, foreign marketing skills, and ability to recruit desired personnel), and environmental effects (ability to respond to adverse changes in such areas as distribution, currency valuation, demand changes, and societal attitudes).

BCG GROWTH SHARE MATRIX

The Boston Consulting Group growth share matrix (Figure 3-8) focuses on portfolios of products and the relationships among them. Using the BCG grid, all company products and businesses are classified according to their positions on two axes: a horizontal axis labeled "Relative market share," and a vertical axis labeled "Market growth rate."

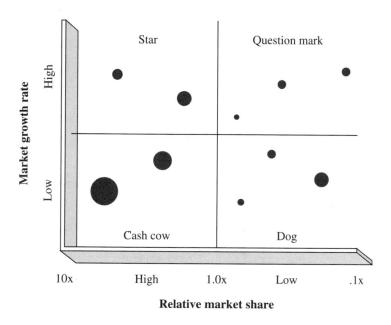

Figure 3–8. The Growth Share Matrix

Products in the high-high quadrant, called stars, typically require considerable cash to finance their rapid growth—often in excess of the revenues the product generates. Key sources of this cash are other products, called cash cows, that occupy the lower left-hand quadrant. Although their market isn't growing at nearly the rate of these stars, these products occupy a high-share leadership position that requires less investment and produces positive profits and cash flows. Question mark products in the upper right-hand quadrant (low market share in a high growth rate industry) typically lack consumer support, have unclear differential advantages, and require a lot of cash to hold share. Dog products in the low-growth/low-share lower right quadrant are unable to attract customers and lag the competition in sales, image, and operating costs.

The location of a product in the growth share matrix helps devise strategies relative to other products in a portfolio depicted on the matrix. For example, as a star, Merton's MM system was selected to spearhead its international marketing efforts. Merton's cash cow programs, spearheaded by its successful line of chip circuits, would help to finance this effort. If the MM marketing program proved successful in global markets, it would be followed by question mark, and even dog products that might fare better in foreign markets.

In modifying the growth share matrix to international markets, Moore substituted countries for a single country along the relative-market-share axis. For example, in Figure 3-9, company A is seen to be a leader in five of the countries in which it markets its products, with cash cows in the United States and Canada, and stars in Great Britain, France, and Germany. Only its Spanish affiliate, a question mark, has not achieved leader status.

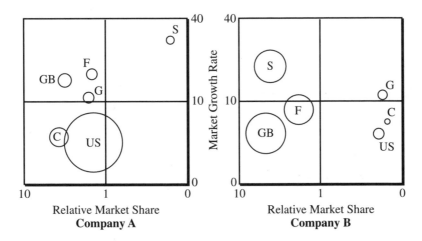

Figure 3–9. International Growth Share Grid

At the same time, Company B, A's main competitor, although not a threat in A's major U.S. market, has a commanding lead in three fast-growing markets—Great Britain, Spain, and France. Comparing the firm's portfolio with those of competitors' suggests strategies to counter competitive initiatives, as illustrated in Global Focus 3-2, which shows how the Whirlpool Company uses global portfolio analyses to position itself in its quest for global status.

GLOBAL FOCUS 3-2

Whirlpool Succeeds Abroad

Holding the top market position in North America, the number 3 position in Europe, and a leading presence in South America, Whirlpool Corporation is, according to a market analyst, "the best positioned appliance company for the 1990s." U.S. rival companies such as Maytag Corporation have struggled with global strategies, but Whirlpool is making its aggressive expansion work. By moving into Europe and developing nations, the firm aims to tap growth areas to complement its mature, slow-growth business in North America.

After acquiring the European appliance business of Philips

Electronics NV, Whirlpool is posting higher profits and bigger market share in Europe, despite the recession and very slow recovery there. In 1993 European shipments rose about 5 percent, even as the overall European appliance business was flat or declining. Further increases are likely over the next few years. Currently, Europe has a collection of 200 appliance brand names, many of them popular in just one country. Whirlpool's strategy is to stand out with strong pan-European brands. President of Whirlpool Europe NV, Hank Bowman, explains that "Research shows that trends, preferences and biases of consumers, country to country, are reducing as opposed to increasing." Although regional preferences will remain, the company sees a chance to profit from the move toward a less-fractured Europe.

When Whirlpool first entered Europe, it used a dual Philips/ Whirlpool brand to introduce consumers to its flagship Whirlpool brand. It is now going it alone, silencing skeptics who thought Europeans would not buy the new American name. According to electronics analyst Andrew Haskins, "Philips had a strong brand name, and Whirlpool has been able to build on that quite considerably."

Source: Robert L. Rose, "Whirlpool is expanding in Europe Despite the Slump," *The Wall Street Journal*, January 27, 1994, p. B4.

PORTER'S COMPETITIVE ANALYSIS MODEL

A third useful planning model Moore used to measure Merton strengths and weaknesses against opportunities and threats in international markets was Michael Porter's "competitive analysis" model,[1] which is based on an assessment of five competitive factors: (1) the threat of new entrants, (2) the bargaining power of suppliers, (3) the bargaining power of buyers, (4) the threat of substitute products, and (5) rivalry among existing firms.

- *Threat of new entrants.* A good entry market for MM systems would be difficult for competitors other than Merton to enter, for a variety of reasons. For example, the MMs strong brand identity, product differences, or cost advantages might deter competitors. Other deterrents could include excessive capital requirements or government policies making entry difficult.

---

[1] Michael E. Porter, *Competitive Advantage*. New York: The Free Press, 1985, Chapter 1.

- *Bargaining power of suppliers.* To be avoided in situations where suppliers of parts and components for MM systems in an entry market are potentially so powerful that they could raise prices or reduce quality at will. Determinants of this kind of power include size and concentration of suppliers, the importance of high volume to the supplier, the presence of substitutes for suppliers' products, and the degree of competition among suppliers.

- *Bargaining power of buyers.* Buyers have the potential ability to force MM system prices down, bargain for higher quality or more services, and play competitors off against each other. The likelihood that they will is determined by such considerations as their concentration, the volume of their purchases, the cost to them of switching from Merton to other providers, substitutes for MM systems, the strength of MM's brand identity, and buyer access to information about Merton and its competitors.

- *Threat of substitute products.* How likely would a substitute product in a global entry market be able to wipe out Merton's strong entry position? Determinants include the technological complexity of the original product, the price and performance superiority of the substitute, and the propensity of buyers to switch to the substitute.

- *Rivalry among existing products.* A high incidence of price competition, advertising battles, new product introductions, and excessive customer service is evidence of a hypercompetitive environment that might undercut entry-and-growth efforts. Rivalry determinants include product differences, brand identities, and concentration among rival firms.

• *STATEMENTS OF STRATEGIC INTENT AND OBJECTIVES*

The SWOT analysis conducted in the second step of the strategic planning process should provide information needed to prepare these statements.

As to an appropriate marketing strategy for entering, or growing, in one or more foreign markets, the four major options are summarized in the product/market opportunity matrix (Figure 3-10), with each option appropriate for different product/market situations.

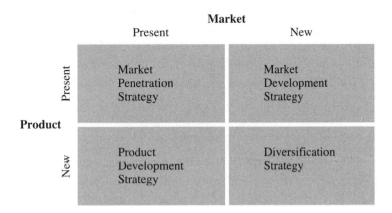

Figure 3–10. Product/Market Opportunity Matrix

- *A market penetration strategy*—marketing existing products more aggressively in existing markets—is appropriate when the market for a product is growing or not quite saturated. More aggressive selling of MM systems to members of Merton's tax accountant target market would be an example. Typically, a penetration strategy brings in revenues and profits by attracting nonusers and competitors' customers and raising the usage rate among current customers.

- *A market development strategy*, which is applicable when a firm seeks to achieve greater sales of present products from new markets, focuses on new geographic or customer segments.

- *A product development strategy*, effective when a firm has a core of strong brands and a sizeable customer following, involves developing new products to attract members of existing markets (e.g., new MM courses to meet the training and development needs among members of Merton's accounting and law target markets).

- *A diversification strategy* involves introducing new products into new markets and is appropriate when more opportunities for growth exist outside the firm's present markets.

Two of these growth strategies—market penetration and product development essentially involve concentration of marketing efforts in a small number of markets, and two—market development and diversification—essentially involve diversification into a number of foreign markets.

As indicated in Table 3-1, data from a SWOT analysis can identify which of the two strategies is appropriate to a given target/market situation. Thus, a concentration strategy would be indicated in situations where the following conditions existed in a prospective entry market: high and stable growth rates, rapid responses to marketing efforts, a strong lead over the competition, the expensive need to tailor the product and the promotion campaign to the needs of the market, and program requirements that mandate extensive interaction with clients and intermediaries.

Table 3–1. Factors Affecting the Choice Between Concentration and Diversification Strategies

Factor	Diversification	Concentration
Market growth rate	Low	High
Sales stability	Low	High
Sales response function	Decreasing	Increasing
Competitive lead time	Short	Long
Spillover effects	High	Low
Need for product adaptation	Low	High
Need for communication adaptation	Low	High
Economies of scale in distribution	Low	High
Extent of constraints	Low	High
Program control requirements	Low	High

Sources: Igal Ayal and Jehiel Zif, "Marketing Expansion Strategies in Multinational Marketing," *Journal of Marketing*, Vol. 43 (Spring 1979), p. 89. Reprinted from *Journal of Marketing*, published by the American Marketing Association.

On the other hand, in target/market situations where product and promotion campaigns can be standardized for all markets, where demand and competitive conditions are similar, a diversification strategy would probably be indicated.

SETTING BUSINESS AND MARKETING OBJECTIVES

Just as the portfolio analyses described previously can help define strategic initiatives appropriate to the needs of customers and companies, they can also help define objectives that these strategies are calculated to achieve. In general, these objectives are first established by top management, based on a researched understanding of resources and opportunities, and with input from staff and line management. They usually encompass a mix of sales, profits, and other long- and short-range expectations.

Marketing objectives, designed to help achieve overall objectives, are usually more customer-oriented, focusing on things like new product acceptance, sales results (in terms of revenues and costs, brand loyalty, repeat purchases, etc.), the appeal of the product to different market segments, and profit results by customer, territory, salesperson, and distribution channel. Marketing objectives are both qualitative (company image, product leadership) and quantitative (dollar sales, share of market), with a growing trend to measure qualitative objectives in quantitative terms (e.g., "innovativeness" measured by number of patents achieved). For sellers of industrial products, marketing objectives usually pertain to profit margins, field sales efforts, new product development, and pricing policies and sales to major accounts or industries; for sellers of consumer products, marketing objectives usually pertain to profits, sales promotion, new product development, pricing, advertising expenditures, and field sales efforts.

• *PREPARE A FORMAL MARKETING PLAN*

Key components of this plan include a situation analysis, objectives and goals, long-term strategies and short-term tactics for bringing together target markets and marketing mixes, an implementation timetable, cost and profit estimates, provision for control, and contingency plans if needed. An important part of this formal marketing plan is provision for a loop between "situation analysis" and "implementation" stages to ensure that decisions are made on the basis of current information. For example, if the control process shows that a particular price or promotional appeal isn't achieving desired results in targeted markets, this information will be incorporated into subsequent SWOT analyses through the marketing information system (discussed in Chapter 4).

THE CONTROL SYSTEM KEEPS PLANS ON TRACK

Having considered organizational and planning systems for Merton's international division, Moore next turned her attention to the control system within the total marketing system.

Control, broadly defined, means making something happen the way it was planned to happen. It requires a clear understanding of the expected results of a particular action (e.g., a price change designed to increase sales by 10 percent), a way to measure the extent to which these expected results materialize, and a way to see that they do when they don't. An effective control system monitors the entire spectrum of environmental variables, including customers, competitors, channel participants, and both controllables (e.g., prices, products, and promotions) and uncontrollables (e.g., political and economic forces). These variables are monitored over both the short- (one year or less) and the long-term (over one year).

In an SBU like Merton's new international division, with operational capability to make MM systems, and strategic capability to market these systems, both operational and strategic control systems would be in place, working to ensure that activities were synergistically coordinated to achieve company and customer objectives.

Operational control involves functions like production control, quality control, and inventory control. Strategic control focuses on monitoring and evaluating the steps of the SMP process, from environmental analysis through strategy implementation. The relationship between operational and strategic control is shown in Figure 3-11.

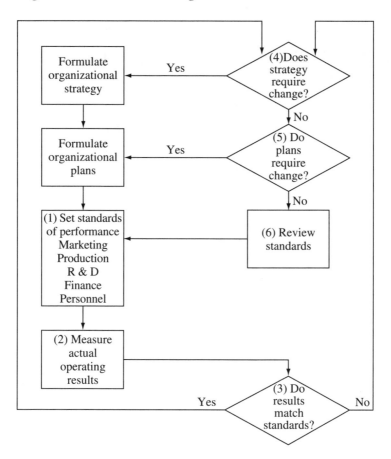

Figure 3–11. Operational/Strategic Control Matrix

Because the control process encompasses and helps to integrate all the firm's operational and strategic activities, it is typically handled at the headquarters level, although largely autonomous SBU subsidiaries like Merton's international division make inputs into the process. For example, Moore would be responsible for developing, as part of the overall strategic plan, budgets that would anticipate (1) revenues from MM global sales; (2) all costs—production, physical distribution, marketing, etc.—anticipated in generating these sales, and (3) the net profit difference between these figures. The figures in this budget, along with other figures defining strategic performance (e.g., sales quotas and net profit per average sale) become standards against which to measure performance.

However, just as Moore's budget encompasses other budgets—for individual customer groups, territories, even individual salespeople—hers must be reconciled with all of Merton's other divisional and group budgets, and appropriate trade-offs must be made at headquarters level.

Regardless of what kind of control system is being installed, it will probably comprise the following three steps depicted on Figure 3-11: measure performance, compare performance with standards, and take corrective action when performance doesn't meet standards.

To illustrate, assume that Moore's strategic plan envisions that use of a particular distribution channel to reach the business/professional market in France will produce so many dollars in sales, at a cost of so many dollars. These "so many dollar" figures become standards against which to measure and assess the actual performance of this distribution channel (steps 1 and 2). If figures come in on target, nothing is done; no control is necessary (step 3). If costs are higher and sales lower than planned, some kind of corrective action will be built into the next plan, such as changing the channel or providing incentives for better channel performance or, perhaps, lowering expectations to more realistic standards (steps 4, 5, and 6). Control will also come into play if channel performance exceeds expectations and costs are lower, and sales higher, than anticipated. Particularly in global markets, this result might be a good reason to try this distribution channel in other areas.

INTERNATIONAL CONTROL PROBLEMS AND PROCEDURES

Establishing standards and measurement tools—necessary control components—is difficult enough in the domestic market, and especially challenging in international markets. Environmental changes, which also change standards, occur at different rates in different countries, and communication problems arise from differences in language and customs and the greater distance between top management and foreign subsidiaries.

To measure performance continuously, Moore incorporated into Merton's Marketing Information System—discussed in the next chapter—standards against which to compare this performance and the means to effectively analyze and distribute emerging information to appropriate decision makers.

CHAPTER PERSPECTIVE

Properly designed and integrated, the four major systems comprising the marketing system generate synergistic output much greater than the sum of their individual components. The organizational system provides a framework for efficient, effective, coordinated activities. The planning system provides a means for generating and implementing strategic marketing plans that achieve mission-related objectives, and the control system provides a means to ensure that proper action is taken when these objectives aren't achieved. The marketing information system, discussed in the next chapter, provides a means of gathering, processing, and disseminating the right information to the right people at the right time in the right form.

KNOW THE CONCEPTS

TERMS FOR STUDY

cash cows
competitive analysis
concentration strategy
decentralization
diversification strategy
dogs
environmental assessment
export department
growth share matrix
international division
market development strategy
marketing control system
marketing planning system
matrix structures
operational control

organizational system
penetration strategy
product development strategy
product structure
question marks
stars
Strategic Business Unit (SBU)
strategic control
strategic marketing plans
strategic planning grid
SWOT analysis
synergy
systems
team building

MATCHUP EXERCISES

1. Match the organizational structure in the first column with the appropriate characteristic in the second column.

1. export department
2. international division

a. most frequently used, worldwide
b. centralizes internal expertise

3. Strategic Business Unit   c. has outside competitors, a distinct mission

4. area structure   d. processes orders for host country middlemen who take title to products

5. matrix structure   e. brings together country, product, and functional specialists

2. Match the statement in the first column with the section of the marketing plan in the second column where it would most likely appear.

1. Initially, distribution will be through agents and brokers in the host country.   a. strategies and tactics

2. At the end of the first quarter, any necessary changes will be made in the marketing mix elements to bring performance in line with planned expectations.   b. objectives

3. Budgeted expectations are for a 10 percent return on investment at the end of year 2.   c. provision for control

4. The promotion campaign will focus, initially, on generating distribution through a "pull" strategy of generating demand among end-users.   d. marketing mix

3. Match the strategic option in the first column with the descriptor in the second column.

1. diversification   a. high growth rates, strong competitive lead, unique product

2. concentration   b. standardized marketing mixes, similar cross-cultural demand

3. product development   c. greater sales of existing products from new markets

4. market development   d. develop new products to attract members of existing markets

QUESTIONS FOR REVIEW AND DISCUSSION

1. Using the Merton Company as an illustrative example, describe the broad components of a marketing system. Why should this system function more efficiently in Merton's domestic market than in a newly entered foreign market?

2. Explain how the four systems comprising the marketing system work together to facilitate the strategic marketing planning process.

3. Explain how and why organizational structures change as they do as the firm evolves from export to global status.

4. What is the significance of each letter in the SWOT acronym in terms of Merton's search for the most worthwhile global entry market?

5. Discuss similarities and differences between the GE strategic planning grid and the BCG growth share matrix. Which would be most appropriate for a multinational or global firm seeking to expand its global reach?

6. What is the difference between operational and strategic control? How are they related?

7. In terms of the steps in the control process, explain why a firm might experience real difficulty in effectively controlling operational and strategic activities in diverse remote locations.

8. Describe the components of a budget and explain its importance in the control process.

ANSWERS

MATCHUP EXERCISES

1. 1d, 2b, 3c, 4a, 5e
2. 1d, 2c, 3b, 4a
3. 1b, 2a, 3d, 4c

QUESTIONS FOR REVIEW AND DISCUSSION

1. Merton's marketing system consists of (1) the company itself, with all the structures, policies, procedures, and objectives that activate, motivate, and control marketing programs; (2) Merton's marketing mix offerings, including product/place/price/promotion strategies supporting a range of product lines in various demand states; (3) target markets for its marketing mix offerings, in consumer, organizational, and governmental market aggregates; and (4) marketing intermediaries that help move offerings to target markets, including distribution channels, banks, advertising agencies, and insurance companies. This marketing system would be more likely to function efficiently in the domestic market because of the unfamiliarity, even hostility, of the foreign market. To some extent, Merton will have to adapt to different economic, political, legal, cultural, competitive and technological

conditions; target markets will be more difficult to identify and define, making marketing mixes to satisfy these markets more difficult to formulate; and marketing intermediaries will often be less reliable and predictable.

2. (1) The organizational system organizes resources so that motivated, specialized people work together effectively to create and carry out marketing plans; (2) the planning system provides the wherewithal to formulate strategic marketing plans that match company strengths with marketplace opportunities to achieve mission-related objectives; (3) the control system provides standards and protocols for comparing actual with planned performance and taking necessary steps when they deviate excessively; and (4) the marketing information system generates and distributes decision information that fuels all the elements of the strategic planning process.

3. From the perspective of the marketing manager, the main purpose of an organizational structure is to direct, motivate, and harmonize human activity toward the achievement of company and marketing objectives in an efficient, economical manner. These objectives, in turn, define the organizational structure that will best achieve them. For example, if these objectives can best be achieved by serving the needs of distributors in foreign markets who take title to merchandise and handle all marketing activities, then a simple export department structure will suffice. However, as more countries are entered, and home country personnel are engaged in host countries, an international division structure might be indicated, with more functions, countries, and products covered. Later, as the most efficient means of achieving objectives results from focusing on broad product groups marketed to customers in large geographic regions, the product, area, or matrix departmental structure might marshall resources most efficiently and economically.

4. The letters in the SWOT acronym imply that a firm is matching its Strengths and Weaknesses against Opportunities and Threats in the marketplace, by way of evolving a strategic plan that will effectively use company strengths to exploit opportunities and counter threats. In Merton's case, an opportunity would be a global entry market most receptive in terms of such considerations as the nature and needs of professionals comprising target markets, a general lack of competitive activity, transportation and communication networks to distribute MM systems, the economic wherewithal to purchase MM systems, and legal, political, and cultural values (language, attitudes toward modern devices, etc.) similar to those in the domestic market.

5. The GE strategic planning grid and the BCG growth share matrix are similar in that each is designed to help formulate product/market strategies that best match company strengths and weaknesses against

threats and opportunities in prospective foreign markets. The significant difference between these two grids derives from the fact that the GE grid makes these matches on a product-by-product basis in terms of the attractiveness of a prospective market and the firm's resources for penetrating this market, while the BCG matrix makes these matches in the context of an entire product portfolio, with cash cows, stars, question marks, and dogs all identified by their locations on axes that depict the growth rate of a market and the relative market share of each product. For a global or multinational firm intent on expanding market reach, the BCG grid would probably be most appropriate in that it helps to define strategies for individual products appropriate to the sweep of products and territories encompassed by the firm's marketing programs. For example, a green light "Go" strategy indicated by a GE grid analysis of market attractiveness and company strengths for an individual product might be a "No Go" strategy when viewed in the context of other products in the firm's portfolio in that entry market.

6. Operational control focuses on operations within the firm concerned with making products for markets, such as production, quality control, finance, research and development, and inventory management; strategic control focuses on strategic plans implemented outside the firm designed to bring together product offerings and target markets. The important role of the control function, in addition to ensuring that performance in operational and strategic areas meets benchmark standards, is to ensure that both areas work together efficiently and economically and that behaviors in different parts of the organization are compatible and support common goals. For example, effective controls will help ensure that production, quality control, and inventory management controls will work with strategic controls to help the ultimate customer get the right product at the right price and place.

7. The steps of the control process entail the following problems when controlling operational and strategic activities in remote locations. (1) Set standards against which to measure performance. A basic principle of effective control mandates that standards must be equitable, realistic, and cover only areas within the firm's control. In international markets, however, differences among diverse markets can practically negate the establishment of such standards. To illustrate, assume that a specified sales or profit return is the mandated standard with different tax, inflation, and monetary exchange ratios, setting equitable, realistic, controllable standards in diverse markets could be next to impossible. (2) Measure actual results as plans are implemented. Once standards are established, means must be devised to measure actual performance. This can be considerably more difficult in foreign than in domestic markets, given cultural and technological

barriers to effective communication. In the domestic market, for example, sophisticated information systems are available to gather and process information pertaining to actual performance; in diverse global markets, such amenities are frequently lacking. (3) Compare actual with planned results. Without the facilities to create comparability and equity among established standards and performance measurements, chances are often slim that this comparison step will produce valid, reliable conclusions on which to base decisions. (4) Revise strategies, plans, and/or standards based on conclusions produced through the control process. Poor controls poorly implemented can create problems in such areas as program coordination, strategic planning, marketing mix performance, and staff motivation.

8. Budgets, a key element in the formalized control process, are short-term guidelines in such areas as operations, investment, and personnel. Usually expressed in dollar terms, they project an outcome (e.g., profit) as well as specific functional costs (e.g., materials, administration, sales) required to produce this outcome. Budgets are used to (1) allocate funds among subsidiaries, (2) plan and coordinate operational and strategic activities; (3) evaluate performance, and (4) exchange information among subsidiaries, product organizations, and headquarters. Thus, supplemented by function reports (on market share, production output, inventory levels, sales, personnel performance, etc.), budgets are involved in all steps of the control process, from setting standards to suggesting corrective actions to be taken when performance and standards don't match.

4

INTERNATIONAL MARKETING RESEARCH I: EXPLORING GLOBAL OPPORTUNITIES

OVERVIEW

In Chapter 3 we examined three of the systems that guide the preparation, implementation and control of strategic marketing plans in international markets. Included were the organizational system, the planning system, and the control system, all interacting synergistically to drive the marketing system. In this chapter and Chapter 5, we examine the marketing information system and the marketing research process that combine to fuel the marketing system by collecting, recording, analyzing, and distributing information about marketing opportunities, problems, and processes during all phases of strategic marketing planning.

MARKETING INFORMATION SYSTEM FUELS OTHER SYSTEMS

A marketing information system (MIS) is an integrated system of data, statistical analysis, modeling, and display formats, relying on computer hard- and software technology, that gathers, sorts, evaluates, stores, and distributes timely and accurate information for use by marketing decision makers to improve planning, organization, implementation, and control.

For Merton's new international division, Moore recognized the critical importance of marketing information in building entry/growth strategies. She also recognized problems to be faced in generating this information in foreign markets separated by time, space, cultural, and technological differences.[1]

To address these needs and problems, she envisioned an MIS system that would encompass the elements depicted in Figure 4-1. This system would work as follows to synthesize information from many sources and convert it into useable form to help her—and other managers associated with the new international division—make faster, smarter decisions:

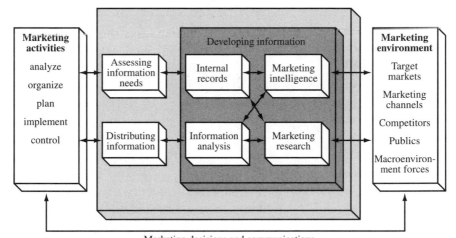

Figure 4-1. A Marketing Information System

- From the *internal records section,* she could tap information developed internally, including records of sales, orders, costs, cash flows, production schedules, shipments, inventories, reseller reactions, competitive activities, and customer needs.

- From the *marketing intelligence section,* she could access information from many sources in the marketing environment, including company personnel, suppliers, resellers, customers, and even competitors. Much of this information would be gathered from online data bases or such suppliers as the A. C. Nielsen Company, which sells data on brand shares and retail sales worldwide.

- From the *marketing research section,* Moore could access information generated through formal and informal studies of specific situations to supplement information from the internal records and marketing intelligence sections. For example, she might want to test pricing or promotion strategies for MM systems in areas where such information wasn't otherwise available.

[1] Sayeste Daser, "International Marketing Systems: A Neglected Prerequisite for Foreign Market Planning," in E. Kaynak, Ed., *International Marketing Management.* New York: Praeger Publishers, 1984, pp. 139–154.

Information from these sections would then be pulled together in the information analysis section of the MIS and presented to Moore in a form that would facilitate activities—from analysis to control—required of the strategic planning process. (Global Focus 4-1 describes computerized information systems used by two companies to generate and disseminate global intelligence that aids tactical and strategic decision making and planning.)

GLOBAL FOCUS 4-1

The Global Spyglass

Both Corning and Digital Equipment Corporation are strong believers in global computer networks for gathering and disseminating competitive intelligence.

Corning started its global system, called the Business Information Exchange Network, with a pilot program in early 1989. One key feature is a news search service that lets users inform the system of topics that interest them. The system then automatically clips articles and places them in the user's electronic mailbox.

Digital Equipment launched its Competitive Information System (CIS) in 1984. Initially, it was mainly used to collect and distribute data on domestic competitors, but after 4 years, it became truly global. CIS contains product descriptions, announcements, internal and external competitive analyses, company strategies, policies and overviews, market analyses, and a direct feed from an external news wire. "Our data serves both strategic and tactical needs," explains Laura J. B. Hunt, Digital's manager of information access services. Digital's competitive analysts use data from CIS for strategic decision making and planning; its sales representatives use CIS data to formulate sales tactics. The system now has more than 10,000 registered employee users and generates more than 100,000 log-ins worldwide.

Source: Kate Bertrand, "The Global Spyglass," in F. Maidment, Ed., *Annual Editions: International Business*. Guilford, Conn.: 1992, pp. 90–92.

Illustrative of the systematic, continuous nature of these MIS processes is environmental scanning, which receives and processes continuous information on international trends and developments (e.g., changing market needs or competitive environments) that help marketers develop long-term policies, broad strategies, action plans, operating programs, and budgets.

Moore had no illusions as to how difficult it would be to build an MIS for the international division. Too little information, incomplete information, dated information, information served up in the wrong form, and information that cost more than it was worth were all problems faced by Merton's domestic MIS. They would be exacerbated in international markets where measurement standards differed from country to country, and many more factors had to be accounted for in gathering and analyzing information.

To address these problems and help ensure the success of the international division's MIS in fulfilling company needs, her needs, and needs of managers, Moore first designed and distributed a questionnaire covering the following points: decisions each manager regularly made, information needed to make these decisions, information that each regularly received, special studies each periodically requested, information each would like to have but didn't get, frequency requirements for each type of information (daily? weekly? monthly? etc.), publications or trade reports each would like to receive on a regular basis, specific topics each would like to be kept informed of, and types of data analysis each would like made available.

Responses, which encompassed the categories shown in Table 4-1, were first edited to eliminate duplicate, irrelevant, or overly expensive information. Information to be used was then integrated into a database to serve the needs of each manager, the department, and the overall organization.

Table 4–1. Categories for a Global Marketing Intelligence System

Category	Coverage
I. Market Information	
1. Market Potential	Information indicating potential demand for products, including the status and prospects of existing company products in existing markets.
2. Consumer/customer attitudes and behavior	Information and attitudes, behavior, and needs of consumers and customers of existing and potential company products. Also included in this category are attitudes of investors toward a company's investment merit.
3. Channels of distribution	Availability, effectiveness, attitudes, and preferences of channel agents.
4. Communications media	Media availability, effectiveness, and cost.
5. Market sources	Availability, quality, and cost.

Category	Coverage
6. New products	Nontechnical information concerning new products for a company (this includes products that are already marketed by other companies).
II. Competitive Information	
7. Competitive business strategy and plans	Goals, objectives. Definition of business: the "design" and rationale of the company.
8. Competitive functional strategies, plans, and programs	Marketing: Target markets, product, price, place, promotion. Strategy and plan: finance, manufacturing, R&D, and human resource strategy, plans, and programs.
9. Competitive operations	Detailed intelligence on competitor operations. Production, shipments, employee transfers, morale, etc.
III. Foreign Exchange	
10. Balance of payments	Government reports.
11. Nominal and real interest rates.	Expert estimation.
12. Inflation rate compared to weighted trading partner average.	PPP theory.
13. Estimate of international competitiveness.	Expert judgment.
14. Attractiveness of country currency and assets to global investors.	Currency demand.
15. Government policy re: country competitiveness.	Expert assessment.
16. Country monetary and fiscal policy.	Expert assessment.
17. Spot and forward market activity.	Market reports.
18. Expectations and opinions of analysts, traders, bankers, economists, business people.	General assessment.

Category	Coverage
IV. Prescriptive Information	
19. Foreign taxes	Information concerning decisions, intentions, and attitudes of foreign authorities regarding taxes upon earnings, dividends, and interest.
20. Other foreign prescriptions and laws	All information concerning local, regional, international authority guidelines, rulings, laws, decrees other than foreign exchange and tax matters affecting the operations, assets, or investments of a company.
21. Home country prescriptions	Home country incentives, controls, regulations, restraints, etc., affecting a company.
V. Resource Information	
22. Human resources	Availability of individuals and groups, employment candidates, sources, strikes, etc.
23. Money	Availability and cost of money for company uses.
24. Raw material	Availability and cost.
25. Acquisitions and mergers	Leads or other information concerning potential acquisitions, mergers, or joint ventures.
VI. General Conditions	
26. Economic factors	Macroeconomic information dealing with broad factors, such as capital movements, rates of growth, economic structure, and economic geography.
27. Social factors	Social structure of society, customs, attitudes, and preferences.
28. Political factors	"Investment climate" meaning of elections, political change.
29. Scientific technological factors	Major developments and trends.
30. Management and administrative practices	Management and administrative practices and procedures concerning such matters as employee compensation, report procedure.
31. Other information	Information not assignable to another category.

Source: Warren J. Keegan, *Global Marketing Management*, 5e, © 1989, p. 407. Reprinted by permission of Prentice Hall, Inc. Upper Saddle River, NJ.

WHAT MARKETING RESEARCH DOES

Marketing research (MR) is the systematic collection, recording, analysis, and distribution of data and information about marketing problems and opportunities. This information applies to each step of the SMP process: identifying environmental threats and opportunities, comparing potential of international markets, selecting target markets, establishing realistic missions and goals, formulating, and implementing goal-oriented strategic plans, and controlling marketing performance. This information can also help marketing management anticipate, and prepare for, global change.

WHO DOES MARKETING RESEARCH?

Every firm that markets things needs MR information. Large firms have their own MR departments, using outside firms for special tasks or studies. Smaller firms are more likely to rely on outside MR firms. In 1990, the 50 largest MR firms in the United States generated revenues of $2.6 billion, 30 percent from research in foreign markets.

And there is no shortage of MR firms in the foreign marketplace. For example, more than 500 marketing research agencies in 17 western European countries offer services, data bases, and bibliographies covering such aspects of international marketing as the business environment, population demographics, and economic forecasts.

PRODUCT/MARKET MR APPLICATIONS

A recent survey of MR activities indicates that the following percentages of U.S. firms conduct, or commission, the following research studies.

- *Sales and market research*—measurement of market potentials (97%), market share analysis (97%), determination of market characteristics (97%), sales analysis (92%), sales quotas and territories (80%), and distribution channels (76%).

- *Business economics*—short-range forecasting (up to 1 year) (89%), long-range forecasting (over one year) (87%), studies of business trends (87%), and pricing studies (83%).

- *Product research*—competitive product studies (87%), testing of existing products (80%), and new product acceptance and potential (76%).

- *Advertising research*—studies of ad effectiveness (76%) and media research (68%).

Moore might easily commission research studies in all these areas in implementing a strategic plan to penetrate the international marketplace. For example, she might begin with a marketing potential study to identify countries and customer groups most likely to respond favorably to the MM offering. Then, a new product acceptance study might be undertaken to define more precisely the response of targeted groups to the MM offering in terms of how they would use it and what features they would expect. Pricing and distribution studies would also be conducted to make sure the MMs were profitably priced and distributed through cost-efficient channels.

Sales forecast, sales territory, and sales quota MR studies would also be undertaken to provide information for allocating dollars and people to bring in the best return. Once profitable sales were generated in selected territories, sales analysis studies would help control the marketing effort by measuring the extent to which sales performance (i.e., revenues and profits generated in different territories by different salespeople) achieved budgeted expectations. Advertising effectiveness studies would provide feedback on how advertising appeals and media strategies were achieving goals.

MR APPLICATIONS DIFFER BY INDUSTRY AND ROLES

The extent to which MR studies are used, and for what purposes, differs within and among organizations. Within organizations, MR applications differ by management level and position. For example, Merton senior management would be more interested in long-range forecasts and information summarizing sales and profitability findings across many products and territories, on which to base decisions for allocating resources to different divisions. Middle and lower echelon managers would be more interested in research information reflecting their positions (e.g., territory, quota, and sales analysis for the sales manager and advertising effectiveness for the advertising manager).

Among companies, MR scope and emphasis differs by markets served and offerings made in these markets. Consumer-oriented firms place more stress on MR studies designed to identify and profile target markets and build attractive marketing mixes. Firms serving industrial markets will more likely stress MR studies concerning distribution, pricing, and selling activities.

KEY MR CONSIDERATIONS: VALIDITY AND RELIABILITY

Depending largely on what they aim to accomplish in what kind of an environment and at what cost, MR studies are subject to a diversity of constraints that should be taken into account in planning research strategies.

To understand these constraints requires an understanding of two key concepts related to any kind of research: validity and reliability. Validity is the extent to which a research study measures what it is supposed to measure. For example, if MR findings indicate that, based on a sample of 100 British accountants, 25 percent will purchase MM systems and between 23 and 27 percent of this targeted population do, indeed, purchase MM systems, then these findings are called valid: They measured, to a desired degree of accuracy, what they were supposed to measure.

When research findings accurately measure variables only in the population surveyed (i.e., British tax accountants), they have internal validity; when findings can be applied to all segments of this population (i.e., all tax accountants), they have external validity. External validity often becomes a problem in international MR when findings from one country are incorrectly assumed to apply to other countries.

Reliability is the likelihood that research results can be repeated. For this study to be reliable, for example, other samples of 100 British tax accountants selected from the same population would also have to indicate a collective intention to buy about 25 MM systems.

Note that it is possible for a study to be reliable—all samples chosen indicate an intention to buy about 25 MM systems—without being valid—none actually purchases more than 10 units.

Validity and reliability are especially important to marketing managers because many MR studies entail considerable cost and risk and can create expensive problems if the information they yield leads to bad decisions. A wrong price, an unpopular product feature, a poorly conceived promotion campaign, or an inefficient distribution channel can put a firm at a competitive disadvantage from which it never recovers.

Unfortunately, due to built-in constraints, validity and reliability are unusually difficult to achieve in domestic marketing research studies, and even more so in MR studies in foreign markets.

KEY MR CONSTRAINTS: SUBJECTS, INSTRUMENTS, AND CONTROLS

To illustrate built-in constraints that limit marketing research validity and reliability, consider two research studies: one, in the physical sciences, to measure the boiling point of water at various pressures and the other a survey of prospective purchasers to measure the likelihood each will purchase an MM system at various price offerings.

- *Complex subjects.* In the boiling point study, subjects being studied—water, heat, pressure—tend to be simple, stable, and predictable. With people, however, the researcher is dealing with complex, dynamic variables like intelligence, feelings, attitudes, and beliefs, which are impossible to define and measure precisely.

- *Crude instruments.* In the boiling point study, finely calibrated instruments measure variables like temperature and pressure with high degrees of precision. The MM survey, on the other hand, must use crude measurement instruments—like questionnaire surveys—that carry a heavy baggage of ambiguities and biases.

- *Poor controls.* In the boiling point study, experimental conditions—temperature, height, weight, etc.—can be precisely controlled. In the MM survey, conditions, like changing environments in which behavior is studied, are much too complex and diverse to control with exactitude.

- *Time constraints.* In the boiling point study, there is usually sufficient time to ensure that study findings are valid and reliable. In marketing research studies, competitive pressures and pressures from a changing environment often result in sacrificing validity and reliability for speed.

PROBLEMS IN CONDUCTING GLOBAL MR

All these problems characterizing MR in general tend to be exacerbated in international MR studies. For example, Moore perceived that Merton's global MIS and MR programs would have to deal with the following differences.

- *Different environments,* including cultures, languages, political systems, societal structures, economies, and infrastructures.

- *Different parameters,* such as currencies, modes of transportation and documentation, port facilities, and business rules and regulations.

- *Different competitors,* including, in addition to direct brand competition that characterized Merton's domestic market, many forms of indirect competition.

These and related differences between Merton's international and domestic markets would combine to define different markets and different strategic plans for penetrating these markets. And as more global markets were entered, the number of different dimensions would increase geometrically, with information on each required to make appropriate business decisions.

Another problem in conducting international MR studies is a general dearth of statistical summary data, especially in less developed countries with primitive data-gathering and research services. Even in countries that do provide productive data sources, the problem of data comparability often arises. Censuses, output figures, trade statistics, and base year calculations are published for different periods in different countries. There are also numerous definitional differences among countries. For example, in Germany, consumer expenditures are estimated largely on the basis of tax receipts; in the United Kingdom, they are estimated on the basis of a combination of tax receipts, household surveys, and production sources. Standard age categories for classifying statistical data covering consumer purchases are defined as follows in four different countries.

Venezuela	Germany	Spain	Italy
10–14	14–19	15–24	13–20
15–24	20–29	25–34	21–25
25–34	30–39	35–44	26–35

These differences among countries often mean that multiple markets must be researched, including poorer countries where a profit potential is questionable, rather than researching a single large market like the United States.

THE MR PROCESS: FORMULATE, COMPILE, ANALYZE, AND RECOMMEND

Recognizing the critical importance of valid, reliable MR information to the success of Merton's strategic plans to market MM systems, as well as the imposing constraints on generating this information in the global marketplace, Moore formulated a systematic protocol for conducting MR studies. This protocol, designed to optimize validity, reliability, efficiency, and economy in the MR process, encompassed seven steps:

1. Define the research problem and objectives;
2. Collect secondary data;
3. Design the research plan;
4. Collect primary data;
5. Analyze data;
6. Make recommendations;
7. Implement recommendations.

We cover the first three steps in this chapter, using Merton's entry into the international market for illustrative examples. The last four steps of the MR process are covered in Chapter 5.

DEFINE RESEARCH PROBLEM AND OBJECTIVES

This research was a collaborative effort among Moore, managers whose decisions would be influenced by research findings, representatives of an outside marketing research firm retained by Merton to conduct the study, and Jim Fist, the marketing research manager for the international division. Moore had a "big picture" understanding of problems to be addressed by research and what information would be needed to address these problems. Other managers knew what decisions they would have to make and what information they would need to fit into this big picture.

In defining problems, researchers usually distinguish between causative (primary) problems and symptomatic (secondary) problems. For example, the fact that MM sales were below expectations in a given territory might only be a symptom of other causative problems, such as competitive inroads or a decline in economic activity. Frequently a good way to begin a research study is to list as many causative problems as possible; each then becomes a hypothesis to be tested or rejected during later stages of the research process. Once primary problems have been identified, research objectives that define types of research and research methodology to be emphasized can be established.

Sometimes the objective lends itself to exploratory research—to gather secondary information that will further define the problem and suggest solutions. Sometimes it is conclusive research—to describe problems statistically or through experimental methods and infer solutions from these descriptions. Frequently, research objectives will change during the course of a study. For example, exploratory research might reveal all the researcher wants to know, or suggest the need for additional conclusive research.

In international markets, a firm's research objectives depend primarily on whether it is engaged in exporting or importing activities.

• *INTERNATIONAL MR OBJECTIVES, EXPORTING*

The most frequent research objectives among exporting firms pertain to foreign market opportunity studies. Typically, these studies begin with a general, low-cost exploration of market variables in prospective foreign markets that will define target markets for the firm's offering. For example, Moore recognized that, to qualify as a market for MM systems, a country must have a certain number of professionals in various fields, earning an average minimum per-capita income. In Merton's case, such cursory studies reduced the number of markets considered for MM entry to a manageable 18.

Next, Merton's research effort focused on individual markets for further evaluation, applying a new set of qualifying criteria to prioritize each in terms of market size, growth rate, and economic/competitive/political constraints for marketing MM systems.

Once prospective markets had been identified and prioritized, research objectives shifted to define supply-demand patterns, dollar potential, and marketing mix offerings best calculated to realize this potential.

• *INTERNATIONAL MR OBJECTIVES, IMPORTING*

The most frequent market research objectives among firms engaged in importing activities involve identifying sources, or potential sources, of needed supplies or materials. As with the research approach to identifying export markets, objectives include acceptability standards against which markets are assessed, such as standards for reliability, quality, and delivery time. Source country environment is also investigated, including such concerns as currency stability, source country export rules, and transportation problems.

COLLECT SECONDARY DATA

Secondary data have already been published or collected for purposes other than those of the researcher. Hence, their usefulness may be suspect and should be carefully assessed in terms of relevance to the current research project, accuracy in terms of validity and reliability, timeliness, and impartiality. For example, a 5-year-old article describing how a training program met the needs of tax accountants in the United States might fail in all criteria areas when applied to training needs in a foreign country.

These quality criteria are particularly applicable to secondary data sources in international markets. Countries are often motivated to distort data (e.g., to attract investment by exaggerating economic growth), and even without such ulterior motives, data availability and collection techniques are often primitive. As a result of these distorting factors, the margin of error for some international statistics can be as high as 25 percent.[2]

SECONDARY DATA SOURCES FOR GLOBAL RESEARCH

Secondary data sources are classified as either internal or external. Internal sources include such documents generated within the organization as sales figures, balance sheets, inventory records, price lists, promotional materials, and P&L statements. Examination of these documents for Merton's domestic operation, and the target markets they highlighted, helped establish criteria against which to identify similar international target markets.

Secondary external sources include documents generated outside the company, including, in the domestic market, publications by federal, state and local governments; reference books, data bases, and periodicals published by private sources such as associations, banks, advertising agencies, newspapers, magazines, and commercial sources (e.g., the Marketing Research Corporation of America and the A. C. Nielsen Company).

GOVERNMENT INFORMATION SOURCES FOR EXPORTERS

In the United States, more than a dozen federal organizations actively collect information from around the world concerning problems and

---

[2] Kavil Ramachandran, "Data Collection for Management Research in Developing Countries," in N. C. Smith and P. Dainty, Eds., *The Management Research Handbook*. London: Routledge, 1991, pp. 300–309.

opportunities for importers and exporters. Much of this information abundance is inexpensive or free. (Global Focus 4-2 shows how one company makes effective use of U.S. Department of Commerce export services to spur its dramatic expansion into global markets.)

GLOBAL FOCUS 4-2

Universal Esthetics Team Up With U.S. Export Services for Global Growth

Marti Cowan, CEO of Universal Esthetic (UE) Inc. of Bristol, Va., knew there was good market potential for the firm's lines of cosmetics and medical/cosmetic equipment in South America, but didn't have specific information on which to build a marketing strategy.

The Commerce Department's Commercial Service (CS) office in Charleston, West Virginia provided the information and answers Cowan needed. Like all CS offices throughout the United States, this office offers a variety of marketing research and trade lead tools designed to fill the needs of client companies at various stages of export marketing campaigns.

In UE's case, the CS consultant referred to such documents as Industry Sector Analyses, Best Market reports, and Country Commercial Guides to narrow UE's South American market to the two or three markets with the best potential.

Cowan explains, "Commercial Service market research reports have helped our company sell product abroad by giving us valuable insights into market potential. As a small business, we feel we needed to carefully evaluate our investment before entering the global marketplace. Because of the information provided by the Commercial Service, we identified our best markets and we are now experiencing a return on our investment—just three months after our first attempt to market in South America."

Source: *Business America*, U.S. Department of Commerce, October 1996, p. 7.

For most practical purposes, however, a small enterprise like Merton's international division, new to the challenges of the international marketplace, is best advised to begin its search for worthwhile global opportunities with the Commerce Department or the Small Business Administration, which integrate information from all sources and tailors it to the needs of individual small to medium-sized firms in specific industries.

To illustrate, here are some of these sources that helped Moore formulate and implement Merton's marketing plan for finding and penetrating high-potential target markets for MM systems in international markets. These sources are sequenced as they were used to (1) identify governmental information sources; (2) get specialized consulting services; (3) find worthwhile target markets, as well as worthwhile customers and distributors in these markets; (4) promote MM systems to these customers and distributors.

• *IDENTIFYING INFORMATION SOURCES*

- *Commerce Department Hot Line* (1 800 872-8723) runs through all federal export programs.

- *Commerce Department Trade Information Center*, a "one-stop shop" for information on assistance from 19 federal agencies, provided Moore with helpful sources of export counseling, international marketing research, leads to distributors and customers abroad, schedules of overseas and domestic trade shows, export financing and information on documentation, and licensing requirements, in addition to state and local programs.

• *GET SPECIALIZED CONSULTATION SERVICES*

- *SBA Small Business Development Centers.* More than 700 such centers offer export counseling.

- *Commerce Department Counseling.* Located at 68 district offices, they provide small companies (under 100 employees) with comprehensive export advice, usually based on the personal experience of trade counselors.

- *Expert legal assistance network* (202-778-3080), cosponsored by the Commerce Department, the Small Business Administration, and the Federal Bar Association, brings new exporters and trade attorneys together to discuss legal aspects of entering world markets.

• *FINDING WORTHWHILE TARGET MARKETS/CUSTOMERS/DISTRIBUTORS*

- *Matchmaker missions*, co-sponsored by Commerce and the SBA, enable first-time exporters in specific fields like electronics and medicine to attend dozens of prearranged meetings with potential customers abroad. Fees for attending firms like MM range between $1,200 and $2,000 (The SBA may pick up $750).

- *Commercial News*, a monthly catalog sent to more than 100,000 buyers in the international market, represents a fast, inexpensive way to generate leads and build a mailing list. Advertisements cost about $250 and are restricted to one product, a photograph, a price, and a company name, address, and phone number.

- *Commerce Department agent/distributor service* provides Trade specialists who tap overseas contacts for distributors willing to sell exporter's products. The search costs $125 and can take 2 months to complete. An additional $100 buys reports on the sales history and credit standing of distributors.

- *Commerce Department Foreign Buyer Program* brings in thousands of overseas buyers to domestic shows sponsored by major trade associations. Signing up is free.

- *Market reports* tap the Commerce Department trade data bank to detail foreign demand for specific goods. Updated monthly, this newsletter is available free or at a nominal charge at Commerce Department district offices and some 400 federal depository libraries. Subscription cost is $360 a year or $35 for any month.

• *PROMOTING PRODUCTS*

- *Catalog and video shows* display a company's catalogs or video demos at "catalog shows" in United States consulates and embassies abroad. Shows are often geared to specific industries like marine equipment and consumer electronics. The Commerce Department advertises each show and passes names of interested parties on to exhibitors. The cost is between $100 and $300.

- Foreign trade shows, sponsored by the Commerce Department, provide small exporting companies with an excellent opportunity to meet buyers and scan the competition. Fees for participating companies average $400, plus travel costs.

SURVEYS OF KNOWLEDGEABLE PEOPLE

These informal surveys are often used to supplement secondary data searches during the exploratory research stage. They are usually restricted to executives and others in the company with an informed knowledge of how to achieve MR study objectives. Later, if this inside information isn't sufficient, the research study will seek information from outside sources. Since little was known about international markets among Merton's domestic personnel, "knowledgeable people" surveyed were primarily international contacts familiar with prospective target markets.

REALISTIC OBJECTIVES EMERGE

Exploratory findings from secondary sources and knowledgeable people helped produce a set of research objectives that were relevant, attainable, and specific to the needs of the strategic plan and managers responsible for making the plan work.

These objectives were calculated to answer these questions:

- In terms of cultural, economic, technological, competitive, and political environments, which country would be most receptive to initial entry with MM systems?

- In terms of income level, educational needs, and work activities, which market segment(s) in this country's business/professional segment would be most receptive to the MM offering?

- How would marketing mix aspects of the MM offering (product features, price, distribution, and promotion) have to be modified to ensure a favorable, profitable market entry?

Note that these objectives are prioritized to generate data in a cost-effective manner. For example, if sufficient demand doesn't exist in a foreign market for MM systems, then research addressing the next two objectives is cancelled.

DESIGN A RESEARCH PLAN

Frequently, the exploratory phase of the research process is sufficient for the decision makers' purposes. For example, the perceived problem is discovered not to be a problem or a solution to an actual problem emerges. Alternately, exploratory research might serve only to define the problem more precisely or to suggest diverse solutions from which to select a single solution. For example, exploratory research might suggest a number of possible global markets for MM systems, but narrowing them down to the most productive entry market and further defining target segments and building marketing mixes attractive to these segments, would require conclusive MR studies. Conclusive research, including approaches and techniques for generating primary data, is discussed next.

CHAPTER PERSPECTIVE

In this chapter, we examined marketing information systems and the marketing research process that work together to help formulate, implement, and control strategic marketing plans. MR applications and needs differ among industries and managerial echelons and can result in cost, waste, and misdirection when validity and reliability are sacrificed to poor planning and ineffective measurement tools. A productive research plan directs and sequences exploratory and conclusive research activities for efficiency and economy through the effective, selective use of seconary data sources, including government agencies and knowledgeable people.

KNOW THE CONCEPTS

TERMS FOR STUDY

advertising research
causative problems
Commerce Department
conclusive research
data comparability
environmental scanning
exploratory research
exporting research objectives
external secondary sources
government information sources
importing research objectives
internal secondary sources
internal validity

marketing information system
marketing research
MR constraints
product research
reliability
research hypotheses
research plan
sales forecasts
secondary data
Small Business Administration
surveys of knowledgeable people
symptomatic problems
validity

MATCHUP EXERCISES

1. Match the MIS information category in the first column with the appropriate information need in the second column.

   1. broad strategic issues

   2. foreign market assessment

   a. What are comparative costs of alternative distribution channels?

   b. Can we afford the customized product and promotion requirements of this prospective market?

3. marketing mix selection   c. To what extent do entry market demographics match those in our domestic market?

2. Match the section of a Marketing Information System listed in the first column with the information it would produce, listed in the second column. This information pertains to an environmental scan of two countries, Saudi Arabia and Egypt, which are customers for water purification systems manufactured by the firm doing the research.

1. marketing intelligence   a. Last year, sales of our systems were down by 20 percent in Egypt, while increasing by 11 percent in Saudi Arabia.

2. internal records   b. Our major competitor increased its share of market by 30 percent in Saudi Arabia and 10 percent in Egypt.

3. information analysis   c. In countries with a per capita income of under $3,000, price increases of 5 percent reduce sales of our units by 20 percent.

4. marketing research   d. Our study showed that price sensitivity toward our products is approximately three times as great in Egypt as in Saudi Arabia.

3. Match the titles in the first column with the types of research information each would likely need to help arrive at a decision as to the desirability of entering the Russian market with a line of used medical equipment.

1. president   a. size and needs of prospective target markets

2. vice president, marketing   b. sales potential by territory and customer group

3. marketing research manager   c. how marketing mix elements will have to be adopted to Russian market

4. sales manager   d. likely return on investment after first and second year in market

QUESTIONS FOR REVIEW AND DISCUSSION

1. Using Merton's search for worthwhile entry markets for MM systems as an example, explain how marketing information systems work with marketing research processes to help identify international market opportunities.

2. How might the following components of a MIS combine to produce a prediction that a price increase for MM systems in country B will not decrease sales, even though a similar increase decreased sales in the domestic market: internal records, marketing intelligence, marketing research, and information analysis.

3. Assume that you publish, in the United States, *The NAFTA Report*, a successful newsletter for small to medium-sized firms interested in entry and growth in North America free trade markets (i.e., the United States, Canada, and Mexico). Currently, you are researching the feasibility of expanding the market for this newsletter to Canada. What are key things you would want to know in the following areas in which information on global market opportunities is typically generated: (1) foreign market assessment and selection and (2) marketing mix assessment and selection.

4. Two research studies, conducted by the National Industrial Conference Board (NICB) on the South American market, presented findings pertaining to (1) the relationship between changes in currency valuations and productivity and (2) attitudes of South Americans regarding joining the North American Free Trade Association (NAFTA). Why would the first study findings tend to be more valid and reliable than the second study findings?

5. Explain how the following prediction can be reliable without being valid. Why is this possibility significant in global marketing research?

   Based on interviews with a randomly selected sample of 200 prospective users, our contract with the Kazakhstan Ministry of Telecommunications to provide a nationwide cellular system for the largest Central Asian state will expand by 100 percent in the second year of the contract to cover more than 100,000 subscribers, and sales volume of over $70 million.

6. List the seven steps of the marketing research process. Why are the first and sixth steps especially important?

7. Why might the following information be suspect in terms of criteria for the acceptability of secondary data?

> According to an article in last June's edition of the Commerce Department magazine *Business America*, NAFTA has created unprecedented opportunities for investment in the growth of the Mexican economy. Studies by the Mexican Board of Trade all indicate that GNP will increase by at least 10 percent per year, most import/export trade barriers have been eliminated, and privatization has created welcoming political and economic climates.

8. Referring to the Mexican Board of Trade study in question 7, how might the following secondary sources have been used: internal secondary sources, external secondary sources, and surveys of knowledgeable people.

ANSWERS

MATCHUP EXERCISES

1. 1b, 2c, 3a
2. 1b, 2a, 3c, 4d
3. 1d, 2c, 3a, 4b

QUESTIONS FOR REVIEW AND DISCUSSION

1. Merton's search for worthwhile entry markets involves, essentially, finding markets in the global marketplace that most resemble Merton's domestic market in terms of such criteria as target market features and needs, the economic ability to purchase MMs, technological infrastructures to transport and communicate about MMs, and friendly legal/political systems. Merton's MIS database contains information about target markets and marketing environments in its domestic market, based on years of continuous accumulated experience. Marketing research studies generate similar information in prospective global entry markets. The MIS has the capability of matching this historical and contemporary information to identify and prioritize worthy prospective entry markets, a process called "environmental scanning."

2. Internal records, such as sales analysis reports of dollar sales by territory in the domestic market, might indicate a drop in sales of MM systems in all territories following a price increase, leading to the hypothesis that the price increase was the main cause of the price decline. Market intelligence, however, might highlight significant differences between foreign market B and the domestic marketplace that would tend to maintain sales volume levels in spite of a price increase. For example, intelligence pertaining to economic and competitive environments might profile a market where a high level of affluence among professionals permits them to easily afford the increased price and where there is practically no competition to exploit Merton's higher price. A marketing research study, perhaps summarizing findings and conclusions from focus group meetings of prospective buyers, might tend to confirm this conclusion, which might further be confirmed by actually raising the MM's price in a test segment of the market. All this information regarding demand patterns in these two markets would be organized, analyzed, and translated into useful decision information by the information analysis section of the MIS.

3. *Marketing mix assessment and selection:* Product: How should format and editorial content of the newsletter be modified in light of the needs the newsletter will fill in the Canadian market? What should the newsletter's mission be in this market? What should its business and marketing objectives be? What should its image be in this market?

   Price: What should the subscription price of the newsletter be in order to be consistent with its image, objectives, competitive offerings, and production/distribution costs in the Canadian market? Should price change for different market segments? What pricing options are available if costs increase or decrease?

   Place—distribution: What types of channels should we use to distribute the newsletter to subscribers (postal service, Fed Ex, agents, or brokers, etc.)? What storage facilities will we require? What will be the distribution cost? What incentives (discounts, allowances, etc.) will we have to offer to achieve distribution objectives? What channels are used by our prospective competitors?

   Promotion, nonpersonal (e.g., advertising and sales promotion): What should our communication objectives (awareness, desire, action, etc.) be? To what extent can the message and media characterizing our domestic promotion effort be adopted to the Canadian market? What should our message be for the Canadian market? What media will most efficiently and economically carry this message? Is this media available in the Canadian market? How much can we afford to invest in promoting the newsletter in Canada? What message and media do competitive newsletters use? Should we retain an advertising agency?

Promotion, personal selling: Will personal selling be needed to generate subscriptions? If so, how many salespeople will we need? Should they be U.S. nationals or Canadian? How should they be selected, trained, motivated, compensated, and evaluated? What kind of sales analysis will we require (sales by territory, customer group, individual salesman, etc.)? How can personal selling be most effectively integrated with nonpersonal promotion and the price/product/place elements of the marketing mix?

Foreign market assessment and selection: Which segments of the Canadian market should you strive to satisfy with your newsletter? What is the dollar potential in the Canadian market for newsletter sales? What are the major economic, political, legislative, legal, social, cultural, and technological trends that will affect newsletter sales? What are the needs that the newsletter will fulfill in Canada? Who decides to subscribe to the newsletter in various target markets? What are the demographic and psychographic characteristics of prospective target market members that would predispose them to subscribe to the newsletter (income, occupation, opinions, interests, etc.)? What are major direct and indirect competitors for the newsletter readership? What are our strengths and weaknesses in positioning the newsletter against this competition? What media are available to promote the newsletter? What channels are available to distribute the newsletter? How will use of these media and channels affect the cost of marketing the newsletter? (e.g., Will advertising and postage rates be higher than in the domestic market?)

4. In the first study, the research findings were objectively determined using, primarily, mechanical and electronic means that are much less subject to invalidating influences found when dealing with people, as was the case in the second study. These influences include biases (interviewer, interviewee, self-selection, nonresponse, halo, etc.), poor measuring devices (i.e., questionnaires), complex subjects (i.e., people), and ineffective controls. To these reasons are added a number of other barriers in global markets (e.g., different languages, poor communication media).

5. To be valid, findings from a marketing research study should measure to a desired degree of accuracy what the study was designed to measure—in this case, number of subscribers and sales volume during the second year of the cellular system contract. To be reliable, this study should achieve approximately the same findings each time a random selection of 200 prospective users is sampled. If this is indeed the case but if actual sales are significantly different (either higher or lower) than projected by the users sampled, then the study is reliable but not valid.

As suggested by this question, marketing research findings are the basis for expensive decisions and decisions based on invalid findings can result in financial and operational setbacks from which the firm never recovers.

6. The seven steps of the marketing research process include (1) define research problem and objectives, (2) collect secondary data, (3) design research plan, (4) collect primary data, (5) analyze data, (6) make recommendations, and (7) implement recommendations.

   Although all the steps of the marketing research process are obviously important, the first and sixth steps are especially important in light of their impact on the decision-making process, which is the ultimate purpose of marketing research. The first step has an impact on decision making, as well as all succeeding steps in the process and the cost and time of the research undertaken. An improperly defined problem or unrealistic research objectives can lead to unnecessary research (e.g., expensive conclusive studies that generate primary data, when secondary data will suffice) or misdirected marketing research (e.g., a study based on the hypothesis that promotion is the problem when it's really distribution) that can dramatically increase the cost of the research while negating the value of decisions based on this research. The sixth step of the process—making recommendations—is important because it integrates data generated by the preceding steps and is the basis for decisions made to activate the final, implementation step, without which the best planned study is just so many useless facts and figures.

7. Before acting on this information, an investor planning to enter the Mexican marketplace might wish to verify (1) the timeliness of this piece (What has happened since it was written? There have been many changes, if this piece appeared before the problems with the peso.); (2) the disinterestedness of the researchers (both the Department of Commerce and the Mexican Board of Trade presumably have an interest in encouraging U.S. firms to invest in Mexico), and (3) the methodology of research undertaken to arrive at this optimistic assessment.

8. Internal secondary sources would include the Board's existing records of various indices of economic activity in Mexico, such as growth in gross domestic product, increases in exporting and importing, and profitability of firms entering the Mexican market. External secondary sources would include sources external to the Board's own internal records that provide generally available data and information either free or for a price. Included could be governmental publications (both in Mexico and the United States), data bases and periodicals published by associations, banks, and commercial sources. Surveys of knowledgeable people could include, for example, groups of U.S. and Mexican company managers that have achieved success importing or exporting goods in the NAFTA aftermath.

5

INTERNATIONAL MARKETING RESEARCH II: GENERATING RELIABLE RECOMMENDATIONS FOR DECISION MAKERS

OVERVIEW

Effectively designed and implemented, conclusive marketing research studies produce recommendations that can be acted on with confidence by marketing decision makers. To achieve this result in the face of constraints in international markets requires effective use of tools and techniques for sampling populations, designing survey instruments, analyzing survey responses, and generating conclusions and recommendations from analyzed information.

DIFFERENCES BETWEEN EXPLORATORY AND CONCLUSIVE RESEARCH

In Chapter 4, we examined the nature, scope, and importance of marketing information systems and marketing research processes and how they work together to formulate, implement, and control strategic marketing plans. We also examined constraints to the generation of valid, reliable, actionable research findings in complex, quixotic international markets, and introduced a systematic approach for addressing these constraints.

This approach began by defining the problem to be studied and collecting secondary data that clarify research objectives bearing on this problem. Frequently, this exploratory stage of the research process is sufficient to achieve research objectives.

Alternately, exploratory research might suggest a diversity of possible causes and cures, at which point the next four steps of the process— collecting primary data, analyzing data, making recommendations, and implementing findings—will be necessary. This is called the conclusive research stage. The end-product of conclusive research is information that helps marketers make better decisions in all areas of the strategic marketing process, from identifying environmental opportunities through defining worthwhile target markets to implementing and controlling marketing mix offerings attractive to these markets.

CONCLUSIVE MARKETING RESEARCH GENERATES PRIMARY DATA

Conclusive and exploratory MR differ in the following significant ways:

- Conclusive MR tests hypotheses rather than seeking to find these hypotheses (e.g., to test the hypothesis that a price decrease of 10 percent will increase sales 20 percent).

- Conclusive MR applies much more rigorous controls.

- Conclusive MR deals with larger numbers and leads to mass data analyses covering classes, averages, percentages, and dispersions.

- Conclusive MR leads to predictions (e.g., a price decrease of 10 percent will increase sales by 30 percent).

Conclusive marketing research also differs from exploratory research in producing primary data, which, unlike secondary data, is collected specifically for the purpose of the investigation at hand by known, controlled methods. Primary data are also usually more current and reliable than secondary data.

Sooner or later, most firms engaged in international trade require primary data to answer issue-specific questions that can't be answered with secondary data, such as psychographic and behavioristic segmentation variables (e.g., lifestyle, attitudes, behavior patterns) that help define target markets and build attractive marketing mixes.

COLLECTING, PROCESSING, AND APPLYING PRIMARY DATA

To illustrate the final four steps of the marketing research process (collecting, analyzing, recommending, implementing), we focus on decisions and actions involved in designing and implementing a conclusive research plan to assess the British marketplace for entry with Merton's MM systems.

Early in this study, the following issues were addressed to determine how and what primary data would be developed and processed.

• *WHO WILL COLLECT THE DATA?*

Generally, three options are available to firms in determining who will do the research:

- *A centralized approach*, whereby the research design and focus are determined at headquarters and forwarded to local country operations for implementation;

- *A decentralized approach*, whereby home country headquarters establishes broad research policies and guidelines and then delegates further design and implementation to local countries;

- *A coordinated approach*, whereby an outside intermediary, such as a marketing research firm, brings headquarters and country operations together.

Centralizing the international research function is generally appropriate when research is intended to influence company policy and strategy and markets are similar. When markets differ from country to country, firms generally move to a decentralized research format. In the process, they gain closer proximity to markets, the ability to respond more flexibly to challenges and opportunities, and the benefits of interaction among home and host country personnel. Often, however, the firm sacrifices control and comparability of data and incurs costly duplication of effort. The coordinated approach, using a reliable, knowledgeable outside intermediary to integrate home and host country research, helps realize the benefits of both approaches. Merton's decision to use an outside intermediary marketing research firm was based on the firm's lack of first-hand knowledge of international markets, and the highly specialized nature of the conclusive research to be undertaken (i.e., a detailed analysis of the nature and needs of prospective target markets among British professionals). Selection criteria stressed the research firm's previous experience in a particular country/industry and the quality of information produced in previous engagements. Merton's search for such an agency was based on assessments of a prospective firm's capabilities compared with capabilities available in-house and from competing research firms.

• *WHAT INFORMATION SHOULD BE COLLECTED?*

Frequently, secondary research will indicate primary research needs by suggesting either hypotheses to be tested or relationships to be defined. These primary data needs are usually posited as research questions that serve as a starting point for the research effort and help define information required. Table 5-1 depicts global marketing research questions that parallel the steps of the SMP process.

Table 5–1. International Marketing Questions Determining Information Requirements

Broad Strategic Issues

What objectives should be pursued in the foreign market?

Which foreign market segments should the firm strive to satisfy?

Which are the best product, place-distribution, pricing, and promotion strategies for the foreign market?

What should be the product-market-company mix to take advantage of the available foreign marketing opportunities?

Foreign Market Assessment and Selection

Do opportunities exist in a foreign market for the firm's products and services?

What is the market potential abroad?

What new markets are likely to open up abroad?

What are the major economic, political, legal, social, technological, and other environmental facts and trends in a foreign country?

What impact do these environmental dimensions have on the specific foreign market for the firm's products and services?

Who are the firm's present and potential customers abroad?

What are their needs and desires?

What are their demographic and psychographic characteristics—disposable income, occupation, age, sex, opinions, interests, activities, tastes, values, etc.?

What is their life-style?

Who makes the purchase decisions?

Who influences the purchase decisions?

How are the purchase decisions made?

Where are the products purchased?

How are the products used?

What are the purchase and consumption patterns and behaviors?

What is the nature of competition in the foreign market?

Who are major direct and indirect competitors?

What are the major characteristics of the competitors?

Table 5–1 *Continued*

What are the firm's competitive strengths and weaknesses in reference to such factors as product quality, product lines, warranties, services, brands, packaging, distribution, sales force, advertising, prices, experience, technology, capital and human resources, and market share?

What attitudes do different governments (domestic and foreign) have toward foreign trade?

Are there any foreign trade incentives and barriers?

Is there any prejudice against imports or exports?

What are different governments doing specifically to encourage or discourage international trade?

What specific requirements—for example, import or export licenses—have to be met to conduct international trade?

How difficult are certain government regulations for the firm?

How well developed are the foreign mass communication media?

Are the print and electronics media abroad efficient and effective?

Are there adequate transportation and storage or warehouse facilities in the foreign market?

Does the foreign market offer efficient channels of distribution for the firm's products?

What are the characteristics of the existing domestic and foreign distributors?

How effectively can the distributors perform specific marketing functions?

What is the state of the retailing institutions?

Marketing Mix Assessment and Selection

Product

Which product should the firm offer abroad?

What specific features—design, color, size, packaging, brand, warranty, etc.— should the product have?

What foreign needs does the product satisfy?

Should the firm adapt or modify its domestic market product and sell it abroad?

Should it develop a new product for the foreign market?

Should the firm make or buy the product for the foreign market?

How competitive is or will be the product abroad?

Is there a need to withdraw the product from the foreign market?

At which stage in its life cycle is the product in the foreign market?

What specific services are necessary abroad at the presale and postsale stages?

Are the firm's service and repair facilities adequate?

What is the firm's product and service image abroad?

What patents or trademarks does the firm have that can benefit it abroad? How much legal protection does the firm have concerning patents, trademarks, etc.?

What should be the firm's product mission philosophy in the foreign market?

Are the firm's products socially responsible?

Table 5–1 *Continued*

Do the products create a good corporate image?

What effect does the product have on the environment?

Price

At what price should the firm sell its product in the foreign market?

Does the foreign price reflect the product quality?

Is the price competitive?

Should the firm pursue market penetration or market-skimming pricing objectives abroad?

What type of discounts (trade, cash, quantity) and allowances (advertising, trade-off) should the firm offer its foreign customers?

Should prices differ according to market segment?

What should the firm do about product line pricing?

What pricing options are available if costs increase or decrease?

Is the demand in the foreign market elastic or inelastic?

How are prices going to be viewed by the foreign government—reasonable, exploitative?

Can differentiated pricing lead to the emergence of a gray market?

Place—Distribution

Which channels of distribution should the firm use to market its products abroad?

Where should the firm produce its products, and how should it distribute them in the foreign market?

What types of agents, brokers, wholesalers, dealers, distributors, retailers, etc. should the firm use?

What are the characteristics and capabilities of the available intermediaries?

Should the assistance of EMCs (export management companies) be acquired?

What forms of transportation should the firm use?

Where should the product be stored?

What is the cost of distribution by channel?

What are the costs of physical distribution?

What type of incentives and assistance should the firm provide its intermediaries to achieve its foreign distribution objectives?

Which channels of distribution are used by the firm's competitors, and how effective are these channels?

Is there a need to develop a reverse distribution system, e.g., recycling?

Promotion—Nonpersonal (Advertising and Sales Promotion)

How should the firm promote its products in the foreign market? Should it advertise? Should it participate in international trade fairs and exhibits?

What are the communication needs of the foreign market?

What communication or promotion objectives should the firm pursue abroad?

What should be the total foreign promotion budget?

What advertising media are available to promote in the foreign market? What are their strengths and limitations? How effective are different domestic and foreign advertising media?

Table 5–1 *Continued*

Should the firm use an advertising agency?
How should it be selected?
How effective and competitive are the firm's existing advertising and promotion
   programs concerning the foreign market?
What are the legal requirements?
Are there foreign laws against competitive advertising?

Promotion—Personal Selling
Is there a need for personal selling to promote the product abroad?
What assistance or services do foreign customers need from the sales force?
What should be the nature of personal selling abroad?
How many salespeople should the firm have?
How should the sales personnel be trained, motivated, compensated, assigned
   sales goals and quotas, and assigned foreign territories?
What should the nature of the foreign sales effort be?
How does the firm's sales force compare with its competitors?
What criteria should the firm use to evaluate sales performance?
How should the firm perform sales analysis?

Source: Adapted from Vinay Kothari, "Researching for Export Marketing," in *Export Promotion: The Public and Private Sector Interaction*, ed. M. Czinkota (New York: Praeger Publishers, 1983), 169–172. Reprinted with permission of Greenwood Publishing Group, Inc., Westport, CT. Copyright © 1993.

In Merton's conclusive study, research questions focused on the feasibility of entering the British professional market and the nature and needs of worthwhile British target markets for MM systems.

DESIGNING THE RESEARCH PLAN

Having determined who would implement the primary research plan (a joint team comprising Merton marketing personnel and personnel from the marketing research firm) and what research questions the plan would address, the next step involves designing a research plan that would define the most effective techniques for generating and processing data on the British professional market.

In deciding on which techniques to use, the research team focused primarily on the nature of the information desired and the people who would presumably provide this information. For example, to what extent was the desired information to be objective (e.g., demographic characteristics in prospective markets) or subjective (e.g., attitudes and behavior patterns in these markets)? Future-oriented (e.g., changing information needs) or oriented toward past experience (e.g., attitudes toward existing methods of generating information)? And what degree of validity and reliability would be required?

As to the audience, to what extent would educational, cultural, and social differences influence peoples' willingness to divulge information, and the selection of information-gathering research techniques? For example, Moore perceived that British reserve would probably make respondents a lot less outgoing than their American counterparts.

Given these considerations and constraints as they applied in the British market, the Merton MR team designed a conclusive research study that stressed observation and survey data-gathering methods.

THE SAMPLING PLAN FOCUSES RESEARCH EFFORT

As the first step in designing the research study, the research team formulated a sampling plan designed to ensure the desired degree of reliability for the type of information generated. For some types of information—such as subjective attitudes toward products—high reliability might not be necessary; for other types of information, such as per-capita income figures among prospective customers, it might be. Thus, the sampling plan was concerned with who would be observed or surveyed, the type of information that would be elicited, and the techniques used to elicit this information.

SAMPLING PLAN DESIGN CONSIDERATIONS

A sample is defined as a limited portion of a larger entity. In a statistical study of income and accreditation characteristics of British tax accountants, for example, the larger entity consisted of all British tax accountants; the limited portion, or sample, could be any number up to one less than the total number comprising the population.

All samples observed or surveyed during marketing research studies are either probability or nonprobability samples. In a probability sample, each member of the population has the same likelihood of being chosen. Thus, if there were 10,000 British tax accountants, and the probability sample chosen comprised 100 of them, each member would have exactly one chance in 100 of being chosen.

A nonprobability sample is selected on the basis of criteria that ensure that some members of the population will have a greater chance of being selected than other members. Thus, members of a judgment nonprobability sample would be selected on the basis of the researcher's judgment; for example, he or she might feel that British tax accountants with a better knowledge of training and development practices should participate in a focus group discussion of how MM systems can improve these practices.

Members of a convenience nonprobability sample are chosen because they are conveniently located; for example, British tax accountants at a single accounting firm might be selected to participate in the round-table discussion. Or, members of a quota sample might be selected based on their representation in the population: for example, if one-tenth of the entire British tax accountant population were partners and one-quarter were managers, this might be the percentage of each reflected in a quota sample.

Nonprobability samples are more applicable during exploratory research, when problems and opportunities are being defined and hypotheses emerge for further testing. During conclusive research, when accurate information is required, probability sampling offers a number of advantages:

- *Less information needed.* Basically, all that is needed to construct a probability sample is a way to identify each universe element and knowledge of the total number of universe elements (e.g., British tax accountants).

- *Measurable accuracy.* Probability sampling is the only sampling method that provides measurable estimates of accuracy. For example, it's possible to come up with a statement like this with a properly selected probability sample: "In 95 cases out of 100, when a sample of 100 accountants is randomly selected from a population of 10,000 accountants, sample members will indicate an intention to purchase a total of between 23 and 27 MM systems when they appear on the market."

Marketing managers who can have this degree of confidence in the accuracy of their research conclusions can also have considerably greater confidence in the accuracy of decisions emerging from these conclusions.

COLLECTING DATA THROUGH OBSERVATION

Observation methods observe and record present behavior or the results of past behavior. In personal observation, the researcher poses as a research subject (e.g., a customer in a store being observed); mechanical observation records behavior through electronic or other means, (e.g., an electric cord across the highway counting the number of passing cars). Observation can be unobtrusive, with subjects unaware that they are being observed, or obtrusive, with subjects aware that they are being observed. In international research, observation is especially useful for shedding light on practices not previously encountered but important for planning purposes. In the MM study, for example, the research plan entailed unobtrusively observing training sessions conducted for British accounting personnel to generate data on terminology, accounting practices, and training needs peculiar to British accounting. A judgment sample of firms presumed to use the most modern methods was selected.

COLLECTING DATA THROUGH SURVEYS

Surveys systematically gather information from respondents by asking them questions, either in person, over the telephone, or by mail. They are particularly applicable for generating specific answers to narrow questions, such as how respondents perceive competitive products or features desired in new products. Because surveys involve communications among people, they are subject to a number of biases including the following:

- *Interviewer and interviewee bias* occurs when the attitudes and actions of either the interviewer or respondent distort questionnaire findings.

- *Nonresponse bias* occurs when people don't respond to a survey, thus potentially biasing findings since the reason they didn't respond might change survey results.

- *Self-selection bias*, the opposite of nonresponse bias, suggests that the reason people volunteer to participate in a survey, such as enthusiasm for a political candidate, might bias survey results.

- *Halo effect bias* is the tendency for respondents to generalize from a favorable part to the whole. For example, responses to a questionnaire measuring attitudes toward a new product might be biased by a favorable experience with existing company products.

A well-trained and supervised staff of field researchers will usually reduce the adverse influences of these biases in survey results. In the global market, recruiting and selecting such a staff is often a big problem. (Personnel management and development problems and approaches are discussed in Chapter 8.)

QUESTIONNAIRE DESIGN: A KEY STEP

The MM study researchers realized that they would be using a number of surveys to explore the entry opportunity in the British market and that properly designing questionnaires would help mitigate biases while achieving desired degrees of reliability. This design process involved decisions as to questionnaire objectives; type of questionnaire; mode of questionnaire communication; question content, wording, and format; and question sequence.

• *QUESTIONNAIRE OBJECTIVES*

Since the main purpose of a questionnaire is to translate research objectives into specific questions, a good starting point in designing a questionnaire is to summarize these objectives briefly. For example, an important objective of the MM entry study was to determine the education needs of various prospective target market groups in the British professional market, along with dissatisfactions with how these needs were being met, what features these groups would expect in MM systems, what they would expect to pay for these systems, and so on.

• *TYPES OF QUESTIONNAIRES*

In terms of information desired and respondents' ability or willingness to provide this information, questionnaires can range from highly structured to unstructured. A highly structured questionnaire, with unchanging question content and sequence, generally elicits uncomplicated information which the respondent is both willing and able to provide (e.g., a job application). An unstructured questionnaire lets the interviewer probe respondents and guide the interview according to their answers, often generating information that respondents were unaware they possessed, or might otherwise have been reluctant to reveal (e.g., a "focus group" of British accountants discussing problems they faced with existing personal computer software programs).

Focus groups comprise seven to ten people who gather for a few hours to talk about a product, service, or organization. Although focus group output is not statistically significant, a skilled leader can help encourage participant interaction that generates a substantial amount of information on perceptions, emotions, issues, and ideas that would not emerge during individual interviews. With advances in electronic communication illustrated by MM systems, focus groups can be carried out internationally, with participants in different countries interacting as if in a single location.

• *MODES OF COMMUNICATION*

Surveys can be conducted person to person, by telephone, or by mail. Although personal interviews are flexible—questions can be stopped or changed at any time—and can generate information not otherwise available, they are the most expensive of the three methods. Telephone surveys are less costly, but they don't generally provide as much depth of information as personal surveys and miss people who hang up or don't have phones. Mail surveys can reach dispersed respondents, have no interviewer bias, and are relatively inexpensive, but they suffer from non-response bias and slow returns. In Merton's feasibility study of the British market, all these modes were available. In studies of other markets, however, the researchers realized that their options might be limited by such constraints as poorly functioning postal and telecommunication systems and limited information on dwellings, their location, and their occupants. In some countries, even street maps aren't available. And even if respondents can be reached through mail, telephone, and personal interviews, cultural factors might negatively affect responses. For example, people in different countries have different degrees of sensitivity to survey questions pertaining to topics like income, age, and political orientation. Thus, in Japan, it's much easier to generate data on consumer needs and preferences from personal visits to dealers and other channel members than from the type of customer surveys typical of research studies in the United States. In Saudi Arabia, the entire population of women is generally inaccessible for any mode of survey. In some countries, entire populations are motivated to provide incorrect information on surveys (e.g., to elude tax collectors or for fear the information will be leaked to the government). And in developing countries, demonstration aids are usually required in conducting surveys among poorly educated people, effectively eliminating mail and telephone surveys.

CONSTRUCTING THE QUESTIONNAIRE

Once researchers have clearly defined questionnaire objectives and decided on questionnaire type and communication method, the stage is set for preparing the questionnaire. This process involves determining question content, wording, format, and sequence.

• *QUESTION CONTENT*
The Merton research team followed these guidelines:

- Avoid unnecessary questions.
- Respondent should be willing to answer the question. For example, potentially embarrassing questions pertaining to personal finances or family life were eliminated or asked in the context of innocuous questions or an explanation of their importance.
- Respondents should have the information required for an answer. For example, questions should be within the respondent's experience and shouldn't require respondents to work to get the information.

- Question content should reflect demographic differences among countries. For example, in an undeveloped country, a white collar worker would be part of the upper class; in a developed country, the middle class.

• *QUESTION WORDING*

The researchers followed these guidelines:

- *Define the issue.* Check each survey question against the who-what-why-when-where-how questions characterizing an effective news story. For example, a question like "what is your income" leaves out an important "what" (what comprises income? salary alone? salary and benefits?) and "when" (weekly? monthly? annually?).

- *Use understandable words.* In any language, many words (such as the word *many*) have different meanings to people, and some locutions (such as the word *locution*) have no meaning at all to some people. Pretest the questionnaire to find and eliminate problem words. One effective test of the understandability of questions in a foreign language is the translation-retranslation approach, which involves first translating the question into the language of the foreign country, then having a translator from this country translate it back into the original language, and finally comparing the two versions.

- *Avoid leading questions or questions that require generalized answers.* Leading questions lead the respondent to an answer, usually by naming the product in a favorable way. Questions that elicit vague, generalized answers are usually phrased that way (e.g., What do you think of professional learning?).

• *QUESTION FORMAT*

Four types of question formats are available for communicating question content, ranging from the unstructured open questions to the more highly structured multiple choice, dichotomous, and rating-scale questions.

OPEN QUESTIONS

Open questions do not suggest alternative answers and thus can be answered as the respondent sees fit. This open question, asked during a focus group discussion of electronic training, illustrates advantages and disadvantages of this format:

"What, in your opinion, are the main advantages and disadvantages of the "electronic classroom" approach to learning accounting principles?

As the first question on a questionnaire, an open question is frequently a good way to familiarize the respondent with the purpose and content of the survey, to interest the respondent in the survey, and to prepare the way for more specific questions. Also, since open questions do not point to possible answers, they can produce unexpected responses, which help solve problems or identify opportunities or, during exploratory research, suggest hypotheses to be tested during the conclusive research stage. These answers can also help design questions for more structured surveys used during the conclusive research stage.

Disadvantages of open questions include difficulty in recording and tabulating answers (they are three to five times more expensive to process than structured questions), interviewer bias resulting from long, rambling answers, and interviewee bias when better-educated respondents give more articulate answers that weight results.

MULTIPLE-CHOICE QUESTIONS

Multiple choice questions, which offer respondents a number of alternatives from which to choose, address most of the problems of open questions while introducing a few of their own. To illustrate, here is a typical multiple-choice question that might appear on the Merton study questionnaire:

Which of the following features would you find most useful in a personal notebook computer?

__ Online conferencing capability

__ Memory capacity

__ E-mail capability

__ Software programs

__ Computational speed

__ User friendly

In addition to the fact that all alternatives listed should be defined more precisely, this excerpt also illustrates the following problems with multiple-choice questions.

- Too many alternatives can cause respondents to lose interest in the entire questionnaire. Four choices are usually considered a reasonable limit. Also, the respondent should be informed if more that one alternative can be selected.

- Alternatives may not include all possible categories (so include an "other" category).

- Alternatives may not be mutually exclusive (e.g., "user friendly" might imply the other attributes).

Other problems peculiar to multiple-choice questions are the following two biases they engender.

- *Position bias,* or the tendency for respondents to select the first alternative in a multiple-choice sequence, and

- *Order bias,* or the tendency to select an alternative in the center of a sequence.

Both biases can be mitigated by rotating question sequence on mailed questionnaires.

DICHOTOMOUS QUESTIONS

Dichotomous questions allow a choice of only one of two alternative answers (yes or no, did or did not, etc.) and are the most widely used of all question formats. In general, the same advantages and disadvantages of multiple-choice questions apply: They eliminate interviewer bias and are relatively easy to edit, code and tabulate, but both alternatives might be true, and other possible answers might be excluded.

SCALING QUESTIONS

Scaling questions are a variant of multiple-choice questions developed mainly to measure subjective variables like motives, attitudes, and perceptions. For example, consumers might be asked to rank various telephone systems in terms of their perceptions of the clarity of each. On the simplest level, an ordinal scale would rank the systems with no attempt to measure the degree of favorability of the different systems (e.g., Sprint, MCI, AT&T).

A variant of the ordinal scales with marketing applications is the Likert scale, which permits respondents to indicate degree of agreement/ disagreement with a series of statements reflecting attitudes toward products and product attributes. Consider the following example.

	Strongly agree	Agree	Undecided	Disagree	Strongly disagree
Continuing education is very important in my profession	___	___	___	___	___
Companies should pay for professional courses employees take	___	___	___	___	___

Interval scales carry ordinal scale rankings a step further by measuring the distance between rank positions in equal units. For example, computer users might be asked to rank personal computer memory capacity along the following interval scale.

	Poor	Average	Excellent
IBM	____	____	____
APPLE	____	____	____
COMPAC	____	____	____

On this scale, the difference between "poor" and "average" is the same as the distance between "average" and "excellent." However, such a scale doesn't permit the conclusion that "excellent" is twice as good as "average, since no zero position has been established.

A variant on interval scales with many marketing applications is the semantic differential in which the respondent selects a point between two bipolar words that best represents the direction and intensity of his or her feelings. For example, here is how such a scale might profile respondent attitudes toward three personal computers, brands A, B, and C.

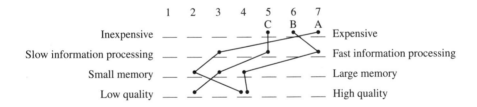

• *QUESTION SEQUENCE*

Here are sequencing guidelines designed to enhance respondent interest and involvement in the survey.

- Place questions that respondent might be reluctant to answer in the body of the questionnaire, to be asked when respondent is at ease with the interviewer or questionnaire content.

- Consider the influence of question placement on succeeding questions; for example, questions that use the product name should appear at the conclusion of the questionnaire.

- Arrange questions in logical order, avoiding sudden topic changes that will confuse the respondent.

The questionnaire should follow this basic sequence.

- A *basic information section* is composed of actual questions asked.

- A *classification information section* provides demographic information (e.g., age, income, education level) that can be related to the respondent's answers.

- An *identification information section* includes identifying data (names, addresses, code numbers, etc.) for all questionnaire participants: interviewer, interviewee, editor, etc.

PRETEST THE QUESTIONNAIRE

Regardless of design or communication approach, the questionnaire should be pretested to eliminate ambiguous phraseology and distortive biases. Ideally, pretesting should be conducted under the same conditions that will be used in the contact situations. At a minimum, the mailing should be pretested on a group comprising experts and members of the population to receive the mailing.

ANALYZING INFORMATION WITH STATISTICS AND EXPERIMENTS

Once gathered and organized, primary (and sometimes secondary) data are analyzed using statistical or experimental methods.

• *STATISTICAL METHODS*

Statistical (descriptive) methods classify data in such a way that inclusion in one category implies inclusion in one or more other categories, often revealing significant relationships among data categories. These relationships can then lead to predictions about future occurrences.

In international markets, statistical research methods are typically used to identify similarities and differences between and among markets and customer groups, with similarities usually leading to standardization strategies, differences to adaptive strategies. For example, Table 5-2 compares two samples, each comprising 100 tax accountants, from the United States and from Britain. Criteria against which the samples are compared—income under $40,000 (or British equivalent) and accreditation status (as Certified Tax Accountant or equivalent)—were found to predict enrollment in professional education courses in the United States.

**Table 5–2. Comparison of U.S. and British Tax Accountants
in Terms of Criteria Predictive of Professional Course Enrollment
(sample size: 100)**

	Income under $40,000 Enrolled in Programs		Not accredited Enrolled in Programs	
	Number	Percent	Number	Percent
U.S. tax accountants	48	48	60	60
British tax accountants	50	50	55	55

These findings, which indicate that the U.S. and British tax accountant markets are quite similar in terms of these predictive criteria, might reinforce a decision by the Merton marketing team to treat the two markets the same in planning a market entry strategy featuring standardized product, price, and promotion offerings.

• *EXPERIMENTAL METHODS*

Although statistical research findings are often sufficiently indicative to act on, they are never conclusive. For example, in the statistical analysis in Table 5-2, it is at least conceivable that criteria different from those predisposing U.S. tax accountants to enroll in professional courses would predispose British tax accountants to enroll.

Experimental (causal) methods are a more effective (and expensive) research approach for identifying and defining cause-effect relationships. Illustrative is a test market experiment involving selecting matched groups of subjects, giving them different treatments, controlling unrelated factors, and checking for differences in group responses. For example, two groups of British tax accountants, closely matched in all significant variables (e.g., income, education level), are each exposed to similar MM offerings with only a 20 percent lower price as a significant difference. If, after this test market has run its course, a check for differences reveals that the group exposed to the 20 percent lower price purchased 40 percent more MM systems, then it might be assumed that the lower price produced the sales increase. Other elements that can be manipulated in the experimental format include product features, promotional appeals, and distribution channels.

However, at least four variables can combine to invalidate these findings.

- *Selection.* Consciously or not, different criteria might have been used to select each group, so they are not truly matched.

- *Mortality.* Members of one group might desert in greater numbers, so even groups that begin as matched might not stay that way.

- *Pretest effect.* When members of a group know they are being selected to participate in a test market study, they might behave in an unnatural way (e.g., purchase MMs to please the researchers).

- *History.* Outside events might bias experiment results (e.g., a competitor might initiate a campaign promoting its MM systems).

TEST MARKETS AS EXPERIMENTS

These invalidating factors, along with high dollar and time costs associated with test market experiments, tend to increase in global markets, where it is especially difficult to hold experimental variables comparable or constant across cultures. As a consequence, many marketers use consumer panels to generate hypotheses and describe situations and opportunities. Panels are cheaper and quicker than test markets and ensure a much higher degree of secrecy, which is important when a new product, or product concept, is being tested.

GENERATING CONCLUSIONS AND MAKING RECOMMENDATIONS

After the research plan had been formulated and followed in collecting and analyzing secondary and primary data pertaining to prospects for successful entry into the British marketplace, the data were tabulated and used as the basis of a report that summarized study findings, conclusions, and recommendations. (Tabulation is the process of summarizing responses by coded categories, with results expressed as totals or percentages.)

The recommendations step is the most important of the entire marketing research process because recommendations are what decision makers rely on. The MM study, for example, concluded that there were no significant differences between British and American accountants with respect to characteristics that would motivate purchase of MM systems and recommended this market as an excellent target for entry. A wrong decision to enter this market, based on faulty research and recommendations deriving from this research, could cost Merton millions of dollars.

Conclusions and recommendations are generally presented in written (in some cases oral) form to decision makers. Since these presentations are often communicated to both headquarters and local managers, all interests should be represented. Study results should be presented clearly and concisely, avoiding lengthy analyses and demonstrations; just note where information of limited general interest can be found. Also, make sure presentations demonstrate how research results relate to original research objectives and are consistent with overall corporate strategy.

IMPLEMENTATION AND FEEDBACK

Finally, the marketing research process comes full circle as findings, conclusions, and recommendations are programmed into marketing information systems and used in the subsequent creation, implementation, and control of strategic marketing plans.

CHAPTER PERSPECTIVE

In this chapter, we examined the last four steps of the marketing research process, involving (1) gathering primary data through surveys and observation; (2) transforming data into decision information using statistical and experimental methods; (3) using the information to generate conclusions and recommendations for further action; and (4) implementing and following up on the recommendations in the strategic planning process. The chapter focused on problems and approaches for generating data in international markets as well as effective sampling, questionnaire design, and statistical and experimental approaches that address these problems.

KNOW THE CONCEPTS

TERMS FOR STUDY

bias	hypotheses
centralized research	interviewer/interviewee bias
communication modes	judgment samples
conclusive research	nonprobability samples
convenience samples	nonresponse bias
coordinated research	observation
data collection	pretesting questionnaire
data processing	primary data
decentralized research	probability samples
experimental methods	question content
exploratory research	question format
focus groups	question sequence

question wording
questionnaire design
questionnaire objectives
questionnaire types
quota samples
report conclusions
report recommendations

research plan
sampling plan
secondary data
statistical methods
surveys
test markets

MATCHUP EXERCISES

1. Match the questionnaire type in the first column with the information needed in the second column (the questionnaire has to do with the needs and attitudes of prospective Russian buyers of expensive dacha-style homes manufactured in the United States and assembled on site in Russia).

1. structured/nondisguised

a. attitudes toward high incomes allowed under new entrepreneurial, free-enterprise Russian environment

2. nonstructured/nondisguised

b. design features that would make it easier to sell the dachas in the Russian market

3. nonstructured/disguised

c. reasons for wanting to purchase an expensive dacha-style home

2. A Mexican winery, intent on entering the U.S. market, is planning a series of surveys to determine U.S. preferences in wine. The wine line that will be marketed will be positioned and promoted to reflect these characteristics and will be aimed at the heavy-user market segment (i.e., the 20 percent of U.S. citizens who consume 85 percent of the wine). Match up the survey type in the first column with the sample selected in the second column.

1. probability

a. One in 5,000 members of the entire population will be selected randomly.

2. judgment

b. Twenty percent of the sample will comprise the heavy-user segment.

3. quota

c. The sample will be restricted to editors of food and drink magazines and newsletters.

4. convenience

d. The Mexican winery's U.S. advertising agency will conduct taste tests among its staff members.

3. Match the form of research study in the first column with information desired in the second column regarding the nature and needs of target markets for MM systems.

1. exploratory: internal secondary

a. relationships between the profession purchasing MMs and profitability generated

2. exploratory: external secondary

b. consensus as to the most worthwhile professions to focus on in market entry campaign

3. conclusive: statistical

c. the extent to which different incentives offered distributors will encourage them to promote MM systems

4. conclusive: experimental

d. distribution of sales among different professions in domestic market

QUESTIONS FOR REVIEW AND DISCUSSION

1. Distinguish between exploratory and conclusive research. How might each be involved in coming up with a prediction that a 10 percent increase in the price of MICROS systems (a modern form of cash register for hotels, restaurants, cruise ships and casinos discussed in Global Focus 18-2) will not decrease sales in the firm's Caribbean market.

2. Discuss advantages and disadvantages of centralized, decentralized, and coordinated approaches for generating information on emerging global markets. Which would you recommend for Merton (1) during its present state as an exporter and (2) if it eventually achieves multinational status?

3. The Cornerstone International Group, a small U.S. company in Minnesota, plans to export, distribute, and sell commercial popcorn equipment and supplies to Russian entrepreneurs. First, however, it needs information on Russian preferences in popcorn, modifications that will have to be made in the equipment offering (i.e., design, price, promotion, distribution) to attract distributors and users of the equipment, and consumers of the popcorn. Discuss how judgment samples, quota samples, and random samples might be used in this research.

4. Why are nonprobability samples more important during exploratory research and probability samples more important during conclusive research?

5. Distinguish between mechanical, personal, obtrusive, and unobtrusive observation methods. How might mechanical and personal methods be used to test student response to a new MM software training course for doctors featuring "virtual reality" surgery experiences?

6. How might the following biases invalidate survey findings indicating that between 40 and 44 percent of the Indonesian female population between the ages of 24 and 50 would be likely to purchase a line of American dishwashers about to be introduced into this market: interviewer, interviewee, nonresponse, and halo effect.

7. Shown here is a semantic differential scale that depicts perceptions toward two brands of lap computers (Brands A and B) in terms of the four dimensions presumed to be of most importance to users: reliability (i.e., it almost always works, even under adverse conditions), speed (i.e., it provides results quickly), portability (i.e., it is easy to pack and travel with), and value (i.e., it is priced right in terms of utilities provided). What would you conclude from this depiction? What product strategy would you recommend for computer B based on these perceptions?

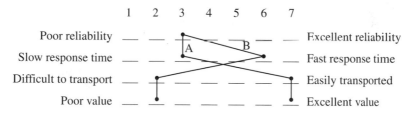

8. As part of its strategy to increase its share of the Canadian market, a U.S. manufacturer of dentifrice products implements a two-city test market for a new kind of dental floss that can simultaneously brush and floss teeth. In each city, 200 randomly selected participants are provided a free 3-month's supply of the dental floss, with the understanding that, at the end of this period, they will fill out a questionnaire exploring their feelings and attitudes toward the floss. This information will then be used to make any necessary modifications of price, product design, and promotion aspects of the offering.

In terms of selection, mortality, and history, why might conclusions derived from this test market be suspect?

ANSWERS

MATCHUP EXERCISES

1. 1c, 2b, 3a
2. 1a, 2c, 3b, 4d
3. 1d, 2b, 3a, 4c

QUESTIONS FOR REVIEW AND DISCUSSION

1. Exploratory research is used mainly to identify hypotheses (i.e., in marketing, hypotheses usually help explain the nature, or resolution, of problems). In the process, exploratory research methods are generally less focused, more free ranging, than conclusive research; they deal with smaller aggregates (e.g., a single focus group) and apply less rigorous controls and statistical methods in gathering, organizing, and analyzing data. Conclusive research, on the other hand, employs rigorous controls and statistical methods and leads to predictions rather than to hypotheses.

MICROS Systems' marketing research manager might have used internal and external secondary sources, as well as knowledgeable people, in arriving at the hypotheses that a price increase for its systems in the Caribbean market would not adversely affect sales. For example, internal records might show that previous increases in this market didn't adversely affect sales; or external reports from MICROS' Association, or the Commerce Department, might indicate a strong, burgeoning hospitality market whose need for MICROS systems transcends concerns over price. To confirm this hypothesis, MICROS might actually raise its price in one representative segment of its Caribbean market; if the hypotheses proves correct, it can raise its price generally.

2. With centralized approaches, research design and focus are decided by headquarters and forwarded to local country operations for implementation. This approach is generally applicable when research is intended to influence company policy and strategy, and the nature and needs of markets are generally similar. With decentralized approaches, home country headquarters establish broad research policies and guidelines and then delegate further design and implementation to local country headquarters. This approach is applicable when markets differ from country to country. It provides closer market proximity, more flexible responses to marketplace threats and opportunities, and the benefits of interaction among home/host country personnel. With this coordinated approach, an outside inter-mediary, such as a marketing research firm, brings home and host country research operations together, helping to realize the benefits of both.

As an exporter to a single country, which is Merton's immediate goal, the company, with no host country personnel in place, must perforce employ essentially a centralized approach. However, it has retained a marketing research firm that is helping the firm to realize its short-term goal and, later, will help to implement a coordinated approach when Merton reaches international status.

3. A judgment sample might consist of entrepreneurs who, in the judg-ment of the researcher, will be most likely to use the equipment (e.g., those who own grocery stores). A quota sample of popcorn con-sumers might be weighted to reflect different ways Russians like their popcorn (e.g., if 50 percent like sweetened popcorn, that is the per-centage of the population that would be represented in this sample). A random sample might be used to determine the percentages com-prising the quota sample (e.g., a questionnaire sent to such a sample requesting feedback on popcorn preferences).

4. During exploratory research, the purpose is usually investigative in nature (e.g., to investigate attitudes toward products, needs to be met, or possible causes or solutions to problems). Frequently, the best way to generate this information is in small, free-wheeling discussion ses-sions, such as focus groups, in which the researcher has no idea of the outcome and statistical analyses would be irrelevant. However, during the conclusive research stage, when hypotheses generated during exploratory research are tested, much larger samples are desired to generate valid, reliable data in a few areas through analy-ses covering classes, averages, percentages, and dispersions.

5. Mechanical observation relies on some sort of mechanical or elec-tronic device (e.g., a radar gun) to observe behavior; personal obser-vation relies on people observing behavior. In obtrusive observation, the observer makes his/her role as an observer known (e.g., an immi-gration officer inspecting the contents of a suitcase); in unobtrusive observation, the observer's role is not revealed to the observed (e.g., an FBI infiltrator of a militant hate group).

Merton could use mechanical observation by having trainees respond electronically to a series of questions about the course; personal obser-vation would occur if one of the students taking the course was also a researcher assigned to monitor reactions of the other students.

6. *Interviewer/interviewee bias:* Attitudes or actions by either the inter-viewer or interviewee can distort responses during personal inter-views. For example, if the interviewer is perceived by the interviewee to have higher socioeconomic status, there would possibly be a

tendency on the part of the interviewee to verbally equalize this difference by exaggerating her responses, while the interviewer's interpretation of her responses might reflect this difference in his or her interpretation of responses. *Nonresponse bias:* The reason a large proportion of the sample refused to answer questions regarding purchase intent might bias the results. For example, they might do their wash in the traditional manner and be too embarrassed to admit unfamiliarity with modern appliances like washing machines. *Halo effect bias:* Words used in the questionnaire, or the way these words are sequenced, can distort responses. For example, if the name of the washing machine manufacturer is familiar to the respondent and is used early in the questioning, she might generalize favorable attitudes toward this name into a statement of intent to buy the washing machine.

7. On a scale of 1 to 7 ("poor" to "excellent"), both computers score equally high on reliability (2.2), so this is not an issue in differentiating the two. Significant differences between perceptions occur in the areas of "speed" and "portability," with B scoring three points higher in speed and A scoring four points higher in portability. Since A is perceived as a better value than B by four points, it can probably be inferred that users place a much higher value on portability than on speed. Given these perceptual differences—and assuming that this is a market in which B wishes to compete against A—a product strategy for B might be to redesign its computer to make it at least as portable as A, even at some sacrifice of speed.

8. The following variables could invalidate findings from this study.

- *Selection.* In spite of efforts to choose samples from similar populations, people in each city might tend to have significantly different attitudes toward dentifrices.

- *Mortality.* Many more people might drop out of one group than the other, so they would no longer be matched.

- *History.* Outside events might bias results. For example, in one of the test cities, a competitor, learning of the test, might seek to skew the results by manipulating marketing mix variables (e.g., a "two-fer" deal on dental floss).

6
POLITICAL AND LEGAL INFLUENCES ON INTERNATIONAL MARKETS

OVERVIEW

Whether on supranational, national, or subnational levels, government political/legal influences affect trade, for better or worse, by promoting, impeding, or actively competing with imports and exports. Adverse influences from either home or host country sources can also negate the elements of a strategic marketing plan, rendering markets inaccessible and marketing mixes ineffective. Positive political/legal environmental influences, on the other hand, can provide importers and exporters with a broad diversity of assists in trade relations from which all participants profit.

POLITICAL/LEGAL ENVIRONMENT AFFECTS STRATEGIC PLANNING

This is the first of three chapters in which we examine elements in the external environment that a firm must understand and account for in formulating strategic marketing plans to penetrate international markets.

In this chapter, we examine political/legal environments, with emphasis on government policies, statutes, and regulations that restrain or encourage international trade. These environments can exist in a firm's home or host country, can derive from bi- or multilateral agreements, and can affect both imports and exports.

We will continue to refer to the Merton company for examples, focusing on its approach for assessing political/legal climates in global markets friendly or hostile to its line of Mighty Mind computer systems.

HOSTILE POLITICAL CLIMATES QUASH ENTRY PLANS

From the perspective of a firm like Merton, searching for congenial foreign markets to enter, an analysis of threats and opportunities presented by political/legal climates is probably the best starting point. This is because this climate can affect, for better or worse, all the elements of the strategic marketing plan, including economic, technological, and competitive environmental climates; the market selected for entry; the means of entering this market; and the marketing mix formulated to attract this market.

This analysis should begin with the firm's home country, where the political/legal climate might effectively exclude exporting its products and services to other countries. If any such initial barriers can be hurdled, then the analysis can be broadened to encompass political/legal climates in prospective host countries and regions.

ASSESSING HOME COUNTRY CONSTRAINTS ON TRADE

Export quotas, export controls, and embargoes are typically the main constraints faced by a home country company in its efforts to penetrate global markets.

• *EXPORT QUOTAS*

Export quotas, which limit the quantity of products that may be exported from a country, are established for a number of reasons. For example, quotas on the amount of redwood and other rare-wood lumber that can be exported from the United States are designed to ensure that scarce natural resources are not depleted and are available to domestic consumers at afforable prices. Export quotas are also established to raise export prices by restricting supplies of the product in foreign markets, as when countries combine to restrict the world supply of commodities like oil and coffee.

• *EXPORT CONTROLS*

Export controls are a more extreme form of export quota designed to deny, rather than delimit, the acquisition of strategically important goods by adversaries. In the United States, the export control system is based on the Export Administration Act and the Munitions Control Act, which combine to control all exports of goods, services, and ideas, usually for reasons of national security, foreign policy, or nuclear nonproliferation. Firms like Merton wishing to export products must first get a license from the Department of Commerce, which has drawn up lists of sensitive products, unreliable countries, and unreliable individual firms (e.g., firms that secretly sold sensitive nuclear materials to Iraq prior to the Persian Gulf War).

Unsensitive products sold to traditional partners may be exported under a general license. Otherwise, especially with hi-tech products sold to unfriendly countries, a validated export license is required.

Since the breakup of the Soviet Union, the export control process has been liberalized. By 1995 the Commerce Department had slashed controls to one-tenth of the products covered in 1989 and denied fewer than 2 percent of the high-tech export applications it received. Now, the focus of export controls is on individual countries or regions such as Iran, Iraq, and North Korea, which are perceived as potentially threatening. Even in these cases, export controls are difficult for the United States to implement: Most countries can make their own strategically important components or acquire them elsewhere; miniaturization of many such components makes them easy to smuggle; and technology transfer is often a personalized affair, inventoried in the minds of experts and difficult to control. The fact that such controls often place U.S. firms at a competitive disadvantage vis-à-vis firms from countries with less severe control systems is discussed in Global Focus 6-1.

GLOBAL FOCUS 6-1

Export Controls Hurt U.S. Firms

Japanese trade practices that exclude billions of dollars worth of U.S. exports are common knowledge. Not so visible are U.S. rules that forbid U.S. companies from selling abroad and block even more export sales.

Syracuse University economist J. David Richardson's comprehensive study of export disincentives estimates their cost to U.S. companies to be $21 to $27 billion a year. By comparison, a study done by the Institute for International Economics puts the annual loss of U.S. exports due to Japanese trade restraints at $9 to $18 billion. According to Richardson, the United States is the world's most aggressive controller of exports, and Washington has been "unduly nonchalant" about the economic effect.

U.S. export controls target high-tech industries that are key to economic growth. Among those hit hardest are makers of computers, telecommunication equipment, machine tools and civilian aircraft.

American Telephone and Telegraph (AT&T) estimates that over the next 5 years, U.S. restrictions dating from the Cold War will cost it $500 million of foreign business. These are sales that probably will go to competitors from Europe or Japan. AT&T chairman Robert E. Allen complained to Congress, "It is unrealistic, perhaps bordering on arrogance, to think that any country would go without advanced information technology just because U.S. companies are forbidden to provide it."

Source: Robert Keatley, "U.S. Rules Dating from the Cold War Block Billions of Dollars in Exports," *The Wall Street Journal*, October 15, 1993, p. A7.

• *EMBARGO*

An embargo is a specific type of quota that prohibits all trade, either imports or exports, on whole categories of products regardless of destination, on specific products to specific countries, or on all products to given countries. Typically instituted for adversarial or political, not economic, reasons, embargoes invariably raise a number of controversial issues. For example, how effective are embargoes in changing other country's policies? (Unilaterally imposed embargoes are usually ineffective.) Even when multilateral embargoes are imposed, who suffers—the people or the government? And, perhaps most important to international marketers, how will firms that suffer when embargoes close their markets be compensated? These marketers are also interested in opportunities created when embargoes are lifted.

ASSESSING HOST COUNTRY CONSTRAINTS ON TRADE

In assessing the impact of political/legal climates in prospective host countries, Merton's major concerns pertained to the country's attitudes toward trade, the stability of its government and currency, and its potential to discourage trade through quantitative and qualitative restrictions.

• *WHAT ARE THE COUNTRY'S ATTITUDES TOWARD FOREIGN TRADE?*

Attitudes toward importing goods from another country range from largely free markets, as exist between the United States and Canada, to a total embargo on the products of another country, as exists, say, between the United States and Cuba. To illustrate some possibilities, consider attitudes of three large Asian markets—Taiwan, Japan, and South Korea—toward United States' goods.

Taiwan, the least resistant, actually has a "Buy American" policy that favors U.S. companies for major purchases and projects (e.g., Japanese firms weren't allowed to bid on Taipai's subway system, but American firms were). In Japan, the *kieretso*—powerful complexes of government, capital, labor, and technology—create trade barriers that are difficult to penetrate and effectively protect many industries. South Korea, fueled by a nationalistic drive to foster development of domestic industry at the expense of foreign competition, has balked at opening its markets to many U.S. products.

• *HOW STABLE IS THE COUNTRY'S GOVERNMENT?*

Two key concerns of firms assessing the stability of a prospective host country's government follow.

- Are government policies and practices consistent and predictable in such areas as taxes, profits, and ownership rights?

- Is there an orderly process for selecting and empowering new leaders?

Unless both of these questions can be answered in the affirmative, the entering company will likely face a climate of instability and discontinuity leading to three kinds of political risk:

- *Ownership risk*, exposing property and life;

- *Operating risk*, exposing the firm's ongoing operations to interference;

- *Transfer risk*, encountered when the firm attempts to shift funds between countries.

Ownership risk generally prevails in countries where civil disturbances, such as coups, guerilla warfare and terrorism, take on a strong antibusiness bias, with U.S. businesses often the most vulnerable targets.[1] The two most likely manifestations of ownership risk include confiscation, or the transfer of ownership to the host country with no compensation (especially affecting mining, energy, public utilities, and banking enterprises), and expropriation, or the transfer of ownership to the host country with compensation (rarely sufficient, usually at the book value of the firm and in the local currency).

---

[1] Michael G. Harvey, "A Survey of Corporate Programs for Managing Terrorist Threats," *Journal of International Business Studies*, (Third Quarter 1993), pp. 465–478.

As a policy tool for unstable governments, both confiscation and expropriation have decreased dramatically over time, from more than 100 such incidents a year in the mid 1970s to fewer than 10 a year in the 1990s. One reason for this decline is a new appreciation by governments of the more subtle, less destructive benefits of domestication, a form of operations risk under which the government demands partial transfer of ownership and managerial responsibility, usually imposing constraints to ensure that the product is produced locally, and a larger share of profit is retained in the country. From the perspective of a firm like Merton, domestication can have calamitous results. For example, local hiring rules can lead to poorly trained, inexperienced managers, unable to communicate and cooperate effectively, and domestic content requirements can force a firm to buy supplies and parts locally, resulting in increased costs, inefficiency, and lower-quality products. Domestication can also result in poor market discipline that makes the company noncompetitive in global markets.

• *HOW WILL THE COUNTRY'S MONETARY POLICIES AND REGULATIONS AFFECT US?*

The White Nights case (Global Focus 6-2) illustrates how a country's monetary policies and regulations can eliminate it as a worthwhile entry target. It also illustrates transfer risk, or the likelihood that host country policies will leave the firm few funds to transfer, or dictate the form in which they must be transferred.

GLOBAL FOCUS 6-2

White Nights Charge into a Russian Ambush

To illustrate the negative impact of a hostile political/legal climate on the best-laid marketing plans, consider the admittedly extreme plight of the White Nights Company, an American firm engaged by the Russian government in 1991 "to bring money, technology, and common sense to the task of salvaging a former enemy's oil fields."

The Americans came to the bleak Siberian city of Raduzhay in July 1991 with a tank full of optimism and loads of fancy equipment. "We expected to kick the dirt and oil would come out," admitted Gary Rinaldi, director of White Nights' Moscow office.

Instead, [the company's] $116 million investment was caught up, and very nearly written off, in the chaos that has engulfed Russia since the collapse of the Soviet Union. Tax codes, to cite one prominent example, change monthly. In May 1992, at the depth of White Nights despair, the tax bill included local taxes of 10 to 20 percent of revenues, a mandatory conversion of half its dollars to rubles at the market rate, a tax on profits from which wages cannot be deducted, a 28 percent value added tax that was supposed to be waived for exports but was often imposed anyway by confused local officials, a 60 percent individual income tax and an export tax of $5.85 a barrel—more than a quarter of the world price.

Since then, Russia has added a mineral use tax, a mineral rehabilitation tax, an excise tax, tariffs on imported goods, port fees and—assuming anyone's made any money—a profit repatriation tax.

Meanwhile, pumps are breaking down and oil fields are drying up from drilling practices that have plugged the pores in oil-bearing rock and fouled oil reservoirs with water.

Source: Ann Imse, "American Know-How and Russian Oil: A Case Study of Why Capitalism and Bureaucracy Don't Mix," *The New York Times*, March 7, 1993. Reprinted with permission.

Ideally, an exporting company like Merton wants its profits in its own currency, or in another recognized world currency (e.g., dollars or marks, not rubles). The importing country, however, might limit the amount of such currency the exporter can obtain for goods or services sold or establish an unfair exchange rate (e.g., the number of dollars received for rubles earned) that can effectively bankrupt the exporter. As when dealing with unstable governments, there are measures the exporter can take to protect its profits against unfavorable monetary policies and regulations. For example, the exporter might be willing to accept a blocked currency—whose removal from the country is restricted—if it can buy other goods in the country that can be sold elsewhere for a needed currency. This, in substance, is what the McDonald's Corporation did in using Russian rubles to purchase potatoes, beef, and other "McMeal" ingredients in Russia, to sell for dollars in its huge Moscow facility.

Other arrangements for protecting profits from unfavorable monetary regulations include:

- *Barter*, involving the direct exchange of goods and services between parties, with no money involved. For example, White Nights (Global Focus 6-2), during its Siberian sojourn, purchased, for rubles, a fleet of brand new Russian jeeps and buses to barter for goods and services.

- *Countertrade*, a form of barter involving money or credit, in which the exporter's products or technology are paid for in full, or partially, by products produced in the importing country. For example, an incentive for White Nights to continue to work with the Russian oil industry is a contractual agreement to eventually share in the profits from oil produced by wells the firm brings in. Countertrade now accounts for about 30 percent of all world trade.

- *Counterpurchase*, a form of countertrade in which two contracts are signed: one in which the exporter sells products for a cash settlement, the other in which the exporter agrees to purchase and market unrelated products from the importer. For example, Pepsi Cola sells its cola syrup to Russia for rubles and agrees to buy Russian vodka for sale in the United States.

HOW FIRMS REDUCE POLITICAL RISK

Often, judicious preparation can mitigate political risks endemic in unwelcoming political/legal climates. For example, the U.S. government's Overseas Private Investment Corporation (OPIC) insures investments in less developed countries against such perils as currency inconvertability, expropriation, and physical damage resulting from war or political strife. OPIC also finances manufacturer foreign direct investment, either individually or as a joint venture, through (1) direct loans from $100,000 to $6 million per project and (2) loan guarantees to U.S. institutional lenders of up to $50 million per project.

An entering firm can also reduce political risk by demonstrating that it is actively concerned with the host country's social and economic welfare, and isn't just another indifferent exploiter. Intensive local hiring, good pay, and socially useful investment are all ways to help create this "good neighbor" image. An entering firm can also reduce political risk by taking on foreign partners, borrowing from foreign governments or banks, or utilizing licensing, contract manufacturing, or management contracting (Chapter 1). From Merton's perspective, however, the most prudent course was simply to eliminate politically unstable countries from consideration.

• *WHAT TRADE RESTRICTIONS WILL WE FACE?*

A country with a hostile attitude toward importing foreign products and services has at its disposal a broad range of trade restrictions for making it difficult, if not impossible, for a firm like Merton to penetrate its well-protected markets.

Examples of these restrictions, as they apply to imports, include:

- *License requirements.* An import license is a privilege permitting a company to sell goods within defined limits in the country issuing the license. Mexico, for example, requires import licenses limiting the importation of certain products to encourage domestic growth of manufacturers of these products. (Many of these licensing requirements have been phased out under the North American Free Trade Agreement [NAFTA], discussed in Chapter 7).

- *Tariffs*. A tariff is a tax on imports stated as a percent of value (ad valorem), or on a per-unit basis. Protective tariffs are designed to protect home industries by reducing imports of protected goods; revenue tariffs, usually lower than protective tariffs, are designed to raise money. Different tariff rates may be applied to different countries, or groups of countries, or a single rate may be applied to all countries. For example, in 1988 the European Community raised the tariff rate (called a duty) on all videocassette recorders from 8 to 14 percent. Governments also impose temporary tariff surcharges on imports to redress a current situation, such as an unfavorable balance of payments. Countervailing duties, usually more permanent than tariff surcharges, are assessed to offset special advantages or discounts, such as an export subsidy. For example, such duties were levied when it was determined that Spain had subsidized shipments of filbert nuts.

- *Taxes*. Some countries, in addition to standard taxes on foreign companies and imports, levy special taxes to serve special purposes. Examples include excise or processing taxes on certain products to provide revenues from local sales (e.g., U.S. automobiles sold in Europe are taxed on the basis of their weight, thus limiting their sales vis-à-vis smaller European cars) and border taxes, levied on imports in European countries to equalize their cost to that of locally manufactured products.

- *Quotas*. These specific provisions limit the amount of foreign products a host country can import. They may be applied to all countries, or on a country by country basis. Absolute quotas limit, absolutely, the amount of a product that may be imported; tariff quotas limit product quantitites imported at low duty rates, while allowing higher quantities in at higher rates. Voluntary quotas ask exporters to voluntarily limit quantities exported until a protected domestic industry has made the necessary adjustments to gain its competitive edge. Also called VERS (Voluntary Export Restraints), these quotas often succeed only in creating confusion and destroying normal marketing operations. For example, when Japan voluntarily agreed to restrict the number of automobiles it sold in the United States, it profited handsomely by selling mainly top-of-the-line cars at top prices, while providing an umbrella under which American automobile manufacturers could maintain artificially high prices.

QUALITATIVE CONTROLS ALSO DISCOURAGE IMPORTS

License requirements, taxes, tariffs, and quotas are all examples of quantitative controls, which specify quantities of goods that can be imported, and/or amounts, and kinds, of payments for these goods.

In addition, host countries also have a number of qualitative controls in their trade arsenals to restrict or discourage imports, including (1) restrictive customs procedures that promulgate complex rules and regulations for classifying and valuing commodities as a basis for levying import duties, making compliance difficult and expensive, and (2) discriminatory government and private procurement policies, such as "Buy British" or "Buy American" campaigns that effectively discriminate against imported products.

• *HOW WILL THE GOVERNMENT PROMOTE TRADE?*

Having systematically eliminated from its list of prospective entry targets countries with hostile attitudes and restrictions toward trade, Merton now turned its attention to the positive side of the assessment ledger: countries whose favorable attitudes toward trade were manifest in a number of supportive promotional activities. These supports exist on supranational, national, and subnational levels and can apply to both imports and exports.

• *SUPRANATIONAL SUPPORTS*

On the supranational level, a country can facilitate both imports and exports by joining organizations set up for this purpose. Examples of such organizations include:

INTERNATIONAL MONETARY FUND

The International Monetary Fund, with a membership of more than 150 countries, was chartered to oversee the management of the international financial system by exercising surveillance over exchange rate policies of members; monitoring developments in the field of international liquidity (e.g., the effect of higher German interest rates on cash flows to other countries); providing temporary balance of payments assistance to member countries in external difficulties; and offering technical aid to promote cooperation in international financial relationships.

ECONOMIC COMMUNITIES

Economic communities are designed to improve trade among member nations through cooperative preferential arrangements. In order of size and influence on trade and the economic well-being of countries and regions, they include: The General Agreement on Tariffs and Trade (GATT), which, in December 1993, committed 117 nations to reduce tariffs around the world by a third and apply free trade rules to agriculture and service industries for the first time; The Asian-Pacific Economic Forum (APEC), created in 1989, which commits all countries in the Asia-Pacific area to a gradual dismantling of trade barriers; The North American Free Trade Agreement (NAFTA), ratified by Congress in 1993, which links Canada, Mexico, and the United States into a single trade zone encompassing 360 million people; and the European Union, which committed 14 European countries to remove all tariffs and trade restrictions on the movement of goods and services by 1992. These and other economic communities are covered in more detail in Chapter 7.

• *NATIONAL AND SUBNATIONAL SUPPORTS*

In addition to supranational agreements and organizations that promote international trade, national governments promote trade in three ways.

- Financial assists, such as export subsidies, including direct subsidies, lower taxes, lower costs, and manipulation of exchange rates;

- State trading companies, which engage governments in buying, selling, and regulating export activities, either in place of or in addition to private traders;

- Information services covering international marketing opportunities for smaller companies.

FINANCIAL ASSISTS

Financial assists generally encompass tax incentives that treat earnings from export activities—such as developing new overseas markets—preferentially, either by applying a lower rate to earnings from these activities or by providing a refund of taxes already paid for income associated with exporting. Other financial assists include allowing accelerated depreciation of export-related assets and outright subsidies to reward export performance. Far Eastern, Latin American, and European trading nations are especially generous in offering these financial assists, often leaving themselves open to retaliatory actions by other nations who feel these assists excessively tip the playing field.

STATE TRADING COMPANIES

State trading companies engage governments in commercial operations, either directly or through agencies under their control. These companies function either in place of private traders—as was the case with Soviet command economies where the state made all exporting and importing decisions—or in addition to these private traders. For example, consistent with its recent industrial policy designed to target overseas industries and markets that show high potential for export growth, the Australian Government formed the Australian Trade Commission that consolidates various export assistance agencies into a single body and effectively grants the government decision-making powers over imports and exports previously made in the private sector.

Whether in place of, or supplementing, private traders, state trading companies, like their private trading company counterparts (best illustrated by Japanese trading companies, a dozen of which are responsible for 80 percent of Japanese imports and exports), present problems for individual companies and entire countries. For example, an exporting company like Merton, dealing with a monolithic state trading company, which often doesn't have to show a profit, has little chance to build loyalty relations with specific customers and is often at the mercy of bureaucratic decisions made with little understanding of marketplace realities. (Functions and benefits of trading companies are discussed in Chapter 18).

GOVERNMENT INFORMATION SERVICES

Government information services offer information assistance to importers and exporters, particularly concerning the location of markets and credit risks, and in promoting products in foreign markets.

In the United States, for example, more than a dozen federal organizations actively collect information from around the world concerning problems and opportunities for importers and exporters. Much of this information abundance is free or inexpensive, if sometimes bureaucratically slow. These sources of information and assistance are covered, along with illustrative examples of their use, in the "Secondary Data" section of Chapter 4.

GLOBAL LEGAL SYSTEMS AFFECT BUSINESS DECISIONS

In addition to largely political and regulatory activities that nations use to promote, impede, or compete with trade, Merton was concerned with the type of legal system in place in a prospective entry country and how this system would influence business decisions.

• *TYPE OF LEGAL SYSTEM*

In general, there are two types of legal systems in place in industrialized countries: the code law system, deriving from old Roman and Napoleonic codes, and the common law system, deriving from English Common Law. Code law, characterizing most of continental Europe, divides the judicial system into civil, commercial, and criminal law divisions, with separate administrative sections, and all-inclusive, relatively inflexible, written statutes for each divison. Common law, on the other hand, characterizing English commonwealth countries and the United States, tends to merge civil, commercial, and criminal law under a single administrative structure, with tradition, past practice, and precedents from previous rulings guiding legal decisions. A significant recent departure from this tendency is the development of the Uniform Commercial Code in the United States which, like code law, brings together a body of specifically designed written rules covering only commercial conduct.

• *HOW LEGAL SYSTEMS AFFECT BUSINESS DECISIONS*

Analyzing how legal systems would affect business decisions was one of the more challenging tasks Merton planners faced in assessing the political/legal environment. To simplify this task, they focused on questions that they perceived would be most critical in successfully entering and growing in the global marketplace.

UNDER WHOSE LAWS WILL MANAGERS FUNCTION?

Some foreign countries (e.g., in Latin America) mandate that foreigners agree to be treated as nationals, forfeiting jurisdiction of their own national laws. This can present real conflicts when a manger's home country mandates this jurisdiction, as is the case with the U.S. Foreign Corrupt Practices Act. This act makes it a crime for U.S. firms to bribe foreign officials for business purposes, with the rationale that business dealings abroad should reflect U.S. moral and ethical leadership and free market competitive forces. In 1988 the act was revised, largely in response to complaints from U.S. businesses abroad that it put them at a competitive disadvantage in countries with no such antibribery laws, against competitors with no compunction to obey such laws. This revision clarified conditions under which U.S. managers were expected to know about violations of the act and distinguished between facilitation of routine governmental actions (e.g., getting licenses and permits) and of policy decisions (e.g., obtaining or retaining contracts). Still, U.S. firms complain that even the revised act puts them in a difficult position vis-à-vis foreign competitors from Europe and Japan, who have no such law and might be more than willing to follow local practices that encourage bribes.

Other situations where U.S. managers are expected by host countries to recognize laws that conflict with general standards of behavior and ethics in the United States abound, including meager safety standards in Mexican firms, Brazil's profligate abuse of its rain forests and other natural resources, and China's human rights abuses and use of prison labor to make products for export.

Still another conflict situation involves U.S. laws pertaining to boycotts implemented by other countries. For example, some Arab nations blacklist firms that do business with Israel, but U.S. laws impose fines and denial of export licenses on U.S. firms that comply with these boycotts.

WILL PATENTS AND TRADEMARKS BE PROTECTED?

This question was of vital importance to Merton, which held patents on computer hardware and trademarks on software. Thus, they assessed prospective entry nations in terms of adherence to such patent agreements as the International Convention for the Protection of Industrial Property (honored by 45 countries), the Patent Cooperation Treaty (39 countries), and the European Patent Convention (11 countries). Under these conventions, Merton would no longer have to patent products in every country it entered.

TO WHAT EXTENT WILL WE CONTROL OUR COMPANY'S DESTINY?

A number of countries require entering companies to dilute their equity. For example, under India's Foreign Exchange Regulation Act, foreign equity participation in local projects is reduced to 40 percent. Merton planners recognized that circumstances might make such dilution feasible, but they would rather avoid it.

HOW FREE WILL WE BE TO COMPETE?

Antitrust laws, long a part of the legal environment in the United States, can apply to international operations of a firm as well. For example, when a U.S. company buys or enters into a joint venture with a foreign company, or makes an agreement with a competing firm abroad, the U.S. Justice Department has the authority to approve or disapprove such an agreement, based on its likely competitive effect on the U.S. market. However, with increasing globalization of business, and concerns about our laws infringing on the sovereignty of other nations, disapprovals are rare.

Of greater concern to domestic firms seeking to succeed in foreign markets is the fact that U.S. antitrust laws have not generally taken root in other nations. For example, although the European Community Commission prohibits agreements and practices that prevent, restrict, or distort competition, it also exempts large categories of "good" cartels to encourage certain businesses to compete effectively with U.S. and Japanese businesses.

Two U.S. laws that address problems faced by U.S. firms competing with foreign oligopolies, monopolies, and cartels are the Webb Pomerene Act, which excludes from antitrust prosecution firms that cooperate to develop foreign markets, and the Export Trading Act which permits small to medium-sized firms to join forces in international market development activities.

WHAT RECOURSE WILL WE HAVE TO ADJUDICATE DISPUTES?

Lawsuits in foreign countries can be long, costly, possibly biased, and conducted in unfamiliar surroundings under different rules. For this reason, Merton established as a condition of entry the existence of arbitration procedings, typically involving a hearing of all parties before a three-member panel, and a judgment that all parties agree in advance to abide by. That such procedings in an entry country would be impartial and professional would be evidenced by membership in such groups as the International Chamber of Commerce, the London Court of Arbitration, and the Inter-American Commercial Arbitration Committee. Also, arbitration clauses would be written into all contracts in entry countries presuming the possibility of litigation.

Given the proliferation of possible legal pitfalls in international markets, Merton strategists decided to give entry market priority to countries, like Canada, that had signed bilateral treaties of friendship, commerce and navigation with the United States and where, in effect, Merton would be treated, from a legal perspective, essentially as in the United States.

WILL WE ADHERE TO INTERNATIONAL LAW?

International law, which comprises the rules and principles that countries consider binding on themselves, faces two severe constraints: (1) the lack of an adequate judicial and administrative framework, or an agreed on body of law, to form the basis of a truly comprehensive international legal system, and (2) the reluctance of most nations to relinquish what they perceive to be vital rights to an international tribunal—and there is little other nations can do if one refuses to submit to arbitration or recognize an unfavorable judgment against it.

CHAPTER PERSPECTIVE

The political/legal environment in a foreign country is typically the single largest incentive, or disincentive, for entry, affecting other elements of the environment (such as economic growth and competitive freedom), the accessibility of markets, and the effectiveness of marketing mix elements. Analysis of this environment usually begins with an assessment of incentives, or disincentives, to trade and then moves on to an examination of the extent to which prospective host countries discourage trade—through unstable governments, unfavorable monetary policies, restrictive tariffs and taxes, etc.—or encourage trade through financial and regulatory assists and information on marketing opportunities. An assessment of the legal environment in a prospective entry country focuses on the type of system in place (code or common law) and adherence to the somewhat nebulous mandates of international law in such areas as managerial freedom, protection of equity, freedom to compete, patent and trademark protection, bribery, and ultimate recourse.

KNOW THE CONCEPTS

TERMS FOR STUDY

arbitration
barter
bilateral agreements
blocked currency
border taxes
boycotts
code law
common law
confiscation
counterpurchase
countertrade
countervailing duties
domestic content laws
domestication
duty
economic communities
embargoes
excise taxes
Export Administration Act
export controls
export license
Export Trading Act
expropriation
Foreign Corrupt Practices Act
general license
government trade supports
inconvertibility
International Monetary Fund

legal climate
license requirements
local hiring rules
mediation
multilateral agreements
Munitions Control Act
operating risk
Overseas Private Investment
   Corporation (OPIC)
ownership risk
patent cooperations treaties
patents
political climate
qualitative restrictions
quantitative restrictions
quotas
regulations
statutes
surcharges
trademarks
tariff quotas
tariffs
taxes
trading companies
transfer risk
voluntary quotas (VERS)
Webb Pomerene Act

MATCHUP EXERCISES

1. Match the concepts in the first column with the definitions in the second column.

    1. export controls

        a. an export license is required to sell supercomputers to China

2. embargo

    b. Arab nations blacklist firms that deal with Israel

3. boycott

    c. American firms are forbidden to sell products to Cuba

4. domestic content law

    d. U.S. firms in India buy supplies and parts locally

2. Match the concept in the first column with the description in the second column.

1. Export Administration Act

    a. U.S. firms that complain it hampers global competitiveness

2. Foreign Corrupt Practices Act

    b. U.S. exporting firms must obtain an export license

3. European Community Commission

    c. U.S. firms overseas still must compete with "good" cartels

4. Export Trading Act

    d. U.S. firms overseas can join forces to develop international markets

3. Match the concept in the first column with the description in the second column.

1. code law

    a. jurisprudence based on tradition, past practices, and precedent

2. common law

    b. Webb Pomerene Act protects U.S. firms in foreign markets from prosecution

3. antitrust law

    c. jurisprudence based on relatively inflexible written statutes

4. International Chamber of Commerce

    d. impartial, professional arbitration

QUESTIONS FOR REVIEW AND DISCUSSION

1. Distinguish between export quotas, export controls, and embargoes, and discuss how each could effectively nullify an effort by a U.S. manufacturer of computer chips to penetrate a foreign marketplace.

2. Argue for and against the proposition that the United States should lift its embargo on Cuba.

3. Panels International, Inc., a small company in Idaho, recently negotiated a joint-venture agreement with a large Russian building company and commercial bank to market and build American-style dachas (i.e., vacation homes) in eastern Russia. The company plans to produce several homes per month. Discuss how this firm might face ownership, transfer, and operating risk in implementing this agreement. Which risk (if any) would be most likely to materialize?

4. Describe how Panels, Inc., could use OPIC to enter the eastern Russian market successfully with its joint venture arrangement and then to protect its investment in this market.

5. Cornerstone International, Inc., a small U.S. company in Minnesota, exports, distributes, and sells commercial popcorn equipment and supplies to Russian entrepreneurs. In 1994 the company expanded its operations to begin growing and processing U.S. hybrid popcorn in Russia. Discuss how Cornerstone might use countertrade and counterpurchase to counteract the affect of a series of new duties, taxes, and other restrictions on importers of foodstuffs into Russia.

6. Give examples of conditions under which Merton would be subject to the following in promoting its computers in the global marketplace: VERS, tariff quotas, countervailing duties, excise taxes.

7. Discuss how supranational and national supports might have been instrumental in Merton's success in global markets.

ANSWERS

MATCHUP EXERCISES

1. 1a, 2c, 3b, 4d
2. 1b, 2a, 3c, 4d
3. 1c, 2a, 3b, 4d

QUESTIONS FOR REVIEW AND DISCUSSION

1. Export quotas, controls, and embargoes are all examples of constraints that home countries place on firms that plan to export products into global markets. Export controls limit the quantity of products that may be exported from a country, usually for economic reasons. For example, Brazil limits the quantity of coffee its growers can export to other countries in order to maintain a desired level of demand and price. Export controls are more severe forms of export quotas that totally ban the export of certain products, usually for strategic reasons. For example, U.S. controls on the sale of nuclear materials to North Korea. Embargoes are controls that prohibit all trade, exports or imports, on (1) whole categories of products regardless of destination; (2) specific products to specific countries; or (3) all products to specific countries. Embargoes are usually instituted for adversarial or political reasons, in the hope of changing a country's policies (e.g., eliminating apartheid in South Africa).

The computer chip manufacturer, particularly during the period prior to the breakup of the Eastern Bloc coalition, could easily fall into any of these categories. For example, quotas could be instituted to maintain the world price of chips, or controls because of their strategic importance to potential enemy countries. And the chips would almost surely be among products included in an embargo imposed for political reasons.

2. In support of the embargo, it might be argued that the country's policies, particularly in the area of human rights, represent a potentially destabling influence in this hemisphere and, hence, must be changed using the most effective tool available, the embargo. A counter argument might be that it's unlikely that a small, poor country like Cuba could destabilize anything beyond its own economy and that its policies are no more inimical to our own than those of other countries we recognize. As a largely unilateral boycott, it might also be argued that it won't work to change Cuba's policies, since other countries can easily fill the trade gap created by the embargo. In the process, these other countries are achieving a competitive advantage in trade with Cuba from which U.S. firms will never recover if and when the embargo is lifted. They argue that it simply isn't fair to penalize, for purely political reasons, the country's economic well-being and companies that could profitably contribute to this well-being.

3. Ownership risk, which would refer to Panel's exposure of life and property, would most likely take one of two forms if initiated by the Russian government (perhaps at the behest of the firm's joint venture partners): confiscation—the transfer of property without compensation—or expropriation—the transfer of property with compensation. Domestication is illustrative of operating risk, whereby the Russian government might demand partial transfer of ownership and management responsibility beyond the provisions of the joint venture agreement with Panel's partners. Transfer risk would be incurred in the event that the Russian government imposes controls on the movement of Panel's profits or investment funds in or out of the country. Such controls could include excessive taxation on such funds, and mandatory conversions of dollars into rubles.

   Assuming any control would be imposed on Panel, Inc., domestication would probably be the most likely outcome, in that it can achieve the benefits of confiscation and expropriation without the negative legal and public relations consequences.

4. OPIC facilitates global trade by helping to finance manufacturer foreign direct investment, either individually or as a joint investment, through direct loans (of from $100,000 to $6 million per project) and/or loan guarantees (of up to $50 million per project). These loans and guarantees could help finance Panel's entry into the eastern

Russian market; as to protecting the firm's investment in this market, OPIC guarantees investments in less developed countries against such risks as currency inconvertibility, expropriation, confiscation, and physical damage from war or political strife.

5. Countertrade is defined as a sale involving obligations by the seller to generate foreign exchange for the buying country. In this situation, Cornerstone's popcorn machines would be paid for in full, or partially, by products produced in Russia—a form of barter (e.g., brand name vodka). The sale of the vodka, in turn, would generate foreign exchange currency (e.g., marks, dollars) for Russia. Counterpurchase (or parallel barter) is defined as a more sophisticated form of countertrade in which participating parties sign two separate contracts that specify the goods and services to be exchanged, with cash making up the difference when exchange values aren't equal. For example, the contracts that Cornerstone signed in this situation might specify, first, that Cornerstone will sell bartered Russian vodka in payment for its popcorn machines and, second, that any difference between the dollar sales volume generated by the sale of the vodka and the value of the popcorn machines will be covered by cash payments in dollars.

6. *Voluntary Export Restraints (VERS):* Merton would be asked to voluntarily limit the number of computers it exports to a host country market in order to protect the host country's fledgling computer industry. *Tariff quotas:* Merton would be permitted to export a given quantity of computers to a host country under a low tariff (i.e., its quota); quantities above this quota would be subject to a much higher tariff. Again, the rationale might be to protect a fledgling computer industry in the host country. *Countervailing duties:* Merton computers are singled out for higher duties when it is determined by the host country that Merton is receiving special subsidies from the U.S. government that allows the company to price its computers so they gain an unfair competitive advantage in the host country. *Excise tax:* This processing tax is assessed locally against Merton computers sold in the host country as a means to generate revenue.

7. On the supranational level, economic communities such as the General Agreement on Tariffs and Trade and the European Union might have been instrumental in Merton's success by actively encouraging trade through the creation of large, integrated markets that cross national boundaries, and the reduction of trade barriers among member nations. On the national level, Merton might have received various direct and indirect financial assists (e.g., an OPIC loan, accelerated depreciation for export-related subsidiaries), as well as assistance in locating markets, gaining distribution, assessing credit risk, and promoting products overseas through such government agencies as the Chamber of Commerce and the Small Business Administration.

7

ECONOMIC INFLUENCES ON INTERNATIONAL MARKETS

OVERVIEW

For the international marketer, the ability to assess economic climates, focusing on the capacity of a region, country, or target market to make, market, and purchase products, is key to selecting entry markets, devising entry/growth strategies, and formulating marketing plans to support these strategies. As with assessments of political/legal climates, assessments of economic climates typically encompass three levels: (1) the national level, focusing on stage of economic development as well as physical and financial attributes conducive to economic health; (2) the subnational level, focusing on demographic, and wealth distribution characteristics defining the economic welfare of specific target markets; and (3) the supranational level, focusing on the impact on trade of global and regional economic communities.

ECONOMIC CONDITIONS CREATE MARKETS

In this chapter, we examine the economic climate that global marketing managers must understand and account for in formulating strategic marketing plans for finding and penetrating worthwhile international markets.

In conducting the search for healthy, welcoming economic climates as entry points for Mighty Mind computers in the global market, Merton marketers began with assessments of economic strengths in specific countries, then among customer groups living in these countries, and finally among the global and regional economic communities these countries belonged to.

Guiding them in these assessments were the precepts of Vilfredo Pareto, a nineteenth century economist who studied the distribution of wealth and concluded that a large proportion of wealth was controlled by a small percent of the population. This Pareto effect, applicable throughout the social and physical sciences, suggests that, if left to its own devices, about 20 percent of a given population will be responsible for about 80 percent of the output attributable to that population. As applied to economic analysis, this means, for example, that a small proportion of companies will produce a disproportionately large amount of goods and services, that a small proportion of the population will consume a disproportionately large amount of this output, and that a small percent of regions, countries, and areas within countries will control a disproportionately large amount of wealth. Examples of the Pareto effect abound. For example, with only 20 percent of the world's population, the United States, Japan, and western Europe control 75 percent of global income; with 15 percent of the world's population, the United States and the European community nations generate more than 60 percent of the world's gross national product; 15 percent of the nations in the world (Japan, Canada, and western European countries) are responsible for more than 60 percent of all world exports and imports; and roughly 80 percent of production is generated in 20 percent of U.S. companies, as are 80 percent of U.S. exports. For international marketers, the implications of this concentration of wealth and productivity are profound: (1) a company can achieve truly global status by concentrating marketing efforts in the dozen or so countries that account for three-quarters of world economic activity and (2) a firm that enters too many national markets will probably find itself managing unprofitable small-scale operations.

ASSESSING NATIONAL ECONOMIC CLIMATES

In assessing the strength and stability of economies of individual countries, the Merton research team applied criteria in three areas: (1) stage of economic development, (2) general economic health, and (3) location and concentration of buying power.

Information sources used in this assessment included World Bank publications, statistical abstracts for individual countries, the Statistical Yearbook of the United Nations, and Department of Commerce sources and services covered in Chapter 4. Together, these sources covered economic, demographic, and technological conditions in countries and regions of interest as potential entry markets.

STAGES OF ECONOMIC DEVELOPMENT

There are probably as many ways to classify the stage of economic development of a country or region as there are criteria on which to base such a classification. For their purposes, Merton researchers found the following five-stage model to be most useful. This model classifies countries according to economic variables found to define markets for Merton computers in the United States, including population, gross domestic product, manufacturing as a percent of national income, infrastructure, and per-capita income.

- *Preindustrial countries*, with per-capita incomes under $500, are characterized by high birth rates and low literacy rates, political instability, little industrialization, much agriculture and subsistence farming, and heavy reliance on foreign aid (e.g., Somalia and Haiti during the early 1990s). Concentrated mainly in Africa, these countries represent limited markets for most products and are insignificant competitive threats.

- *Less developed countries*, with per-capita incomes of under $2,000, are at the early stages of industrialization, with factories erected to supply growing domestic and export markets. With consumer markets expanding, these countries represent an increasing competitive threat as they mobilize cheap and highly motivated labor. Together with preindustrial nations, these countries, concentrated in Asia, possess two-thirds of the world's population but less than 15 percent of world income.

- *Developing countries*, with per-capita incomes averaging about $4,000, are moving rapidly from an agricultural to an urbanized industrial base. Good worker skills, high literacy rates, and significantly lower wage costs than in advanced countries make these countries formidable competitors in export markets. Examples include many Latin American countries discussed in Chapter 9, such as Uruguay, Peru, Colombia, Chile, and Argentina.

- *Industrialized countries*, with per-capita incomes of about $9,000, are major exporters of manufactured goods and investment funds. They trade goods among themselves and also export them to other types of economies (developing, postindustrial) for raw materials and finished goods. High wages, strong infrastructures, a highly educated population, and a large middle class make these countries rich markets for all kinds of goods and formidable competitors in export markets. Taiwan and South Korea are examples of industrialized countries, poised to make the leap to postindustrialized status.

- *Postindustrialized countries*, with per-capita incomes in excess of $14,000, are distinguished by an increased importance of the service sector (which accounts for more than 70 percent of GNP in the United States); the key importance of information processing and exchange; the ascendancy of knowledge over capital and intellectual technology over technology. Other distinguishing features: an orientation toward the future, the importance of interpersonal and intergroup relationships, and sources of innovation that are derived increasingly from the codification of theoretic knowledge rather than from random inventions. Examples include Japan, Germany, Sweden, and the United States.

FINDING HEALTHY, WELCOMING ECONOMIES

In determining the extent to which economies in prospective entry countries would facilitate entry and profitable growth, Merton researchers assessed these economies against quantitative and qualitative criteria pertaining to basic political/economic orientation, geography, infrastructure, fiscal/monetary policies, and quality of life.

• *BASIC POLITICAL/ECONOMIC ORIENTATION*

On the North American continent, practically all economic systems are democratic and capitalist, with the means of production strongly skewed toward private ownership. In the rest of the world—particularly in the freed-up communist bloc countries—the trend is also away from statist, command economies, toward democratic, capitalist market economies. While it is obviously possible for countries with different—even opposed—political/economic systems to profitability trade with each other, it seems equally obvious that certain types of political/economic systems are more conducive to growth and free trade, and that nations with similar political systems are better positioned to trade with each other. This is evidenced by political/economic similarities among members of successful economic groups, such as the European Union (EU), discussed later in this chapter.

• *GEOGRAPHY*

This criteria category encompasses a country's physical characteristics, including distances, or the physical separation of the marketer from customers; topography, or land and water barriers between marketers and customers; and climate, or the degree to which weather conditions change as distance and topography change. Of particular concern to Merton marketers was the extent to which these physical characteristics would affect marketing planning. For example, extensive distance and topography barriers could make it prohibitively expensive to enter a country or, if entered, mandate marketing mix changes in price and distribution strategies to counter these costs. Climactic conditions could also affect marketing mixes; for example, how products are packaged and transported to withstand weather extremes. Taken together, all these physical characteristics could play an important role in defining target markets, in that they can define cultural and economic conditions in a society.

• *INFRASTRUCTURE*

The components of a country's infrastructure pinpoint its importance to marketers:

- *Communication amenities* to tell customers about products;

- *Transportation amenities* to distribute products to customers, and

- *Energy amenities* to power production and marketing activities.

Indicators of the extent of a country's communication networks include number, and quality, of telephone, print media, and broadcast media; indicators of the extent of land, rail, air, and waterway transportation services include numbers of passenger cars and buses, rail freight tons per kilometer, air miles traveled, and pipeline mileage. Per-capita energy consumption is a standard measure of energy capacity.

In addition to sufficiency, other important considerations in assessing a country's infrastructure pertain to quality (e.g., are communication and transportation amenities subject to frequent breakdowns?), compatibility (e.g., are current and voltage compatible with products marketed?), affordability (can prospective market members afford to tap into infrastructure networks?) and synergy (e.g., do the networks mesh together efficiently so that, for example, products can be produced and distributed to people who have been sold on them?).

• *FISCAL AND MONETARY POLICIES*

A country's fiscal policies pertain to taxation and expenditures; its monetary policies pertain to efforts by its central bank to vary the supply of money. Working together, fiscal and monetary policies influence a country's inflation rates, interest rates, and the stability of its currency—all of significance in assessing the health and strength of an entry country's economy. High interest rates can have a dampening effect on economic activity by pricing money needed to make, market, and buy products out of the reach of producers and consumers. High inflation rates can have a similarly depressing effect by devaluing currency and creating uncertainty for marketers, who may have to change their offerings (e.g., lower product quality or increase prices) to cope with advancing prices. While stifling productivity and purchasing power, excessively high interest and/or inflation rates also work to cut productivity, corporate profits, employment, and the Gross National Product and increase national indebtedness—all anathema to the economic health of prospective entry markets. (Table 7-1 shows global consumer price indices—the main index of inflation rates. Note the general downward trend of these rates coincident with the growing influence of regional economic blocs and market economies.)

Also affecting a country's economic health is the stability of its currency. When a foreign currency fluctuates widely in relation to an entering country's currency (for Merton, dollars), sales and profits are affected. For example, from mid-1988 to 1989, the value of the Colombian peso against the U.S. dollar fell from 290 to 361 pesos per dollar. This meant that, in 1989, a Colombian consumer had to spend 361 pesos to buy a one dollar U.S. product and that foreign firms, because of these higher prices, had greater difficulty exporting products to Colombia. It also meant Colombian goods were cheaper in other countries, encouraging exports from Colombia.

• *QUALITY OF LIFE*

Many countries that were able to generate double-digit growth during the decade of the 1990s did so at a social expense reflected in things like urban congestion, political repression, exploited labor, battered infrastructures, environmental destruction, and deteriorating health standards. Given the strong correlation between social welfare and economic growth and health—including the ability of a country to attract outside investment—Merton researchers consulted the Physical Quality of Life Index (PQLI) in assessing prospective entry markets. This index, a composite measure of a country's social welfare, has three components—life expectancy, infant mortality, and adult literacy—and is among the few indicators that compare social progress through time in all countries of the world.

Table 7–1. Global Consumer Price Index

Country	1986–1987	1987–1988	1988–1989	1989–1990	1990–1991	1991–1992	1992–1993
United States	3.7	4.0	4.8	5.4	4.2	3.0	2.8
Argentina	131.3	343.0	3,079.8	2,314.0	171.7	24.9	16.0
Australia	8.5	7.2	7.6	7.3	3.2	1.0	1.8
Austria	1.4	1.9	2.6	3.3	3.3	4.0	3.3
Bangladesh	9.5	9.3	10.0	8.1	7.2	n.a.	3.6
Belgium	1.6	1.2	3.1	3.4	3.2	2.4	2.6
Bolivia	14.6	16.0	15.0	17.3	21.0	n.a.	n.a.
Brazil	229.7	682.3	1,287.0	2,937.8	440.8	n.a	28.6
Canada	4.4	4.0	5.0	4.8	5.6	1.5	.8

Country	1986-1987	1987-1988	1988-1989	1989-1990	1990-1991	1991-1992	1992-1993
Chile	19.9	14.7	17.0	26.0	21.8	15.4	10.6
Colombia	23.3	28.1	25.8	29.1	30.4	27.0	21.0
Ecuador	29.5	58.2	75.6	48.5	48.7	54.6	n.a.
Egypt	19.7	17.7	21.3	16.8	19.8	13.6	12.0
France	3.3	2.7	3.5	3.4	3.2	2.4	1.9
Germany	.2	1.3	2.8	2.7	3.5	4.0	2.5
Ghana	39.8	31.4	25.2	37.3	18.0	n.a.	25.0
Greece	16.4	13.5	13.7	20.4	19.5	15.8	12.2
Guatemala	12.3	10.8	11.4	41.2	33.2	10.0	9.6
India	8.8	9.4	6.2	9.0	13.9	11.8	9.1
Indonesia	9.2	8.0	6.4	7.5	9.2	7.5	8.7
Iran	28.6	28.7	22.3	7.6	17.1	22.9	n.a.
Israel	19.8	16.3	20.2	17.2	19.0	11.9	10.8
Italy	4.7	5.1	6.3	6.5	6.4	n.a.	5.2
Japan	—	.7	2.3	3.1	3.3	1.7	1.0
Malaysia	.9	2.0	2.8	2.6	4.4	n.a.	3.5
Mexico	131.8	114.2	20.0	26.7	22.7	45.5	52
Netherlands	-.7	.7	1.1	2.5	4.0	n.a.	2.7
Norway	8.7	6.7	4.6	4.1	3.4	2.3	1.7
Pakistan	4.7	8.8	7.8	9.1	11.8	9.5	11.2
Peru	85.8	667.0	3,398.6	7,482.0	409.5	73.5	33
Philippines	3.8	8.8	10.6	12.7	18.7	8.9	8.5
Portugal	9.4	9.6	12.6	13.4	11.4	8.9	5.9
Romania	.5	2.9	.6	4.7	n.a.	n.a.	n.a.
South Africa	16.1	12.8	14.7	14.3	15.3	13.9	12.8
South Korea	3.0	7.1	5.7	8.6	9.7	6.2	6.2
Spain	5.3	4.8	6.8	6.7	5.9	5.8	4.9
Sweden	4.2	5.8	6.4	10.5	9.3	2.3	3.2
Switzerland	1.4	1.9	3.2	5.4	5.8	4.0	4.0
Thailand	2.5	3.9	5.4	5.9	5.7	n.a.	6.3
Turkey	38.8	75.4	69.6	63.6	66.0	70.1	78.9
United Kingdom	4.1	4.9	7.8	9.5	5.9	3.7	2.8
Venezuela	28.1	29.5	84.2	40.8	34.2	31.4	56

n.a.—Not available.

Source: *International Financial Statistics.* Washington, D.C.: International Monetary Fund, monthly.

ASSESSING GLOBAL TARGET MARKETS

Of primary concern to Merton researchers who were assessing individual markets within prospective entry countries were statistics pertaining to distribution of wealth and income among a sufficiently large segment of the population to constitute a market. For some low-cost products perceived as necessities—such as cigarettes and soft drinks—population size alone might be a sufficient measure of market potential. And for marketers of such products, indicators of present population size as well as projected growth would be the key demographic data required (See Table 7-2).

Table 7–2. Population Projections by Region and Countries, 1990 to 2025

Region and Country	1990	1995	2000	2025
World, total	5,248.5	5,679.3	6,127.1	8,177.1
More developed[a]	1,208.8	1,242.8	1,275.7	1,396.7
Less developed[a]	4,039.7	4,436.4	4,851.5	6,780.4
Africa	645.3	753.2	877.4	1,642.9
Eastern Africa[b]	189.7	224.7	266.2	531.4
Burundi	5.3	6.1	7.0	11.0
Kenya	25.4	31.4	38.5	82.9
Madagascar	11.6	13.4	15.6	29.7
Mozambique	16.2	18.8	21.8	39.7
Somalia	5.9	6.2	7.1	13.2
Tanzania	27.0	32.5	39.1	83.8
Uganda	18.8	22.5	26.8	52.3
Zimbabwe	10.5	12.6	16.1	32.7
Middle Africa[b]	71.9	83.0	96.1	183.5
Angola	10.0	11.5	13.2	24.5
Cameroon	11.1	12.6	14.4	25.2
Zaire	38.4	44.8	52.4	104.4
Northern Africa[b]	143.8	164.3	185.7	295.0
Algeria	26.0	30.5	35.2	57.3
Egypt	52.7	58.9	65.2	97.4
Morocco	27.6	31.9	36.3	59.9
Tunisia	8.1	8.9	9.7	13.6
Southern Africa[b]	42.3	48.1	54.5	90.7
South Africa	36.8	41.6	46.9	76.3
Western Africa[b]	197.6	233.1	275.0	542.4
Ghana	15.9	18.7	21.9	37.7
Guinea	6.1	7.0	7.9	13.9
Ivory Coast	11.5	13.4	15.6	28.1
Mali	9.3	10.7	12.4	21.4
Nigeria	113.3	135.5	161.9	338.1
Senegal	7.5	8.7	10.0	18.9
Latin America	453.2	501.3	550.0	786.6
Caribbean[b]	34.6	37.7	40.8	57.7
Cuba	10.5	11.2	11.7	13.6
Dominican Republic	7.0	7.7	8.4	12.2

Region and Country	1990	1995	2000	2025
Haiti	7.5	8.6	9.9	18.3
Middle America[b]	119.7	134.4	149.6	222.6
El Salvador	6.5	7.5	8.7	15.0
Guatemala	9.7	11.1	12.7	21.7
Mexico	89.0	99.2	109.2	154.1
Nicaragua	3.9	4.5	5.3	9.2
Temperate South America[b]	49.1	52.3	55.5	70.1
Argentina	32.9	35.1	37.2	47.4
Chile	13.1	14.0	14.9	18.8
Uruguay	3.1	3.2	3.4	3.9
Tropical South America[b]	249.8	276.9	304.1	436.3
Bolivia	7.3	8.4	9.7	18.3
Brazil	150.4	165.1	179.5	245.8
Colombia	31.8	34.9	38.0	51.7
Ecuador	10.9	12.7	14.6	25.7
Paraguay	4.2	4.8	5.4	8.6
Peru	22.3	25.1	28.0	41.0
Venezuela	21.3	24.2	27.2	42.8
Northern America[b]	275.2	286.8	297.7	347.3
Canada	27.1	28.3	29.4	34.4
United States	248.0	258.3	268.1	312.7
East Asia[b]	1,317.2	1,390.4	1,470.0	1,696.1
China: Mainland	1,119.6	1,184.2	1,255.7	1,460.1
Hong Kong	6.1	6.6	6.9	7.9
Japan	122.7	125.1	127.7	127.6
North Korea	22.4	24.9	27.3	37.6
South Korea	43.8	46.8	49.5	58.6
South Asia	1,740.2	1,909.4	2,073.7	2,770.6
Eastern South Asia[b]	440.4	480.8	519.7	684.7
Indonesia	178.4	191.9	204.5	255.3
Malaysia	17.3	19.1	20.6	26.9
Philippines	61.4	68.3	74.8	102.3
Singapore	2.7	2.9	3.0	3.2
Thailand	56.2	61.1	66.1	88.3
Vietnam	55.4	71.7	78.1	105.1
Middle South Asia[b]	1,189.9	1,279.9	1,386.7	1,815.9
Afghanistan	19.3	21.7	24.2	35.9
Bangladesh	115.2	130.3	145.8	219.4
India	831.9	899.1	961.5	1,188.5
Iran	51.8	58.7	65.5	96.2
Pakistan	113.3	128.0	142.6	212.8
Western South Asia[b]	129.9	148.7	168.3	270.0
Iraq	18.5	21.6	24.9	42.7

Region and Country	1990	1995	2000	2025
Israel	4.7	5.0	5.4	7.0
Lebanon	3.0	3.3	3.6	5.2
Saudi Arabia	13.5	16.1	18.9	33.5
Turkey	56.0	62.4	68.5	99.3
Europe (excluding former nations of the Soviet Union)	499.5	506.5	513.1	526.9
Central Europe	115.7	118.2	121.0	131.2
Bulgaria	9.4	9.6	9.7	10.2
Czechoslovakia	16.0	16.3	16.8	18.8
Hungary	10.8	10.8	10.9	10.9
Poland	39.0	40.2	41.4	45.9
Romania	23.9	24.8	25.6	29.2
Northern Europe[b]	82.6	83.0	83.4	83.6
Denmark	5.2	5.1	5.1	4.8
Finland	4.9	5.0	5.0	4.8
Ireland	3.8	4.0	4.2	5.2
Norway	4.2	4.2	4.2	4.3
Sweden	8.2	8.2	8.1	7.5
United Kingdom	55.8	56.0	56.2	56.4
Southern Europe[b]	146.4	150.0	153.1	162.8
Greece	10.2	10.5	10.7	11.8
Italy	57.4	57.9	58.2	56.9
Portugal	10.4	10.7	11.0	11.9
Spain	40.5	42.0	43.4	49.2
Western Europe[b]	154.8	155.3	155.6	149.3
Austria	7.5	7.5	7.5	7.3
Belgium	9.9	9.9	9.9	9.8
France	55.4	56.3	57.1	58.5
Netherlands	14.7	14.9	15.0	14.6
Switzerland	6.2	6.0	5.9	4.9
Germany	77.3	76.8	76.4	75.9
Former nations of the Soviet Union	291.3	303.1	314.8	367.1
Oceania[b]	26.7	28.5	30.4	39.5
Australia	16.7	17.7	18.7	23.5
New Zealand	3.4	3.6	3.7	4.2

[a] Regions
[b] Includes countries not shown separately
Source: Bureau of the Census, *Statistical Abstract of the United States, 1991*. Washington, D.C.: Government Printing Office, 1992, pp. 830–832.

For expensive computer systems, however, affluence of a sufficiently large proportion of the population to constitute a target market was the main consideration. The composition of this population would also be important; for example, there would probably be more professionals in need of Mighty Mind systems in Singapore (population 2.9 million) than in China (population 1.2 billion). Other population variables of interest to international marketers include:

- *Average household size*, which tends to be smaller in more advanced countries;

- *Average age of the population*, which tends to be older in advanced countries;

- *Concentration of population*, which tends to be more urbanized in advanced countries (for example, only 6 percent of the population is urbanized in Burundi, as compared to 97 percent in Belgium).

To the extent that they combine to identify target markets (e.g., recreation and health care products for the over-65 segment), and where and how to reach these markets, these population variables are of continuing interest to global marketers.

HOW WEALTH IS DISTRIBUTED

In turning its attention to the distribution of wealth and income in developing, developed, and postindustrial economies, the Merton research team recognized the following considerations:

- Even though per-capita income is generally the best indicator of the potential ability of members of a market to purchase products, it is not the sole measure of purchasing power, which should also take into account prices, savings, and credit availability.

- Even though income is a useful index for screening markets, it is not always valid in specific cases. Depending on the product or service purchased, a high per-capita income in one country could be equivalent to a low per-capita income in another country. In Moscow, for example, monthly rent for a subsidized apartment costs one-fifth of what it does in Washington, D.C.; on the other hand, a color TV set will cost this same Moscovite 22 times what it costs the D.C. resident.

- Also distorting per-capita income as an index of purchasing power is the consideration that certain products are not available for purchase in certain countries, or are received free-of-charge. In Tanzania, for example, per-capita income under $500 hardly reflects the fact that the sun, the local well, and community healers replace expensive utility and health bills in other countries.

- Changing exchange rates can also distort per-capita income figures as indicators of real purchasing power, as when the value of local currencies are measured at the U.S. dollar's foreign exchange rate. The use of purchasing power parties (PPP) instead of exchange rates help avoid these distortions and give a truer picture of per-capita purchasing power. A PPP says, in effect, that a change in relative inflation must result in a change in exchange rates in order to keep the prices of goods in the two countries fairly similar (i.e., one unit of a currency should buy the same amount of goods and services, regardless of different inflation rates).

- Raw per-capita income figures overlook an extremely important measure of national wealth and purchasing power—the way income is distributed among members of a population. For example, per-capita income could be distributed in at least four ways in a country: (1) practically all low per-capita incomes; (2) some high per-capita incomes, many low per-capita incomes; (3) a roughly equal number of low, medium, and high per-capita incomes; or (4) roughly the entire population with medium per-capita incomes.

From Merton's perspective, the second and third options were preferable because they ensured at least a segment of the population with the wherewithal to purchase MM systems. Of these two, the third option was preferable for two reasons: (1) This distribution ensured a larger number of affluent prospects, and (2) as countries become more developed, the lowest third of the population generally receives a higher proportion of gross domestic product as actions are taken (e.g., more progressive taxation, unionization, transfer payments) to change the normal course of the Pareto effect, with more wealth accruing to fewer people. Thus, countries with distribution patterns characterized by higher percentages of income received by the lowest third of the population would probably qualify as countries whose stage of economic development could support Merton's marketing programs.

There is a close relationship between income distribution and consumer spending priorities. People in low, medium, and high average per-capita income classifications tend to spend income in different, generally predictable, ways. This was the major conclusion of the nineteenth century Prussian statistician Ernst Engel, who studied how spending patterns were affected by changes in people's incomes. He found that as family income rises, the percent spent for basic necessities like food and clothing declines, the percent spent on housing remains constant (except for utilities like gas and electricity, which decreases), and the percent devoted to savings and spent on other items like luxuries, recreation, self-help, and education increases. Engel's findings, helpful in understanding spending patterns in global markets, are reflected in Table 7-3, which shows income percentages spent for various consumer product categories throughout the world. As an initial screening tool, this table helped Merton researchers identify worthwhile markets for Mighty Mind computers, which are covered in the "leisure and education" category.

Table 7–3. Consumer Spending by Category, as Percent of Total Spending

	Food, Beverages, Tobacco	Clothing Footwear, Textiles	House-hold Fuels	House-hold Goods	Housing	Health	Leisure and Education	Transport and Communi-cations	Other
Argentina	39.6	4.5	6.3	5.1	11.5	4.2	4.8	5.5	18.5
Australia	28.1	7.2	3.0	5.5	16.8	5.1	13.9	17.9	2.5
Brazil	29.6	5.0	6.1	5.0	28.3	5.2	5.0	9.1	6.9
Canada	17.6	5.0	3.5	6.7	19.9	4.4	7.6	10.1	25.3
China	54.1	13.4	1.5	10.1	0.7	1.5	5.6	1.2	11.8
CIS[a]	43.3	19.2	3.8	8.0	3.2	2.7	8.3	2.9	8.0
Colombia[a]	48.2	6.1	1.7	6.0	9.1	5.4	5.5	14.5	3.6
Germany	17.5	7.8	3.6	7.1	15.3	14.3	10.0	16.0	8.5
India	46.4	9.8	n.a.	2.6	9.7	2.1	2.5	7.0	20.0
Indonesia	53.4	4.5	n.a.	8.0	15.2	n.a.	1.9	3.4	13.5
Israel	24.8	5.4	3.8	9.9	21.8	14.0	9.7	9.9	0.6
Japan	27.2	7.3	5.5	4.1	5.1	2.8	14.0	9.3	24.8
Mexico	33.7	10.0	n.a.	11.6	8.4	4.9	4.8	11.8	14.8
Singapore	24.0	8.6	0.0	10.5	11.1	5.3	18.9	16.3	5.3
South Korea	32.2	8.1	4.2	5.7	10.4	5.3	13.3	8.6	12.3
Thailand	32.1	13.8	2.0	2.0	7.5	9.4	14.0	10.6	8.7
United Kingdom	21.9	5.4	3.7	5.9	12.7	1.4	9.8	13.2	25.9
United States	15.9	5.4	2.9	7.6	14.8	14.8	5.9	11.4	21.2
Zimbabwe[a]	35.6	12.1	8.6	n.a.	7.4	1.9	7.5	7.4	19.5

n.a.—Not available.
[a] 1990 data.
Sources: *International Marketing Data and Statistics 1993* (London: Euromonitor, 1993), p. 411; *European Marketing Data and Statistics 1994* (London: Euromonitor, 1994), pp. 276–277.

ASSESSING SUPRANATIONAL ECONOMIC COMMUNITIES

Global and regional economic communities, designed to improve trade among signatory members through cooperative preferential arrangements, range from agreement among two or more nations to reduce trade barriers to the full-scale economic and political integration of many countries. Table 7-4 lists major regional economic communities.

Table 7–4. Major Regional Trade Associations

AFTA	**ASEAN Free Trade Area** Brunei, Indonesia, Malaysia, Philippines, Singapore, Thailand
ANCOM	**Andean Common Market** Bolivia, Colombia, Ecuador, Peru, Venezuela
APEC	**Asia Pacific Economic Cooperation** Australia, Brunei, Canada, China, Hong Kong, Indonesia, Japan, Malaysia, New Zealand, Philippines, Singapore, South Korea, Taiwan, Thailand, United States
CACM	**Central American Common Market** Costa Rica, El Salvador, Guatemala, Honduras, Nicaragua
CARICOM	**Caribbean Community** Anguilla, Antigua, Bahamas, Barbados, Belize, Dominica, Grenada, Guyana, Jamaica, Montserrat, St. Kitts-Nevis, St. Lucia, St. Vincent and the Grenadines, Trinidad-Tobago
ECOWAS	**Economic Community of West African States** Benin, Berkina Faso, Cape Verde, Gambia, Ghana, Guinea, Guinea-Bissau, Ivory Coast, Liberia, Mali, Mauritania, Niger, Nigeria, Senegal, Sierra Leone, Togo
EU	**European Union** Belgium, Denmark, France, Germany, Greece, Ireland, Italy, Luxembourg, Netherlands, Portugal, Spain, United Kingdom
EFTA	**European Free Trade Association** Austria, Finland, Iceland, Liechtenstein, Norway, Sweden, Switzerland
GCC	**Gulf Cooperation Council** Bahrain, Kuwait, Oman, Qatar, Saudi Arabia, United Arab Emirates
LAIA	**Latin American Integration Association** Argentina, Bolivia, Brazil, Chile, Colombia, Ecuador, Mexico, Paraguay, Peru, Uruguay, Venezuela
MERCOSUR	**Southern Common Market** Argentina, Brazil, Paraguay, Uruguay
NAFTA	**North American Free Trade Agreement** Canada, Mexico, United States

In assessing the impact of supranational economic communities on plans for globally marketing its computers, Merton researchers found it useful to first categorize them. The main criteria defining these categories is the extent to which (1) trade barriers between and among countries participating in the integration effort are reduced. and (2) factors of productivity, including goods, services, capital, labor, and technology, are mobile and interchangeable within the integrated nations (i.e., factor mobility). Thus, as degree of integration moves from free trade areas through customs unions and common markets to full economic union, trade barriers are reduced and factor mobility is increased, to the point where a fully integrated economic union resembles, conceptually, the political, financial, social, and economic integration of the United States.

Free trade areas, the loosest, least restrictive form of economic integration, remove barriers to the sale of goods and services among member nations to enhance international competitiveness, economic growth, and job creation. However, each member nation maintains barriers against nonmembers. The three major examples of free trade areas in the world today are the General Agreement on Tariffs and Trade, the North American Free Trade Agreement, and Asia Pacific Economic Cooperation.

GATT BENEFITS: WEALTH AND GROWTH

In 1993, 117 member countries signed a pact designed to bring order and predictability to world trade by reducing tariffs and rewriting free trade rules for the General Agreement on Tariffs and Trade. Under this pact, tariffs on manufactured goods are cut an average of one-third, and free trade rules are broadened to cover agriculture and some service industries for the first time. Additionally, quotas on textiles and clothing and government subsidies to farmers will be phased out or cut, and member countries will be constrained from imposing quantitative restrictions on products from other countries, such as the United States imposed on Japanese automobile exports in the 1980s. Other provisions cover international investment flows, protecting intellectual property rights, and streamlining the settlement of disputes. One key feature of GATT is the formation of the World Trade Organization (WTO) to supervise and adjudicate GATT agreements and encourage future negotiations; another feature is the most-favored nation principle, which allows every nation covered by the agreement to obtain the best contract terms received by any single member nation. A major exception to GATT, increasingly significant as nations integrate economically, allows member countries to participate in regional economic communities with fewer trade barriers among member nations than among nonmember nations.

Advocates claim that, over the next decade, GATT will add hundreds of billions to the world economy and create millions of jobs by eliminating trade barriers that keep consumers from buying the products of other countries. More specifically, these advocates argue that the trade liberalization provision of GATT will accomplish the following:

- Spread the benefits of comparative advantage by encouraging member countries to specialize in products they make best for which international demand exists. This specialization will then channel workers from inefficient to efficient industries, enhancing competition and making employment more profitable. (Most studies show that, just as trade liberalization increases the wealth of nations, trade-related jobs pay above the average.)

- Lower the cost of many products, effectively increasing the real purchasing power of workers. These lowered costs will also increase the profitability of employers who use these products in producing products and services.

- Generate the innovation, invention, and imitation that have largely replaced natural resources in creating growth and economic well-being.

Although most of GATT's benefits will accrue to industrialized and postindustrialized member countries, developing and less developed countries will also benefit. Many of these countries still pursue protectionist, inward-oriented growth strategies; GATT will commit them to lower tariff barriers to open their markets and share in free-market prosperity.

From the perspective of wealthier nations, the economic wealth and growth of semi-industrialized countries is significant. For example, $5 of every $10 spent on jets, tractors, grain, movies, and other U.S. exports in 1995 were paid by other than Japan, Canada, and European countries. And even conservative forecasts suggest that the economies of less developed countries should grow two to three times as fast, on average, as industrialized and postindustrialized countries through the 1990s.

NAFTA AND AFTER

The North American Free Trade Agreement, passed by the U.S. Congress in November 1993, links the economies of Canada, the United States, and Mexico into the largest trade zone in the world—360 million consumers with spending power of $6 trillion.

The main argument favoring NAFTA's passage was that, while older, less competitive industries might suffer (and would probably suffer without NAFTA) in the short run, in the longer run job creation depends, largely, on exports. Also, NAFTA, by eliminating trade barriers along U.S. borders north and south, would dramatically increase trade with the two countries that have traditionally been our largest trading partners. Other arguments favoring NAFTA's passage follow.

- It is entirely consistent with the free trade philosophy characterizing U.S. foreign policy since the 1920s.

- It will give U.S. negotiators more clout in negotiations with Asian and European countries.

- It will preclude a return to protectionist policies characterizing past trade relations between the United States and its southern trading partners.

Another argument favoring NAFTA passage looks to the future, and to the potential of countries south of Mexico that might also eventually become members of the NAFTA family.

Arguments against NAFTA's passage were typical of arguments against other proposals for economic integration, focusing on issues of economic stability and sovereignty in arguing that NAFTA would do the following:

- Lose jobs in the United States and Canada to the low-wage Mexican economy (Ross Perot's "great sucking sound").

- Reduce wages and health and safety standards in the United States to the level of Mexico, which, they claimed, was politically, socially, economically, and financially behind the United States and Canada.

- Threaten the sovereignty of all member nations through use of international tribunals empowered to issue binding decrees to resolve trade disputes.

- Achieve competitive advantages for member nations at the expense of nonmember trading partners in Asia and Europe, whose cooperation is vital for global security and economic progress.

ECONOMIC IMPLICATIONS OF APEC

By location and tradition, the United States is a Pacific nation, too, depending on Asian trade for a large measure of economic growth and prosperity. One reflection of this dependence is volume of trade. In 1994, the United States did $394 billion in merchandise trade with Asia Pacific countries, far more than the $285 billion it did with Canada and Mexico, or the $258 billion with western Europe. In 1994, almost three million jobs in the United States were dependent on this trade.

Another reflection of the economic interdependence between North America and the fast-growing economies across the Pacific is the Asia Pacific Economic Cooperation forum, or APEC, created in 1989 and comprising the United States, Canada, New Zealand, Australia, Japan, China, South Korea, Hong Kong, Taiwan, Singapore, Thailand, Indonesia, Malaysia, the Philippines, and Brunei.

This economic community envisions a gradual dismantling of trade barriers among member nations, culminating in a free trade area encompassing eastern Asia, Australia, and parts of the western hemisphere. In addition to helping to forge strong institutional ties among Asian and North American trading partners, advocates claim this organization should help the United States counter Japan's growing economic power base across Asia and the Pacific.

• *CUSTOMS UNIONS*

Customs unions are identical to free trade areas, except that members establish a common trade policy with respect to nonmembers. For example, in 1921, the Benelux countries formed a customs union that was eventually broadened in 1994 into the European Union. (It is discussed later under economic unions.) Illustrative of contemporary customs unions are the Latin American Integration Association (Argentina, Bolivia, Brazil, Chile, Ecuador, Mexico, Paraguay, Peru, Uruguay, and Venezuela) and the Association of South East Asian Nations (Brunei, Indonesia, Malaysia, the Philippines, Singapore, and Thailand).

• *COMMON MARKETS*

Common markets carry customs unions a step farther. In addition to the prohibition of duties on imports and exports among members and the adoption of a common external tariff with respect to nonmembers, factors of production are mobile among members, with restrictions on immigration and cross-border investment abolished. The Central American Common Market (Costa Rica, Guatemala, El Salvador, Honduras, and Nicaragua) is an example of a common market.

• *ECONOMIC UNIONS*

Economic unions require integration of monetary, fiscal, social, and countercyclical policies, as well as the establishment of a supranational authority whose decisions are binding on member states. In addition to economic integration, economic unions also imply a degree of political and financial integration, with the establishment of a Central Bank to facilitate uniform monetary policies. In the world today, the nearest any global or regional group of nations has come to achieving a true economic union is illustrated by the European Union.

THE EUROPEAN UNION

According to the dream of the European Union (EU), by the end of 1996, 14 member states—Portugal, Spain, France, Denmark, Ireland, Finland, Sweden, Germany, the United Kingdom, the Netherlands, Belgium, Luxembourg, Italy, and Spain—would be integrated into a single market of 350 million sophisticated consumers with a spending power of $5 trillion. In this new era of unity and prosperity, there would be a totally free flow of products and services among member nations. A common currency would be created, banking systems consolidated, taxes standardized, and tariff barriers and border checks eliminated. Labor and capital would move freely to areas of high return. As trade barriers fell and economic integration took hold, outsiders, no longer facing a hodgepodge of trade restrictions, economic conditions, and political tensions, would be welcomed to keep the productivity fires stoked.

On the microeconomic level, businesses that had been held down by regulations and government monopolies, such as advertising and television, would experience growth surges. Joint recognition of professional licenses would dramatically expand professional activities. Uniform standards and economies of scale resulting from increased free-market competition would make European firms more efficient, cost conscious, and competitive. Marketing skills would become more important in an environment stressing competition and product differentiation.

Unfortunately, a number of setbacks have come between the dream and the reality. Although economic integration—still lacking a common currency—was largely accomplished by 1994, many member states were still finding it difficult to abdicate economic and political sovereignty voluntarily to unelected bureaucrats in Brussels. Then, there is the increasing clamor by nearly a dozen nonparticipating European states—including Austria and such freed-up eastern European nations as Hungary, Poland, and the Czech Republic—to join the club. Some are much less developed than existing members, and all bring unique needs that will have to be integrated into the mix.

ECONOMIC COMMUNITY TRENDS: INCLUSION AND EXCLUSION

Two major trends affecting the growth and scope of supranational economic communities include a tendency to include as members many ex-members of communist command economies (Slovakia, Poland, Hungary, etc.) and a countervailing tendency to discriminate, economically and politically, against nations that are not members of these communities. For example, the United States currently finds it impossible to export many categories of farm products to European Union member countries.

STRATEGIC RESPONSES TO ECONOMIC INTEGRATION

Economic integration among nations creates both opportunities and problems for firms seeking entry and growth in global markets. Opportunities exist in the basic rationale for integration—to create favorable conditions for intraregional trade. For a firm established in a regional economic community, these favorable conditions mean larger markets that cross national boundaries, scale and standardization efficiencies in both making and marketing products, few if any trade barriers, and a greater ability to productively mobilize and move factors of production. Combined, these conditions spell volume and profit opportunities that often justify even the most expensive entry effort.

Between the conditions and the profits, however, problems can intrude. One problem could be a negative response to outsiders from various stakeholders in the prospective entry market, including government, producers, and unions. Facing such opposition, the global marketer can sometimes influence change and facilitate entry by bringing information, such as test results or general benefits of entry, to the attention of policymakers. These lobbying efforts are usually made at multiple levels; for example, within the European Union, contact levels include the European Commission in Brussels, the European Parliament, and EU national governments. Entering firms should not overlook the often invaluable assistance in these lobbying efforts of various agencies of the U.S. government discussed in Chapter 4.

Another problem could be the competitive environment in the prospective integrated economy. Companies like Merton entering a market where competition is already well entrenched may have to form alliances with established firms to create and sustain a competitive presence. In situations where the existing competitive presence is weak, the entering company will probably face expensive challenges in building markets and finding sources to sustain this effort. Combined, these challenges can mandate company organization and staffing changes to achieve closer coordination between home and host country personnel in executing regional marketing programs with an understanding of differences in consumer behavior across markets.

CHAPTER PERSPECTIVE

In this chapter, we discussed economic climates that marketers must assess and account for in formulating and implementing strategic plans for entry and growth in international markets. The economic climate affects planning on three levels: (1) the national level, where considerations like stage of economic development, currency stability, and infrastructure sophistication combine to define worthwhile markets; (2) individual markets, where considerations like population size and composition and size and distribution of income define worthwhile purchasing power and potential; and (3) the international level, where most world markets are integrated into global and regional economic communities that present problems and opportunities to marketers.

KNOW THE CONCEPTS

TERMS FOR STUDY

APEC
common market
currency stability
customs union
developing countries
economic climates
economic unions
Engel's law
exchange rates
factor mobility
fiscal policies
free trade areas
GATT
geographic variables
income distribution
industrialized countries
inflation
infrastructures
interest rates

less developed countries
monetary polices
most-favored nation
NAFTA
national economic climates
PPP
PQLI
Pareto effect
per-capita income
population concentration
postindustrialized countries
preindustrial countries
purchasing power
quality of life
subnational economic climates
supranational economic climates
transportation amenities
WTO

MATCHUP EXERCISES

1. Match the concept in the first column with the descriptor in the second column.

1. less developed countries

2. postindustrialized countries

a. major exporters of manufactured goods and investment funds

b. moving rapidly from agricultural to urbanized industrial bases

3. industrialized countries

    c. although in early stages of industrialization, ability to mobilize cheap and highly motivated labor represents an increasing competitive threat to more industrialized countries

4. developing countries

    d. knowledge, technology, and services

2. Match the concept in the first column with the descriptor in the second column.

1. fiscal policies

    a. money value doesn't fluctuate against entering currency

2. currency stability

    b. tax and spend

3. monetary policies

    c. make more money available

4. price indices

    d. money is losing its value

3. Match the concepts in the first column with the descriptors in the second column.

1. PQLI

    a. truer picture of purchasing power

2. PPP

    b. social welfare of a society

3. GATT

    c. Asian and North American countries

4. APEC

    d. most-favored nations

4. Match the concepts in the first column with the descriptors in the second column.

1. population age

    a. higher in advanced countries

2. household size

    b. smaller in advanced countries

3. urbanization

    c. greater in advanced countries

QUESTIONS FOR REVIEW AND DISCUSSION

1. The Automotive Division of Allied Signal Company of Morristown, N.J., makes and markets products for the automobile industry (e.g., spark plugs, oil filters, turbochargers). In exploring new opportunities in global markets, Allied is focusing on that portion of the automobile original equipment market that deals with emissions standards, which is a profitable, growth phase of its business. How would the Pareto effect help Allied identify these markets?

2. Discuss why all five criteria defining an effective infrastructure might be important in successfully penetrating a foreign market for Merton Mighty Mind computer systems.

3. Why, in spite of an effective infrastructure, might Merton Company marketers decide not to attempt to enter a foreign market where both interest and inflation rates are unusually high?

4. In terms of its relative effect on purchasing power, explain how the devaluation of the Mexican peso with respect to the U.S. dollar was largely responsible for wiping out the U.S. trade surplus with Mexico.

5. Panels International (PI) of Idaho recently negotiated a joint venture with a large Russian building company and a commercial bank to market and build American-style dachas (vacation homes) in eastern Europe. From the point of view of the principals in the venture, explain why purchasing power, defined in terms of all its components, would be a key indicator of market potential for these dachas.

6. Assume two expatriate executives for a large American manufacturer —one stationed in Japan, the other in Australia—earn the same salary in U.S. dollars in 1995. Explain how the following variables could markedly change the actual purchasing power of each salary: exchange rates, inflation rates, product requirements, and product costs. How could purchasing power parities point up these differences?

7. How might Engel's law apply in predicting sales of the following products in China and Canada: Mercedes Benz automobiles, a Mediterranean cruise, fuel for home heating, cigarettes, rent on an apartment, and health care.

8. The world-leading footwear industry is concentrated within a 100-mile area in Northern Italy. Why might the president of a company in this industry welcome Italy's membership in the European Union? Why might the president of a shoe manufacturer in the United States not welcome membership in NAFTA?

ANSWERS

MATCHUP EXERCISES

1. 1c, 2d, 3a, 4b
2. 1b, 2a, 3c, 4d
3. 1b, 2a, 3d, 4c
4. 1a, 2b, 3c

QUESTIONS FOR REVIEW AND DISCUSSION

1. The Pareto effect, as applied in this case, suggests that a large amount of purchasing power for a particular class of products is generated by a small percentage of buyers (i.e., the 80-20 ratio). In this case, the small percentage of buyers would be located in the small number of countries that manufacture automobiles in sufficiently large quantities to represent a viable market and are concerned with emissions standards as a matter of public policy. Once this highly concentrated market is identified, Allied's marketing efforts can be targeted on it much more efficiently and effectively than if the company used a scattershot approach of covering a vast geographic area. "Targeted" is the operative word here, since the Pareto effect applies across a broad range of products for consumer and organizational markets and is the basis for concepts like market segmentation, target marketing, and positioning (discussed in Chapter 12).

2. The five criteria of an effective infrastructure, from Merton's perspective, encompass sufficiency (there are enough infrastructure amenities, such as telephones, bridges, and power plants), quality (the amenities are reliable, not subject to breakdowns), compatibility (they are compatible with those in Merton's domestic market), affordability (people can buy and use them), and synergy (they operate in harmony with each other). To focus on the "promotion" aspect of the marketing mix, for example, there would have to be a sufficient number of communication outlets (e.g., electronic and print media) to carry Merton's message persuasively; Merton should be able to count on these outlets to work; they should work in a manner compatible with Merton's domestic market media (e.g., state-owned media in command economies probably would not); prospective Mighty Mind customers should be able to afford these media (TV sets, magazines, etc.); and the media should work in harmony with other infrastructure amenities (e.g., transportation amenities should make the Mighty Mind computers available to customers when they have been "sold" by the communication media).

3. High interest and inflation rates generally combine to create an unstable, recessive economy with negative consequences for both buyers and sellers. Especially for buyers of expensive products like the Mighty Mind computer, usually purchased on time, high interest rates increase the cost of borrowing money and, effectively, the price of the product. Also increasing the price of the product are high inflation rates, further eroding consumer purchasing power. From the seller's perspective, high inflation and interest rates, in addition to eroding the purchasing power of target markets, also lever higher prices by making it more expensive to perform all the interest-sensitive activities involved in making and marketing products (e.g., financing production, carrying inventory) and forcing a pricing strategy that must anticipate continuing price increases.

4. The devaluation of the Mexican peso vis-à-vis the U.S. dollar meant, in effect, that each U.S. dollar could buy more pesos, as well as products and services produced in Mexico with labor and materials denominated in devalued pesos. Since Mexican products and services were now cheaper with respect to U.S. dollars, they were perceived as bargains in the U.S., encouraging exports to the United States. Imports from the United States to Mexico, on the other hand, were not perceived as bargains, since the devalued Mexican peso now bought many fewer of the dollars that went into their production. Since a trade surplus is defined as the surplus of the value of a country's exports over its imports, the devaluation of the peso resulted in an increase in Mexico's trade surplus with the U.S. that wiped out the U.S. trade surplus with Mexico that existed when the peso was devalued.

5. In addition to income, components of purchasing power include prices, savings, and credit availability, and all generally enter into a capital purchase like a home. In the Russian market, for example, a prospective buyer, even with a good income, might not be able to afford the dacha if it is too expensive (price). Even if the price is reasonable, and the buyer has a sufficiently high income to afford to maintain the home, he or she will almost certainly require a mortgage loan to cover the purchase price on the home. Thus, credit availability now becomes an issue, as does the extent of the borrower's savings, as an indicator of ability to pay off the loan and possibly contribute to the initial purchase price.

6. In 1995, the Japanese yen was stronger against the U.S. dollar than was the Australian dollar, meaning that the expatriate would not be able to buy as much in Japan as in Australia. On the other hand, the inflation rate in Japan was about one-third what it was in Australia, meaning that, at the end of the year, the salary of the expatriate in Japan would be worth more in purchasing power than the salary of the expatriate in Australia. In Australia, however, product requirements would probably be less, overall, since the climate is warmer than in Japan, meaning considerable savings on clothing, housing, and utilities. Additionally, products that would be required by U.S. expatriates in these countries—such as apartments, homes, restaurant meals, and most durable goods—are usually less expensive in Australia than in Japan.

Purchasing power parities, based on a formula that expresses purchasing power as an equation relating the percentage change in the exchange rate between two currencies to the inflation rates for the two currencies, has proven to be a reliable predictor of price changes over extended periods, as well as required differences in income to account for these differences.

7. According to Engel's law, as family income rises, the percentage spent on food declines, the percentage spent on housing remains constant (except for such utilities as gas, electric, and public services, which decrease), and both the percentage spent on other categories and that devoted to savings increase. Given the relative difference in average incomes in China and Canada, Engel's law would indicate that, as a percent of this income, the average Canadian citizen would spend a larger percent of this income for the Mercedes Benz, the Mediterranean cruise, and health care, while the Chinese citizen would likely spend a larger proportion of this income for fuel and cigarettes, while each would spend about the same percent for rent.

8. An important difference between the EU and NAFTA is that the first is an economic union and the latter a free trade area. Even though both forms have similar objectives—growth, job creation, and global competitiveness through lower trade barriers—they differ in a way that would be of importance to the two company presidents. As an economic union, the EU is modeled along the lines of the United States, with integrated economic policies; harmonized monetary, taxation, and government spending policies; and the free flow of goods, services and factors of production across borders. Thus, the president of the Italian footwear company, as a member of the EU, could look forward to the same kind of growth that a leading company in the United States could look forward to, with no barriers across state borders, the ability to set up shop anywhere in the union, and legislated protection from unfair competition or exchange rate vicissitudes. (For these conditions to exist, the EU mandates rough political/economic parity among members as a condition of entry.)

As compared to an economic union, a free trade area is merely an agreement among separate countries to lower tariff barriers across their borders, with each reserving the right to maintain trade barriers vis-à-vis nomembers. However, the free trade format offers few protections against drastic exchange rate changes, or unequal competition in the form of, for example, lower wage rates in one of the countries. Thus, the president of the U.S. footwear company might express some concern that other signatories to the agreement could put his firm out of business with their exports of shoes made by much cheaper labor paid in a devalued currency.

8

CULTURAL INFLUENCES ON INTERNATIONAL MARKETS

OVERVIEW

A country's culture is learned, shared, transmitted, inherently conservative, and continuous. From the international marketer's perspective, cultural variables (e.g., values, attitudes, language, and religious beliefs) can be used to identify and define target markets, plan entry strategies, and build marketing mixes. Approaches for identifying and measuring significant cultural variables include observational fieldwork, content analysis, value measurement surveys, and searches for cultural universals. Approaches for preparing marketing personnel for cultural diversity focus on addressing culture shock and the self reference criterion in such areas as recruiting, selecting, training, motivating, and compensating.

CULTURAL COMPETENCE AND GLOBAL STRATEGIC PLANNING

Culture is a complex whole, learned and shared by members of a society, encompassing beliefs, values, language, religion, art, morals, law, education, customs, habits, and capabilities. Culture is handed down from generation to generation and reinforced by such social institutions as schools and churches. Culture provides individual members of a society a sense of identity and well being. Cultures are inherently conservative, in that they resist change and foster continuity.

As the globalization of business grows, so does the need for intra- and cross-cultural competence to deal with culturally diverse publics that influence the health and growth of the enterprise, including customers, employees, facilitating agencies, and entire communities. A firm's level of cultural competence can be the primary determinant of its level of involvement in a given market and how effectively it understands and addresses the nature and needs of this market. Cultural incompetence can lead to millions of dollars in wasted negotiations, lost sales, and calamitous customer relations.

In the context of the crucial role of culture in the strategic planning process, it's the job of the global marketing manager to identify significant intra- and cross-cultural variables (such as a shared value or belief) that point to opportunities and threats and then account for them in the marketing plan. Sometimes these cultural variables will predispose people to purchase classes of products (e.g., washing machines) or specific product brands (e.g., Maytag washing machines). This information can then influence every aspect of the strategic marketing planning process, from defining the nature and needs of target markets to building marketing mixes that appeal to these markets.

Among significant cultural variables that can help marketing managers define and develop international markets are values, language, and religion.

VALUES GUIDE BEHAVIOR

The values component of culture—defined as widely held beliefs that some activities, relationships, feelings or goals are important to a community's identity or well being—have the following characteristics of interest to marketers:

- They guide culturally appropriate behavior;

- They are difficult to change;

- They are widely accepted; and

- They incline people to respond to specific stimuli in standard ways.

To illustrate, a value associated with culture in the United States is humanitarianism—a strong and enduring sense of personal concern for the rights and welfare of others. This shared value produces such standard responses to stimuli as aid in mass disasters and a huge philanthropic system devoting time and money to such organizations as the United Fund, the Red Cross, and CARE.

Values can also be associated with products. For example, widely held values pertaining to the desirability of getting married and raising families implies spending on a broad diversity of products such as matrimonial services, furniture, appliances, clothing, vacations, baby food, toys, and doctors' visits.

The task of identifying values, even in domestic markets, can be daunting. First, there are all the problems and biases associated with practically any effort to generate information in the marketplace (discussed in Chapter 4). Then there are problems associated with the complex, changeable nature of values themselves: They overlap other values, they can change slowly or abruptly, and they are often difficult for people to articulate (e.g., what does "I'm religious" mean to different people?).

Perhaps the main problem in culture value research derives from problems in relating cultural values to buying behavior. To illustrate, a study of soft drink consumption patterns among American and European consumers identified cultural elements as only one of ten significant motivating factors. (Other factors included price, quality, taste, advertising expenditures, availability of distribution channels and raw materials, and income levels.)

All these problems encountered in the relatively homogeneous domestic market are magnified in international markets, where cultures and cultural values often differ appreciably among or within countries and language barriers and mistrust of strangers are common. Marketing planning mistakes resulting when cultural differences aren't recognized can be appalling, as illustrated by the following.

- *Product.* Pepsodent toothpaste failed in southeast Asia because it promised white teeth in a culture where black or yellow teeth are symbols of status.

- *Promotion.* In Mexico, a Braniff Airlines campaign advertising that passengers could sit in comfortable leather seats was a predictable failure (*sentando en cuero* translates to sit naked).

- *Price.* In Japan, Procter and Gamble discovered that low prices for its detergents hurt the reputations for these items because price discounting is not a regular practice.

- *Place.* U.S. food manufacturers doing business in the United Kingdom discoverd that British culture assigns a different role to supermarkets. Instead of the large American versions they were constructing, the British prefer substantially smaller stores, consistent with values of British housewives that view shopping as a social experience, done in local stores within walking distance of home.

- *Target market selection.* There is little demand in Europe for fabric softener dryer sheets because most people use clotheslines.

VALUE CATEGORIES THAT HELP RESEARCHERS

Values can be perceived from a number of perspectives helpful to researchers in defining markets and market opportunities:

• *CORE AND SECONDARY VALUES*

Core values are highly persistent; secondary values much more likely to change. As examples, persistent core values include getting married and raising families; secondary values include getting married later in life and raising smaller families. Emerging secondary values, such as a new appreciation for low fat foods, can represent opportunities for marketers who can relate their offerings to these values. Disappearing secondary values, such as the communist menace, can lose opportunities for marketers who stay with them too long.

• *SUBCULTURE AND CULTURE VALUES*

Subcultures are separate segments of a culture organized around such factors as race, nationality, religion, or geographic location. Common values shared by members of discrete subcultures—in food, recreation, politics, religion, child rearing, etc.—frequently represent marketing opportunities not available in the culture at large.

• *INSTRUMENTAL AND TERMINAL VALUES*

Instrumental values focus on modes of conduct; terminal values focus on end-states of existence. For example, a member of our society might believe that ambition and self-discipline (instrumental values) will lead to prosperity and happiness (terminal values).

• *MATERIAL AND NONMATERIAL VALUES*

Material values pertain to things, including things people buy ("most store brands are as good as advertised brands") and places where they buy them ("WalMart has the best selections and prices"). Nonmaterial values, which pertain to ideas, customs, and beliefs, can also condition consumer behavior, especially toward less tangible services and religions or political orientations.

LANGUAGE COMPETENCE CREATES TRUST

Language, as a cultural variable, includes words used, how they are used, and nonverbal elements of the communication process, such as gestures and eye contact. As a component of the marketing process, language is important to a company like Merton in achieving access to an entry market (and allaying concerns about the firm's intentions); gathering and evaluating information (e.g., attitudes and needs regarding products and services); interpreting contexts in which communications will take place and actually communicating with prospects, customers, staff members, and facilitating personnel. A manager's competence in a foreign language must go well beyond simply understanding and speaking words to include contexts in which communication takes place and idiomatic meanings (in England, for example, *tabling a proposal* means immediate action must be taken and a *bombed* negotiation is a smashing success).

Language problems usually arise through misunderstandings and translation errors, as illustrated by the examples in Global Focus 8-1.

GLOBAL FOCUS 8-1

Block Those Language Blunders!

Many U.S. multinationals have had difficulty crossing the language barrier, with results ranging from mild embarrassment to outright failure. Seemingly innocuous brand names and advertising phrases can take on unintended or hidden meanings when translated into other languages. Careless translations can make a marketer look downright foolish to foreign consumers, as shown by these classic language blunders:

- When Coca-Cola first marketed Coke in China in the 1920s, it developed a group of Chinese characters that sounded like the product name but translated to mean bite the wax tadpole. Today, the characters translate as happiness in the mouth.

- Several car makers have had problems when their brand names crashed into the language barrier. The Chevrolet Nova translated into Spanish as *no va*—it doesn't go. General Motors changed the name to Caribe and sales increased. Ford introduced its Fiera truck only to discover that the name means ugly old woman in Spanish. And it introduced its Comet car in Mexico as the Caliente—slang for streetwalker. Rolls Royce avoided the name Silver Mist in German markets, where *mist* means manure. Sunbeam, however, discovered the Germans had little use for a manure wand when it entered this market with its Mist Stick.

- Advertising themes often lose—or gain—something in the translation. The Coors beer slogan, "Get loose with Coors," came out in Spanish as "Get the runs with Coors." Coca-Cola's "Coke adds life" theme in Japanese translated into "Coke brings your ancestors back from the dead."

Such classic boo-boos are soon discovered and corrected, and they may result in little more than embarrassment for the marketer. But countless other more subtle blunders may go undetected and damage performance in less obvious ways. The multinational company must carefully screen its brand names and advertising messages to guard against those that might damage sales, make it look silly, or offend its customers.

Source: David A. Ricks, "Products That Crashed into the Language Barrier," *Business and Society Review* (Spring 1983), pp. 46–50. Reprinted with permission.

One way to address communication problems is to retain advertising and marketing research agencies located in unfamiliar entry markets. Another, applicable for promotion and other written communication, is the back-translating approach, whereby a message translated into a foreign language (e.g., Chinese) is translated back to the original language by a person other than the one who made the first translation.

Nonverbal language is composed of conditions under which communication takes place, and cues, other than words, with which people communicate. Of special concern in this area are differences in time and space. In the United States, punctuality is seen as a virtue, with people usually arriving early for a business appointment. In a foreign country, the concept of punctuality may be radically different. In many Arab, Latin American, and Asian countries, for example, time is flexible to the point where it is considered discourteous to arrive at an appointment at the invited time.

Another aspect of nonverbal communication is the amount of space people want to separate them from others. For example, South Americans like to sit or stand very close to each other when they talk business—almost nose to nose. The American business executive tends to keep backing away as the South American moves closer, which may be taken as a negative reaction.

Body language is another aspect of nonverbal communication that differs from country to country. For example, the "yes" of a Greek or Turk is indicated by a head movement identical to the negative shake used in the United States, and the thumb and finger sign that connotes success in the United States means "money" in Japan and "I will kill you" in Tunisia. In negotiations, southern Europeans tend to involve their bodies a lot, while northern Europeans are comparatively stiff and reserved.

RELIGION CREATES COHESION AND CONFORMITY

Religion, which in most cultures is a dominant force toward group cohesion and conformity, is also of interest to global marketers in terms of its formal strictures and protocols. For example, food taboos and holidays can represent opportunities for marketers in meeting local needs (e.g., holiday artifacts, nonalcoholic beverages in Arab countries). On a larger scale, religious strictures often define the relative role of the sexes, with marketing consequences. For example, in Japan and the Mideast, women are not permitted the freedom to function as they do in the West, with implications for hiring policies among global firms (e.g., women may not be employed as managers), and their role as consumers (they may have less input into buying decisions, and may be reached only through female sales personnel, direct marketing, and women's specialty shops).

THE MARKETER'S TASK: IDENTIFY AND USE PREDISPOSING VARIABLES

In accommodating marketing plans to cultural values, the marketer's first task is to identify variables, or combinations of variables, most likely to predispose people to buy the marketed product. The marketer's second task is then to incorporate predisposing variables into such marketing plan aspects as the market targeted and the marketing mix aimed at this market.

Four approaches for identifying significant cultural variables include observational fieldwork, content analysis, value measurement surveys, and searches for universal values. Each has supporting assumptions, advantages, and drawbacks that tend to differ as applied in domestic and global markets.

• *OBSERVATIONAL FIELDWORK*

This approach typically involves trained researchers observing the behavior of a small sample of people from the culture being studied. For example, Merton researchers might observe responses to Mighty Mind computer models at international computer trade shows. Field observation usually takes place in a natural environment, with or without the subject's awareness.

• *CONTENT ANALYSIS*

Using this approach, researchers make inferences about changing social and cultural values based on the content of verbal and pictorial communications. For example, the way minority groups and females are depicted on television or in newspaper articles could lead to broader inferences about value changes in the entire culture.

Both observational and content analysis approaches for identifying significant cultural variables suffer from limited applicability, the need for expensive trained researchers, and/or difficulties in relating variables to class or brand-specific buying behavior. Value measurement surveys and universal value searches address these shortcomings.

• *VALUE MEASUREMENT SURVEYS*

This approach involves the direct measurement of values using scaled questionnaires, called value instruments, to show how people feel about various values and related behaviors. Two examples of these direct measurement studies include the Rokeach Value Survey (RVS)[1] and SRI International's Value and Lifestyle (VALS)[2] survey.

RVS SCALE

The RVS scale groups and profiles respondents in terms of (1) terminal values designed to measure the relative importance of "end states" of existence (i.e., personal goals); (2) instrumental values designed to measure the relative importance of various approaches an individual might follow to achieve these goals; and (3) related buying behaviors. For example, one RVS survey identified the following value clusters as defining liberals and traditionals.

	Values	Social Issues	Consumer Products
Liberals	Exciting life equality self-respect intellectual logical	air pollution freedom of the press housing discrimination	compact cars outdoor recreation
Traditionals	national security salvation social recognition family values	crime control drug problem pro life	standard size cars stylish clothes videocassette recorders

---

[1] Milton Rokeach, "Change and Stability in American Value Systems," *Public Opinion Quarterly*, Vol. 38 (Summer 1974), pp. 222–238.
[2] Niles Howard, "A New Way to View Customers," *Dun's Review* (August 1981), pp. 42–46.

VALS SCALE

The VALS scale, another example of the application of value measurement to consumer behavior, combines value and life-style information with demographic data to create four general consumer profiles to predict product purchases: (1) need-driven consumers, (11 percent of the domestic population); (2) outer-directed consumers (66 percent); (3) inner-directed consumers (21 percent), and (4) integrated consumers (2 percent). Each group is then defined in terms of value/life-style orientations and buying behavior patterns.

SURVEY LIMITATIONS IN GLOBAL MARKETS

Because VALS and RVS surveys were generally conducted in the domestic market, their findings are not necessarily indicative of relationships among value systems and buying behavior in global markets. Furthermore, they are expensive to conduct and subject to most of the problems and biases endemic to survey research, as discussed in Chapter 4.

Given the limitations of observational, content analysis, and value measurement surveys in conducting global cultural studies, the "Search for Cultural Universals" approach is gaining adherents.

• *SEARCH FOR CULTURAL UNIVERSALS*

Unlike the other approaches covered, which assume that cultural values—and their relationship to behavior patterns—differ with place, time, and situational variables, this approach assumes that certain universal cultural values can be identified and related to behavior patterns.

To the extent that these universal values exist and prove predictive of product class or brand choice, it is possible for the global marketer to standardize various marketing plan components. For example, assuming similar cultural values predisposing people to purchase Mighty Mind computers in the United States and Taiwan, the same target market(s) in each country could be subject to the same marketing mix, adjusted for language differences and geared to these universal values. Advantages of standardizing marketing plans in international markets include quicker penetration of markets with a single marketing mix and cost savings from fewer product models, distribution channels, promotional appeals, and media outlets.

Although the notion that such universal values exist across a broad spectrum of products is debatable, there is general agreement that they exist for some products (e.g., Coca-Cola). There is also general agreement that a diversity of trends, including population mobility, economic integration among countries, computers, and cross-boundary communications are working to increase the number of universal values and work toward "cultural convergence," whereby the time required for a culture to adopt an innovation is shortened.[3] For example, the lag time between the penetration of the U.S. market on the one hand and the European and Japanese markets on the other, shortened dramatically between the introduction of black-and-white television sets (10 years), compact disks (1 year), and videocassette recorders, (3 years, with the United States lagging).

Examples of global marketing approaches that assume measurable universal values include Murdock's list of universals,[4] Kluckhohn's value orientations,[5] and Hall's High/Low Context Cultures.[6]

• *MURDOCK'S LIST OF UNIVERSAL VALUES*

Murdock's list of universal values includes athletic sports, bodily adornment, cleanliness training, cooking, courtship, dancing, division of labor, education, ethics, folklore, food taboos, inheritance rules, kinship, joking, law, medicine, mourning music, nomenclature, population policies, property rights, puberty customs, religious rituals, status differentiation, surgery, toolmaking, trade, weaning, and weather control.

Assuming the universality of these values, the role of the international marketer is to identify those deemed important to members of the society studied and able to motivate interest in the product class or brand being marketed. For example, in marketing Mighty Mind computers in the domestic market, highly regarded values like "education" and "status differentiation" were incorporated into a promotional campaign that stressed the importance of professional education in achieving higher status positions. If these values were also highly regarded in other countries, the same campaign might be successfully implemented.

• *KLUCKHOHN'S VALUE ORIENTATIONS*

Kluckhohn's value orientations combine individual values into clusters said to define five basic orientations thought to be universal among nations: human nature, relationship of man to nature, sense of time, activity, and social relationships. Each orientation runs a spectrum of beliefs shown in Table 8-1.

Here, the marketer's task involves understanding what types of value orientations predominate in a given society (e.g., along the "human nature" spectrum, do members of society perceive people to be evil, both good and evil, or basically good?) and then relating marketing plans and programs to this orientation. In Merton's domestic market, for example, a "future-oriented" time sense, "doing" activity, and "individualistic" social relations were all woven into strategic planning for Mighty Mind computer systems.

[3] "The New Japanese Consumer: Affluent and Ready to Shop for the Right Products," *Business International* (January 27, 1992), p. 23.

[4] George P. Murdock, "The Common Denominator of Culture," in Ralph Linton, Ed., *The Science of Man in the World Crisis*. New York: Columbia University Press, 1945, p. 145.

[5] Clyde Kluckhohn and Henry A. Murray, Eds., *Personality in Nature Society and Culture*, 2d ed. New York: Alfred A. Knopf, 1953, p. 346.

[6] Edward T. Hall, *Beyond Culture*. Garden City, N.Y.: Doubleday, 1976.

Table 8–1. Variations in Value Systems

Orientation	Range		
Human nature	*Evil* (changeable or unchangeable): Most people are basically evil and can't be trusted.	*Mixture of good and evil* (changeable or unchangeable): There are evil and good people in the world.	*Good* (changeable or unchangeable): Most people are basically good and can be trusted.
Man nature relationship	*Subjugation-to-nature:* Life is largely controlled by outside forces.	*Harmony-with-nature:* Live in harmony with nature.	*Mastery-over-nature:* Man should challenge and control nature.
Time-sense	*Past-oriented* (tradition bound): Man should learn from and emulate the glorious past.	*Present-oriented* (situational): Make the most of the present moment. Live for today.	*Future-oriented* (goal-oriented): Plan for the future in order to make it better than the past.
Activity	*Being:* The spontaneous expression of impulses and desires. Stress on who you are.	*Being-in-becoming:* Emphasizes self-realization, development of all aspects of the self as an integrated whole.	*Doing:* Stressing action and accomplishment.
Social relations	*Lineal* (authoritarian): Lines of authority are clearly established with dominant-subordinate relationships clearly defined and respected.	*Collateral* (group-oriented): Man is an individual as well as a group member participating in collective decisions.	*Individualistic:* Man is autonomous and should have equal rights and control over his own destiny.

Source: Adapted from Florence R. Kluckhohn, "Dominant and Variant Value Orientations," in Clyde Kluckhohn and Henry A. Murray, Eds., *Personality in Nature, Society, and Culture*, 2d ed. (New York: Alfred A. Knopf, 1953), p. 346.

• *HALL'S HIGH- AND LOW-CONTEXT CULTURES*

Hall suggests the concept of high- and low-context cultures as a way of identifying and relating to cultural orientations perceived as universal in groups of countries. The universal "language," written and verbal, is the basis for this perception. In a high context culture (e.g., Hall cites Japan and Arab countries) less information is contained in the verbal component of a message, since much more is implicit in the context in which the message is sent and received, including the background, associations, and values of the communicators. In low-context cultures (e.g., Hall cites the United States and northern European cultures), the message itself is the focus of negotiations.

Negotiating a business deal illustrates characteristics of high- and low-context styles. As compared to low-context negotiations, in high-context negotiations, the words describing terms and conditions are less important than the negotiating context; more important are shared cultural values, a sense of connection and trust among the negotiators, and a strong sense of honor and personal obligation in fulfilling the conditions of the deal. Time is less important; more important is getting to know one another. Social distance is shorter and more personal; negotiations tend to be lengthier; legal sanctions (and lawyers) are less important than a person's word in consumating the deal; responsibility for errors is taken at highest levels, not pushed to lower levels; competitive bidding is less frequent. (Global Focus 8-2 shows how an understanding of context helped American marketers succeeded in global market negotiations.)

GLOBAL FOCUS 8-2

It Helps to Know the Negotiating Context

Illustrative of how an understanding of cultural context can help succeed in global markets is the experience of Judith Sans, founder of Judith Sans Internationale of Atlanta, and Henry F. Henderson, Jr., president and CEO of H.F. Henderson Industries of West Caldwell, N.J.

Judith Sans began marketing her natural cosmetics and skin care salons and schools overseas in 1985, when she joined a trade mission in the Far East to meet representatives of foreign businesses. Her firm now sells in more than 20 countries, with exports accounting for 46 percent of total sales volume in 1993. Ms. Sans now regularly attends worldwide specialty trade shows to meet potential customers and check over the competition (a Hong Kong show opened the door for her products in China; an Italian show got her firm's products distributed in Italy and Germany).

In her dealings with foreign businessmen, Ms. Sans credits "cultural flexibility" and an understanding of context, from a woman's perspective, as important to her firm's success in global markets. For example, in Saudi Arabia, she never meets alone with a male client, and she knows when it's acceptable to be polite but aggressive (e.g., acceptable in China but not acceptable in Japan).

Henry Henderson, who chooses to sell his firm's automatic weighing systems directly to foreign customers rather than through overseas agents or distributors, emphasizes travel and the ability to adapt to language and cultural differences. Henderson and his associates have made dozens of trips to countries like China, Australia, South Korea, Hong Kong, France, Russia, Switzerland, Austria, Hungary, Italy, Finland, England, Costa Rica, and Brazil and have adopted their negotiating styles to each. Some differences noted by Ben Martyn, a Henderson marketing manager: Americans "force terms and conditions, and insist that all the boilerplate be legally sanctioned and lived up to . . . for the Chinese and Japanese, a handshake is enough; to back down from an agreement would mean to lose face. So they don't need lawyers, but they must have the last word . . . for the English, it's usually sufficient to agree that they'll do the best they can."

Source: *Business America*, U.S. Department of Commerce (June 1993).

AVOIDING CULTURE SHOCK AND THE SELF-REFERENCE CRITERION

In addition to objective problems inherent in any marketing research effort to identify cultural values in global markets, researchers face two subjective problems: culture shock, or psychological jolts engendered in encountering a wide variety of unfamiliar value systems, and the self-reference criterion (SRC), or the unconscious tendency for an individual to assume that everyone else should share his or her values, attitudes, and life-style.

To help address these subjective problems, James A. Lee[7] offers a four-step approach that gradually exposes the researcher to foreign value systems so as to recognize and account for unconscious biases. This approach worked as follows when Moore engaged in negotiations with a team of Japanese businessmen to distribute Mighty Mind computer systems in Japan[8]:

---

[7] James A. Lee, "Cultural Analysis in Overseas Operations," *Harvard Business Review* (March–April 1966), pp. 106–114.
[8] Ideas pertaining to differences in negotiating styles are adapted from John L. Graham and Roy A. Heberger Jr., "Negotiators Abroad—Don't Shoot From the Hip," *Harvard Business Review* (July–August 1983), pp. 160–168.

• DEFINE PROBLEM/GOAL IN TERMS OF HOME COUNTRY CULTURAL TRAITS, VALUES, OR NORMS

Moore's objective was to negotiate mutually satisfactory conditions and terms under which Mighty Mind computer systems would be distributed in Japan. In the United States, such negotiations would be characterized by informality, the assumed equality of participants, and a direct, linear approach that states the case "up front" and marshalls arguments favoring the desired outcome. Frequently, in negotiating with foreigners, impatient American negotiators consider "feeling out" prospective partners to be a waste of time and have difficulty perceiving their needs and feelings— including feelings of irritation when Americans resort to hard-sell approaches.

• DEFINE PROBLEM/GOAL IN TERMS OF THE FOREIGN COUNTRY'S CULTURAL TRAITS, HABITS, AND NORMS

Preparatory to the negotiations, Moore had done her homework, obtaining information on Japanese customs and class structures from various primary and secondary sources. She recognized that her Japanese counterparts would need to develop a sense of connection and personal trust in order to feel comfortable about doing business—especially since they weren't used to dealing with women as business equals—and that this would take time. She also recognized that much of this time would be consumed in polite indirections and seeming irrelevancies, as each team of negotiators felt each other out. A spirit of inquiry and a flexible ability to change perceptions and understand those of prospective partners would be key.

• ISOLATE SRC INFLUENCE ON THE PROBLEM AND EXAMINE IT CAREFULLY TO SEE HOW IT COMPLICATES THE PROBLEM

Moore hoped that her own studied understanding of the context in which the negotiations would take place would be sufficient to mitigate the self-reference criterion influence in her own behavior. She even took an intensive, 3-week course in conversational Japanese to help relate to her prospective partners. Her main concern focused on two of the other three members of her negotiating team (the third was a Japanese national who would serve as advisor and interpreter and who had coached Moore on Japanese negotiating style).

- ### *REDEFINE THE PROBLEM WITHOUT SRC INFLUENCE AND SOLVE FOR THE FOREIGN MARKET SITUATION*

Moore put the two negotiators through the same training she had undergone (with the exception of the 3-week course in conversational Japanese) to hopefully eliminate the SRC influence.

PREPARING PERSONNEL FOR CULTURAL DIVERSITY

The diversity of roles, status, and tenure among people engaged in international marketing activites, added to the diversity of cultures they are likely to encounter, presents problems in personnel management hardly imagined in the domestic market. Exacerbating these problems is the comparative lack of intercultural competence among U.S. firms competing in global markets, where lack of foreign language and international business skills costs millions of dollars in inefficient management, weak negotiations, and lost sales.

Evidence of the importance, worldwide, of competent intercultural skills and abilities is a survey of European executives that found a shortage of international managers to be the single largest constraint on expansion abroad.[9] Evidence of the general indifference in the United States toward preparing such managers is found in a UNESCO study of 10- and 14-year-old students in nine countries which placed Americans next to last in comprehension of foreign cultures.

The challenge of adapting U.S. management and marketing practices to foreign countries entails a number of other challenges. For example, how well will such "American" values as independent enterprise, selection on merit, and the individual as master of his or her destiny play in ex-communist bloc command economies, with their strong tradition of collectivism and state planning of individual destinies? This challenge pervades all aspects of managing personnel in international markets, from preparing job writeups, through selecting, training, motivating, and compensating home and host country personnel to assessing performance.

Following are considerations involved in recruiting, selecting, training, motivating, and compensating marketing personnel in global markets and guidelines for implementing personnel management policies and practices consistent with global diversity and goals of employees and employers.

---

[9] "Expansion Abroad: The New Direction for European Firms," *International Management,* Vol. 41 (November 1986), pp. 20–26.

• *RECRUITING*

This critical first step of the process, designed to attract a pool of attractive candidates from which to select employees, begins with formal job descriptions that consider long- and short-range company goals and needs and requirements indigenous to specific countries. These descriptions should also spell out advantages and disadvantages of the foreign position in terms of prospective employee needs and goals. In addition to traditional domestic personnel sources (current salespeople, employment agencies, job ads, etc.), global recruiters should consider foreign students attending domestic colleges; other companies selling in foreign markets; foreign expatriates who want to go home; and acquisition, or joint venture arrangements, with foreign companies and their pools of prospective employees.

• *SELECTION*

Recruiting will attract applicants from which the company must select the best, a procedure that can vary from a single informal interview to lengthy interviewing and testing of such measures as sales aptitude, analytical and organizational skills, and personality traits. Regardless of procedure, of key importance are such personal attributes related to foreign assignments as intelligence, ambition, appearance, speaking ability, sales and business background, sensitivity toward other cultural differences, interpersonal communication skills with host country contacts, the ability to make decisions and work independently without home office support, knowledge in many areas relating to a new cultural environment, and a favorable outlook toward an international assignment.

Given the difficulty, importance, and cost of selecting expatriate employees, many companies are including employee families as part of the selection process, especially in light of evidence that unsuccessful family adjustment is the main reason for expatriate dissatisfaction. Interviews with family members frequently reveal unexpected antagonisms toward potentially painful adjustments to new foods, languages, cultural values, schools, friends, and status.

Many of these attributes—such as the ability to adopt to a foreign culture or speak the language—can be assumed when a company is recruiting and selecting host country nationals to work in the host country, but selection procedures should be at least as rigorous, especially in light of stringent laws protecting host country worker rights in most European, oriental, and less-developed countries (e.g., in Venezuela, a terminated employee national is legally entitled to 1 month's severance pay and 15 day's salary for every month of service exceeding 8 months, plus an additional 15 days pay for each year employed, plus a mandate that he or she be replaced by another national, at the same salary, within 30 days).

• *TRAINING*

In addition to content of programs that train marketing people in domestic markets (e.g., objectives, products, and markets; product features and benefits; competitor characteristics and strategies; customer needs, motives, and habits; effective sales presentations), programs designed to train expatriates to work in foreign markets include content on developing cultural skills and customs, values, social, and political institutions of the host country. Objectives of a typical intercultural program include abilities and skills required to (1) communicate verbally and nonverbally and convey a positive regard and sincere interest in people and their culture; (2) tolerate ambiguity and cope with cultural differences and frustration; (3) display empathy for other peoples' needs and differences from their viewpoint; and (4) be nonjudgmental regarding the values and standards of others.

Training programs for host country nationals are similar to domestic programs, emphasizing the company, its products and markets, technical information, and selling methods. Since both expatriates and nationals tend to cling to their own attitudes and behavior, an important goal of both programs is to establish an open-minded ability to see things from the perspective of others. Continuation training is generally more important in global than in domestic training programs because of the lack of routine contact with the home office.

• *MOTIVATION*

The overall goal of most motivation programs—to persuade employees to blend personal objectives with company objectives—is difficult enough to achieve in the domestic market, where marketing jobs frequently involve hard work, long hours, travel away from home, aggressive competitors, and, often, isolation from associates.

To boost morale and encourage people to work at their best level in the face of these obstacles, management typically relies on the motivational force of (1) an organizational climate that encourages participation and communication, holds marketing people in high esteem, and rewards outstanding performance; (2) quotas, or standards, that are achievable with a moderate amount of extra effort; and (3) both monetary and nonmonetary incentives (bonuses, meetings, honors, and opportunities to meet with "company brass").

In international markets, however, these traditional motivation methods don't always work. Often, the very nature of an expatriate's situation isolates him or her from other company personnel. Cultural differences can also affect motivation method effectiveness. For example, in Japan, a tradition of paternalism, collectivism, lifetime employment, and seniority can render recognition for individual performance acutely embarrassing to an employee who doesn't want to appear different from his or her peers. Similarly, in countries with the fatalistic philosophy that Allah, rather than the individual, is responsible for achievement, it is often difficult to reward individual enterprise effectively.

Management should take these differences into account in developing motivation plans in international markets where, given the high cost of turnover and low morale, they can be even more important than in the domestic market. Of particular importance is making criteria for promotion and other rewards clear and following through quickly and fairly.

• *COMPENSATION*

Especially in managing international personnel, compensation plans can be used to reward, recruit, develop, motivate, and retain personnel, although they tend to get unwieldy if they try to do too much.

Before deciding on the mix of goals a compensation plan will aim to achieve, the manager should consider how circumstances in global markets will modify these objectives. For example, in high-tax countries, more emphasis is often placed on liberal expense accounts and fringe benefits, which can account for up to 60 percent of salary in a high-tax country like France. Another circumstance involves differences in compensation between expatriate and home personnel working for the same company. If the group receiving the lesser amount feels aggrieved and mistreated, it can be reflected in performance and turnover costs. And there will be differences: short-term expatriate assignments usually involve payment of overseas premiums, all excess expenses, and allowances for tax differences. Longer expatriate assignments can include home-leave benefits and travel allowances for spouses and children, often exceeding the base salary. (One study showed that fringe benefit costs for a base salary of $40,000, over a 3-year period, ranged from $138,300 in Canada to $427,000 in Nigeria.) Indeed, sometimes the amount paid to expatriates to persuade them to take a foreign assignment can make it difficult to repatriate them back to a much higher cost of living in the home country.

CHAPTER PERSPECTIVE

In this chapter we examined aspects of cultures, including values, beliefs, languages, and religions, that influence all elements of the strategic planning process, from defining target markets and entry strategies to formulating marketing mixes. Problems involved in researching the nature and impact of cultures in global markets include identifying and defining values that motivate class- or brand-specific purchasing behavior; measuring the relative impact of these values; and overcoming biases and barriers associated with global marketing research. To address these problems, various approaches for identifying, categorizing, measuring, and applying class- or brand-specific cultural values were examined, including observational fieldwork, content analysis, value measurement surveys, and searches for cultural universals. Also examined were strategies for preparing marketing personnel to compete effectively in global markets by developing intercultural competence.

KNOW THE CONCEPTS

TERMS FOR STUDY

back translating	material values
body language	nonverbal language
content analysis	observational fieldwork
core values	personnel management programs
cross-cultural competence	predisposing variables
cultural convergence	religion
cultural universals	self-reference criterion (SRC)
culture	subcultures
culture shock	taboos
expatriate	value measurement surveys
high-context cultures	value research
low-context cultures	values

MATCHUP EXERCISES

1. Match the concepts in the first column with the statements in the second column.

1. core values	a. passing a CPA exam
2. secondary values	b. belief in God
3. instrumental values	c. school prayer
4. terminal values	d. achieving high social status
5. material values	e. purchasing a BMW automobile

2. Match the concepts in the first column with the statements in the second column.

1. outer-directed consumers	a. people who are driven toward success
2. RVS scale	b. salvation, prolife, standard cars
3. religion	c. late arrival for an appointment
4. nonverbal communication	d. food taboos, holidays

QUESTIONS FOR REVIEW AND DISCUSSION

1. Explain, with examples, how language, as a cultural variable, would affect Merton's efforts to identify target markets for Mighty Mind computers in Germany and to design marketing mixes to penetrate these target markets.

2. Describe a study designed to identify and define a target market for a diet soft drink. This study should make use of these cultural variables: subcultures, instrumental values, and core values.

3. The Dugal Corporation of Miami, Florida, exports its complete line of fashion jewelry to countries in Europe, southeast Asia, the Middle East, and South and Central America. Important to the success of the firm's global marketing efforts is co-founder Joanna Ponimal's attendance at worldwide jewelry trade shows, where she makes contacts and negotiates contracts. Discuss how the following studies might help explain Mrs. Ponimal's success in designing jewelry that meets customer needs: observational fieldwork, value measurement studies, and content analysis. In terms of cost vs. benefits in probing global markets, which approach would probably be least effective?

4. Select four Universal Values from Murdock's list that might be useful in positioning and promoting a new tennis racket developed by the Prince Sports Group of Bordentown, N.J. This racket, called the Long Body, will supplement the oversized heads pioneered by the company with longer handles (29 in. vs. the traditional 27 in. length) said to impart more power, spin, reach, control, and comfort. Following the racket's success in the United States, Prince plans to introduce the racket into European and Pacific Rim markets and hopes that, by relying on universal values, the company will be able to use a standardized promotional campaign.

5. Distinguish between Murdock's list of Universal Values and Kluckhohn's value orientations, and speculate on how each approach might be used to identify target markets in the global marketplace for a management consulting service specializing in American techniques for developing and successfully launching new products.

6. Describe a situation in which the high-context negotiating style of the seller meets the prospective buyer's low-context style. What would be the likely result of such a meeting?

7. Eagle Bear Associates, a Michigan-based company, joined with other American companies to put American farm centers in a number of grain areas of Russia. Although the centers will use U.S. technology and equipment to improve retained grain yields, all managers and employees will be Russian nationals. What might be the rationale for Eagle Bear's decision in terms of recruiting, selecting, training, motivating, and compensating expatriate personnel?

ANSWERS

MATCHUP EXERCISES

1. 1b, 2c, 3a, 4d, 5e
2. 1b, 2a, 3d, 4c

QUESTIONS FOR REVIEW AND DISCUSSION

1. Language would play an important role in identifying and defining German target markets in that much information would have to be generated about these markets from these markets (e.g., computational needs and perceptions of competing computers) using both written and verbal media in which the ability to write and read German would be key. Once target markets have been defined, the task of building marketing mixes attractive to them would also depend mainly on a knowledge of German. For example, (1) Product design: the design of software and instruction manuals accompanying Mighty Mind computer models would have to be in proper German; (2) Distribution: fluency in German will be required to, first, persuade German distributors to carry the Mighty Mind line and, second, to work with these distributors in implementing physical distribution, inventory management, training and motivation, etc., programs; (3) Promotion: whatever form the promotion program assumes (e.g., emphasizing publicity, direct marketing, direct selling, advertising, and/or sales promotion) will have to be in understandable, persuasive German; (4) Price: the price paid by German buyers of Mighty Mind computers will have to reflect additional costs incurred for adapting the product to the German market, including costs for communicating to and through distributors to end users.

2. In this situation, subcultures, defined as separate segments of a culture organized around such factors as race, nationality, religion, or occupation, might comprise people in professions (e.g., dancers and athletes) where weight is an important issue. These subculture members would all probably subscribe to a similar core value with respect to the desirability of not getting fat, as well as to a similar instrumental value of achieving this desired end through dieting.

3. Observational fieldwork involves observing the behavior of a sample of people from the culture being studied. The worldwide jewelry trade shows she attends, which are also attended by members of Dugal target markets from around the globe, provide a perfect opportunity to observe, converse, and record information on the nature and needs of prospective customers, limited only by the size of the sample observed and her ability to interpret this information. Value measurement studies use scaled questionnaires to identify values common to known customer groups that relate to the product/service marketed. Possibly Mrs. Ponimal could have such questionnaires available at the Dugal booth at the worldwide trade shows she attends, with an offer of a premium for completing each. Content analysis involves making inferences about changing social and cultural values based on the content of verbal and pictorial communications (e.g., newspapers and TV shows). Checking competitive jewelry advertisements in fashion magazines in targeted countries illustrates how Mrs. Ponimal might use this technique.

Of the three techniques, value measurement would probably be least effective. First, it would suffer from most of the biasing factors characterizing surveys in general (e.g., self-selection, halo effect, interviewer) plus biases from value surveys specifically (e.g., relating products to values). Additionally, it would be much more expensive than the other approaches.

4. Among presumably universal values, Prince might use to build a standardized promotional campaign for the Long Body are sports, status differentiation, courtship, and bodily adornment. For example, the campaign might stress, directly or implicitly, the value of excellence in a prestige sport like tennis for achieving status in life and attracting members of the opposite sex. Building on this message, the campaign would stress the value of the new Long Body racket for achieving these desired outcomes.

5. Murdock's list of universal values lists individual values that the marketer is free to combine so as to relate product/service values to values of members of target markets. Kluckhohn's value orientations do this grouping for the marketer, combining individual values into value clusters that define five presumably universal orientations, including human nature, relationship of man to nature, sense of time, activity, and social relationships. Using either approach, the consulting firm might begin with a value measurement study to identify values characterizing its customer base in the United States. Then, assuming the universality of Murdock's and Kluckhohn's lists, base promotion programs in other cultures on individual values or value clusters that characterize the U.S. customer base.

6. In a high-context negotiation, the actual content of the message (e.g., words describing terms and conditions) would be secondary to the context in which the message is communicated, including trust, friendship, shared values, and associations of the participants. In a low-context situation, the message itself would be the focus of the

negotiation, with much less emphasis on values and backgrounds of the participants. When a high-context style (e.g., a Japanese or Arab businessman "feeling out" his American counterpart with much indirect and apparently irrelevant conversation aimed at building a context of shared feelings of trust and obligation) meets with a low-context style (e.g., the American businessman engaged in linear, focused discussions of the negotiation issue, complete with precise specifications and legalisms), the result is bound to be frustration for both parties leading, often, to botched negotiations, bad feelings, and lost sales.

7. Beyond the likelihood that the host country, Russia, might mandate the hiring of its own people as a condition of the deal, Eagle Bear Associates would probably have a number of practical purposes for using local rather than expatriate personnel to operate the farm centers. A major consideration motivating this decision would be the cost and difficulty of recruiting, selecting, training, motivating, and compensating people in the United States for employment in Russia. First, there just aren't that many with the knowledge of the Russian language, social and political institutions, agriculture market, and culture required for the job, and training them would be so time-consuming and expensive as to be prohibitive. Even if they could be found (perhaps among Russian emigres to the United States), there would be expensive problems in relocating them in Russia, a task made doubly difficult if families, who might be making this move reluctantly, are involved. Motivation problems would also probably be magnified with expatriates who, unlike host country personnel, would be away from their chosen home and isolated from associates. Compensation plans designed to motivate expatriates to take a foreign assignment could also be a source of friction with host country personnel, who perceive them receiving more for the same work. Even in domestic markets, the cost of low workforce morale and high turnover is often high enough in itself to force a firm into receivership; using expatriate personnel in foreign markets can result in multiplying this cost.

9

PROSPECTS AND OPPORTUNITIES IN INTERNATIONAL MARKETS

OVERVIEW

This chapter examines the effects on international markets of the economic, technological, cultural, political, and competitive forces discussed in earlier chapters. We focus on countries within three large economic communities—NAFTA, APEC, and the EU—that represent America's major markets and on threats and opportunities these countries present now and in the future.

THE GROWTH OF GLOBAL MARKETS

Since the mid-1980s, an eclectic series of revolutions, including the fall of communist command economies and the wildfire spread of democracies and free-market economies, have dramatically expanded and altered international markets and produced a mixed bag of outcomes: dislocation and consolidation, growth and decline, new alliances and old alienations, and many new competitive opportunities and threats.

Another key outcome was an acceleration of the race to create global and regional economic communities among the countries of the world, with more than 90 percent of the world's nations belonging to economic communities by 1996. Reasons for this integration invariably entail the freeing up of trade among nations by reducing or eliminating political, legal, financial, technological, and competitive barriers.

APEC, GATT, NAFTA, AND THE EU

This race among nations to affiliate in economic communities culminated, within a 5-year period, in four agreements that effectively integrate most of the world's production, population, and buying power.

In 1989, the Asia Pacific Economic Conference (APEC) was created to gradually dismantle trade barriers among 15 Pacific nations. In 1993, the ratification of the Maastrict Treaty created the European Union (EU), with a commitment to a common European currency by 1999. Also, in 1993, the North American Free Trade Agreement (NAFTA) passed Congress, linking Canada, the United States, and Mexico into a trade zone of 360 million people and a GNP of $6 trillion. Also, in 1993, 117 member countries agreed to provisions of the General Agreement on Tariffs and Trade (GATT), which will reduce tariff barriers and foster free trade. (APEC, NAFTA, the EU, GATT, and other economic communities are discussed in more detail in Chapter 7.)

In the remainder of this chapter, we examine countries comprising these economic communities, focusing on their present state of development, future prospects, and opportunities for trade they represent. We begin with our own continent and then circle the globe from West (the Pacific Rim and eastern Asia) to East (western Europe). Figure 9-1 shows the regions covered in this analysis, and an index of the relative stage of development of countries comprising each region (i.e., number of data transmission devices per ten thousand of population).

THE AMERICAS, NORTH AND SOUTH

From north to south, this market is composed of Canada, the United States, Mexico, Belize, Guatemala, El Salvador, Honduras, Nicaragua, Costa Rica, Panama, Colombia, Venezuela, Ecuador, Peru, Brazil, Bolivia, Paraguay, Uruguay, Argentina, and Chile. We begin our discussion of this market with the three northernmost countries, brought together economically by the NAFTA pact and then focus on the economic revolution in the nations south of them.

CANADA AND THE UNITED STATES: CAUTIOUS FRIENDS

Although Canada's population is only one-tenth the size of that of the United States, the two countries are quite similar in a number of respects. Per-capita GNP is roughly the same (about $20,000), as are consumer-spending categories. Both Canadians and Americans spend similar percentages of income for transportation and communication; leisure and education; and clothing, footwear, and textiles. Canadians, with universal health care, spend significantly less for health, and Americans spend

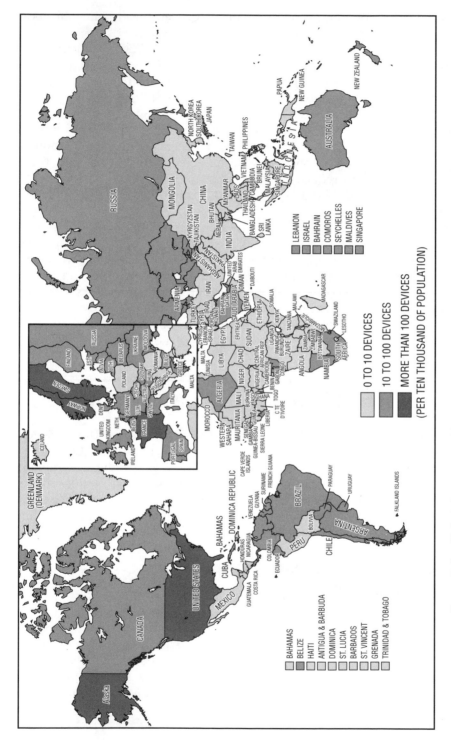

Figure 9–1. Global Comparison Map: Data Transmission Devices per 10,000 Population

somewhat less for housing. In 1996, both countries had about the same GDP growth rate (2.6 percent) and low rates of inflation and unemployment.

In one statistical respect, however, Canada differs markedly from the United States. As one of the world's preeminent exporting countries, Canada generated a trade balance surplus of $18 billion in 1996, as compared to a concomitant U.S. deficit of $176 billion. (This colossal U.S. trade deficit accumulated despite the generally weak dollar that would normally favor exports over imports and despite an increase in U.S. exports of from 7.2 to 10.2 percent of GDP between 1985 and 1995. Demand for imports generated by the growth of the U.S. economy simply overwhelmed these considerations.)

A significant cultural difference between Canada and the United States pertains to language and life-style variables that effectively divide Canada into two countries: French and English Canada. In 1980, French separatists lost in a sovereignty referendum by a 60 to 40 percent margin; in 1995, the vote for an independent, French-speaking Canada was much closer: 49 to 51 percent. From a marketer's perspective, the fact of these two distinct cultures—the staid, efficient, uprightness of English Canada and the exuberant, creative spirit of French Quebec—must be addressed when dealing with Canada. For example, separate communication programs are needed to reach each market, since neither group reads the other's books or newspapers or watches the other's TV, and rational promotional appeals are said to work more effectively in English Canada, whereas emotive appeals work more effectively in Quebec. Quebeckers also tend to identify more with the United States, support free trade agreements, and fell less threatened by American culture than do English Canadians.

In 1989, after three failed attempts in this century, the United States and Canada signed a free trade agreement that created a single $5 trillion economy, 10 percent larger than the United States' own economy and 15 percent larger than that of the European Union. A large part of the problem in finally getting this agreement signed derived from Canada's desire to preserve its cultural identity alongside the colossus to its south that dominates broadcast, film, publishing, and similar industries in Canada. The agreement finally signed aims to preserve Canada's cultural industries, with free trade arrangements for less-sensitive sectoral areas (e.g., automobiles) implemented immediately and then gradually broadened to include more sensitive sectors (e.g., textiles and steel).

MEXICO: BOOM AND BUST

After the United States-Canada free trade agreement was expanded in 1994 to include Mexico in the NAFTA agreement, U.S. trade with Mexico surged to over $100 billion in the first year, thrusting Mexico ahead of

Japan as the United States' second largest export market behind Canada. During this period, U.S. exports to Mexico—mainly of automobiles, agricultural products, consumer electronics, iron, steel, and other metals—increased by over 20 percent, as did imports from Mexico. In dollar terms, however, this increase in trade further exacerbated a Mexican trade deficit that began in 1987, when Mexico, along with most of its South American neighbors, implemented a mix of free market initiatives that opened its economy to a flood of formerly restricted imports and helped generate a $30 billion trade imbalance within 6 years. With domestic savings low, the only way to cover this imbalance was with foreign investments, usually raised through the sale of Mexican treasury bonds and notes. To entice investors, Mexico guaranteed that the peso would not be devalued and backed this promise with a policy of buying pesos that traded outside the parameters of a rigidly controlled range.

Then, a series of political and economic shocks—political intrigues and assassinations, a peasant revolt in Chiapis, and higher interest rates in the United States and other developed and emerging countries—stimulated a flow of investment funds out of Mexico to other investment opportunities. Meanwhile, Mexico's Central Bank was spending billions a month to support the peso, now trading outside its controlled range, while failing to prevent the surging growth of the domestic money supply. The dam burst when the Central Bank ran out of foreign currency to buy back the pesos it had been pumping into the economy to keep interest rates low and the economy booming. In desperation, the Mexican government devalued the peso from its precrisis exchange rate of 3.5 pesos to the dollar to a rate of around 6 pesos to the dollar.

The predictable results of this devaluation were widespread. In Mexico, living standards—already low by developed nation standards—dropped further, as did the value of personal savings. Investor confidence in the government, and its ability to negotiate free markets, was diluted, leading to a further flight of capital. Many businesses that owed money in dollars were ruined. Inflation began an upward spiral to 52 percent in 1995.

On the positive side, Mexico's products, produced by workers whose already low wages declined 50 percent after devaluation, were suddenly much more competitive in world markets, transforming Mexico's $18 billion trade deficit of 1994 into a $7.4 billion trade surplus in 1995 and releasing Mexico from the deficit drag that had been slowing economic growth. This new competitiveness also benefited companies and consumers in other countries, who now paid less for Mexican goods. However, the fact that Mexican consumers could no longer afford American products quickly turned the U.S. trade surplus with Mexico into a deficit of $8.6 billion in 1996, which, by the rule of thumb that 17,000 jobs are lost for each $1 billion of negative trade balance, translates into 146,000 additional jobs lost to Mexico.

These economic pluses for the Mexican economy, combined with a draconian economic plan involving frozen prices and wages, spending cutbacks, and enforced savings, began to turn the economy around perceptively beginning in 1995, making Mexican securities again attractive to foreign investors. As evidence of this turnaround, in June 1996 Mexico paid back, 3 years ahead of schedule, $4.7 billion of the $10 billion it borrowed from the United States to help weather its financial crisis.

THE REMARKABLE LATIN AMERICAN ECONOMIC MIRACLE

From the mid-1940s to the mid-1980s, the Latin American component of the hemispheric market was statist, protectionist, and anti-United States. By the mid-1980s, all of Latin America was close to economic collapse. Hundreds of billions of dollars, lent by banks and international lending organizations to governments and state-owned businesses, went to cover budget deficits and finance projects plagued by bureaucratic tangles, corruption, and mismanagement. Constant defaults on these debt payments threatened the stability of the international banking system. Dealing with dictatorships on the right and left, foreign companies encountered attempts at nationalization, protectionist policies favoring local companies, and spiraling inflation rates. High tariff barriers discouraged trade, and economic cooperation among Latin American nations was minimal.

Then, preceding the fall of communism in eastern Europe, a political revolution swept Latin American, led by Chile, which lowered or removed tariffs, got rid of import licensing, and generally integrated its economy into the global economy. By 1993, most Latin American nations had followed suit to the point where all governments were free-market democracies. Economic approaches embraced by most Latin governments— emphasizing open markets, low inflation, and balanced budgets—enabled them to reduce once-onerous debt levels. Tariffs were reduced, exports increased, taxes cut, capital markets modernized, small business growth encouraged, business red tape and regulations reduced, and judicial processes changed to ensure equal protection for foreign investors. Entire industries were privatized to relate output to market needs and face the discipline of competition.

Many problems remain. Maldistribution of wealth and income still oppresses Latin America's burgeoning underclass. And throughout the region there is an acute shortage of banking services, computerization, telecommunications, shopping centers, supermarkets, hotels, insurance, and a host of other services. Many of the new democracies are fragile. To keep investment dollars coming, central banks have kept interest rates high, a drag on growth. There is pressure on governments to follow the Mexican lead and devalue currencies to make exports more competitive.

Judging from the response of the rest of the world, however, it would seem that the pluses of Latin America's dynamic new economic look easily outweigh the minuses. Led by consumer products, technology, and service sectors, businesses in the United States, Japan, and Europe quintupled their investment in Latin America between 1991 and 1996, from $30 billion to over $150 billion. In 1994, Latin American countries raised over $20 billion in bond and stock offerings in the international marketplace, up from an annual average of under $1 billion through the 1980s. According to projections by the World Bank and the International Monetary Fund, Latin America and Asia will be the primary world growth areas in the twenty-first century.

Led by countries like Chile and Peru, Latin America's economies grew dramatically in the early 1990s, reaching a 4.6 percent increase in GDP in 1994, when the financial crisis in Mexico, combined with another in Argentina, were largely responsible for a GDP growth increase of only 0.6 percent in 1995. In 1996 however, the growth curve again tilted upward.

As discussed in Global Focus 9-1, South American countries, with their Mercosur free trade agreements, are combining to leverage their economic growth in the manner and scale of their NAFTA neighbors to the north.

GLOBAL FOCUS 9-1

Hands Across the Andes

When Mercosur began hesitantly in 1991 as a free trade agreement between South America's two giants, Brazil and Argentina, and two neighboring minnows, Paraguay and Uruguay, it seemed just another patch in a quilt of subregional pacts covering the western hemisphere. Yet Mercosur is developing fast. In January 1995, its members agreed to form a customs union, setting a common external tariff. Already, trade between the Mercosur countries has risen fourfold since 1990. Now the group is expanding. On June 25, 1996, at a meeting of presidents held near the Argentine city of San Luis, Chile signed a free trade agreement with Mercosur, due to come into effect on October 1, 1996. Bolivia hopes to do the same by the end of the year. Venezuela may follow.

Chile, which has the most open economy in South America, at first stood aloof from its more protectionist neighbors across the Andes. Instead, it hoped to join NAFTA, the free trade agreement linking the United States, Mexico, and Canada. But since Mexico's currency collapse has turned its trade deficit with the United States into a surplus, enthusiasm for expanding NAFTA southward has cooled in Washington. Chile's change of course means that Mercosur will amount to a market of 200 million people with a combined GDP of nearly $1 trillion and total trade of $175 billion. That makes it a potentially powerful southern counterpoint to NAFTA.

This is important in the wider argument about how to construct a free trade area covering the Americas as a whole, something the hemisphere's leaders have agreed to do by 2005. It appears increasingly likely that the United States will have to negotiate with Mercosur as a block, which it has been reluctant to do. And Mercosur's leaders have wider ambitions: They have signed a framework agreement aimed at developing free trade with the European Union, also by 2005, and they see Chile's Pacific ports as a route to expanding trade with Asia.

Source: "South America Getting Together," *The Economist* (June 29, 1996), p. 42.

The following are among the most attractive Latin American markets:

- *Chile*, with its robust, export-led economy, attracts more investment for its size than any other Latin American country. Even in the recessive Latin American economy of 1995, Chile's GDP grew by 8.4 percent, increasing by 41 percent since 1990.

- *Peru*, in 1994, recorded the world's largest growth rate—of 12 percent—with foreign investment doubling to over $6 billion. Much of the credit for this growth goes to the liberalized economic climate created by the Fujimora government, featuring programs for selling off government-owned companies, reducing inflation (from 7650 percent in 1990 to 15 percent in 1995), liberalizing foreign investment codes and generally neutralizing the activities of the shining Path guerrilla movement.

- *Colombia*, despite guerrilla and drug-related violence, has grown at a steady 3 percent annual rate for two decades, including a 6 percent growth rate in 1995. Its Central Bank has tried to keep a flood of drug-related dollars from pushing up inflation, which peaked at 20 percent in 1995, third only to Venezuela (64 percent) and Brazil (22 percent) in Latin America.

- *Argentina*, where deep economic reforms lowered inflation from 5000 percent in 1989 to 14 percent in 1994, and where privitization of state companies brought in almost $8 billion in cash and debt reduction over this period, still remains an attractive market despite a Mexico-type devaluation crisis in 1995, which produced a negative 8 percent growth rate.

- *Brazil*, where inflation still persists and where generally corrupt governments lack public confidence and keep the economy mired in recession, is still an attractive market. With an economy larger than Russia's and twice as large as Mexico's, it has belatedly committed to a free-market economy, which, it anticipates, will put it on the path of its fast-track neighbors.

THE ASIA PACIFIC MARKET

The Asia Pacific countries—Japan, China, South Korea, Hong Kong, Taiwan, Singapore, Thailand, Indonesia, Malaysia, Brunei, the Philippines, Vietnam, Cambodia, Australia and New Zealand—today represent the most powerful economic region in the world, with a staggering Gross National Product of $14 trillion. During an almost unbroken growth period from the early 1960s, the Asia Pacific region saw its collective percentage of global output increase sixfold, from 4 to 25 percent. In 1993, the Asia Pacific share of total world trade of $7 trillion was almost 35 percent, $2.3 trillion. In 1989, the United States and Canada joined these Asian nations to form the Asia Pacific Economic Conference (APEC), which envisions the gradual dismantling of trade barriers, and an eventual free trade area, among member countries.

Another index of the region's economic growth, and the importance of a resurgent China in this equation, are figures on the growth of individual nation's GDP in 1995: China, 11 percent; Malaysia, 9 percent; Thailand, 9 percent; Taiwan, 6 percent; Singapore, 9 percent; Indonesia, 7 percent; Hong Kong, 5 percent; and South Korea, 10 percent. Only Japan, mired in a seemingly endless recession, experienced negative growth figures.

Following are profiles of key Asia Pacific countries.

JAPAN, A HUMBLED GIANT

The Japanese economy has proven to be a phoenix, rising from the ashes of World War II to unparalleled heights. Some of Japan's growth is attributable to its role as a supplier and staging area for U.S. forces during hot and cold war engagements in Korea and Vietnam. Most of it is attributable to hard, smart work, based on a culture that fosters discipline; a government industrial policy that takes the long view in supporting and subsidizing growth industries; a highly educated workforce able to move easily to these growth industries from declining, phased-out industries; a unique ability to import, integrate, and improve technology; and interlocking systems of businesses, financial institutions, and trading companies (the *kieretsu*) that effectively bar unwelcome offshore competitors. Japan also has the high savings rate needed to capitalize growth industries, with a population that saves 14 percent of disposable income, compared to 5 percent in the United States.

Today, Japan has the world's most technologically advanced manufacturing plant and the largest pool of investment capital. Japan is also the world's richest creditor nation, with a 1996 trade surplus of $135.4. (The United States, with a 1996 deficit of $176 billion, is history's largest debtor nation.)

As the world's largest creditor nation, Japan is also the world's largest investor nation, with a 17:1 ratio of investment in other countries versus their investment in Japan (similar ratios for the United States and the United Kingdom are 1.05:1 and 1.19:1, respectively). Japan's investments in other countries have largely financed the U.S. debt since the late 1970s (as long as interest rates were attractively high) and represents the largest source of investment funds in southeast Asia. As Japan uses its strong yen to buy, at bargain prices, more and more factories in cheap labor markets, it is also lowering its labor costs at home and offsetting the effects of a higher yen on its exports.

Yet, with all these financial, cultural, political, technological, and economic strengths, Japan has been mired in a recession since 1992, thanks largely to a cumbersome, inefficient financial system; a strong yen; and a series of crises (e.g., political corruption scandals, earthquakes, disfuntional protectionist policies, and nerve gas attacks) that distracted the country from its competitive mission.

Japan's recession continues, only managing to reach a 1 percent growth rate in one year between 1991 and 1996. Unemployment remains high, wages and earnings are flat, and property values are depressed (saddling financial institutions with at least $400 billion in bad real estate loans). Economic deregulation and revamping, necessary for sustained, broad-based vitality in other countries, have had little impact in Japan.

To understand the impact of Japan's malaise on its relations with the United States and other countries, consider the Japanese domestic automobile monopoly, which is representative of many other product monopolies in Japan's protected markets. In 1953, the U.S. share of the Japanese automobile market was 60 percent; by 1960, it was less than 1 percent and has remained there since. (Eighty percent of U.S. dealers sell foreign cars alongside domestic cars; only 7 percent of Japanese dealers do, and they are usually not American cars.)

The fact that Japanese cars generate more than a 25 percent share of the huge U.S. automobile market has resulted in a trade imbalance that is the single largest component of the United States' worldwide trade deficit. However, the fact that the yen, since 1985, has been soaring in value against the dollar means that Japanese cars made in Japan (in 1996, almost 60 percent of Japanese cars sold in the United States were made in America with American-made parts) are harder to sell in the United States and generate much smaller profits. These profits lost in the United States are recouped by profits made on Japanese cars sold in the protected Japanese market, at the expense of Japanese consumers who can't shop in a competitive, free-market environment.

In an attempt to redress this imbalance and persuade the Japanese to open their markets for automobiles and other American products, the United States, periodically since the 1970s, has been threatening and, occasionally, implementing trade sanctions (tariffs, quotas, licensing requirements, etc.) against Japanese products. The results of these initiatives have generally been unproductive. Typically, commitments to open their markets are ignored or otherwise evaded by the Japanese, or retaliatory measures are taken against American products that leave our current account (i.e., the trade deficit) and employment picture unchanged. In recent years, there has also emerged a general feeling among the world's nations that the United States is using the wrong tactics in dealing directly with Japan, instead of using the offices of the World Trade Organization (WTO) set up for that purpose.

However, with the world's second largest economy and an embarrassment of export wealth, Japan is likely to grow out of its doldrums and dominate new technologies like biotechnology, superconductivity, and microelectronics.

FOUR GROWING, GROWLING TIGERS

South Korea, Taiwan, Hong Kong, and Singapore, Asia's "four tigers," are effectively following the Japanese model, with hard working, well-educated labor forces; strong government aid to business; and an aggressive emphasis on moving into new fields (e.g., automobiles and computers) and regions. Like Japan, they are not adverse to protecting their markets, to the point where they accounted for more that 20 percent of the U.S. trade deficit in 1995.

A large part of the growth of these economies related to the explosive growth in demand by the Chinese and Indonesian economies for high-technology and heavy-industry products including steel, machinery, petrochemicals, consumer electronics, and automobiles (e.g., in 1995, the Chinese bought 22 percent of South Korea's auto exports).

As labor moves from low-wage, low-productivity industries into services and higher value-added industries, it is quickly closing the gap between industrialized and post-industrialized status. This transition is occurring so rapidly that it doesn't show up in the statistics, with unemployment under 3 percent in all four economies between 1992 and 1996.

CHINA'S ECONOMIC MIRACLE

Part of China's extraordinary economic growth over the past decade, which has seen urban incomes increase 400 percent and rural incomes increase 300 percent, can be explained by the relatively low productivity base from which it made its great leap upward.

Even now, China's per-capita income of under $2,000 is but a fraction of most of its Asian neighbors, although, with China's 1.1 billion population, it is sufficient to make China's economy the third largest in the world, behind the United States and Japan. At its present growth rate, China, with Taiwan and Hong Kong (to be annexed in 1997), will be the world's largest economy by the turn of the century.

Among the reasons to expect that China's economy will continue to grow:

- An economy moving tentatively away from the cumbersome communist command model toward free-market institutions;

- A culture that values hard work, education, savings and investment;

- An enormous need for outside assistance (in spite of present size and future growth prospects, China's economy is still backward; it has huge infrastructure needs—roads, railroads, communication networks—and modernization of antiquated, labor-intensive manufacturing industries);

- A steady supply of investment dollars to finance growth and modernization from the likes of Japan, the United States, and overseas Chinese.

Opportunities for American companies in China's resurgent economy are reflected in the following examples. Coca-Cola sales have grown an average of 54 percent a year in China since 1985, making China Coke's fastest-growing market; sales of Motorola pagers have leaped from 100,000 in 1991 to 4 million in 1995; Kentucky Fried Chicken franchises will be opening in 31 cities by 1996; Apple, IBM, Hewlett Packard, and Compaq formed a joint venture to build and distribute 30,000 personal computers a year (with only one computer for every 5000 people in China in 1996, the market for computers is expected to grow by 30 percent per year for the rest of the decade). Heavy demand is also expected to grow in the fields of financial services, heavy industry, transportation, jet technology, automobiles, cellular telephones, agriculture, power plants, and branded consumer products to feed increasingly affluent tastes. Overall, the United States is expected to get more than 60 percent of the sales in these fields.

Behind these success stories, however, many building blocks of a successful market economy are still missing in China. Its currency is not yet convertible, its banking system is antiquated and unsound, financial regulation is absent, corruption is rampant, and commercial law is arbitrarily enforced (in 1994, the world's largest McDonald's was unceremoniously evicted from a prime location in Beijing despite a 20-year lease). Also, its communist government, in spite of the roaring success of its free-market experiments, still insists on churning out laborious 5-year plans and subsidizing a huge network of unprofitable, poorly managed state enterprises (of 17 China-based companies listed on the Hong Kong stock exchange in 1991, only one—Shanghai Petrochemical—was trading at more than its original price in 1996).

Companies planning to do business in China have to expect government meddling and red tape at all stages of entry and development. Approvals to open plants are required on numerous governmental levels; operational constraints can be onerous governing things like joint ventures, expansion plans, and markets to target; and tax policies can be capricious (in 1995, Beijing canceled $6 billion in tax rebates promised to export businesses). This difficulty of doing business in China, as compared to the relative ease of entering the U.S. market, is at least partially responsible for China's growing trade surplus with the United States, which grew 30 percent in 1994 to $30 billion. (China's ratio of 4:1 of quantities exported versus quantities imported is higher than Japan's ever was with the United States.)

Problems affecting trade between the United States and China go well beyond the operational level to encompass human rights violations, arms sales to unfriendly countries, nuclear proliferation, aggressive behavior toward Taiwan and Hong Kong, and the piracy of American software, music, and movies. In 1995, the United States and China negotiated an agreement on piracy under which China, among other things, agreed to take immediate steps to curtail infringements on intellectual property. In 1996, a new agreement was negotiated, under threat of sanctions (e.g., tariffs, removal of most-favored nation status, and entry into the World Trade Organization) when it became obvious that the first agreement was being largely ignored.

VIETNAM: HUNGRY FOR INVESTMENT

With a population of 74 million industrious, literate, low-wage people, more than 50 percent of whom are under 21, Vietnam is busily attracting foreign investment, technology, and markets to help build a market economy from the ground up. In 1993, the United States removed its trade embargo against Vietnam, agreed to low-level political and economic liaisons, and provided the means for American companies to enter the Vietnamese marketplace in force. One thing these entering firms are discovering is that someone beat them to it. For example, Australia dominates the phone system and British Petrol controls the oil segment, while

Singapore advises on the legal code. In 1996, the United States ranked only thirteenth in investments in Vietnam by country, with Hong Kong, Taiwan, and South Korea the biggest investors, all contributing to a 9 percent growth rate.

Another thing entering firms are discovering is that Vietnam's needs are great. Denied access to the World Bank and other development lenders by the American trade embargo, Vietnam is among the poorest nations in the world, with an average annual income under $300, few reliable power sources, and a crumbling infrastructure in desperate need of roads, bridges, airports, and hospitals.

Still another thing these firms are discovering is what American investors in China discovered, the communist command economy habits die hard, in spite of a commitment to free markets. American investors complain of being blocked by layer upon layer of bureaucracy and rampant corruption, which puts U.S. companies at a competitive disadvantage vis-à-vis countries like Japan and Germany that have no Foreign Corrupt Practices Act. They are also blocked by a legal system that barely functions: Vietnam has no commercial code, and its bankruptcy law has no regulations to support it. Another complaint is over the outrageous cost of every aspect of doing business in Vietnam, from making phone calls to renting office space, which can quickly overwhelm savings from its low-wage work force.

INDIA: AN AWAKENING GIANT

Since 1991, when after 40 years of socialist economic policies, India implemented a radical economic overhaul program that embraced market forces and foreign investment, American firms have been the leading investors in many diverse sectors, including breakfast cereals, computers, soft drinks, power plants, and telephone systems. The main attraction of the Indian market is its sheer size: 890 million people with a middle class almost as large as the entire U.S. population. Other attractions include India's democratic form of government, with an independent court system capable of settling disputes, and the widespread use of English. Also, India seems partial to U.S. investment, which accounted for 40 percent of all proposals accepted by India's watchdog agencies between 1991 and 1996 and increased from $350 million to $800 million between 1985 and 1995.

Against these positives, investors in India encounter many of the same obstacles they face in China and Vietnam: bureaucratic interference in all aspects of doing business; a vast network of loss-ridden, state-owned industries; bans and punitive tariffs on many foreign-made consumer goods and equipment for new projects; a crumbling infrastructure; and backward living standards for the vast majority, who have a 60 percent illiteracy rate. Other negatives include a history of nationalizing industries and draconian labor laws that mandate, for example, that no Indian worker can be laid off.

These negatives have combined to help hold India's growth rate since 1991 to only 3.5 percent, about half of what it needs to catch up with fast track eastern Asian neighbors like Malaysia, Thailand, Singapore, South Korea, and Thailand, all of which have annual per-capita incomes many times higher than India's $350.

THE SLUGGISH EUROPEAN UNION

Between 1960 and 1996, what began as the European Free Trade Area evolved into the European Community and, finally, the European Union, uniting 14 countries into an economic union. As such, member countries are committed to allow the free movement of people, products, services, and capital and to surrender large measures of national sovereignty to supranational authorities such as the European Parliament in Strasbourg and the European Commission in Brussels. Member nations will also be expected to harmonize government spending, taxation, and monetary policies, anticipating a common currency, with fixed exchange rates, in 1999.

It is primarily in this latter area that major problems are anticipated and arising. Specifically, in order to create the economic conditions required to implement a single currency (the Eurodollar), participating European governments will have to achieve healthy, stable economies, moving in lockstep, by 1999. One key requirement will be to cut budget deficits to 3 percent of Gross Domestic Product, which might prove challenging, at best. In 1991, Europe was hit by a recession that, like Japan's, seems interminable. Some figures tell the story. In 1996, growth among EU countries remains sluggish, at about half the level of the United States, and a third that of the average Pacific Rim country (e.g., 1.6 percent for France and Germany and 2.1 percent for Sweden, Britain, Holland, and Austria). Unemployment levels are about twice that of the United States and three times that of Pacific Rim countries (e.g., 14 percent in Belgium, 12 percent in France, 11 percent in Germany, 12 percent in Italy, and 24 percent in Spain). In 1995, deficits among EU countries averaged 5.5 percent of GDP, as against 2 percent in the United States.

Exacerbating these recessive conditions, and militating against moves to create healthy, growing economies by 1999, are these problems facing EU countries individually and collectively.

- *More aggressive global competition.* In the 1980s, Europe was one of the most competitive regions in the world. Now, in the 1990s, it has to deal with what the United States had to deal with in the 1980s: the Asians, with their more productive economies and a United States that grew more competitive largely in response to aggressive Asian trade initiatives. Today, European technology is well behind that of Asia and the United States in a number of critical areas, with high wages and inflexible labor laws further dulling Europe's once keen competitive edge.

- *An extensive social welfare system,* which the Europeans can no longer afford in the competitive global economy, including expensive systems of health care, pensions, unemployment insurance, and family aid that have defined European social and economic policies since World War II. In Germany, for example, 37-hour work weeks, fully paid maternity leaves, and 40 days off each year are mandated; In France, the 4-day work week is becoming a mandated reality. These social payments help keep deficits high and, with no broad consensus to change the welfare systems, are difficult to cut. Since World War II, Britain is the only government elected on a plank to reduce the size of government; in France, labor protests paralyzed parts of France at the prospect of minor cuts in social payments in 1996.

- *An immigrant tide into western European countries from western and northern Africa, eastern Europe, Asia, and Turkey* that is further straining welfare systems and economies. Germany, whose generous asylum laws have been tightened in response to this influx, is particularly hard-hit. Of the millions seeking asylum in western Europe, two-thirds try to enter Germany.

- *The enormous burden of German unification.* Germany, traditionally the engine of European economic recovery and growth, finds its economy stagnating under the load of reunification and dragging down other continental economies in the process. East Germany, with unemployment hovering around 30 percent, a decrepit infrastructure that will cost trillions to modernize, and no training in democracy or free-market enterprise, is proving to be more an albatross than an asset. Largely as a result of the cost of unification and emigration, Germany has a huge budget deficit that puts continual pressure on the central bank to raise interest rates—increases that radiate throughout Europe to further stifle productivity and exacerbate the recession.

- *The end of the cold war and, with it, the end of a unifying force that held European countries together in a common cooperative purpose.* Since the fall of the Berlin Wall, European confidence in

U.S. leadership has been eroded by a number of cautions and crises, including the end of NATO as a strong unifying force and conflicting strategies for ending the Bosnian civil war. Trust in the United States has been further eroded by what many Europeans perceive as economic opportunism using the weak dollar to penetrate European and other world markets. Many also perceive that the United States can no longer be relied on as the main guarantor of Europe's security with all its other interests in Asia and the western hemisphere.

- *A big company mentality.* Another prospective damper on European competitiveness that isn't being affected by EU agreements is the dominance of European economies by big companies that are less flexible and creative than smaller companies from which most technological breakthroughs emerge.

- *A protectionist tradition that extends across the continent,* notably in France (which insists on protection for its subsidized farmers even in the face of strong pressures from GATT and EU trading partners), Germany, and the Benelux countries. One manifestation of this tradition is a growing notion among Europeans that they can maintain satisfactorily high incomes and living standards without depending on the global economy. Presently, 80 percent of Europe's trade is internal—about twice that among Asia Rim countries—and the EU is often perceived as a shield behind which to maintain this situation, making Europe a much less attractive trading partner than was envisioned when the Berlin Wall came tumbling down.

Measures taken to address problems enervating the European economy are earnest if generally ad hoc and insufficient. For example, Germany cut coal subsidies by $7 billion and is making some effort to cut spending, reduce welfare state largesse, and raise taxes; however, when taxpayers are already paying 45 percent of Gross Domestic Product in taxes—49 percent in France—there isn't much wiggle room. Italy pushed through welfare changes in 1995 aimed at saving $60 billion through 2005, Sweden made big cuts in its social safety net, and France raised its value added tax to 20.9 percent.

However, while the slumping European economy stands in sharp contrast to the dynamic vigorous economies of Asia and the Americas, there is little talk of broad-based initiatives of the sort that are dramatically invigorating these economies, such as extensive privatization of industry and reduction of social benefits and tax policies to globally competitive standards.

CHAPTER PERSPECTIVE

Dramatic changes in the international economy, brought on by the fall of communist bloc command economies and the worldwide spread of free-market economies, have multiplied global threats and opportunities. Threats emerge from the proliferation of economic communities among nations—including GATT, NAFTA, the EU, and APEC—and the possibility they will exclude trade with outsiders. Opportunities emerge from the dynamic growth in productivity and purchasing power that these economic communities help engender by toppling trade barriers and encouraging the efficient flow and use of labor, capital, and expertise. Regions and countries that have most benefited from the new free-market, free-enterprise environment are those that have used it best, including almost all Latin American and Pacific Rim countries.

KNOW THE CONCEPTS

TERMS FOR STUDY

APEC
big company mentality
command economy
common currency
devaluation
European Union
foreign investment
GATT
immigrant tides
inflation rates

infrastructures
international lending organizations
Mercosur
NAFTA
protectionism
reunification
social welfare systems
tariff barriers
trade balance
unemployment rates

MATCHUP EXERCISES

1. Match up the events in the first column with the consequences listed in the second column.

1. immigration and unification

2. Latin America adopts free-market policies.

a. An estimated 146,000 jobs are lost to Mexico.

b. Canada refuses to sign a series of free trade agreements with the United States.

3. A government perceives threats to its cultural identity.
4. The peso is devalued.

c. Germany's budget deficit balloons.
d. Foreign investment quintuples between 1991 and 1996.

2. Match up the regional economic community in the first column with the descriptor in the second column.

1. Mercosur

a. Mexico becomes the United States' second largest trading partner.

2. APEC

b. dismantles trade barriers among 15 Pacific nations

3. NAFTA

c. a potential counter to NAFTA

4. EU

d. plans for a common currency by 1999

3. Match up the country in the first column with the descriptor in the second column.

1. Peru

a. unemployment rate three times that of Korea

2. Italy

b. world's largest GDP growth rate in 1994

3. Brazil

c. rapidly achieving postindustrial status

4. Korea

d. an economy twice as large as Mexico's

5. Vietnam

e. most open economy in South America

6. Chile

f. no commercial code or workable bankruptcy laws

QUESTIONS FOR REVIEW AND DISCUSSION

1. Although hemispheres apart, China and Chile are representative of countries that have maintained double-digit growth rates from the mid-1980s to the mid-1990s. What factors common to both economies explain these growth rates?

2. Using Mexico as an example, discuss the relationship between exchange rates and economic growth and well being.

3. Explain significant differences between Pacific Rim and European Union countries that help explain differences in their respective growth rates.

ANSWERS

MATCHUP EXERCISES

1. 1c, 2d, 3b, 4a

2. 1c, 2b, 3a, 4d

3. 1b, 2a, 3d, 4c, 5f, 6e

QUESTIONS FOR REVIEW AND DISCUSSION

1. First, both countries started their growth spurts from relatively low productivity bases, so even slight improvements would tend to be magnified as a percent of overall GDP. More significantly, both countries have adopted policies designed to increase trade, including lowering tariff barriers; encouraging foreign investment with tax, licensing, and other incentives; privatizing industry (to a lesser extent in China); encouraging entrepreneurship; working to modernize banking, investment, and judicial processes to stimulate and direct growth; and joining economic communities (for China, APEC, and for Chile, Mercosur) to achieve benefits of leverage and comparative advantage.

2. Mexico is an example of a country with a weak currency (devalued from 3.5 to 6 pesos to the dollar in 1994). This means that its exports are going to be lower priced in foreign markets (e.g., foreign currency will buy more of the peso-denominated goods), but imports to Mexico will be higher priced, since devaluation will reduce the purchasing power of the peso. This difference in exports versus imports explains the dramatic shift from a deficit to a surplus in Mexico's trade balance with the United States. Devalued pesos, in addition to reducing purchasing power, also reduce wages and living standards for Mexicans, but represent an attractive investment opportunity for companies that can lower their production costs by investing in Mexico (e.g., Japan is doing by investing extensively in low-wage countries in the orient). This increase in investment, combined with growth in export sales, can work to reverse the deteriorating economic conditions in the country whose originally weak currency will probably gain strength as the economy strengthens and, presumably, wise economic policies guide this growth.

3. In the years between 1990 and 1995, there was a fairly consistent relationship among vital economic statistics characterizing Pacific Rim (PR) and European Union (EU) countries, with PR countries having higher growth rates and lower rates of unemployment and deficit growth in approximately a 3:1 ratio to EU countries. Reasons for these differences can probably be traced largely to conditions in EU countries that don't generally prevail in PR countries. In EU countries, for example, inflexible labor laws, high wages, and a broad-based social welfare system (encompassing amenities like health care, unemployment, and job benefits) combine to make labor less productive than in PR countries, where workers are much more likely to be paid less and save (and invest) more. Also, EU countries incur other costs (e.g., unification and immigration) not incurred by PR countries, further increasing budget deficits and dragging down growth rates. Additionally, EU countries, perhaps responding to a "big company" mentality that tends to stifle innovation and a growing protectionist orientation that rejects foreign incursions, are not as technologically advanced as PR countries, further reducing their ability to compete.

10
INTERNATIONAL CONSUMER AND ORGANIZATIONAL MARKETS

OVERVIEW

An understanding of buyer behavior in consumer and organizational markets is critical in planning and implementing marketing strategies that identify and define target markets, build marketing mixes keyed to the nature and needs of these markets, measure market size, forecast sales, and assess marketing performance. Understanding consumer behavior involves identifying intra- and interpersonal influences that trigger the buyer decision process and building strategic plans on this knowledge. The international organizational market, which is composed of manufacturers, trade industries, and governments, differs from consumer markets in a number of significant respects that affect strategic marketing planning: demand patterns fluctuate more, are more derivative and dependent, respond more to elasticity and reciprocity arrangements, and evidence more sophisticated, collegial buying practices.

CONSUMER BEHAVIOR DEFINES TARGET MARKETS AND MARKETING MIXES

In the four previous chapters, we focused on environmental components of the strategic marketing planning process, examining how they combine to define worthwhile global markets where political, economic, competitive, cultural, and technological conditions are favorable to entry and growth. Now, in this chapter, we narrow our focus to examine how prospective customers shaped by these environmental components behave, both as individuals and as organizations. We include in our definition of consumer behavior the full range of decisions and activities involved in evaluating, acquiring, using, and disposing of goods or services. For example, referring to Merton's global strategy, planners will want to know how buyers in prospective markets learn about MM computer systems; how they assess these computers against competitive models; who or what, influences the selection of an MM system over competitive makes; how these computers are used; what benefits and features are desired; and what happens to MMs when they become obsolete.

Answers to these and related questions about the nature and needs of target market members will prove helpful to Merton planners in a number of ways. First, it will help them segment broad market aggregates into smaller target markets, each comprising groups of prospective consumers with similar buying behavior favorable to the purchase of MM computer systems (segmentation concepts are covered in Chapter 11).

This information on global consumer and organizational markets will also help in measuring and forecasting sales and marketing potential (covered in Chapter 12), in preparing budgets, and in controlling the effectiveness of sales efforts. Perhaps the most important use of information on consumer behavior is in building marketing mixes calculated to appeal to members of each target market. For example, with an understanding of how, why, from whom, and for what price MMs are purchased by members of a given target market, Merton planners will be much better positioned to reach them with a product positioned, priced, and promoted to meet these needs.

RESEARCHING GLOBAL CONSUMER BEHAVIOR: PROBLEMS AND PLUSES

Developing information on consumer and organizational buying behavior is almost always more difficult in heterogeneous international markets than in comparatively homogeneous domestic markets. Differences in language, cultures, economies, legal, and political systems, as well as deficiencies of marketing research tools and techniques (discussed in Chapter 5) create sizable problems in access, reliability, and validity of data—especially data pertaining to inter- and intrapersonal influences like reference groups, motives, and attitudes. Somewhat offsetting these problems is the growing recognition of the universality of much consumer behavior, especially among countries that have achieved higher levels of development. For example, results of a survey of 100 senior executives of 27 leading multinationals in consumer package goods industries found that 63 percent of total marketing programs—including product, price, distribution, and promotion components—were highly standardized, this is, practically identical from country to country.[1] In promotion—the marketing mix element most responsive to differing cross-cultural characteristics and needs—study findings showed that almost three-quarters of advertising messages had been standardized.

STIMULI THAT INFLUENCE CONSUMER BEHAVIOR

Stimuli that influence consumer decision-making processes can be classified as interpersonal (between people) or intrapersonal (within people). Interpersonal influences include social and cultural groups to which people belong or would like to belong, such as family- and gender-based groups. Intrapersonal influences include drives, perceptions, and attitudes that shape consumer behavior. Primarily, Merton planners were searching for strong underlying values and behaviors that were broadly similar among diverse cultures, that tended to differentiate one group, or market, from another, and that predisposed these groups toward Merton products.

The planners used this information on strengths, similarities, and differences in prospective global markets to define worthwhile target markets, with similar values and behaviors favorable to MM systems, and to address questions pertaining to the MM's marketing mix strategy. For example, how would MM systems have to be modified to harmonize with current and evolving values and behaviors in different target markets? (If these values and behaviors were sufficiently similar across cultures, no modification might be required.) What means of communication (advertising, direct marketing) would apply across cultures, and what modifications would be needed (language, taboo avoidance, etc.) consistent with cultural differences?

HOW INTERPERSONAL VARIABLES INFLUENCE CONSUMER BEHAVIOR

In understanding and integrating consumer behavior into MM marketing plans, Merton planners started with an examination of the influence of larger groups such as cultures, subcultures, and social classes on consumer behavior and then narrowed to focus on the influence of smaller peer and reference groups. In general, the smaller the group, the greater its influence on consumer behavior.

---

[1] Ralph Z. Sorensen and Ulrich Weichmann, "How Multinationals View Marketing Standardization," *Harvard Business Review*, May–June 1975.

CULTURES AND SUBCULTURES SHAPE BEHAVIOR

Employing analytical tools and techniques examined in Chapter 8, Merton planners identified cultural and subcultural values relating to consumer behavior toward MM systems in prospective entry markets. Later, these values would shape marketing plans calculated to stimulate favorable buying decisions. In Japan, for example, cultural values stressing the importance of cooperation, interdependence, and loyalty to the organization would require a much different marketing appeal for MM systems than would a culture stressing individual self-expression, competition, and independence.

In examining subcultures—separate segments of a culture organized around such factors as race, nationality, religion, or geographic location—the planners focused primarily on characteristics that would predispose members to purchase MM systems. In Asia, for example, they identified regional and ethnic subcultures that were highly imbued with an entrepreneurial, market economy ethic, which the planners perceived could be furthered with MM programs. In analyzing subcultural groups, the planners also recognized that, even in the most homogeneous of groups, there are usually as many differences as similarities within each subculture.

SOCIAL CLASS PREDICTS BUYING BEHAVIOR

A social class is a relatively homogeneous and enduring division of a culture whose members share similar values, interests, and behavior. Social classes are hierarchically structured—ranging from low to high status—with an individual's position in a given stratum based on a number of variables, including amount and type of income, occupation, type of house, and area of residence. Members of a given social class show distinct product and brand preferences in such areas as clothing, home furnishings, and automobiles. In the United States, lines between social classes are not fixed; over their lifetimes, people can move up and down among the hierarchies. This mobility is generally less characteristic of other developed and developing countries such as India, England, and Japan. In less-developed economies, upward mobility is often impossible.

A number of studies indicate that similar social class hierarchies are broadly dispersed among countries at similar stages of development (e.g., postindustrialized). For example, the nature and needs of members of the upper-middle class stratum would be basically similar in Sweden, England, and the United States. The size of this stratum will differ from country to country, as will some culturally conditioned attributes. For example, while overall patterns of occupational perceptions are universal (e.g., professionals are held in higher regard than ditch diggers), the social prestige accorded specific occupations will vary (e.g., in the United States, with its focus on money, physicians are held in higher regard than professors; in Japan, it's the opposite).

The universal aspect of social structures makes the task of the global marketer similar to that involved in seeking and relating to universal cultural values. First, identify the social stratum—or strata—whose values predispose purchase of the product class or brand being marketed; then, identify countries with sufficiently large proportions of the population occupying this stratum to be considered a worthwhile target market. Finally, build a marketing mix that will attract target market members. Global Focus 10-1 shows how this process worked in marketing ostrich meat in domestic and international markets.

GLOBAL FOCUS 10-1

Ostrich Rancher Looks to Feather His Nest in Overseas Markets

As general manager and vice president of Zion View Ostrich Ranch in St. George, Utah, Rick White oversees a 10-person, 250-acre operation that raises ostriches for meat and other products. The meat is marketed through specialty meat distributors and grocery stores, which order thousands of pounds a week.

"The biggest advantage of eating ostrich is that it is 98 percent fat-free and makes for a tasty and healthful meal, without the high fat content in beef or the potential for salmonella poisoning," White says. To reinforce this point, the ranch's promotional literature describes ostrich as "A versatile red meat with mildly beefy flavor that makes a flexible addition to any menu."

"We've had great success here in the United States for different reasons," says White, citing the growing popularity of low-fat ostrich meat being sold in retail and health food stores. "In addition, ostrich is a favorite of the lobster tail crowd who patronize pricey 'white tablecloth' restaurants, and of patrons who enjoy dining on unique foods like venison," he says.

Zion View first entered the domestic marketplace with ostrich meat in 1995, and began to tap the Japanese and European markets in 1996 as part of its long-term strategic marketing plan. "One of the major appeals for doing business in Japan and Europe is that people spend more time dining at fine restaurants in those countries than in the United States," he says, "So obviously we are concentrating heavily on those marketing segments."

The Japanese and Europeans, like Americans, are becoming more conscious about their eating habits and are looking to reduce fat intake without diminishing the overall dining experience. "Ostrich is healthy eating without the sacrifice in taste," says White.

Source: Curtice K. Cultice, "Where's the Beef?," *Business America*, U.S. Department of Commerce, October 1996.

HOW REFERENCE GROUPS INFLUENCE CONSUMER BEHAVIOR

Reference groups have a direct (face to face) or an indirect influence on consumer attitudes and behavior. Major reference group categories include:

- Membership groups the individual already belongs to,

- Aspirational groups the individual would like to join, and

- Disassociative groups whose values the individual rejects.

In Poland, Czechoslovakia, and Hungary, for example, a newly emerging class of free-market entrepreneurs aspire to values of their counterparts in western Europe, while rejecting values of the communist command economies they helped overthrow. Marketing plans to reach this group would certainly reflect these aspirational and disassociative values. Membership and aspirational groups influence people in a variety of ways of interest to marketers. They expose people to new products and behaviors, influence an individual's attitudes and self concept, and create pressures to conform to group norms. The force of this influence depends on:

- The cohesiveness of the group, with highly cohesive groups, such as a religious cult, exerting more influence;

- The people being influenced by group norms and values, with "other-directed" people, who adopt values of reference groups, more likely to be influenced than "inner-directed" people, who act more on personal values;

- The product concept, with group influence strongest when products are highly visible and can be seen in use by others, as with MM systems.

Family, gender, and age-based reference groups are of particular interest to global marketers in that they differ appreciably in form and substance among nations.

FAMILY-BASED GROUPS

As the smallest reference group with which the consumer interacts, the family is also the most important buying influence in society. Two kinds of family—the family of orientation and the family of procreation—exert this persuasive influence. The family of orientation, consisting of the consumer's parents and siblings, imparts behaviors and values toward religion, politics, economics, feelings of personal ambition, and product worth. This family can even influence the buyer's unconscious behavior. The family of procreation, comprising consumer's spouse and children, has a more direct influence on buying behavior than any other group.

Key differences among family-based groups in different countries relate to the size, strength, and cohesion of the family unit. From a marketer's perspective, the average size of a household—which is a good measure of family size, although it includes related and nonrelated occupants—in a prospective entry market often defines the nature and size of a market for such products as appliances and prepared foods. For example, Norway (average household size: 2.1) would likely be a much better customer for single-serving portions of frozen food than Colombia (average size: 6).

Strength and cohesion of family units are also key indicators of market potential for many products. In Mediterranean and Latin American countries, for example, the family constitutes the most important membership group, with family membership often exceeding individual accomplishment as a measure of social status. In these countries, families can exert strong leverage in shaping consumer behavior. Also helpful in shaping consumer behavior is family cohesion; for example, in countries like Greece and Korea, strong family cohesion manifests itself in cooperative business ventures (restaurants, retail outlets, etc.), that are customers for diverse products and services.

GENDER-BASED GROUPS

Country-specific attitudes toward males and females are of interest to global marketers in that they help define the nature and size of markets as well as marketing mixes that best meet the needs of these markets. To varying degrees, for example, most Asian and Islamic countries exhibit male preference, manifested in China by the widespread practice of aborting female fetuses and in Saudi Arabia by the downgraded socioeconomic status of women, who must attend separate schools, are generally restricted from working outside the home (and then mostly in professions with no male contact), and are legally prohibited from driving cars or riding in a taxi without a male escort. Even when women constitute a large portion of the working population, there are dramatic differences in types of jobs regarded as "male" or "female." In Sweden, for example, more than

45 percent of administrative and managerial positions are held by women, compared to less than 5 percent in Spain. Thus, for a company like Merton, an understanding of the relative socioeconomic status of the sexes can help answer a number of questions pertaining to consumer behavior, such as how large each market is, what products each needs, who makes purchasing decisions, and how each market can best be reached.

HOW INTRAPERSONAL VARIABLES INFLUENCE CONSUMER BEHAVIOR

Having identified significant interpersonal variables—such as cultural and social values—that defined target market characteristics and needs as well as marketing mix strategies for reaching target market members, Merton planners next focused on intrapersonal variables predisposing individual target market members toward the purchase of MM systems. For example, what would be the effect of a respondent's age and economic condition on a decision to purchase a MM system? What personal motivations would such a purchase satisfy? How would life-style and personality characteristics predispose purchase?

In exploring the nature and impact of these variables on consumer behavior, the planners began with demographic intrapersonal variables—including age, occupation, and economic circumstances—and then explored psychographic intrapersonal variables, including motivation, learning, perception, attitudes, personality, and life-style.

DEMOGRAPHIC INTRAPERSONAL VARIABLES

Information on demographic variables, which pertain to such state-of-being characteristics of human populations as size, density, location, age, sex, and race, are relatively easy to come by and frequently correlate well with buyer behavior. Thus, in every market studied, Merton planners found significant relationships among three demographic variables—age, occupation, and income—and interest in purchasing MM systems. They found, for example, that "middle management" in accounting, banking, and insurance fields, primarily in the 30–50 age group, had the strongest interest in purchasing MM systems, and sufficient discretionary income and borrowing power to fulfill this interest.

PSYCHOGRAPHIC INTRAPERSONAL VARIABLES

Unlike demographic variables, significant psychographic variables (motives, attitudes, perceptions, etc.) are generally difficult to identify and measure, especially in complex, dynamic foreign markets. Often it's worth the effort, however, since these variables can be the most useful of all for segmenting markets and building persuasive marketing mix offerings that relate to potent emotive responses.

Following are brief definitions of motives, perceptions, attitudes, and life-styles, and the Merton planners' conclusions pertaining to the effect of each on consumer responses to MM marketing mix variables.

• *MOTIVATION*

A motive, or drive, is a stimulated need that an individual seeks to satisfy. Until it is satisfied—or otherwise eliminated—it will continue to generate an uncomfortable tension. Stimulated needs can be classified as primary buying motives (associated with broad product categories such as computers) or selective buying motives (associated with specific product brands such as MM computers). Marketing activities can be viewed as a way to both stimulate motives (e.g., to feel a need for a computer system) and to satisfy motives (e.g., to make an offering that meets this need that the buyer can't refuse).

• *PERCEPTION*

Perception is the process by which people derive meaning from the selection, organization, and interpretation of stimuli from within themselves (e.g., a feeling of frustration) or from the external environment (e.g., an advertisement for an MM computer system). Three perception-related concepts are of particular interest to marketing managers. Here is how each might influence a promotional campaign for the Merton MM.

SELECTIVE EXPOSURE

Selective exposure means that people only have the mental capacity to process a small percentage of the millions of stimuli competing to "get through" to our cognitive centers. Stimuli (e.g., an advertisement or sales presentation) that relate to an anticipated event, show how the audience can satisfy needs, or represent a significant change in intensity from other stimuli have been found more likely to be selected. Thus, a full-page advertisement (intensity change) might announce a free special seminar to learn about MM systems (anticipated event) and explain how this seminar can satisfy needs for increased income and an improved life-style (need satisfaction).

SELECTIVE DISTORTION

Selective distortion means that people change the meaning of dissonant stimuli so it becomes consistent with their feelings and beliefs. For the marketer, this means that the offering should be consistent with these feelings and beliefs or the intended meaning will be lost.

SELECTIVE RETENTION

Selective retention means that people are more likely to remember stimuli that support preconceived feelings and beliefs and forget stimuli that do not. In general, people tend to ignore, or quickly forget, stimuli that they perceive as a functional risk (the product will not perform as claimed) or a psychological risk (the product will not enhance the prospect's self-concept or well-being). For stimuli promoting the MM, this suggests appeals stressing proofs of performance.

• *ATTITUDES*

Attitudes are relatively stable tendencies to perceive or act in a consistent way toward products or classes of products. They are formed or adjusted by what is learned from families, peers, and other social groups, from information received, and from previous behavior. Although attitudes are second only to intentions as predictors of behavior, they are difficult to define, measure, and relate to product classes (e.g., computers) or specific brands (e.g., Merton).

To mitigate this difficulty, Merton marketers found it useful to define and measure the influence of attitudes toward product purchases in terms of four product-related functional areas:

- *Utilitarian*, or the ability of the product to help achieve desired goals (e.g., a productive career path);

- *Ego-defensive*, or the capability of the product to defend the buyer's self-image against internal or external threats;

- *Value expressive*, or the degree of consistency of the product with the buyer's central values or self-image;

- *Knowledge*, or the ability of the product to give meaning to the individual's beliefs and experiences.

For example, a measurement of these attitudinal dimensions (using rating scales discussed in Chapter 5) among middle managers might show confusion as to how the MM could achieve utilitarian or ego-defensive goals, which could be addressed in MM promotional literature.

• *LIFE-STYLE*

Distinguishing combinations of activities, interests, and opinions that lead to relatively consistent and enduring responses to the environment comprise an individual's life-style. The usual technique for defining an individual's life-style, called psychographics, involves measuring attitudes, interests, and opinions (AIO) in diverse areas (work, politics, recreation, etc.) by soliciting agree-disagree responses on lengthy survey instruments. Once distinctive life-style groups are revealed through similar AIO response patterns, an attempt is made to relate these groups to demographic and marketing mix variables. Although problems involved in generating and interpreting life-style data can be formidable, they often provide multidimensional views of target market segments that suggest new product and product positioning opportunities, improved communications, and generally improved marketing strategies.

COMPONENTS OF THE ORGANIZATIONAL MARKET

The organizational market comprises the industrial producer market, the trade industries market, and the government market. The following discussion covers characteristics of each market of concern to international marketing planners, including relative size, demand patterns, products purchased, and purchasing policies and practices.

THE INDUSTRIAL PRODUCER MARKET

Throughout the world, the industrial producer market consists of individuals and organizations that acquire goods and services used, directly or indirectly, in the production of other products and services that are sold, rented, or otherwise supplied to others. Included are manufacturing firms; farmers and other resource industries; construction contractors; and providers of such services as transportation, public utilities, finance, insurance, and real estate. This market is typically the largest and most diverse of all the organizational market aggregates, frequently offering the largest sales and profit potential and the most formidable competitive challengers.

Table 10-1, which shows the transactions involved in purchasing a single MM computer system, also shows reasons why the industrial producer market is typically the largest of all the aggregates, organizational or consumer. Note that the consumer market is involved in only one of the five transactional areas in which products are bought and sold, whereas the industrial producer and trade industries markets are each involved in two. In terms of the U.S. market, this translates into total annual sales of $3 trillion worth of goods and services in the industrial producer market, and $2.5 trillion worth of goods and services in the trade industries market, a total almost three times that of the total buying power of the entire consumer market. These relative figures don't differ significantly in other developed economies and highlight the need for international marketers to think in terms of a number of transactional levels leading to the final, consumer level.

Table 10–1. Organizational Market Transactions in Producing One Product

Raw Material Processor	Merton Consumer Products Div.	Wholesaler	Retailer	Consumer
BUYS:	BUYS:	BUYS:	BUYS:	BUYS:
Copper, plastics, silicon Equipment Labor Energy	Wire Plastic forms Chip circuits Equipment Labor Energy	Personal computers Space Equipment Labor Energy	Personal computers Space Equipment Labor Energy	Personal computer
SELLS:	SELLS:	SELLS:	SELLS:	
Wire, Plastic forms, etc.	Personal computers	Personal computers	Personal computers	

INDUSTRIAL MARKETS DIFFER FROM CONSUMER MARKETS

Industrial markets differ from consumer markets in terms of purchased products, demand patterns, and purchasing practices. For illustrative purposes, we will refer to a German automobile manufacturer.

This automobile manufacturer buys millions of marks worth of products and services in the course of a typical year, but practically all can be classified into four broad product categories:

- *Long-lived capital goods depreciated over time*, including heavy equipment and installations;

- *Short-lived accessory items*, like tools and office machines, that don't become part of the finished product;

- *Expense items,* including raw materials used in production processes, and components, such as tires and small motors, that become part of the finished automobiles (i.e., original equipment, or OEM, items);

- *Supplies,* including maintenance, repair and operating (MRO) items, like brooms, nails, paper clips that don't go into the final product.

Marketing mix attributes of these products are discussed in Chapter 13.

PRODUCT NEEDS CHARACTERIZING STAGE OF DEVELOPMENT

The stage of development of a prospective foreign market is a strong determinant of industrial products purchased and emphasis on such product attributes as service, quality, performance, and costs. Here are industrial product purchase needs characterizing stages of development discussed in Chapter 7.

- *Preindustrial stage,* primarily agricultural, subsistence economies. Most industrial products purchased are used in production and transportation of country's basic resources, including specialized, expensive construction equipment (e.g., oil rigs).

- *Less developed,* beginning to develop the capability to supply growing domestic and export markets. Industrial products purchased are used to develop primary manufacturing capabilities and process resources which, in the preindustrial stage, were shipped in raw form (e.g., bleaching powder for sugar and empty jute bags).

- *Developing countries,* making the transition from an agrarian to an urbanized industrial base. Growth of manufacturing facilities for non- and semidurable consumer products creates a demand for entire factories (new and used); associated OEM, MRO, capital, and expense products; construction and mining equipment; motor vehicles and parts.

- *Industrialized countries,* major exporters of manufactured goods and investment funds, with strong infrastructures and skilled, educated, well-paid workers. Main demand for industrial goods relate to rapidly growing consumer demand (autos, refrigerators, etc.) and to production of specialized goods for world markets.

- *Postindustrial countries*, with declining emphasis on manufacturing, more on service sector, information processing, and exchange. Strong demand for consulting services, and "electronic highway" products representing confluence of computer, telecommunications, and television technologies. Tendency to specialize in certain products for world market often creates opportunities for sales of industrial products in which country doesn't specialize. For example, Japan, in spite of its dominance of many segments of the electronics market, is a good customer for electronic bookkeeping and accounting equipment.

KEY EXPORT INDUSTRIES GENERATE JOBS AND GROWTH

Beginning in 1994, a part of its National Export Strategy, the U.S. Department of Commerce identified six industry sectors given high priority for export to Big Emerging Markets (BEMs) expected to "more than double their share of world exports, to 27 percent, by 2010."[2] These sectors were selected on the basis of (1) the potential of the industry for creating "a significant number of high-paying U.S. jobs"; (2) growth prospects of the sector; (3) superior U.S. competitiveness in the sector; and (4) the extent to which government action, in concert with the private sector, can further improve U.S. global competitiveness. (Global Focus 10-2 illustrates the extent to which government agencies are prepared to support U.S. company initiatives to penetrate these markets.)

Table 10-2 identifies and defines these industry clusters in terms of major component technologies comprising each, present size and prospective growth prospects of each cluster in global markets, key global markets for each cluster, and major competitors for each cluster. Growth prospects for these six industry clusters are projected to range from 5 percent (for transportation and environmental technologies to more than 8 percent for information, health, and energy clusters.

---

[2] *Business America*, National Export Strategy, Vol. 115, No. 9 (October 1994), p. 58.

GLOBAL FOCUS 10-2

SIVAM: Case Study in Successful Advocacy

Following intense advocacy efforts by the U.S. government, the government of Brazil selected a U.S. consortium—led by Raytheon—to build a $1.5 billion Amazon environmental surveillance and air traffic control system (SIVAM). SIVAM will provide Brazilian government agencies with the capability to collect and process the information required to protect the environment, combat illegal mining and drug trafficking, improve population and public health controls, and strengthen border security.

The selection of the Raytheon-led group of companies to produce the SIVAM project in the face of stiff competition from a European group of companies led by the French firm Thomson CSF was partially a result of:

- Personal support from President Clinton via a letter to President Franco of Brazil;

- Several meetings with Brazilian Ministers and SIVAM officials in Brazil by Commerce Secretary Ronald Brown;

- Support by our embassy in Brasilia, including the Ambassador, Deputy Chief of Mission, and US&FCS staff;

- Active monitoring by key senior officials, through the TPCC Advocacy Network, of the status of the bidding process;

- Advocacy letters from Secretary Brown, Ex-Im Bank Chairman Brody, TDA Director Grandmaison, Environmental Protection Agency Administrator Brower, Federal Aviation Administration Administrator Hinson, National Oceanic and Atmospheric Administration Under Secretary Baker and members of Congress.

- Assistance from the Ex-Im Bank in developing a package competitive with the French government package, and additional financing by OPIC, if necessary.

Source: *Business America*: National Export Strategy, U.S. Department of Commerce (October, 1994), p. 22.

Table 10–2. Six High Potential Industry Clusters

	Environmental Technologies	Information Technologies	Health Technologies
Major component technologies	Design and construction services; stationary and mobile source air pollution control; solid, hazardous waste management; contaminated site remediation.	Computer hardware and software; telecommunication services; electronic components; semiconductor manufacturing equipment; information services; satellites; computer network services.	Medical and dental devices and supplies; pharmaceutical, biotechnologic, and health care services.
Present status and growth prospects	The United States is the leader and largest producer and consumer of environmental goods and services, which produced more than $140 billion in revenue in 1995. Worldwide market for these services is expected to grow to over $400 billion by year 2000, with U.S. exports accounted for about 10 percent of total.	Small and medium-sized companies comprise bulk of industry in United States with annual exports of over $20 billion expected to more than double by year 2010. U.S. computer systems and packaged software firms control 75 percent of information technologies world market, which is expected to grow at an annual rate of 7 percent, reaching $300 billion by 2010.	U.S. is world's leader in terms of research, patents, and number of products brought to market, with healthcare management companies expanding globally. U.S. share of global medical device industry is 52 percent, 50 percent for pharmaceuticals, with U.S. exports expected to rise to over $14 billion by 2010 (over $9 billion to BEMs).
Major BEM markets	Demand for environmental technologies is forecast to increase an annual rate of 20 percent by year 2000 in BEMs in Asia (Indonesia, India, S. Korea and Chinese Economic Area), and over 15% in Latin American BEMs (Argentina, Brazil, Mexico).	Roughly 26 percent of growth gain in international markets will come from exports to BEMs, including South Africa, Poland, India, China (stressing telecommunications), Brazil, South Korea, Mexico, South Africa, and Taiwan (computer hard- and software); and China (information services).	Key BEM markets for health technology products include Russia, South Africa, Central Asia, Mexico, and Eastern Europe.
Major competitors	Germany, Japan, France, and the United Kingdom are strongest competitors—Japan and Germany especially in air pollution control technologies; France and Britain in wastewater treatment. Germany is attempting to get its standards, practices, and testing protocols adopted by the EU.	Japanese have narrowed technological and market gaps in computer equipment by building a strong domestic base in semiconductors and other enabling technologies. However, rising challenges from U.S. and South Korean challengers are eroding this lead in high-volume devices like memory chips. In telecommunications satellites, United States has lead, but Europeans are catching up, with diversified R&D and production across the EU.	Although U.S. medical device and pharmaceutical industries maintain global leadership position, West European and Asian companies, especially in Germany and Japan, gained ground in last decade, especially in exploiting emerging markets in Eastern Europe and China.

Defined by BEMs[a] Markets and Competitors

Transportation Technologies	Energy Technologies	Financial Services
Aerospace technologies, automotive industry, and transportation infrastructure, including airports, ports, road, and railroad projects.	Gas and oil field equipment and infrastructure; conventional and renewable energy power generation equipment, facilities, and services; infrastructure facilities; engineering and related services	Commercial banks, investment banks, securities dealers, and insurance companies.
The U.S. aerospace industry leads all other industry sectors in exports and manufactured goods, with $45 billion in exports in 1995. In 1995, the automotive industry, which encourages the development of new products and advanced technologies, accounted for about 5 percent of total U.S. manufacturing employment. The United States remains the global leader in engineering, management, and financial talent for foreign transportation infrastructure, responsible for 45–50 percent of foreign construction work.	The United States is internationally competitive both in advanced petroleum and power generation equipment, with exports of newly made power generation equipment increasing from $4 billion to $8 billion between 1980 and 1996.	U.S. securities firms are world leaders in financial innovation and development of financial instruments for raising capital through debt and equity. Income from international activities of U.S. financial service firms is expected to double, from $8 billion in 1993 to $17 billion by 2010.
Aerospace technologies: Asia and Latin America represent biggest markets (China alone expected to need over $40 billion in new aircraft over next 20 years); *Automotive:* including light, commercial, and specialized vehicles and small and medium-sized parts manufacturers will see major growth in Latin America, India, East Europe and South Korea; *Transportation infrastructure:* Major growth throughout Asia, primarily airports, subway systems, rail and road projects.	BEMs are expected to account for two-thirds of projected global growth in power generation equipment by 2010. China's electric power generation capacity is expected to increase by 55 percent by year 2000; Mexico's demand increases by 8 percent annually; OPEC countries will continue to be largest market for oil and gas field equipment; also countries with major oil and gas exploration operations (e.g., Russia, Indonesia, China, India, Mexico).	Recipients of private capital flows in 1996 were generally middle-income Asian and Latin American countries, especially China, India, and Indonesia. The markets of Mexico, Brazil, and Argentina led bond issuers, followed by Turkey and South Korea. China was the largest receiver of foreign direct investment and commercial credit in 1995.
European aerospace manufacturers, often government subsidized, have formed partnerships and alliances to spread risk and gain leverage from resources. European and Japanese automotive manufacturers offer challenging competition to U.S. manufacturers in mature, saturated markets.	Barriers to increasing exports include incompatibility of U.S. standards and technical specifications, competitive financing to foreign suppliers with government subsidies, and regional "Buy National" policies. Petroleum equipment manufacturers face strong international competition from strategic alliances forged between European suppliers.	Primarily, developed European and Asian nations engaged in exploiting growth potential in BEMs.

[a]Big Emerging Markets (BEMs) include the Chinese Economic Area (China, Taiwan, Hong Kong), Indonesia, India, South Korea, Mexico, Argentina, Brazil, South Africa, Poland, and Turkey.

DEMAND PATTERNS CHARACTERIZING INDUSTRIAL MARKETS

As compared to demand patterns in consumer markets, demand patterns in global industrial markets tend to be more concentrated, more direct, more dependent on demand patterns in other markets, more elastic initially and inelastic subsequently, and more likely to be dependent on purchases of related products and reciprocal arrangements.

• *CONCENTRATED DEMAND*

As compared to demand in consumer markets, demand in industrial markets is much more concentrated geographically and by industry—with fewer, larger manufacturing plants in related industries located in countries and areas close to such resources as transportation, skilled workers, and power. Here are some examples. In Italy, the world-leading footwear industry is concentrated within a 100-mile area in northern Italy; some 300 firms produce cutlery in one German town, making it a world center of that industry; and most of the world's racing cars, including almost all of the Indianapolis 500 racers, are built in a region north of London.

According to Porter,[3] this concentration among industries in industrial and postindustrial countries creates "hotbeds of competition" that help these industries overcome formidable obstacles and spur innovation:

> The health of such clusters is the key to the economic vigor of countries. . . . Most nations rely on a few dozen industrial clusters and a few hundred companies to provide most of their exports, raise productivity and improve national living standards.

Industrial demand is also concentrated by purchasing practices, with most purchasing offices for large manufacturers located in large metropolitan areas. Finally, demand concentration is displayed in a disproportionate relationship between size and productivity, with a relatively small number of plants, consistent with Pareto's principle, employing most of the production employees and generating most of the value added by manufacturing.

This high degree of concentration affects key aspects of the seller company's marketing mix. For example, it is easier to communicate with customers and prospects—the "promotion" aspect—and product distribution channels tend to be shorter than for final customers.

---

[3] "Think Locally, Win Globally," *The Washington Post*, April 5, 1992; also Michael E. Porter, *The Competitive Advantage of Nations*. New York, Free Press, 1990.

• *DIRECT PURCHASING*

Industrial buyers are more likely to purchase products directly from manufacturers, and in larger quantities, than are consumers. This is particularly true for products that are complex and expensive, like factory automation equipment used by automobile manufacturers.

• *DERIVED DEMAND*

Demand for industrial products derives largely from demand for final consumer goods. For example, if MM computers sell well among managers and professionals—ultimate consumers—the producers of MM computer components will also do well.

• *FLUCTUATING DEMAND*

Small changes in consumer demand can lever much larger changes in industrial demand. To illustrate, assume demand for a popular car introduced by the auto manufacturer exceeds the firm's capacity to produce them. The company must then either build, or otherwise acquire, new plant facilities to handle this excess demand and anticipated future demand. This will result in massive purchases of industrial goods and services to accommodate demand that might only be slightly more than anticipated. Conversely, sales of this automobile might drop, say, 5 percent below expectations, but as a result the manufacturer might cut back purchases of OEM items more than 50 percent, relying on inventory until conditions improve. The disproportionate change in industrial demand caused by changes in consumer demand is called the accelerator principle.

• *ELASTIC DEMAND INITIALLY, INELASTIC DEMAND SUBSEQUENTLY*

Because many suppliers are actively competing on price for contracts, industrial demand can be extremely elastic during the early negotiation stages of the purchasing process, with demand increasing substantially with small decreases in competitive prices. Once contracts are negotiated, however, demand is inelastic to the extent that demand for many industrial products is not influenced by short-run price changes. For example, assume that the automobile manufacturer contracts to purchase 1,000,000 fuses at a cost of $0.15 per fuse, and streams them into the production of its automobiles. If the price of the fuses then drops to $0.13 a piece, the company will not purchase additional quantities of fuses because the cost of storing them would exceed the small savings. Nor is the manufacturer likely to renegotiate its contract with the fuse manufacturer if a competitor comes in with the $0.13 price; it would be too expensively disruptive to change suppliers in midstream. Of course, if the competitor's price were appreciably less—say, $0.10 per fuse, where big cost savings resulted—the automobile manufacturer might change suppliers.

• *JOINT DEMAND*

Frequently, demand for some industrial products is related to demand for other industrial products. For example, if the automobile manufacturer has delivery problems with fuse boxes, it will probably cut back on its purchases of fuses.

• *RECIPROCAL ARRANGEMENTS*

Frequently, in global markets, industrial buyers will select as suppliers firms that also purchase their products. For example, the automobile manufacturer might agree to purchase its fuses from a large electronics firm that agrees to specify the manufacturer's automobiles for its automobile fleet.

With the Japanese kieretso system of interlocking manufacturers, distributors, and financial agencies, for example, these arrangements are not only common but also institutionalized, often making it difficult for offshore firms to compete. (In the United States, both the Federal Trade Commission [FTC] and the Justice Department forbid such reciprocity arrangements if it can be proved they unfairly shut out competition.)

Possibly the most prevalent form of reciprocity in global markets are offsets, a form of countertrade that mandates various forms of business activities as a condition of purchase. Typically, they obligate a seller of major purchases (e.g., military hardware) to minimize any trade imbalance or other adverse impact caused by the outflow of currency required to pay for such purchases. Among the forms offsets take are licensing, subcontracting, or joint ventures. For example, when Saudi Arabia purchases military aircraft from U.S. producers, the cost is usually offset through investments in the country's resources.

THE INDUSTRIAL BUYING PROCESS

Largely because of the costs, risks and opportunities associated with the industrial buying function, it is frequently viewed as an important profit center, where the investment in goods and services purchased can be managed and controlled to improve the firm's profits and competitive posture. With this emphasis on profitability, purchasing departments have integrated many functions (e.g., traffic, production scheduling, warehousing, and inventory control) not traditionally associated with core procurement functions.

This broadened perception of the procurement function as an integrated, professionalized profit center, combined with the application of modern management techniques and controls in implementing this function, can spell opportunity for marketers who understand and can relate to these trends. Even in countries that haven't reached this level of procurement sophistication, considerations involved in dealing with it (e.g., systematically relating product value to customer needs) can serve the seller well.

THE "BUYING CENTER" CONCEPT

The increasingly complex and professional nature of the procurement function has led to the development of the buying center concept, defined as all individuals and groups that participate in the purchase decision process because they share common risks and goals arising from buying decisions. Membership in buying centers varies with the cost and complexity associated with buying situations, or buyclass categories. These are classified as straight rebuy, modified rebuy, and new task situation.

- *Straight rebuy* situations involve purchase of a routine, repetitive nature, such as office supplies or inexpensive plant maintenance items. Such products require no modifications and are generally purchased on a regular basis from suppliers on the customer's list.

- *Modified rebuy* situations are essentially straight rebuy situations that have been taken out of this category by a change in price or specification. For example, a competitor might offer the present MM customer a similar system at a considerably lower cost.

- *New task* situations involve products never purchased before, thus entailing a higher degree of cost and risk than usually associated with straight or modified rebuy situations (e.g., purchasing expensive MM systems for the first time). These situations typically involve a larger number of people and a greater need for product information focusing on product specifications, price limits, delivery, service, payment terms, order quantities, and vendor acceptability standards.

Understanding how a company's products are perceived in terms of these buyclass categories can help salespeople recognize competitive threats and opportunities and do a more creative job of serving customer needs. Here are some of these threat/opportunity situations:

- *Threat:* A competitor tries to transform a straight rebuy situation involving an MM system into a modified rebuy or new task situation involving a system claimed to be superior.

- *Opportunity:* The salesperson turns a competitive straight rebuy situation into a modified rebuy situation favoring the MM system.

- _Opportunity:_ The salesperson creates new task situations for MM systems by creating request-for-proposal situations in which she dramatizes savings and efficiencies.

ROLES OF BUYING CENTER MEMBERS

Understanding and responding to buyclass situations also requires an understanding of the various roles assumed by buying center members involved in these situations. For example, in preparing her presentation in behalf of the MM electronic training and development system, the salesperson dealt with:

- A _gatekeeper_ who controls the information flow; in this case, a chief procurement officer who assessed her concept and decided whether, and in what form, it warranted further consideration.

- Two _influentials_, in the form of EDP and T&D managers, who were enthusiastic about installation of the new system and helped develop specifications for the system.

- A _decider_, in the form of the human resources manager who made the final decision as to whether the system would be purchased and from what supplier.

- A _buyer_, with whom the salesperson negotiated details of the sale.

- The _user_, the T&D manager responsible for the operation of the system, who identified the need for it in the first place.

In modified rebuy and new task situations, planning the sales presentation typically involves anticipating which roles will be supportive and hostile to the purchase decision, and how they will interact.

In the case of simple, inexpensive straight rebuy products, major influences motivating favorable purchase decisions are usually personal in nature, often based on social friendships between buyer and seller. As products become more complex and costly, however, industrial salespeople must deal with more people assuming more roles and with more customer concerns in a variety of areas. Typical economic concerns, for example, focus on cost/benefit relationships, product and supplier reliability, and product guarantees and warranties. Environmental concerns focus on the likelihood of materials shortages, competitive advantages, and technological obsolescence. Organizational concerns focus on the compatibility of products with the firm's systems and procedures.

BUYPHASE ACTIVITIES

In addition to classifying product procurement situations into buyclasses, modern materials management departments and salespeople calling on these departments also classify procurement activities into buyphases, which they relate to each buyclass situation. Table 10-3 outlines such buyclass activities typically associated with each buyclass situation to provide guidelines for covering each situation efficiently and productively.

Table 10–3. Buyphase Activities Related to Buyclass Situations

STAGES OF THE BUYING PROCESS (BUYPHASES)	BUYING SITUATIONS (BUYCLASSES)		
	New task	Modified rebuy	Straight rebuy
1. Problem recognition	Yes	Maybe	No
2. General need description	Yes	Maybe	No
3. Product specification	Yes	Yes	Yes
4. Supplier search	Yes	Maybe	No
5. Proposal solicitation	Yes	Maybe	No
6. Supplier selection	Yes	Maybe	No
7. Order routine specification	Yes	Maybe	No
8. Performance review	Yes	Yes	Yes

Source: Adapted from Patrick J. Robinson, Charles W. Faris, and Yocam Wind, *Industrial Buying and Creative Marketing* (Boston: Allyn & Bacon, 1967), p. 14.

Buyphase activities, all of which would probably come into play in a new task situation, entail first recognizing a problem (e.g., the need for more efficient training and development methods) and then describing the need in terms of performance standards to be achieved in addressing this problem. Subsequent steps would involve translating his need into product specifications and then embarking on a supplier search for the vendor best able to meet these specifications. Proposals solicited from possible vendors would be the basis of a final supplier selection, which might use a rating scale depicted in Table 10-4, which shows how a selected vendor achieved a score of 3.6 in terms of criteria the buyer considered most important.

**Table 10–4. Vendor Analysis Rating Scale Evaluation of
Performance of Merton's Industrial Division**

ATTRIBUTES	RATING SCALE				
	Unacceptable (0)	Poor (1)	Fair (2)	Good (3)	Excellent (4)
Technical and production capabilities					x
Financial strength				x	
Product reliability					x
Delivery reliability				x	
Service capability					x
4 + 3 + 4 + 3 + 4 = 18					
Average score: 18/5 = 3.6					

The final two steps of the buyphase process involve the following activities.

- *Order routine specification.* The purchasing agent on the buying team writes the final order for the supplier (or suppliers) selected to develop the new system. Covered in this order are technical specifications for system components, delivery times, performance standards, costs, and warranties.

- *Performance review.* This final buyphase stage encompasses procedures for monitoring the supplier's performance to ensure compliance with the contract. Essentially, performance is evaluated against criteria used during the supplier selection stage to review proposals.

As shown in Table 10-3, the number of buyphase stages involved varies with the buyclass situation, with only product specification (stage 3) and performance review (stage 8) typically involved in a straight rebuy situation. An effective industrial salesperson can recognize, and often create, buyphase stages and become actively involved in each stage. For example, during the buyphase stages leading up to the purchase of the MM, the salesperson helped buying team members recognize and describe the problem (stages 1 and 2), design the system to help solve the problem (stage 3), and establish standards for supplier acceptability (stage 4), which she knew Merton could meet. During stage 5, she prepared a proposal that was as much a sales as a technical document, and that helped assure Merton's selection during stage 6. In effect, she was working as a member of the manufacturer's buying team, helping to define and solve problems and ensuring that specifications drawn up would include Merton's products. For firms selling industrial products in international markets, it is important to recognize different conventions regarding spec- ifications in working with customers to create sales. For example, margins of error allowed on specifications differ dramatically; generally, in Europe and Japan, they are exact. For example, if a beam is purchased to carry 20,000 pounds, that is the maximum weight it can carry. In the United States, the beam will usually have a sufficiently large safety factor built in to cover overload situations.

This anatomy of a sale also illustrates systems buying, whereby firms find it more profitable to purchase an entire turnkey operation system from one or two vendors than to purchase and combine system compo- nents themselves. For sellers, systems buying represents an opportunity to create profitable modified rebuy and new task situations to help win and hold accounts by promoting groups of interlocking products.

THE RESELLER MARKET

The reseller market consists mainly of retailers and wholesalers who pur- chase products to resell or rent to others at a profit. Sometimes these resale products are finished goods (e.g., automobiles or appliances) that are mar- keted to consumers; in other instances, some processing or repackaging may take place, as when lumber dealers process car loads of lumber to the specifications of individual customers. Like the producer market, the reseller market in industrialized and postindustrialized countries is usually larger than the entire consumer market. Reseller markets will be covered in greater detail in the Chapter 18 discussion of the place component of the marketing mix.

INTERNATIONAL GOVERNMENTS

As noted in Chapter 6, government policies and practices are responsible, in large measure, for the size, growth, competitiveness, and openness of many global markets in developed economies. Additionally, these govern- ments represent excellent markets themselves, with unique characteristics and purchasing practices that marketers should account for in strategic planning.

From the perspective of the global marketer selling in increasingly democratic international markets, the fact that governments must respond to the will of the electorate has a number of significant implications. To ensure public review, many products are purchased through a mandatory bidding procedure, and governments often are required to accept the lowest bid. Contracts for products not easily described, or without effective competition, can be negotiated directly but, in any case, the ability to write clear specifications and precisely identify costs is important to marketers interested in serving the government market. Also important is an understanding of the environmental, organizational, and interpersonal factors that influence government buying decisions. These are generally similar to those in the producer segment, except that government buying decisions are more likely to be influenced by noneconomic criteria such as the needs of depressed industries, the perceived need for weapons, or the mandates of policies favoring various constituencies, such as small businesses, the elderly, or protected industries. A tolerance for considerable paperwork involved in dealing with complex bureaucracies characterizing government purchasing practices is also helpful.

CHAPTER PERSPECTIVE

An understanding of consumer and organizational buying behavior in international markets is critical to ensure successful marketing planning, help segment markets, devise marketing mix strategies, measure potential, forecast sales, and control marketing effectiveness. In consumer markets, information for marketing planning is based on an understanding of the influence of inter- and intrapersonal variables on buying decisions. In organizational markets, which are composed of industrial producers, trade industries, and governments, marketing planning is based largely on an understanding of unique needs and characteristics of this market. Particularly in developed countries, it is much larger and more concentrated than the consumer market, creating excellent sales and profit opportunities. However, it is an extremely price-conscious market, often dependent on what happens in consumer markets, the availability of other products, and reciprocity arrangements.

KNOW THE CONCEPTS

TERMS FOR STUDY

accelerator principle	better terms
attitude	buyclasses
best vendor situation	buying center

buyphases
capital items
concentrated demand
consumer behavior
decider
derived demand
direct purchasing
elastic/inelastic demand
expense items
family of orientation/procreation
financial risk
fluctuating demand
gatekeeper
gender-based groups
government market
industrial producer market
influentials
interpersonal variables
intrapersonal variables
joint demand
leasing
life-style

membership groups
modified rebuy
motives
MRO items
new item situation
new task situation
OEM items
offsets
organizational market
perception
performance risk
profit center
reciprocal arrangements
reference groups
reseller market
social class
social risk
straight rebuy
systems buying
trade industries
turnkey operations
users

MATCHUP EXERCISES

1. Match up the promotional campaign outcome in the second column with the group that most influenced this outcome listed in the first column.

1. aspirational group

2. disassociative group

3. families of orientation

4. gender-based groups

a. Campbell Soup stresses convenience in promoting soup to mothers in Poland, where 98 percent of soups are homemade.

b. Levi Strauss features Iowa teenagers in advertising its jeans in Indonesia.

c. Dial soap achieves global success with its "Aren't you glad you use Dial" standardized campaign.

d. Harley-Davidson improves its product and image to attract a new market in Japan—young managers who don't want oil spilled on their Gucci loafers.

2. Match the campaign strategy in the second column with the associated purchase risk listed in the first column.

1. performance risk	a. Perrier mineral water promoted itself as being served in the best restaurants.
2. psychological risk	b. General Mills' Toy Group's European subsidiary, launching its G.I. Joe product line, has to change its commercials in Germany and Belgium, which ban advertising with violent or military themes.
3. financial risk	c. Zippo lighters offer an unconditional money-back guarantee.
4. social risk	d. The Rich Lumber Company of Beardstown, Illinois, ships a British contractor a trial container of kitchen cabinet doors to quality-test for 6 months.

3. Match the industrial product in the second column with the product category listed in the first column.

1. capital items	a. At Goodyear's R&D center in Akron, Ohio, computerized workstations test tire durability, traction, fuel efficiency, and compatibility with new car designs.
2. expense items	b. A division of Textron makes gas turbine engines for the M1 tank.
3. MRO items	c. Schaffer Eaton sells pens and paper products to law and accounting firms.
4. OEM items	d. E-Z-Go makes utility vehicles used in factory materials handling operations.

4. Match the types of organizational market transactions in the first column with the situations described in the second column.

1. modified rebuy	a. Rosegate Technology, a Cincinnati-based distributor of used equipment, enlists the help of Russian physicians to upgrade ultrasound equipment in Russian hospitals.

2. new task

    b. Crystal International Corp. of New Orleans receives another order for its popular hot sauce from its Jordanian distributor.

3. straight rebuy

    c. Allied Signal Corp. of Morristown, N.J., sells turbocharger, filters, and other automotive aftermarket products to Mexican carriers to help them conform to new NAFTA-mandated truck emissions standards.

5. Match the roles involved in the industrial buying process listed in the first column with the situation described in the second column pertaining to efforts by the Toys 'R' Us Corporation to construct retail outlets in Japan.

1. gatekeeper

    a. Japanese consumers complain about the exorbitantly high prices they must pay for toys, largely because of the Large Store law, which effectively protects politically powerful small Japanese storekeepers from large retailers.

2. decider

    b. Following the law, the Japanese Ministry of trade and industry (MITI) often manages to stall incursions into the Japanese market by large retailers, even local ones.

3. buyers

    c. By 1990, under pressure from the U.S. government and Japanese consumers, MITI changes the Large Store law to permit larger discount retailers to compete in Japan. However, local councils, comprising consumers, merchants, and professionals, often erect barriers to large discounters.

4. influentials

    d. By 1995, Toys 'R' Us had 20 outlets in Japan, each generating at least $15 million.

QUESTIONS FOR REVIEW AND DISCUSSION

1. In the context of the strategic marketing planning process, explain the importance of understanding consumer behavior concepts and processes.

2. Discuss how motives, perceptions, and attitudes might combine to activate the purchase of a Merton MM computer system by a manager in an accounting firm intent on achieving partner status. What would be the general role of marketing in this process?

3. Discuss the difference between organizational and consumer markets with respect to number of transactions and number of products/services involved in these transactions. How would these differences complicate the job of penetrating global organizational (as against consumer) target markets?

4. In the 3 years following the signing of the NAFTA pact, Panamax, Inc., of San Rafael, California, experienced a 1000 percent increase in sales to Mexican distributors of surge protectors used primarily with personal computers and accessories, although sales to end-user consumers increased by only half this amount. Explain how derived demand and the accelerator principle might have accounted for this dramatic increase in demand and for the equally dramatic decrease in demand when the peso collapsed in early 1994 and again in 1995.

5. Following up on question 4, describe how concentrated demand, direct purchases, and reciprocal arrangements might have characterized Panamax's successful entry into the Mexican market.

6. In 1986, the Finnish Air Force (FAF) decided to modernize its fighter fleet by replacing the aging Swedish-made Drakens and Soviet-made MIG 21s that comprised this fleet. In 1992, after protracted negotiations, the Finnish government selected the McDonnell Douglas (MDC) Hornet over a number of competitive models from Sweden, France, and the United States. At the onset of these negotiations, MDC, which wasn't among the aircraft companies invited to submit proposals, figured it had only a 5 percent chance of closing the deal but decided the size of the contract made it worth the effort. The $2 billion deal finally signed involved delivery of 57 F/A-18 Cs and 7 F/A-18 Ds between 1995 and 2000. Representing the Finnish government in these negotiations were the following agencies: (1) the Ministry of Defense, which, working with the FAF general staff, determined criteria for selection (e.g., specifications, delivery dates, prices), and made final purchase decisions but turned most of the actual negotiating over to (2) the Ministry of Trade and Industry, assisted by a (3) Technical Working Group. Also involved in negotiations was (4) the Finnish Offset Committee, which was composed of technical special-

ists and representatives of business and government who determined offset commitments by the winning bidder.

a. Speculate on (1) the roles of the Finish agencies and committees involved in these negotiations during the six buyphases of the organizational buying process and (2) MDC's role during these buyphases. (Note: MDC's group was called the F-18 Team.)

b. Discuss buyer roles that might have been assumed by members of Finnish government negotiating agencies and committees that the F-18 Team could relate to.

7. Discuss how the following products would have been involved in the manufacture of the F/A 18s discussed in question 6: expense items, capital items, MRO items, and OEM items.

8. The Second Chance Company of Central Lake, Michigan, markets bullet-resistant vests to foreign countries through a network of native police and military personnel. Discuss how, on a given day, Second Chance representatives might encounter straight rebuy, modified rebuy, and new task transactions. How would the degree of buyer involvement and the approach of Second Chance sales personnel, differ with each type of transaction?

ANSWERS

MATCHUPS

1. 1b, 2c, 3a, 4d
2. 1c, 2b, 3d, 4a
3. 1a, 2c, 3d, 4b
4. 1a, 2c, 3b
5. 1b, 2d, 3a, 4c

QUESTIONS FOR REVIEW AND DISCUSSION

1. The strategic marketing planning process involves identifying and defining target markets, and matching marketing mix offerings to the nature and needs of these markets. This matching process is done in the context of a company mission, business and marketing objectives that derive from this mission, and strategies based on a researched understanding of how company strengths and weaknesses relate to marketplace threats and opportunities. In terms of this definition of the SMP process, everything—missions, objectives, marketing mix

offerings, strategies—begins with, and depends on, an understanding of consumer behavior: what needs prospective customers have, what products and services the company can profitably market to meet these needs, how these products and services can best be positioned, and so on.

2. A motive is a stimulated need that an individual seeks to satisfy; a perception is the process by which people derive meaning from the selection, organization, and interpretation of stimuli; and an attitude is a tendency to act in a consistent way toward products or classes of products. An example might illustrate how these three variables come together to activate an accountant's purchase of an MM computer system. First, we understand that the accountant is motivated to achieve partner status (the unsatisfied, stimulated need). Further, he or she might perceive (1) that an intensive training program might help to achieve this goal and (2) that the MM computer system, with associated training hardware, is the best such training system available. These perceptions will help condition an attitude tending toward the purchase of the MM system. The role of marketing in this process is to activate motives (e.g., the unfulfilled need to achieve partner status), condition perceptions toward products that will satisfy unfulfilled needs, and, in so doing, also condition favorable attitudes (and actions) toward these products.

3. Because industrial producer and trade organizational markets are intermediaries between the producers of raw materials and ultimate consumers that purchase products made from these raw materials, there are many more transactions, products, and dollars involved in organizational than in consumer markets. For example, the process of making a single pair of shoes for a consumer involves multiple transactions among hide tanners, shoe manufacturers, wholesalers, and retailers involving a diversity of products and services. Reflecting all these transactions, aggregate purchasing power among these industrial producer and trade organizational markets, at least in developing, industrialized, and post-industrialized countries, is invariably much greater than that of consumer markets (in industrialized and post-industrialized countries, usually more than three times greater). This size, diversity, and complexity of the organizational market usually makes it much more challenging and expensive to penetrate than the consumer market.

4. Derived demand means that demand for a product derives from the needs of ultimate customers—in this case, consumers in the Mexican market who used the surge protectors with their personal computers and accessories. When sales of these products increased sharply, Mexican wholesalers handling them ordered much larger amounts for their inventories from Panamax, in anticipation of a continued profitable growth of this market (many also ordered products from other

suppliers to build facilities to handle this inventory). However, when the value of the peso dropped sharply in 1994 and again in 1995, throwing Mexico into a recession in which many U.S. imports became prohibitively expensive, many of these same Mexican distributors that earlier overbought surge protectors now stopped ordering them completely, as a means of reducing now-excessive inventory levels. Thus, purchases, in relation to actual consumer demand, were accelerated at each end of this buying cycle, consistent with the accelerator principle.

5. Although ultimate, end-user demand for Panamax surge protectors are diverse and geographically widespread, the number of distributors (primarily, three large chains of consumer electronics retailers) that had to be contacted directly to reach this market was concentrated both as to number and location (e.g., buyers in Mexico City and environs were responsible for more than 50 percent of sales volume). Reciprocal arrangements might have taken the form of various offsets, such as might relate to coproduction, licensing, subcontracting, investment/technology development, export development, and tourism development in Mexico.

6a. The first buyphase stage of the process—problem recognition—would probably have been the responsibility of the general staff of the Finnish Air Force. The next two stages—preparing general need descriptions and product specifications—would probably have been the responsibility of the Ministry of Defense, working with the FAF general staff. Since actual negotiating was delegated to Ministry of Trade and Industry, this group would be responsible for the next three stages—supplier search, proposal solicitation, and supplier selection. During these buyphases, these groups would be working closely with the Finnish Offset Committee to determine countertrade requirements incorporated into the contract (in the final contract, MDC was obligated to complete an offset program by the year 2002 through a number of elements, including marketing assistance, export development, technology transfer, team purchases, and investment financing). Final approval of the selected firm would be made by the Ministry of Defense. The final two stages—order routine specification and performance review—would be performed by the FAF once the deal was closed.

MDC's role during these buyphases was to continually be ready and able to help the customer with information and assistance. Toward this end, MCD was the only company considered that actually set up a full-time office in Helsinki and was involved with all the constituencies in a full range of activities, such as setting up tests, helping write specifications, and performing background research. Naturally, most of these activities were focused on the F-18 as the aircraft best suited to Finland's needs.

6b. Possible gatekeepers, controlling the flow of information, would include, primarily, the Ministries of Defense and Trade and Industry. Influentials, who could help persuade the negotiators to favor MDC over competitors might include members of the Finnish parliament and high-ranking officers of the previously mentioned ministries. The main decider was the Ministry of Defense, although all involved agencies made key decisions in such areas as supplier selection, specifications, and offsets. The Finnish government (through its purchasing office) was the buyer of the aircraft, and the FAF was the user.

7. Expense items are short-lived goods and services charged off against revenues as used, including raw materials, component materials, and fabricated parts that are relatively inexpensive on a per-unit basis (e.g., batteries and small motors used in the F-18). Capital items are goods used in the production process that do not become part of the final product, including expensive, long-lived installations and accessory equipment such as punch presses and wind tunnels used in manufacturing F-18s. MRO items could be any product—including expense and capital items—used in operating the plant or maintaining and repairing plant equipment. Examples would include lathes, paint, fork-lift trucks, brooms, and polishing cloths. OEM items would include any products used as original equipment in the F-18s such as tires and batteries.

8. In a straight rebuy situation, a buyer would routinely recorder the same Second Chance vests previously ordered; in a modified rebuy situation, the buyer would specify Second Chance vests with some change in price or other specification. For example, the firm might want a lower price for the same vests or be willing to pay the same price for an upgraded model. In any event, some degree of negotiation would be indicated, thus taking this situation out of the routine. A new task situation would entail purchasing bullet-resistant vests for the first time, thus entailing a higher degree of cost and risk in which considerable decision making is undertaken by more decision participants seeking more information on alternative products and suppliers, product specifications, price limits, delivery terms and times, service, payment terms, acceptable suppliers, and the supplier under consideration (Second Chance). Because different decision participants can influence each decision (e.g., users, buyers, influencers), Second Chance salespeople seek to provide product information and other assistance to as many key buying influences as possible. In straight rebuy situations, the salesperson's role is negligible or nonexistent; in modified rebuy situations, where a prospective customer wants to modify product specifications, terms, prices, or suppliers, "out" salespeople are often provided with an opportunity to gain new business by making a better offer.

11

INTERNATIONAL SEGMENTATION, TARGETING, AND POSITIONING STRATEGIES

OVERVIEW

Market segments are groups of high-potential prospective customers with common characteristics and needs that distinguish them from other high-potential market segments. By identifying, defining, and targeting these groups, global marketers improve all aspects of the strategic marketing planning process, including devising attractive marketing mix offerings, formulating segmentation and product positioning strategies for efficiently reaching target markets, and controlling overall plan effectiveness.

A systematic market gridding approach involves applying demographic, geographic, psychographic, and behavioristic criteria to identify and define consumer and organizational target market segments in global markets. Information emerging from this analysis is the basis for choosing appropriate segmentation strategies and effectively positioning products.

TARGET MARKETING IMPROVES MARKET PLANNING

In previous chapters, we examined environmental influences that affect strategic marketing planning and shape buying behavior among members of global consumer and organizational markets. In this chapter, we build on this background and offer a systematic approach for segmenting large market aggregates into smaller groups of customers, called target markets, each of which differs from the others in terms of its response to marketing mix offerings. To illustrate, Procter and Gamble has identified six different market segments for Crest toothpaste, based on age and ethnic differences (e.g., children, Latinos, African Americans) and attempts to appeal to each using different promotion, distribution, and product positioning strategies.

Most products sold internationally in consumer and organizational markets lend themselves to a segmentation strategy, which is basic to formulating, implementing, and controlling strategic marketing plans. An important advantage of a segmentation strategy is its consistency with the Pareto principle: Typically, a relatively small proportion of total potential customers will purchase a disproportionately large share of product. Figure 11-1, for example, shows this relationship among consumers of beer in the United States. Note that only 32 percent of the entire population drinks all the beer consumed, with 16 percent of the population responsible for almost 90 percent of beer consumption. Included among many other products for which this general pattern holds are cereals, shampoo, paper towels, dog food, soaps and detergents, industrial metals, and MRO and OEM products.

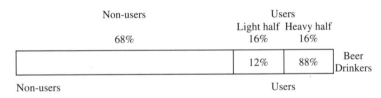

Figure 11–1. Beer Consumption Pattern in the United States

From the marketer's perspective, this disproportionate market size/purchase potential relationship offers a diversity of pluses in the strategic planning process. First, economies and efficiencies derive from tapping most of the buying power in a given market by targeting a small percentage of the market's population. Additionally, by specifying target customers and their needs, a segmentation strategy helps marketers position products and create marketing mixes responsive to these needs, enhancing customer loyalty and competitive posture.

An effective segmentation strategy also helps to measure overall market size (covered in Chapter 13); recognize, and respond to, competitive threats; and budget and control marketing performance. In sum, an effective segmentation strategy leads to the selection of the most attractive combination of markets and products and to the strategic elements best calculated to bring them together.

SEGMENTATION STRATEGY OPTIONS

Essential to any segmentation strategy are decisions defining how many market segments will be encompassed by the firm's marketing program and how boundaries for these segments will be established. At one extreme, the marketer might elect to consider all actual or prospective customers as comprising a single market and design a single offering to satisfy needs in this single market. At the other extreme, the marketing manager might consider each customer a unique, discrete market in itself and devise distinctive offerings to appeal to each. An example of this is large airframe manufacturers (Lockheed, Boeing) serving a relatively small number of large airlines (Lufthansa, United, Qantas, etc.).

Along this spectrum from total to individual target market segments, three segmentation strategies can be identified: undifferentiated (mass marketing), concentrated (product differentiated), and differentiated (target marketing).

• *UNDIFFERENTIATED*

The undifferentiated strategy attempts to appeal to an entire market with a single basic marketing strategy intended to have mass appeal. For example, at one time, Coca-Cola produced only one drink for the entire soft drink market. The major advantage of this strategy is mass market economies of scale from mass production and marketing efficiencies. The major disadvantage is that "cherry picker" competitors, with offerings attractive to subsegments of the mass market, can undercut the mass marketing strategy.

• *CONCENTRATED*

The concentrated strategy provides multiple offerings to the same well-defined target market. For example, Coca-Cola, to maintain its competitive lead, packaged its soft drinks in different sizes and containers in order to offer variety to its basic market rather than appeal to different segments within this market. The main advantage of this strategy is higher sales and brand loyalty among members of the targeted market. The main disadvantage is that the "all eggs in one basket" philosophy means that the firm depends on conditions in a single market and is vulnerable to competitors who segment their markets using a differentiated target-marketing strategy.

• *DIFFERENTIATED*

The differentiated strategy selects and develops offerings tailored to the needs of specific target market segments. For example, Coca-Cola now produces soft drinks for the diet segment (Diet Coke and Tab), the sugared-cola segment (Coca-Cola Classic, Cherry Coke), and the no-caffeine segment (Caffeine Free Coke). For most products sold in consumer markets, this strategy helps identify marketing opportunities more effectively than does the mass marketing approach and avoids dependence on a single market characterizing the product differentiated strategy. However, as the number of market segments served increases (each with its own marketing mix offering), total costs increase while economies of scale decline.

CRITERIA THAT DEFINE WORTHWHILE SEGMENTS

In working to identify, define, and prioritize worthwhile target market segments for its MM computer systems in international markets and to decide on the most appropriate segmentation strategy to reach these segments, Merton marketing planners applied five criteria designed to identify the optimum number of market segments beyond which overall profits will begin to decline: (1) substantial, (2) homogeneous within, (3) heterogeneous with respect to other segments, (4) accessible, and (5) operational.

To illustrate these criteria, consider one segment of Merton's domestic market: lawyers. Beginning with "Administrative and Government Law" to "Worker's Compensation," there are at least three dozen recognized legal specializations for which Merton could develop computer software packages. Some, like "Corporation," "Divorce and Family Law," and "General Practice" were large practices; others, like "Computer Law," "Entertainment Law," and "Landlord and Tenant Law" were small, but growing.

To qualify as a segment of Merton's target market, the prospective segment would first have to be sufficiently large—substantial—to justify the effort and expense of developing a discrete marketing mix, including software design, distribution, and promotional programs geared to member needs. Then, its members would have to be sufficiently homogeneous with respect to MADR criteria that define them as a market segment: They can afford MM systems (money), have the authority and desire to use them, and will respond similarly to the same marketing mix offering.

Additionally, members of sufficiently substantial, homogeneous markets should be sufficiently different from other prospective groups (i.e., heterogeneous) to justify treatment as a discrete entity. For example, environmental lawyers would require completely different software programs, and promotional appeals, than corporate lawyers.

Particularly important in international markets would be the fourth criteria—accessibility—meaning that the segment, no matter how desirable, could be profitably reached by Merton communication and distribution programs.

Finally, the segment should be operational to the extent that characteristics of the segment (e.g., size, purchasing power, and basic needs) can be measured. For example, in certain ex-communist bloc countries, few data exist regarding the nature and needs of various legal specialties common in the United States.

Note that these five segmentation criteria can be viewed as either qualifying or determining in nature—an important distinction when devising a segmentation strategy. Qualifying criteria are the same for all market segments. For example, all segments of the legal profession served in Merton's domestic market were sufficiently substantial and accessible to justify developing offerings to meet their needs. Also, the needs of all these target market members can be measured and used to develop these offerings, so the operational criteria is met. However, each segment also possesses determining characteristics that distinguish it from other segments (e.g., "homogeneous within" and "heterogeneous without" software needs), and these characteristics will determine how Merton's offering will differ from offerings designed for other segments of the legal market.

In international markets, these determining criteria are particularly important in distinguishing and defining markets among nations and between other nations and the United States. Consumers in different countries have varied geographic, demographic, economic, and cultural characteristics, leading to different needs and wants. To the extent that these characteristics are similar among countries, a standardized marketing approach might be indicated to reach these consumers.

BASES FOR SEGMENTING MARKETS

Larger market aggregates may be subdivided into smaller target markets on the basis of geographic, demographic, psychographic, and behavioristic criteria. A key problem for global marketers is determining criteria most appropriate for specific situations, and the order in which to apply them.

• *GEOGRAPHIC CRITERIA*

Geographic criteria focus on locating prospective target markets and distinguishing characteristics associated with each location. Marketing managers can focus on a single area, a few areas, or many areas, depending on such considerations as the size of each geographic area and the cost of serving it. If more than one area is selected, offerings may be tailored to different natures and needs among these areas. In Switzerland, for example, three different languages—German, French, and Italian—are spoken in three contiguous areas, the only significant difference in qualifying markets in these areas.

• *DEMOGRAPHIC CRITERIA*

Demographic criteria refer to such state-of-being measures as age, sex, family size, family life-cycle stage, income, occupation, and nationality. All can be used to identify and define target markets and to develop offerings attractive to each segment. Examples of these criteria follow.

Variable	Possible Segments	Products
Age	Child, adult, senior citizen	Toys, Medigap insurance
Sex	Male, female	Cosmetics, sporting equipment
Family size	1, 2, 3, 4 or more	Packaged soup, minivans
Occupation	Professional and technical, managers, clerical, sales, students, retired, unemployed	Work shoes, MM computer systems
Nationality	American, British, Italian, Japanese	Ethnic foods, movies

Largely because of country-to-country differences in economic, cultural, political and technological environments, international markets tend to be more heterogeneous than domestic markets with respect to these demographic variables.

• *PSYCHOGRAPHIC*

Psychographic criteria are "state-of-mind" variables that have a direct influence on buyer behavior. They include social class, personality, and life-style, as measured by such instruments as the AIO (Attitudes, Interest, Opinions) test. For example, here is how psychographic segmentation was used to identify and define target markets for soft drinks in Australia.

Soft Drink Brand	AIO Profile Related Positively to Brand	AIO Profile Related Negatively to Brand
Solo	Adventure seeker, extrovert Australian chauvinist	Economic conservative, social conservative, authoritarian
Swing	Cynic, extrovert, social conservative	Family cohesion, critical consumer, Australian conservative
Tab	Family cohesion, thrifty consumer, critical consumer	Cynic, extrovert, social conservative

Note that most of the AIO profile characteristics that predict a favorable response to one soft drink also predict an unfavorable response to others, an important finding in positioning (or repositioning) a soft drink brand to appeal to a defined market segment or in developing a marketing mix to support this positioning strategy.

• *BEHAVIORISTIC*

Behavioristic criteria define target market groups in terms of how market members behave, as consumers, toward a seller's offering: how frequently they use it, how loyal they are toward it, what benefits they seek from it, and so on. These criteria are useful both in defining dimensions of a target segment and in devising marketing mixes to appeal to defined segments.

Here are some behavioristic variables Merton planners used to define target markets and design attractive offerings for prospective Merton target segments in the legal profession.

OCCASIONS

Market segments can be identified in terms of occasions when its members get the idea to actually buy or use the product. For example, the planners identified periods during the year when tax accountants would have most use for MM systems and timed promotional programs to coincide with these periods.

BENEFITS SOUGHT

An unusually effective base for behavior segmentation focuses on benefits to which market segments will respond favorably. For example, among tax attorneys, Merton planners found that the major benefit desired in a tax and financial planning software was the timeliness of content. This and other desired benefits were incorporated into products and promotions designed for each group.

USER STATUS

Frequently, market segments can be defined and cultivated based on the extent to which segment members use the product. Merton planners, for example, developed profiles of groups that were not interested in using personal computers (nonusers); groups that had purchased a Merton personal computer in the past and then purchased another brand (ex-users); and groups that relied exclusively on Merton MM systems (regular users). Analyses of these profiles provided insights into the size and characteristics of prospective target market segments and strategies to attract or keep worthwhile customer groups.

USAGE RATE

As noted earlier, many products sold in consumer and organizational markets can be defined in terms of the relatively small percent of the population that purchases a disproportionate quantity of that product. Merton planners found that, in their training programs, three legal practices— divorce and family law, corporate law, and tax law—purchased more than 80 percent of Merton systems purchased. Analyses of reasons for this concentration suggested strategies for maintaining the loyalty of these segments and attracting other practices to MM systems.

LOYALTY STATUS

This behavioristic measure focuses on degrees of product loyalty as defined by usuage patterns. For example, the following profiles of MM users were used in positioning, pricing, and promoting MM systems to different legal practices.

- Hard core loyals repurchased Merton computers and associated Merton software.

- Soft core loyals purchased a diversity of computers and software in addition to Merton systems.

- Switchers were generally loyal to Merton computer systems but were willing to switch brands if a better offer was made.

BUYER READINESS

At any point, actual and prospective buyers may be in different stages of readiness to purchase products or services. With respect to MM systems, some might be completely unaware of their features and benefits; others may be aware but not especially interested; still others may be informed, others interested, and others eagerly desiring to purchase a Merton MM system. Segmenting markets in terms of these buyer-readiness stages can provide useful cues for positioning and promoting products. For example, in different foreign markets, any of these responses to the Merton MM— from unawareness to desire—might be anticipated and responded to in designing promotional materials and positioning MM systems.

EVALUATING AND USING SEGMENTATION BASES

In general, demographic and geographic criteria are not as useful as psychographic or behavioristic variables in determining what actually motivates people to buy products and devising appealing marketing mixes based on this understanding. For example, knowledge of a woman's motives for purchasing a particular brand of perfume or of the benefits she expects from this perfume would be considerably more useful in promoting this perfume than the demographic fact of her gender or the geographic fact that she lives in Houston. However useful, these demographic and geographic criteria must be incorporated into the mix if only to qualify prospective customers (e.g., can they afford the product? are they accessible?). This is especially the case in global markets, with their diverse, heterogeneous markets.

The key to successful segmentation, discussed next, is to group significant criteria variables (demographic, psychographic, etc.) into clusters that maximize within-group similarities and between-group differences, while suggesting strategies for melding marketing mix components.

IDENTIFYING AND DEFINING MARKET SEGMENTS

We will now demonstrate a procedure for identifying, defining, and prioritizing worthwhile market segments as used by Merton in exploring opportunities in international markets.

SELECT PRODUCT/MARKET AREA

The first step in the process involved determining which target markets in the global marketplace would be served from Merton's portfolio of computers and associated software. While, conceivably, a full range of Merton computers and software could be marketed globally, the initial decision was to go with the two markets that had proven most profitable in the United States—accountants and legal firms—and the MM models, with associated software, to serve these markets.

QUALIFY PROSPECTIVE INTERNATIONAL MARKETS

The first series of segmentation criteria applied to international markets was designed to qualify countries deserving of further study. These qualifying criteria included factors examined earlier in discussions of political, economic, competitive, technological, and cultural considerations, including the country's stage of economic development, population size and makeup, per-capita income, political stability and attitude toward trade, social structures, and cultural and technological conditions favorable to Merton's profitable entry and growth. Qualifying criteria were then applied to markets within countries that weren't screened out, including existence of legal and accounting markets that met desired standards (accessible, substantial, operative, etc.), competitive conditions in these markets, and market growth trends.

In applying these qualifying criteria to countries and markets, Merton planners used a market gridding approach that showed the cumulative impact of a cluster of segmentation variables within and among countries. Figure 11-2, for example, shows the interaction of 3 variables—GNP growth rate, per-capita income growth rate, and specific country.

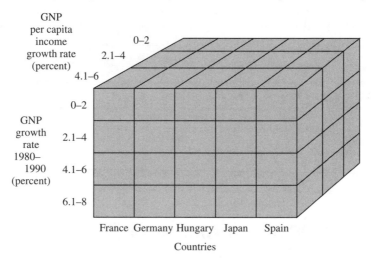

Figure 11–2. Segmentation of International Market by Three Variables

DETERMINE WORTHWHILE TARGET MARKETS

After qualifying segmentation criteria had been applied to countries and markets, product-related determining criteria were applied to markets that were not screened out by the qualifying criteria. Included were demographic (occupation, education, etc.), psychographic (life-style, personality), and behavioristic (benefits, purchase occasion, etc.) criteria that tended to define product acceptance and profit potential in the U.S. market.

PROFILE AND PRIORITIZE SEGMENTS

This final step in the process involved briefly profiling each segment in terms of the cluster of segmentation variables characteristic of each, and listing these profiled segments in priority order according to three factors—sales potential, prospective return on investment, and ease of market entry.

CHOOSING A SEGMENTATION STRATEGY IN THE CONSUMER MARKET

After identifying, defining, and prioritizing prospectively profitable international market segments, Merton planners faced the problem of choosing a suitable segmentation strategy for markets selected for entry. Table 11-1 shows some considerations involved in the selection of three possible strategies—undifferentiated mass marketing, product differentiated, and target marketing:

Table 11–1. Segementation Strategies Related to Product/Market Characteristics

PRODUCT/MARKET CHARACTERISTICS	SEGMENTATION STRATEGY OPTIONS		
	Undifferentiated	Concentrated	Differentiated
Company resources	Sufficient	Limited	Sufficient
Product homogeneity	Homogeneous (e.g. steel)	Capable of being differentiated	Capable of being differentiated
Product life-cycle stage	Introductory stage	Introductory stage	Mature stage
Market homogeneity	If buyers have same MAD R characteristics	Buyer groups have different MAD-R characteristics	Buyer groups have different MAD-R characteristics
Competitive strategies		Competitors practice undifferentiated strategies	Competitors practice undifferentiated strategies

Based on this matrix data, for example, the planners would select an undifferentiated mass marketing strategy in situations where all prospective buyers had the same MADR characteristics (e.g., if the only really substantial market in a territory comprised tax accountants), the product was new to the country, with no competition (introductory stage), and Merton resources were sufficient to undertake the mass production and marketing initiatives required to serve this mass market.

Then, as these conditions changed (e.g., multiple profitable markets, with diverse product needs, are identified, along with a changed competitive environment characterizing more mature life-cycle stages), product differentiated and target marketing strategies are indicated.

CHOOSING A SEGMENTATION STRATEGY IN THE ORGANIZATIONAL MARKET

Many of the same criteria used to segment consumer markets can be used to segment producer and reseller components of organizational markets, including geographic bases and such behavioral bases as benefits sought, user status, usage rate, loyalty status, and readiness stage. As shown in Table 11-2 a number of other criteria also come into play relating to industrial consumer demographics, operating characteristics, purchasing approaches, situational factors, and personal characteristics.

Table 11–2. Major Segmentation Variables for Industrial Markets

Demographic
> *Industry:* which industries that buy this product should we focus on?
> *Company size:* what size companies should we focus on?
> *Location:* what geographical areas should we focus on?

Operating variables
> *Technology:* what customer technologies should we focus on?
> *User/non-user status:* should we focus on heavy, medium, or light users or non-users?
> *Customer capabilities:* should we focus on customers needing many services or few services?

Purchasing approaches
> *Purchasing function organization:* should we focus on companies with highly centralized or decentralized purchasing organizations?
> *Power structure:* should we focus on companies that are engineering dominated, financially dominated, or marketing-dominated?
> *Nature of existing relationships:* should we focus on companies with which we already have strong relationships or simply go after the most desirable companies?
> *General purchase policies:* should we focus on companies that prefer leasing? Service contracts? Systems purchases? Sealed bidding?
> *Purchasing criteria:* should we focus on companies that are seeking quality? Service? Price?

Situational factors
> *Urgency:* should we focus on companies that need quick and sudden delivery or service?
> *Specific application:* should we focus on certain applications of our product rather than all applications?
> *Size of order:* should we focus on large or small orders?

Table 11–2. *Continued*

Personal characteristics
  Buyer-seller similarity: should we focus on companies whose people and values
    are similar to ours?
  Attitudes toward risk: should we focus on risk taking or risk avoiding customers?
  Loyalty: should we focus on companies that show high loyalty to their suppliers?

Source: Adapted from Thomas V. Bonoma and Benson P. Shapiro, *Segmenting the Industrial Market* (Lexington, MA: Lexington Books, 1983).

Frequently, as with consumer segmentation strategies, criteria can be combined, as illustrated in the Figure 11-3 flowchart showing options for a manufacturer of chip circuits. Three potential markets include (1) resellers that will sell the chips to retailers that, in turn, will sell them to electronics hobbyists; (2) manufacturing firms that will use the chips as original equipment in products they manufacture (such as laptop computers); and (3) manufacturing firms that will use the chips in machinery (e.g., robotics, computers) that will be used in production and maintenance operations. In terms of customer size, planners determined that the most lucrative market was businesses that will use the chips for OEM applications, which was more than twice as large as the next largest category. Subsequent analyses identified industries with the greatest demand for the chips, as well as benefits desired and readiness stages.

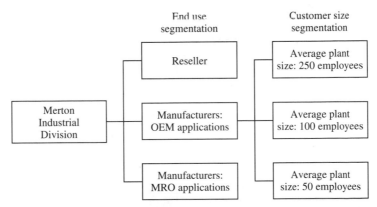

Figure 11–3. Segmenting the Industrial Market with "End User" and "Customer Size" Segmentation

MARKET POSITIONING: FIND A SAFE NICHE

Once the market for the product has been segmented and a segmentation strategy decided upon, marketers must decide what positions the product can most profitably occupy in each selected segment. The concept of product position is an extension of the brand image concept, defined as the sum of perceptions, favorable or unfavorable, about attributes of a product based on consumers' experience and knowledge of the product. In brief, a product's position is its brand image with respect to competing products—the way the product is competitively defined by consumers on key attributes.

The three-dimensional perceptual map in Figure 11-4 illustrates an approach for deciding on a product positioning strategy in defined target market segments. This map assumes three major attributes of concern to managing partners in law firms in selecting computer systems for professional personnel: timeliness, in that software content reflects current developments in such areas as tax and environmental law; efficiency, in that the material can be conveyed quickly and effectively to extremely busy, costly attorneys; and cost of the systems.

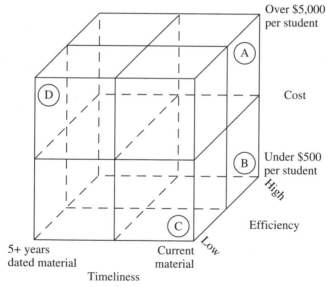

Figure 11-4. Perceptual Map Helps Determine Positioning Strategies

Given these criteria, the Merton MM might be positioned as perceived by consumers in the A quadrant of the map, as extremely efficient, timely, and costly. This perceptual map also assumes that competitors are already positioned in two other map quadrants (i.e., low cost, timely, and efficient [B] and low cost, timely, and less efficient [C]).

Here are some guidelines for deciding where to position a product in terms of perceived important attributes and in relation to other competitors. The product should be positioned in an unoccupied quadrant if:

- There are a sufficient number of buyers to justify the position (not too likely in the unoccupied low efficiency, high cost, low timeliness portion of unoccupied quadrant D).

- The position is feasible (e.g., consistent with the firm's mission, affordable, and technologically doable).

The product should be positioned in a quadrant occupied by competitors if:

- The preceding conditions for positioning the product in an unoccupied quadrant prevail.

- The product can be made (or be perceived to be) superior to competitive offerings.

Given these conditions and limitations, Merton planners had experienced difficulty in effectively positioning MM systems in cluttered quadrants of the domestic market and looked forward to positioning the systems in less cluttered international target market segments. Global Focus 11-1 illustrates this process of building an effective international marketing strategy around a strong product position.

GLOBAL FOCUS 11-1

Non-Alcoholic Wine Exporter Toasts World Markets

As owner of San Francisco-based Creative Juices (CJ), Lori Foster is marketing her non-alcoholic wine substitutes to users in the United States and most recently in Europe.

"Our wine substitute is superior to other wine imitations because of its exemplary taste," she says. "This is because our product never has any alcoholic content to begin with—all the other non-alcoholic wines on the market are actually wines with the alcohol removed."

"Taking the alcohol out of wine requires a heating process that also destroys the original flavor of the wine," says Foster. "Our wine is never fermented," she says, "so you get the original flavor of our Chardonnay and Zinfandel grapes without the alcohol."

Creative juices distributes most of its wines under the private labels of large chain stores, high-end gift stores, and catalogs. Major market segments include upper-level high-schoolers who wish to enjoy the drinking experience without consequences of alcohol beverages, and adults seeking health benefits associated with reduced alcohol consumption.

Structuring her marketing strategy around its position as the non-alcoholic wine with an exemplary taste, Foster achieved profitable growth in the U.S. domestic market, and hadn't really considered the export market until she heard about a "Women in Trade" mission to Amsterdam and London in September 1995.

Foster signed up, and was one of 22 businesswomen to participate. "My biggest surprise in Amsterdam was finding out how willing they were to try a new product," she says. "I started showing a bottle to the Amsterdam distributor, and he actually grabbed it out of my hand and ran to show his friends."

As a result of the trade mission, Foster ultimately won a contract to supply Creative Juices to a grocery store chain in Amsterdam. "Through the stores, we sold 1,500 cases of our wine substitute in just two weeks," says Foster, who credits the healthy Dutch life style for her product's wide appeal in that country.

Creative Juices is also exploring opportunities with major airlines, restaurants, and interest from the United Arab Emirites, Canada, and Asia.

Source: Curtice K. Coultice, "Bottoms Up," *Business America*, the U.S. Department of Commerce (October, 1996), pp. 25–27.

CHAPTER PERSPECTIVE

Identifying and defining profitable, high-potential target markets can upgrade all aspects of the strategic marketing process, including devising attractive marketing mixes, evolving strategies for bringing mixes and markets together, and controlling marketing effectiveness. Important aspects of global segmentation processes include the systematic application of geographic, demographic, psychographic, and behavioristic criteria to identify countries and customer groups that meet the standards defining productive target markets (i.e., substantial, homogeneous within, heterogeneous without, accessible, and operational). An important by-product of the segmentation process is information on how to position products in selected segments and the most appropriate segmentation strategy (undifferentiated, concentrated, differentiated) for penetrating entry markets.

KNOW THE CONCEPTS

TERMS FOR STUDY

behavioristic bases
benefits segmentation
brand image
buyer readiness stage
concentrated strategy
demographic bases
determining criteria
differentiated strategy
end-user segmentation
geographic bases
heterogeneous segments
homogeneous segments
loyalty status
market gridding

mass marketing
occasions segmentation
perceptual map
positioning
product differentiated marketing
psychographic bases
qualifying criteria
segmentation bases
segmentation strategies
segment size criteria
target marketing
undifferentiated strategy
usage rate
user status

MATCHUP EXERCISES

1. Match up the customer characteristic in the second column with the organizational segmentation variable listed in the first column.

1. demographic
2. operational

3. purchasing

4. personal

5. situational

a. Customer leases all its vehicles.
b. Customer maintains strong working relationships with suppliers.

c. Customer insists on prompt deliveries.
d. Customer relies on supplier servicing capability.
e. Customer employs 200 production workers in main plant.

2. Colgate Palmolive is launching its Plus toothbrush into the German marketplace. Match the concepts in the second column pertaining to how this product will be positioned and promoted with the definitions in the first column.

1. attribute

a. have higher than average level of oral care involvement

2. position

   b. as compared to Oral B Indicator and Advanced Design Reach (competitors) is perceived as more effective in removing plaque and tartar

3. perceptual map

   c. superior brushing by cleaning teeth and caring for gums

4. target market

   d. has rippled bristles

3. Match the consumer market segmentation variable in the first column with the characteristic of a typical buyer of a Merton Mighty Mind system in the accounting profession listed in the second column.

1. psychographic

   a. has an active social life, which he mixes with business activities

2. behavioristic

   b. makes sure he has the most state-of-the-art software

3. geographic

   c. male, in his early thirties

4. demographic

   d. works for a large Tokyo public accounting firm as a manager, with expectations of soon becoming a partner

QUESTIONS FOR REVIEW AND DISCUSSION

The first three questions are based on the following short case:

When Peter Johns, an American entrepreneur with 30 years experience in direct marketing, made plans to distribute a mail order catalog promoting upscale American products to affluent consumers in Mexico City, he faced an unexpected problem: a lack of useful marketing information on this segment of the Mexican market. Government census reports failed to break down income levels over $35,000, and the few lists available were dated, incomplete (for example, no zip codes), and/or exhorbitantly expensive. So Johns developed his own lists, by soliciting membership lists from organizations with which affluent Mexicans would affiliate, such as exclusive country clubs and private schools. By 1995, Johns had a customer base of 10,000 families, each spending an average of $750 annually on the products represented in his catalog.

1. Based only on case facts, what bases did Johns use to segment the Mexican market? What other bases could he have used?

2. In terms of criteria that define worthwhile market segments, assess the viability of the target market that emerged from Johns' segmentation efforts.

3. How does Johns' successful segmentation effort illustrate the Pareto principle justification for target marketing?

4. Textron, Inc., the Providence, R.I., conglomerate, follows a deliberate strategy of targeting both government and consumer segments in marketing its lines of aerospace technology and commercial and financial products and services. In so doing, it aims to achieve the flexibility that some of its behemoth competitors are denied (e.g., the Northrup Corporation realizes 91 percent of its sales from government contracts). This diversification strategy also dictates different marketing strategies for products and services in Textron's product portfolio (i.e., undifferentiated, concentrated, differentiated). Which strategy would you recommend for each of the following products, and why? (1) gas turbine engines for M-1 tanks; (2) E-Z-Go golf carts; (3) Schaeffer pens and paper products.

The next two questions are based on this case:

> In 1988, the Alpnet Company entered the language translation services market, buying up foreign translation services and using translation software it had developed to speed productivity at its 40 offices worldwide. Each of these offices is a "one-stop" shop that translates dozens of languages and offers typesetting, printing, graphics, and publishing services. Alpnet's primary targets are multinational clients that perform the following activities requiring translation: issue securities that will be sold abroad, perform extensive sales and promotion activities in global markets, create access to technology flowing from foreign countries (especially Japan), and communicate with many foreign national employees.

5. Describe how Alpnet would follow the steps of the market segmentation process for identifying and defining its target market.

6. In identifying and defining Alpnet's target market, what would be qualifying and determining criteria?

7. Describe how geographic, psychographic, and behavioristic criteria might have been used to develop the basic offering for a $5000-per-person New Year's Eve party featuring a Concorde flight to Paris for a gourmet meal and a show at the Follies.

ANSWERS

MATCHUPS

1. 1e, 2d, 3a, 4b, 5c
2. 1d, 2c, 3b, 4a
3. 1a, 2b, 3d, 4c

QUESTIONS FOR DISCUSSION AND REVIEW

1. Johns used demographic and geographic bases to segment the Mexican market, producing a list of affluent Mexicans (demographic) residing in affluent neighborhoods in Mexico City. He could also have used a number of behavioristic bases to further define this target market so as to improve his offering (e.g., products, prices, and promotional appeals in his catalogs). For example, Johns might have uncovered cultural differences between American and Mexican customers that would affect his offering using these behavioristic bases:

- Usage rate: Per capita, do affluent Mexicans tend to use more of certain products (e.g., jewelry, fashion clothing)?

- Buyer readiness: What products familiar to American buyers are new to Mexican buyers (e.g., consumer electronics)?

- Occasions: Are there special occasions when Mexicans exchange gifts (e.g, special religious observances)?

- Benefits: Do Mexicans seek different benefits from products than do American buyers?

2. Judging from the success of Johns' mail order catalog venture, his target market (based on his early conclusion that there is "a sense of consumer deprivation in the luxury market of Mexico City") meets all the criteria for viability: It is (1) substantial enough to generate excellent sales and profits; (2) homogeneous within and heterogeneous with respect to other market segments (the affluent luxury market in Mexico City is well defined in relation to other socioeconomic groups); and (3) it is accessible, through a functioning postal system, to Johns' catalogs. Initially, due to a lack of defining marketing information, it was not operational, but Johns changed that by creating his own mailing lists (which he now sells along with space in his catalogs).

3. According to the Pareto principle, a small percentage of a given population will be responsible for a disproportionately large percentage of economic activity (roughly, a 20/80 ratio). In this case, a very small percentage of the Mexican population (less than 5 percent) purchase more than 90 percent of luxury products. Thus, Johns can efficiently and inexpensively cover this entire market by focusing on this small affluent group.

4. For (1) the M-1 tank engines, conditions indicate an undifferentiated strategy wherein the marketer goes after the entire market with a single offering. The product is homogeneous as to government specifications; the market is also homogeneous as to its needs; and the company has sufficient resources to implement this strategy. For (2) the E-Z-Go Golf Cart, a concentrated strategy is indicated, whereby the company goes after a large share of one or a few submarkets (i.e., golf courses) instead of after a small share of a large market. The product itself is capable of being differentiated into different models to meet differing buyer needs, and the company can achieve economies and the benefits of a strong market position through this strategy. For (3) Schaeffer pens, a differentiated strategy is indicated, whereby the company would design different offerings (e.g., ball point, luxury pens) for several different target market segments (business offices, students, etc.). The product, in the mature state of its life cycle, is capable of being differentiated, and there are discrete, definable target markets for these offerings.

5. First, Alpnet selected its product/market area—a full range of translation services for multinational firms. Then, Alpnet qualified prospective market members by locating and identifying all the multinational firms in the global areas it was set up to serve. Next, Alpnet identified worthwhile target markets by applying to these multinational firms organizational market segmentation criteria that further defined them as needing Alpnet services (e.g., technology dependence, large cadres of foreign employees, aggressive foreign communications programs). Finally, Alpnet prioritized and profiled each target market group and began planning and developing marketing plans to attract each to its offering.

6. Qualifying criteria included the prospective customer's status as a multinational and location in Alpnet's trading area. Determining criteria included demographic, operating, purchasing, and situational variables that combined to more precisely define each prospect as needing Alpnet services.

7. The relatively small, select target market group that could afford to attend this event—or would even want to—would have behavioristic characteristics (e.g., benefits desired and user status), psychographic characteristics (e.g., attitudes and interests), and demographic characteristics (e.g., age and income) that could be used to develop this offering. For example, the cost of the party (price) would derive from income segmentation; the product itself (e.g., the Concorde flight and the menu at the French restaurant), from Attitude-Interest-Opinion psychographic segmentation; and the promotion campaign, from psychographic variables pertaining to attitudes, motives, and perceptions. A media strategy for effectively delivering this message would also require an understanding of where party members resided (geographic segmentation).

12
MEASURING INTERNATIONAL MARKET AND SALES POTENTIAL

OVERVIEW

Forecasts of the nature and extent of potential demand in international market segments underpins all aspects of the strategic planning process, including establishing realistic marketing objectives, allocating resources to achieve these objectives, monitoring competitive and other aspects of the external environment, and keeping marketing efforts on track.

International market forecasts typically encompass direct and analogy measures of national, industry, and company sales in consumer and organizational markets along time, area, and product dimensions. Specific quantitative and qualitative forecasting techniques employed include correlation, time series, market factor, chain ratio, total market demand, market buildup, and surveys of expert, sales force, and buyer intentions.

FORECASTS PROJECT MARKET AND SALES POTENTIAL

In Chapter 11, we examined strategies for identifying, defining and prioritizing worthwhile consumer and organizational segments in international markets and positioning products to competitive advantage in these segments. In this chapter, we examine strategies and techniques for forecasting market and sales potential in these target market segments.

Market potential is the prospective volume of a specific good or service that would be bought by a defined customer group over a specific time period in a defined geographic area and marketing environment and under a defined level and mix of industry marketing effort. Sales potential is the prospective proportion of market potential for a specific good or service that could be purchased from a specific seller, like Merton. Market potential is what consumer and organizational markets could purchase from all sellers; sales potential is what they could purchase from an individual seller.

A forecast is what the seller projects market or sales potential volume to be, usually stated in monetary or product units. Market share is the percentage of market potential that the seller actually gets. For example, if market potenial for the Merton MM is $20,000,000 in a given market segment (i.e., what customers could purchase from all sellers), and Merton is only getting $2,000,000 of this potential, then its market share is 10 percent. Using the MM as an illustrative example, Figure 12-1 (a) and (b) shows some of the ways market and sales potential can be perceived and used to set goals and formulate strategies.

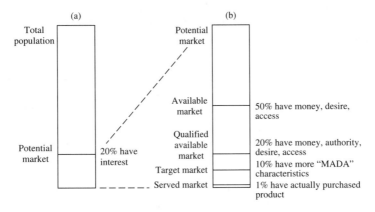

Figure 12–1. Divisions of Potential Market in Terms of Money/Authority/Desire/Access Characteristics

Figure 12-1(a) depicts two key potential dimensions:

- *Total population*, which is composed of all the people in a given country who may or may not be interested in buying a Merton MM system.

- *Potential market*, which is composed of people among the total population who profess some level of interest in procuring an MM system.

Figure 12-1(b) begins with the 20 percent of the total market that represents the potential market for MMs and further defines and delimits this market. Thus, of this potential market, only 50 percent constitute its available market, comprising people who are interested in, can afford, and have access to MM systems. Assuming, however, that Merton is interested in selling MM systems only to accredited professionals such as lawyers and accountants its qualified available market (20 percent of the potential market) would be limited to people who possess these credentials.

The target market is composed of that 50 percent of the qualified available market that Merton decides most justifies cultivation, and the penetrated market is composed of that 10 percent of target market members who have actually purchased Merton MM systems.

Viewing markets in terms of these categories is a useful starting point for planning marketing strategies. For example, forecasts depicting the nature and scope of these market segments might show Merton planners that a given target market isn't being effectively penetrated (10 percent of the potential market might be considered too small). They might then suggest initiatives (e.g., a more innovative, intensive promotion program) for converting target market members into members of the served market. Or, Merton might decide to lower its accreditation requirement to increase the size of the qualified available market, change its marketing mix to attract more members of the available market, or include more professional groups to increase the size of the potential market.

RELATIONSHIPS BETWEEN MARKETING EFFORT AND DEMAND

Figure 12-2 depicts another useful aspect of the forecasting process—the time dimension. On this model, the horizontal axis shows different possible levels of marketing expenditure in a given time period, and the vertical axis shows demand levels associated with each expenditure level. Point Q_0, the market minimum, represents sales volume that would result without any expenditures. For example, word-of-mouth promotion alone would result in the sale of some MM systems. Greater expenditures would yield some sales and push the sales response curve (i.e., the extent to which sales change with expenditure changes) closer to the market potential line, which represents what all prospective customers could purchase of these products. The distance between the market minimum Q_0 and market potential Q_1 shows the overall marketing sensitivity of demand. If the distance is great, the market is capable of greater growth (i.e., it is highly expandable) and will be more likely to respond to marketing expenditures than if the distance is small. The market for innovative new products, or existing products introduced as new to global markets, is usually more expandable and responsive to marketing efforts than existing products in competitive domestic markets.

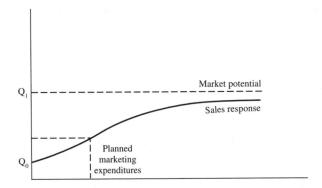

Figure 12–2. Sale Responses as a Function of Planned Expenditures

THE MANY DIMENSIONS OF FORECASTING

As shown in Figure 12-3, market and sales potential can be forecast along a diversity of dimensions. Along the area dimension, for example, Merton's marketing planners might want to measure the sales potential of a single large customer or of all the customers in a given territory or region, the entire domestic market, or the entire global market.

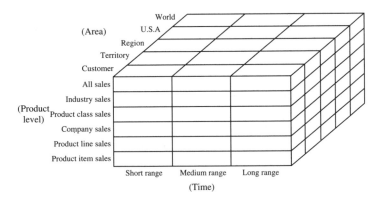

Figure 12–3. Product/Space/Time Dimensions Identify 90 Categories

Along the product level dimension, the marketing planners might want to know what demand is for MM systems designed for one professional group (product item), all computer system models Merton markets to professional groups (product line), or all the diverse consumer electronics products Merton makes and markets (product class).

Merton planners might also want to know how the company is doing in relation to its competition, so industry sales will also be forecast. Additionally, they might want to know about how Merton's sales, and sales of its competitors, are doing as compared to sales of all products in this country and globally, so these forecasts will also be made.

Along the time level dimension, any of these product/area level forecasts might be made for a short-range period (up to 1 year); a medium-range period (1–3 years); or a long-range period (more than 3 years).

In its initial efforts to enter the global marketplace, Merton's forecasting efforts would focus on a single product item (the MM) to defined customer groups, in a few regions of the world, over medium-range time periods. Then, assuming these efforts proved successful, Merton's forecasts would encompass additional area product, and time level dimensions.

FORECASTS HELP PLAN AND ACHIEVE MARKETING GOALS

Figures 12-2 and 12-3, which depict measures of market and sales potential, dimensions along which potential can be measured, and relationships among potentials, expenditures, and response curves, also highlight the value of forecasts in strategic marketing planning.

To illustrate further, assume that Merton, using approaches and techniques discussed next, has come up with dollar estimates of market and sales potential for MM systems in the "accountant" target market in Mexico. This information can help Merton marketers to:

- *Monitor the external environment.* For example, a reliable forecast of sales and profits will take into account such environmental factors as the state of the Mexican economy (and its impact on purchasing power), political roadblocks to successful market entry, technological factors that will help to manufacture and market MMs for the Mexican market, and the nature and extent of competitive initiatives.

- *Establish realistic sales and profit objectives.* Estimates of dollar potential of a target market segment are necessary for budgeting marketing effort and dollars to achieve a desired level of sales and profits; setting these goals begins the strategic planning process.

- *Allocate resources to achieve these established objectives.* Understanding the nature, needs, and dollar potential in a target market segment provides information on which to base goal-oriented resource allocation decisions in such areas as product quantities and distribution, pricing strategies, and promotional campaigns.

- *Control marketing efforts.* If marketing efforts result in sales or profits that are excessively above or below forecasted expectations, appropriate measures can be taken to bring actual figures back in line with projected expectations.

FORECASTING APPROACHES FOR GLOBAL MARKETS

Poor forecasts can inflict an awful price in lost sales, profits, and goodwill on otherwise happy, healthy enterprises. But reliable forecasts are generally more difficult to come by in international than in domestic markets, where environments—economic, political, and cultural—change dramatically within short space and time frames and can have a devastating impact on the unwary and unprepared.

The following approach to measuring potential in international markets is designed to address these difficulties.

DIRECT AND ANALOGY FORECASTING APPROACHES

In general, there are two approaches for forecasting international potential, each based on a different assumption:

- The *direct approach* assumes that the firm has no experience on which to base forecasts of potential in foreign markets.

- The *estimate by analogy* approach assumes that demand develops in much the same way in different countries and can be measured with the same indices used in the country that serves as the basis of the analogy.

The estimate by analogy approach might assume, for example, that, since disposable income is the best predictor of sales of MMs to professionals in the United States, this indicator, and its anticipated growth during the next decade, will also predict sales of MMs in the Mexican market.

A variant on the estimate by analogy approach, called the time displacement approach, assumes a different kind of analogy between countries that are dissimilar in terms of growth stage and other defining variables. Specifically, this approach assumes an anology between stages of development in both countries, and the time each stage is reached. Thus, for example, this approach might assume that the Mexican professional market for MMs will achieve parity with the U.S. market, say, in 10 years, and a sales projection line can be drawn based on the assumption that demand growth will follow the same pattern as in the United States.

Still another variant on the estimate by analogy approach assumes an analogy between similar products. For example, Japanese consumption of beef, sugar, liquor, and dairy products grew, between 1970 and 1990, at a rate closely paralleling that in the United States in an earlier period. This growth rate also closely paralleled the relative growth of per-capita income in the two countries. As a result, marketers could base forecasts of sales of these products, and products similar to them (e.g., other sweeteners or foodstuffs) in Japan on projections of per-capita income growth in the United States.

The prospective flaw in all analogy approaches is the assumption of similarity. In the Mexican example, other factors, unique to Mexico, might be dominant in determining product purchases. Also, it is at least possible —perhaps likely—that technological and social factors might permit the country to leapfrog previous development stages in the United States, helping Mexico achieve parity in less than 10 years. And there might be enough differences among apparently similar products to significantly change demand patterns of each.

Given these constraints, it's important, when applying analogy approaches, to know the needs a product serves domestically before similar needs and potential can be measured in foreign markets. It is also important to have a sufficiently long historical record of the bridging variable or variables to ensure the validity and reliability of these indices. For example, if per-capita income growth serves as a reliable indicator of sales of dairy products in both Japan and the United States for 10 consecutive years, then its validity, reliability, and usefulness as a forecasting tool for these products can probably be assumed.

FORECASTING GLOBAL POTENTIAL DIRECTLY

Given that products do not necessarily have reliable, valid indices that conveniently correlate with experience in a prospective entry market, the direct approach to potential measurement is typically used to replace or supplement analogy approaches.

Essentially, the direct forecasting approach encompasses a group of quantitative and judgmental techniques that produce estimates of market and sales potential. Typically, combinations of these approaches are used in forecasting potential, acting as checks on each other. As with market research initiatives in general, the number of approaches used is limited by cost/benefit considerations. For example, if two or three techniques used in combination have historically produced highly accurate, reliable forecasts, adding others would unnecessarily increase the cost. However, as the data on which all quantitative and judgmental forecasts are based become less accessible or reliable, more techniques are added to the mix, which usually means more forecasting techniques are used as prospective foreign entry markets become less similar to the home country.

THE THREE-STEP DIRECT FORECASTING APPROACH

Although marketers entering global markets are initially most interested in measuring short-range potential for product classes in defined, targeted territories, these figures become more meaningful when compared to forecasted figures for the country's economy as a whole, and the firm's industry as one component of the national economy.

To illustrate the usefulness of these three forecast levels—national, industry, company—assume a situation in which the Merton MM proves to be a commercial success in the English market and attracts other competitors with similar electronic offerings. Also assume that, in an upcoming year, Merton forecasts a 10 percent increase in MM sales in England. If the actual increase is only 5 percent, does this indicate subpar performance in implementing Merton's marketing plan and the need to revise this plan? Perhaps so, if industry forecasts show that Merton MM sales are losing market share to competitors. However, forecasts of the English economy, and industry performance in general, might indicate that, in spite of its 5-point sales decline, Merton is actually picking up market share in a recessive economic environment. The point is that the significance of Merton's forecast can best be understood, and acted upon, in a broader context of general economic and industry forecasts.

Generally, national economic forecasts are available from a number of sources listed in Chapters 4 and 6—including the U.S. Chamber of Commerce, foreign embassies and agencies, United Nations reports, industry associations, trade magazines, banks, and private research organizations. From these sources, marketers can usually find a single forecast or combination of forecasts that have worked well in the past to forecast trends and developments in a country.

Many of these organizations also prepare sales forecasts for specific industries. Unfortunately, these forecasts are usually made for broad business categories (e.g., services, steel, housing, electronics) rather than for specific submarket categories (e.g., "notebook computer" or "tax accountant" markets). Thus, marketers need to look to their own forecasting tools and techniques to generate useful, focused forecasts.

FORECASTS RELY ON NUMBERS, JUDGMENT, OR BOTH

In general, approaches for forecasting industry and product sales potential can be categorized as either quantitative or judgmental in nature.

Quantitative techniques rely primarily on sales volume and other numbers (e.g., disposable income) generated in the past and presumed to have predictive value into the future. In the specific quantitative techniques discussed next, these numbers are added, multiplied, and/or related to other figures in developing projections.

Judgmental techniques rely on the judgment of people presumed to have a special knowledge of the impact of different variables on sales. Salesmen, for example, or prospective customers, would presumably have a first-hand knowledge of how customers and markets will respond to a firm's products, and the environmental factors influencing these responses.

QUANTITATIVE AND JUDGMENTAL FORECASTING TECHNIQUES

In this section, we examine quantitative and judgmental techniques used to forecast market and sales potential in consumer and organizational markets. For each technique examined, we will first discuss how it might be applied in the domestic market and then how it might be modified to apply, via analogy approaches, in global markets.

Quantitative techniques for forecasting consumer markets include input-output, correlation, market factor index, chain ratio, and total market demand analyses to convert market potential figures into sales potential figures for specific products in specific areas.

• *INPUT-OUTPUT ANALYSES*

Input-output analyses show resources used by different industries for a given output as well as the interdependence of economic sectors. Through the use of input-output tables, now published by many countries, production (output) of one sector is shown as the demand (input) for other sectors. For example, steel output becomes input for such sectors as automobile and airframe manufacturers, households, government, and the foreign sector. Using these tables first for the U.S. domestic market, Merton analysts developed a profile of input-output features of the consumer electronics market, which was then matched to similar profiles of prospective entry markets (where timely, reliable profiles existed). To the extent that parallels existed between the two profiles, similar market conditions were assumed to exist and were used as a basis for forecasting market potential, sales for Merton products, and purchases in different market sectors. For example, assuming that Canada had the same input-output pattern of products to and from the consumer electronics sector, but only one-third the volume as the United States, rough forecasts in Canada would be factored as one-third that of the United States.

• *CORRELATION ANALYSIS*

This technique measures the degree of association (correlation) between potential sales of a product and a market factor that has closely paralleled sales of this product in the past. Typically, this market factor is a measurement of economic activity, called a leading series, which changes in the same direction but ahead of product sales being measured. For example, historical experience showed Merton researchers that consumer disposable income correlated closely with MM sales in Merton's domestic market and had been projected into the future with unusual accuracy by a number of private and government economists. In a typical year, the consensus among these forecasters was that disposable income would increase by 5 percent. Since total domestic sales of MM systems had been $20 million the previous year, Merton researchers projected MM sales at $20,100,000 for the coming year.

Two other correlates of particular value in identifying growth potential in foreign markets are indices of income elasticity and production growth.

- *Coefficients of income elasticity* correlate prospective purchases with increases, or decreases, in income. As discussed in the Chapter 7 section on Engel's law, purchases of certain categories of products, like recreation and education, increase at a faster rate than do increases in income. For example, if purchases of MM systems increase by 1.2 percent for each 1 percent income increase, the income coefficient of elasticity for this product is 1.20, a figure that can be projected into the near term and correlated with forecasted sales of MMs.

- *Production growth trends*, especially useful as indicators of sales potential for any products or services required in manufacturing processes, are usually adjusted to include imported products used in production processes and to subtract inventories of finished goods.

Two major limitations of correlation analysis follow.

- It requires a lengthy sales history to develop relationships—at least 20 quarters of sales records.

- It is an expensive, time-consuming approach, invariably requiring computerized data bases. It is often beyond the skills of researchers.

• *MARKET FACTOR INDEX*

The market factor index technique was used as a check on the correlation analysis to develop data on overall MM sales potential. In Merton's experience, the buying power index formula, published each year by *Sales and Marketing Management* magazine in its "Survey of Buying Power" section, had accurately reflected sales of MM systems among professional groups in Merton's domestic market. This formula is based on three weighted factors: an area's share of the nation's disposable personal income y_i, retail sales r_i, and population p_i. Hence, the formula for buying power is

$$B_i = 0.5y_i + 0.3r_i + 0.2p_i$$

In one segment of Merton's domestic market, for example, the respective y, r, and p shares of national totals were 0.06, 0.08, and 0.07, respectively; hence, this area could account for 0.068 of total potential demand for MM systems $(0.5 \times 0.06 + 0.3 \times 0.08 + 0.2 \times 0.07) = 0.068$. Thus, if national demand for MM systems was estimated to be, say, $30,000,000, demand in this segment would be estimated at $2,040,000 ($30,000,000 × 0.068).

In global markets, percentage figures plugged into the basic buying power formula were modified to reflect local conditions. In Japan, for example, where a strong savings ethic contrasts to the spending ethic characterizing the U.S. culture, much less weight was placed on the retail sales component of the formula.

• *CHAIN RATIO*

The chain ratio technique involves multiplying a base number, such as total number of buyers in a market, by various qualifying criteria that refine this base number to reflect specific characteristics of submarkets under study. For example, in Merton's domestic trading area, researchers estimated a total of 100,000 accounting professionals with interest in and access to MM system purchases—the potential market. Of this total, however, only 30 percent were estimated to have the disposable income to afford an MM system. Thus, Merton's qualified available market was composed of 30,000 accountants (100,000 × 0.30).

In adopting this approach to global markets, Merton again plugged in figures that best reflected specific characteristics and needs. In France, for example, "clients served" turned out to be a much more predictive qualifying criteria than disposable income.

• *TOTAL MARKET DEMAND*

The total market demand approach builds up to a total market demand figure Q by multiplying total number of buyers n by the quantity q purchased by the average buyer by the price p of an average unit. Thus, for example, starting with the 30,000 accountants figure emerging from the chain ratio calculation, and assuming that one in ten of these accountants would purchase an MM system at an average cost of $3,000, Merton estimated its sales potential in this area to be $9,000,000 ($Q$ = 30,000 × 0.10 × $3,000). In foreign markets, all the components of this formula were modified to reflect local situations, including price differences, and the quantity of MMs likely to be purchased in relatively undeveloped markets.

ORGANIZATIONAL MARKET FORECASTING STRATEGIES

In forecasting sales of MM systems to large professional legal and accounting firms in its domestic organizational market, Merton's most commonly used forecasting approaches were market buildup and time series analyses.

• *MARKET BUILDUP*

The market buildup approach involved building up to total potential figures for an entire trading area by adding together potential figures for specific industries in this area. The U.S. government's Standard Industrial Classification (SIC) system, which assigns numerical codes to broad categories of industries comprising the organizational market (Table 12-1), is the basis for this approach in domestic markets. For example, here is how Merton arrived at market potential estimates for MM systems in two target segments of the organizational market—accounting (SIC 7658) and law firms (SIC 7617)—in one territory in the firm's domestic market:

SIC Code	Number of Employees	Number of Firms	Potential Sales Per Employee ($)	Market Potential ($)
7658	20,000	250	500	10,000,000
7617	15,000	200	400	6,000,000

This analysis shows that, based on surveys of a sampling of the accounting and law firm populations, market potential—what these firms could purchase from all suppliers of computer systems—was $16,000,000. This figure assumes that each of the 20,000 accountants in 250 accounting firms would purchase, on average, $500 worth of computer systems, and each of the 15,000 lawyers, an average of $400 worth.

Table 12–1. Organizational Market Categories

Functional Category	SIC Category	Size Categories		Employees per Organization
		No. of organizations	No. of employees	
INDUSTRIAL PRODUCERS				
Agriculture, forestry, fishing	01–09	3,486,000	3,571,000	1
Mining	10–14	181,000	1,028,000	6
Construction	15–17	1,412,000	5,756,000	4
Manufacturing	20–39	569,000	20,286,000	36
Transportation, utilities	40–49	570,000	6,552,000	11
Finance, Insurance, Real estate	60–67	2,179,000	6,270,000	3
Services	70–89	4,777,000	30,090,000	6
TOTAL		13,174,000	73,553,000	6
TRADE INDUSTRIES				
Wholesalers	50–51	383,000	4,120,000	11
Retailers	52–59	1,855,000	16,638,000	9
TOTAL		2,238,000	20,758,000	9
GOVERNMENTS				
Federal	91–97	1	2,862,000	
State		50	3,747,000	
Local		82,290	9,324,000	
TOTAL		82,341	15,933,000	
OVERALL TOTALS		15,494,341	110,244,000	8

Source: U.S. Bureau of the Census, *Statistical Abstract of the United States: 1992* (112th edition) Washington, DC: U.S. Government Printing Office.

To adopt this market buildup approach to the global marketplace, Merton planners replaced SIC figures with equivalent Harmonized Commodity Classification figures, which perform essentially the same function as SIC figures in international markets. Merton planners then conducted surveys of target market samples to build market potential estimates.

• TIME SERIES ANALYSES

This approach assumes that changes in sales levels in previous periods (i.e., the time series) can be used as a basis for predicting sales in the future. In Merton's domestic market, these changes generally reflected four components:

- A *long-term trend T*, reflecting an underlying pattern of sales found by fitting a straight or curved line through past sales.

- An *intermediate-term cycle C*, reflecting cyclic changes in economic or competitive activity, depicted by wavelike changes in the trend line.

- A *seasonal component S*, reflecting any recurrent weekly, monthly, or quarterly changes in sales patterns.

- An *erratic events component E*, reflecting unexpected events (strikes, floods, fads, etc.) that might influence sales.

In using time series analyses to forecast sales volume in domestic markets, Merton marketers had sufficient data to compile trend, cycle, and seasonal components, to which they added a figure reflecting their best assessment of the nature and likelihood of possible erratic events. For example, in a year when the possibility of government initiatives in worldwide economic and military conflicts was expected to have an impact on the economy for better or worse, Merton projected a 10 percent sales increase T, to which was added another 5 percent resulting from an anticipated cyclic growth spurt C. Another 5 percent was added for the spring and fall seasons—typically the busiest in Merton's year S, and, finally, the total forecasted figure was reduced by 5 percent as the anticipated result of unusually high budget cutbacks in the public sector.

In adopting time series analyses to the global marketplace, Merton marketers initially faced the problem of the lack of a sales trend line on which to append modifying C, S, and E influences, which could usually be identified. Typically, their only alternative was to use substitution approaches, assuming a trend line in an entry economy similar to the domestic economy.

JUDGMENTAL FORECASTING TECHNIQUES

Groups whose judgment is typically solicited in preparing judgmental forecasts include experts, salespeople, and prospective customers. Here is how each group was used in compiling sales forecasts for MM systems in Merton's domestic market.

• *SURVEY OF EXPERT OPINION*

This approach relies on the opinion of people with presumed knowledge of different variables affecting sales. Merton's own executives, with their "big picture" understanding of various environmental influences, might constitute one such group; another might be a trade association of manufacturers of computer systems or publications serving Merton's professional target markets that gather and disseminate statistics from many sources, including manufacturers, sellers, and government researchers.

In developing such expert information from Merton executives, researchers made use of the Delphi technique, whereby estimates of future sales were sent back to the people who originally submitted these estimates until a consensus figure emerged. For example, one estimate ranged, initially, from a predicted sales decline of 6 percent to a predicted increase of 12 percent. These estimates were ranked, with supporting rationales, and returned to the executives with requests that they state their agreements and disagreements with the rank order and rationales, make any desired changes in their initial projections, and return the estimates. After several rounds, a consensus figure projecting a 4 percent increase emerged.

• *SURVEY OF BUYER INTENTIONS*

Typically making use of independent marketing research firms to maintain anonymity, Merton had a number of surveys of customers and prospects conducted to determine the likelihood that firms would purchase MM systems in general and Merton systems in particular. A typical survey instrument used in these probes, the purchase probability scale, uses rating scale probabilities of from 0.00 (no chance) through 0.50 (fair chance) to 1.00 (certain) to measure purchase intentions. Among many domestic organizations that publish forecasts of buyer purchase intentions, the Survey Research Center of the University of Michigan, with its consumer sentiment measure, is probably the best known.

• *COMPOSITE SALES FORCE OPINION*

Similar to the survey of expert opinion, this approach bases sales forecasts on the opinion of salespeople. Logically, salespeople, closer to happenings in the marketplace, should be able to provide reliable estimates, although it is frequently argued that they lack a "big picture" overview of factors affecting sales. It is also argued that salespeople might have incentives to estimate low (e.g., to get a lower quota) or, conversely, that the optimistic nature of the sales personality might encourage high estimates.

ADOPTING JUDGMENTAL APPROACHES TO GLOBAL MARKETS

Of the three judgmental forecasting techniques mentioned in the last section, the first two—expert opinion and buyer intentions surveys—are the easiest to implement in foreign markets, usually with the expertise of a locally based marketing research firm. Indeed, many firms interested in entering the global marketplace make such forays as a relatively inexpensive way to get the feel for an entry market before committing resources to a large-scale, possibly futile, marketing effort. Another advantage of such early research is the production of data to implement more sophisticated quantitative forecasting methods (e.g., finding effective leading indicators for correlation analyses, or qualifying criteria to adjust chain ratio figures).

Obviously, polling sales force opinion is not feasible if the firm has no sales force in a prospective entry market, but sometimes salespeople from other firms can be polled, as when an association or publication generates information from salespeople on market prospects.

Whether conducted in domestic or foreign markets, all of these judgmental techniques lend themselves to two techniques designed to improve accuracy and validity of findings while keeping costs low:

- *Focus group panels* (discussed in Chapter 5), usually consisting of 8 to 12 members of a knowledgeable group (customers, salespeople, executives) who discuss, in an in-depth, free-wheeling manner, products, markets, threats, and opportunities.

- The *Delphi technique*, discussed previously, usually conducted with groups of between 20 to 30 participants.

GAP ANALYSIS SCANS AND COMPARES

Once estimates of market or sales potential are made in a given international market or markets, gap analysis is a useful technique for putting these figures into a meaningful perspective. This is done by comparing gaps in a number of areas and taking appropriate action based on this understanding. Consider, as examples, gaps between (1) sales forecasts for countries A, B, C, and D; (2) sales forecasts and forecasts of market potential; and (3) sales forecasts for product A and competitive products B, C, and D. In situations where these gaps are significantly large, further investigation is usually indicated to identify, and rectify, their causes, which may be due to a diversity of factors, including customer attitudes, competitive initiatives, promotional failures, product (or price) inadequacies, or distribution failures.

CHAPTER PERSPECTIVE

Valid, reliable market and sales forecasts, in both consumer and organizational markets, are basic to formulating and implementing strategic marketing plans, including setting objectives, assigning resources, and controlling marketing effectiveness. Quantitative and judgmental techniques are generally combined in generating forecast data, with the number used dependent on such variables as data availability and cost constraints. Direct methods for generating sales and market forecasts in domestic markets include input-output and correlation analyses, chain ratio and total market demand techniques, and surveys of expert, sales force, and customer opinion. In generating forecasts for the global marketplace, various analogy approaches are typically used, all based on the assumption that there are measurable similarities between the home country serving as the basis of the analogy and the foreign country where various dimensions of sales and markets are being forecast.

KNOW THE CONCEPTS

TERMS FOR STUDY

analogy approaches
available market
buying power index
chain ratio technique
coefficient of income elasticity
company sales potential
correlation analysis
Delphi technique
expandable demand
focus groups
forecasting dimensions
gap analysis
input-output analysis
judgmental approaches
leading indicator
market buildup method
market factor index method

market forecast
marketing sensitivity of demand
market potential
market share
penetrated market
potential market
production growth trends
qualified available market
quantitative methods
sales force opinion
sales response function
survey of buyer intentions
survey of expert opinion
time displacement approach
time series projection
total market demand

MATCHUP EXERCISES

1. Match up the market component in the first column with the situation listed in the second column that best describes it.

1. potential market	a. These people are most likely to want to take a cruise on the Holland-America Line.
2. target market	b. These people have already taken a cruise on the Holland-America Line.
3. served market	c. These people would like to take a cruise on the Holland-America line, if circumstances permit.
4. qualified available market	d. These people would like to take a cruise on the Holland-America line, can afford to, and have access to a port of departure.

2. Match up the quantitative forecasting technique in the first column with the example listed in the second column

1. coefficient of income elasticity	a. Increases in disposable income and retail sales should push sales of Merton Mighty Minds up by 20 percent this quarter.
2. market factor index technique	b. As disposable income increases by 1 percent, jewelry sales increase by 1.5 percent.
3. chain ratio	c. In Taiwan, 80 percent of automobile buyers can't afford a BMW; among the remainder, one in ten will purchase a BMW within the next 5 years.
4. correlation analysis	d. There is a strong relationship between annual precipitation in the Ukraine and the amount of wheat purchased abroad.

3. Match up the qualitative forecast technique listed in the first column with the defining situation listed in the second column.

1. Delphi technique	a. have "big picture" understanding of market forces
2. survey of expert opinion	b. purchase probability scale

3. survey of buyer intentions   c. summarizes and resubmits
                                       estimates

4. Composite sales force opinion   d. closer to the customer

QUESTIONS FOR REVIEW AND DISCUSSION

1. A large multinational manufacturer of sporting equipment is undertaking a sales forecast for 1996 in one of five industrialized Latin American countries where total sales of the firm's golf clubs totalled $50,000,000 in 1995. Using market factor index and chain ratio forecasting techniques, estimate the sales of the manufacturer's golf clubs in this country given the following data:

   - This country has 0.09 percent of total income of the five countries, 0.12 percent of retail sales generated in these countries, and 0.15 percent of the total population of the five countries.

   - This country has 800,000 golfers, of which 20 percent will purchase (or receive as a gift) a new set of golf clubs during the coming year. One in ten of this group will buy or receive a set of the manufacturer's golf clubs paying, on average, $400.

   From your answers, what can you conclude about when and why to meld a number of forecasting techniques to arrive at sales forecasts? Explain how two judgmental forecasts might have supplemented these quantitative forecasts.

2. In terms of marketing control, what is a "gap analysis" and how might such an analysis be used by the multinational sporting goods manufacturer (question 1) after developing forecasts in the five industrialized countries that comprise the company's Latin American market? How might the following concepts be involved in implementing activities emerging from this analysis: potential market, penetrated market, qualified market, and available market.

   The next three questions are based on the following facts and figures pertaining to the salad/cooking oil market in general, and, more specifically, the olive oil segment of this market, and the leading olive oil processing companies:

   In the United States, olive oil generated, in 1995, about $250 million, or 15 percent of the $1.5 billion salad/cooking oil market and 7 percent of total volume sales. (The average price of a 16-oz bottle of olive oil is about $4.25 versus $1.50 for a similar bottle of vegetable oil.) Between 1985 and 1995, olive oil consumption in the United States doubled, to about 70 million pints. The market leader is Bertolli USA, owned by S.M.E. International, a $2.5 billion Italian food company. Bertolli, the only brand with a truly national presence, sells 37 percent of the olive oil consumed in the United States; Berio, a distant second, sells 19 percent, and Pompeian sells 18 percent. A major reason for the increasing popularity of olive oil is the increasing concern for dietary correctness among American consumers and the fact that olive oil is among the lowest of all oils in both cholesterol and saturated fats. A major reason for Bertolli's surge ahead of Berio—which was No. 1 in 1985—was its invention and aggressive marketing of "light" olive oil, a blend of oils selected for light color, mild taste, and conformity to finicky American tastes—notably, an aversion to the "olive" taste of olive oil. It took Berio more than 3 years to come out with its own "light" version, Mild & Light. Now, with Extra Virgin, it has a complete line to promote in its efforts to win back market share against Bertolli and the Wessons, Puritans, and Criscos that still control most of the market with a diversity of other oils (e.g., peanut, cannola, corn, vegetable) able to compete effectively on health grounds

3. Discuss how Berio's sales forecasts would (1) take time, product level, and area dimensions into consideration and (2) explain relationships among demand levels, marketing expenditures, and the forecasts themselves.

4. Explain how Berio's forecasts at the various levels would assist in establishing objectives, allocating resources, and controlling marketing effectiveness in the firm's efforts to regain No. 1 status.

5. What costs would Berio incur for forecasts that excessively under- or overestimate actual demand? Under what conditions might an accurate forecasted increase in sales volume actually be very bad news?

The next question is based on the following case.

Searching for new global markets and business opportunities, Ian Ward, president of Lakewood Forest Products in Hibbing, Minnesota, discovered an unmet need for chopsticks in the orient, where the chopsticks industry was generally fragmented, technologically backward, and lacking in natural resources (e.g., there were 450 chopsticks factories in Japan alone, serving a market demand for 130 million pairs of disposable wooden chopsticks per day). Ward perceived that his plant in Hibbing was ideally positioned to serve this market: the decline of mining in the area had created an excellent labor pool and a regional desire for new industry; Hibbing had an abundance of unmarred aspen wood ideal for making chopsticks; and Ward himself had the financing and production know-how (with the help of sophisticated equipment purchased from Denmark) to create an automated production line with a capacity of up to 7 million chopsticks a day. With a unit manufacturing cost of $0.03, and a unit selling price of $0.057, Ward had no trouble preselling his first 5 year's output to Japan, earning a pretax profit of $4.7 million in 1989, his first year.

6. Subsequent to his original contract with customers in the Japanese market, Ward undertook searches in other countries—both oriental and otherwise—to identify and measure markets and to build production capacity to meet market needs. Of these three approaches—estimate by analogy, time displacement, and analogy between similar products—which would be most appropriate (and why) in measuring potential in these countries: Taiwan, China, the United States.

ANSWERS

MATCHUP EXERCISES

1. 1c, 2a, 3b, 4d
2. 1b, 2a, 3c, 4d
3. 1c, 2a, 3b, 4d

QUESTIONS FOR REVIEW AND DISCUSSION

1. Using the market factor index forecasting technique, estimated 1996 sales for the firm's golf clubs in this country will be $5,500,000:

$$0.5 \times 0.09 + 0.3 \times 0.12 + 0.2 \times 0.15 = 0.111, \text{ multipled by } \$50,000,000$$
$$\text{Total five-country sales} = \$5,500,000$$

Using the chain ratio forecasting technique, estimated 1996 sales will be $6,400,000:

> 800,000 golfers
> × 0.20 will buy (or receive) a set of golf clubs
> 160,000 golfers
> × 0.10 will buy mfrs. clubs
> 16,000 golfers × $400 per golfer = $6,400,000 sales

The dollar difference between the two estimates—almost a million dollars—suggests that the data from this country that forecasters have to work with (e.g., percentages in the market factor index formula that reflect the situation in the United States) is not overly reliable and that additional forecasting techniques should probably be added to the mix. Two judgmental techniques that might be added include (1) a survey of buyer intentions, in which a sampling of golf club buyers (e.g., pro shops, sporting goods distributors) are asked to estimate their probable purchases of the manufacturer's golf clubs, based on their understanding of market conditions in this country, and (2) a survey of expert opinion, in which knowledgeable people (e.g., company marketing executives, editors of golf magazines) are surveyed, perhaps using the Delphi technique to reach a consensus. Possibly, in using this technique, the estimates from the quantitative methods used ($5,500,000 and $6,400,000) could be the parameters for the final estimates.

2. In global marketing terms, a gap analysis is a tool for comparing a company's performance in different countries in order to calculate how well the company is doing in each and to take appropriate action when actual performance doesn't meet expectations (marketing control). In the case of the sporting goods manufacturer, for example, assume actual sales in three of the five Latin American countries for which forecasts were prepared closely adhered to forecasted figures. In the fourth country, however, sales were dramatically lower than forecast, and in the fifth country they were dramatically higher. These gaps between performance and expectations suggest some action by marketing management. In the first case, management needs to find out what went wrong and to do something about it (e.g., revising the forecast for next year or changing the marketing mix to reflect marketplace realities). In the second case, management might find out what went right in this country and see if it could be effectively applied in the other countries. In general, approaches used would entail the following strategies: (1) increasing the size of the potential market penetrated and/or (2) expanding the size of the qualified market or the available market (e.g., by changing qualifying standards).

3. All strategic marketing planning—such as Berio's strategic plan to regain market share from Bertolli—is essentially a matter of deciding where you are now, where you can hope to be at a future point in time, and how you will get there. Sales forecasting is essential for knowing where you are now and where you can hope to be, so it covers the time dimension—in the case of Berio's forecast, the 5 years it plans to regain No. 1 status in the U.S. olive oil market. Berio's sales forecasts will also cover the product level, in that the firm's planning will have to recognize projected sales of (1) all products with which olive sales correlate (i.e., trends toward "light" menus featuring salads and low-fat cooking oils); (2) all competitors in the salad/cooking oil category (corn, cannola, etc.); (3) Berio's competitors in the olive oil product class; and (4) each product in Berio's product line (Mild and Light, Extra Virgin, etc.). These forecasts will provide Berio marketing management with invaluable information for planning long- and short-range strategies and tactics. For example, they will learn which

usage areas are growing and declining, which competitors (brand, generic, and form) are gaining and losing market share relative to Berio's experience, and which of Berio's product lines is competing most effectively. This information will help Berio marketing management effectively position and promote itself in terms of matching its strengths against competitive weaknesses in exploiting market opportunities. The area dimension would also be of critical importance in Berio's strategic planning. As a multinational, the firm would need the preceding information on time and product level forecasts for all the regions, countries, and territories in which it markets its products, right down to individual customers (e.g., a large food wholesaler or supermarket buying office) that are prospective buyers of its products.

4. The forecasts Berio develops along product, time, and area dimensions will provide the basic raw material and point of departure for establishing business and marketing objectives that are specific, realistic, and attainable (e.g., improving market share vis-à-vis specified competitors by improving sales to specified target markets). By suggesting what can be done, forecasts also suggest ways to allocate resources to do it (e.g., promoting the taste and health benefits of light olive oil to the health and diet-conscious segment of the market). These forecast projections, incorporated into specific goals, also serve as benchmarks against which to measure performance and take appropriate measures when performance falls short of objectives.

5. Berio's costs for underestimating demand—leaving distributors and customers without the product—would be more than the tangible loss of sales and profits represented by these demanded but undelivered goods. For example, a less tangible cost of lost goodwill, and a less measurable cost of competitor's gain, would probably also be exacted. The main cost of overestimated demand would be measured by the cost of the excessive unsold inventories that would have to be maintained by Berio and its distributors—a cost that, in a typical quarter, can easily eat up any possible profit on sales of the product.

6. In Taiwan, with a state of socioeconomic development similar to that of Japan, an estimate by analogy approach would probably be the most effective way to estimate potential for Lakewood chopsticks. In substance, potential per-capita consumption of the chopsticks would be assumed to be the same in Taiwan as in Japan. In the case of China, with its state of socioeconomic development well behind that of Japan, a time displacement approach might be most appropriate. Thus, chopstick usage in Japan at a point in its history when the country was on a socioeconomic level with China might be found to approximate China's per-capita consumption, and consumption projections for future sales in China based on assumptions as to the time required to reach Japan's present socioeconomic status. As to the U.S.

population of oriental descent (and assuming a latent interest among this population to use traditional eating implements), an analogy among similar products approach might be most productive. That is, the number of knives and forks purchased on a per-capita basis in this community might serve as a surrogate estimate for the number of chopsticks that could be purchased.

13

INTERNATIONAL PRODUCT PLANNING I: PRODUCT/MARKET GROWTH STRATEGIES

OVERVIEW

Whether marketed domestically or globally, products and services largely determine a firm's customers, its competitors, its allocation of resources, and its supportive price/place/promotion marketing mix elements. Existing and new products can be defined in terms of objective features, extended features, benefits, and marketing mix implications in both consumer and organizational markets. As products move from local to global status, leverage benefits accrue, including economies of scale and transferability of skills and resources. Products also move through different stages of the product life cycle, with each stage dictating different marketing mix strategies. These strategies are also influenced by characteristics of products that lend themselves to various degrees of adaptation, from standardized to customized plans, where marketing mix elements change to accommodate the nature and needs of specific national markets.

PRODUCTS DEFINE CUSTOMERS, COMPETITORS, AND MARKETING MIX

To this point, we have examined strategic marketing planning processes whereby global marketers (1) understand and account for favorable and unfavorable environmental influences on prospective entry markets and (2) identify, define, and measure target market segments most consistent with company missions, objectives, and resources.

In the next seven chapters, we focus on the four components of the marketing mix—product, price, promotion, and distribution—which marketers combine to achieve company objectives by satisfying market needs. We start with the product component as the dominant marketing mix element. To a large extent, products define the firm's business, including its customers, competitors, resource requirements, and supportive distribution, pricing, and promotion strategies. This chapter views products from a number of perspectives that help to segment markets and formulate marketing strategies, including (1) actual, augmented, and core product characteristics; (2) consumer versus industrial products; (3) products versus services; and (4) local, multinational, international and global products. We will also discuss the importance of new products in successful global entry/growth strategies and how product life-cycle models help shape and guide these strategies.

PRODUCTS DEFINED: BUNDLES OF SATISFACTIONS

In the broadest sense, products, whether marketed in domestic or global markets, are defined as anything offered for attention, acquisition, use, or consumption that is capable of satisfying needs. Figure 13-1 shows how a marketing manager might view the need-fulfilling satisfactions his firm's products offer along a broad spectrum from highly tangible pure goods to highly intangible psychic satisfactions.

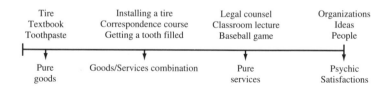

Figure 13–1. The Goods-Services Spectrum

The largest segment of goods along this spectrum represents some combination of goods and services. A tire, for example, is a pure good, although its purchase price may also include the service of installing and balancing it. The Merton Mighty Mind system illustrates products along this spectrum. At the "goods" extreme is the computer with accompanying accessories and software that allow it to be used in a diversity of applications, such as computer-assisted design, spreadsheet analyses, and on-line training and development (T&D) sessions. The T&D software represents a combination of tangible goods (e.g., CD ROMS) and services (e.g., the lectures carried on the CD-ROMS). Intangible ideas are represented by the content of the lectures.

In addition to being defined in terms of their location on this tangible-intangible spectrum, products can be defined in terms of attributes exhibited at any point on this spectrum. On the uppermost level is the actual product, defined in terms of such intrinsic features as quality level, taste, size, price, styling, color, efficiency in use, brand, and packaging.

Next, a level down, is the augmented product, which encompasses the tangible elements of the product as well as an accompanying cluster of image and service features. The augmented MM, for example, would include software programs, instructions for use, guarantees and warrantees, maintenance agreements, brand name associations, and promptness of service. To the consumer, the augmented product is part of the total product, with augmented features often used to distinguish otherwise similar products. For example, the simple fact that a wine was produced in France or an automobile in Germany might be sufficient augmentation to distinguish these products for consumers.

For marketers, a key product management decision is determining how, and how far, to augment the product. Frequently, this decision entails examining buyer consumption patterns as they relate to the product, including where, when, why, how, and by whom it was purchased.

Finally, another level down, is the core product, defined in terms of benefits it offers or problems it solves for the buyer. For example, MM T&D software, as a core product, might be defined as a convenient way to increase productivity and earning power of professionals. To the extent that marketers sell benefits, they generally focus on the core product in developing marketing strategies. Some examples follow.

- "In the factory we make cosmetics, in the drugstore we sell hope" (Charles Revson of Revlon).

- "One million quarter-inch drills were sold not because people wanted quarter-inch drills, but because they wanted quarter-inch holes" (Theodore Levitt, Harvard professor).

In international markets, this complex of tangible and less tangible elements defining individual products will tend to differ from market to market more than in the domestic marketplace, if only because the nature and needs of markets differ more.

CONSUMER/INDUSTRIAL PRODUCTS DEFINED

Another way to define products that helps in developing product/market strategies is in terms of the nature and needs of consumers and industrial buyers. Tables 13-1 and 13-2 summarize classes and categories of products purchased in each market, domestically and internationally; buying behaviors typically displayed with respect to these products by consumer and industrial buyers; and marketing mix implications of interest to marketing planners.

CONSUMER PRODUCTS

In consumer markets, products are defined in terms of their life span and in terms of the buying behavior or shoppers toward them.

• *LIFE SPAN*

Products that are consumed in one or a few uses (e.g., paper clips or candy bars) are called nondurable goods; tangible actual products that survive many uses (e.g., furniture or heavy appliances) are called durable goods.

• *BUYING BEHAVIOR OF SHOPPERS*

Convenience goods are purchased often, quickly, and with little comparison or effort. Shopping goods involve product comparisons on such bases as quality, price, style, and suitability. Specialty goods possess unique attributes for which a significant group of buyers will make a special effort. These shopping characteristics, in turn, determine marketing mix emphasis for each product type. For example, the often impulsive nature of convenience goods purchases stresses the "place" element to make sure that these products are available and visible, whereas the "brand insistence" status of specialty goods emphasizes promoting the product brand name.

INDUSTRIAL PRODUCTS

From the marketing planner's perspective, industrial products are typically categorized in terms of how they are used in productive processes, as defined in terms of the people who purchase them. As noted in Chapter 10, this buying behavior differs appreciably from buying behavior in consumer markets. For example, demand for industrial products typically derives from demand for consumer products, is more inelastic, fluctuates

Table 13–1. Consumer Products: Buyer Behavior and Marketing Mix Attributes

Consumer Product Classifications	Examples	Buying Behavior	Marketing Mix Attributes			
			Product	Price	Place	Promotion
CONVENIENCE Inexpensive habit or impulse purchases; little service or selling costs • Staples • Impulse • Emergency	food, drug items; TV Guide, candy bar; umbrellas	Purchases often planned in store, based on "best buys"; Fast, unplanned purchases; based on strong felt need; Purchased when need great; little shopping done	Branding, packaging, labeling important to encourage impulse purchases; inform buyers	Low unit price for staples, impulse goods; higher for emergency goods	Carried by many outlets; impulse goods in highly conspicuous locations, near checkout counters; emergency items often carried as "fill in" items	Mass market advertising main element in promotion mix
SHOPPING Products perceived as worth a time and effort to compare with competition • Homogeneous (perceived basically the same) • Heterogeneous (perceived as different)	certain sizes, types of refrigerators, TV sets; relatively expensive supermarket items (coffee, butter), furniture, cameras, clothing	Looks for lowest price; Compare on basis of preconceived quality standards, features	Extended product attributes (installation, credit, follow-up, delivery, services) developed; wide assortments needed to satisfy individual tastes	Usually cost more than convenience goods	Location convenience stressed	Homogeneous products stress extended product features (service, quality); Heterogeneous competitive features, benefits. Personal selling key part of mix
SPECIALTY Perceived as worth a special trip	Mercedes automobiles, Gucci boots, Cabbage Patch dolls	Buyer wants a specific product; no comparison required; will expend considerable time and effort to acquire	Brand identification important; also extended product attributes like service, packaging; product line extension decisions important	Unique product characteristics, brand name associations permit high price	Location of outlets, rather than number, most important	Stresses unique product attributes and associations; Advertising appeals and media decisions reflect product image; personal selling important
UNSOUGHT Customers don't want product, or are unaware they can purchase it	New unsought: 500 channel cable TV; smoke detectors; Known unsought: life insurance, encyclopedias	Need exists, but buyer not motivated to satisfy it; No product search	Extended product attributes (service, guarantees) important	Must be competitive to overcome buyer resistance, but high enough to cover selling costs	Unsought status requires many outlets often in-house presentations	Require strong emphasis on all elements of promotion mix, especially advanced personal selling methods; Benefits rather than features emphasized

Table 13–2. Industrial Products: Buyer Behavior and Marketing Mix Attributes

Industrial Product Classifications	Examples	Buying Behavior	Marketing Mix Attributes			
			Product	Price	Place	Promotion
INSTALLATIONS Long-lived capital goods depreciated over time	Buildings (used); Buildings (new); Fixed equipment customized standardize	Motives primarily economic (return on investment) multiple, high-level buying influences negotiation with vendors important	Purchase expense and risk often makes leasing more attractive than buying; form of product doesn't change; very low consumption rate	High per-unit price; demand tends to be inelastic, especially during economic upswings with attractive ROI; otherwise, competition on bid basis	Usually purchased directly from manufacturer	Indirect promotion (advertising, publicity) much less important than personal selling; can be focused in centralized market, but to meet needs of individual buyer
ACCESSORY EQUIPMENT Short-lived items that don't become part of finished product	Tools, equipment for production, office activities (portable drills, typewriters, etc.)	Many more potential customers, but fewer buying center influences than for installations; smaller order size	More standardized than installations; leasing attractive in some target markets; engineering services less important	Medium per-unit price; demand tends to become more elastic as equipment becomes more standardized	Market geographically dispersed, so use more middlemen	More use of the indirect promotion (especially sales promotion)
RAW MATERIALS Unprocessed expense items that enter production process	Natural and nurtured resources (crude oil, iron ore, lumber); also farm products	Low-level decision making; supply continuity, cost efficiency key motives; prefer sorted, graded products; may encourage contract purchasing to control supply	Perishable, seasonal, not expandable in short run	Often depends on supply, which is difficult to adjust to demand; generally, inelastic for industry, elastic for individual firms	Constant demand, seasonal production mean emphasis on storage transportation, grading; dispersed producers, centralized distributors mean large, centralized distributors vertical integration	Products difficult to differentiate, so direct selling important component of promotion mix
COMPONENTS Expense items that require more processing than raw materials; also enter production process	Parts (finished or nearly finished, ready for assembly); tires, small motors Materials (need further processing) wire, yarn, iron	Modified rebuy or new task situation if components are important, expensive; straight rebuy for standards economic needs (price, availability, quality, important); usually many back-up sources	Highly rapid consumption puts emphasis on service and continuity	Industry demand derived and basically inelastic, but elastic for individual firms, with price a key factor in mix; unit price low	Many suppliers create competitive market conditions	OEM, and after markets, especially attractive
SUPPLIES MRO items; don't become part of final product	Paint, nails, brooms, nuts, paper clips, lubricating oils	Require backup sources; usually straight rebuy, with few buying influences, little shopping; may negotiate contracts to create straight rebuy situation; reciprocity often expected	Branding important to make buying easier; packaging for easy storage; rapid consumption puts emphasis on reliability; should offer full line	Unit prices very low; highly elastic demand in short run	Many suppliers create competitive conditions	Media advertising, sales promotion support direct selling efforts
SERVICES •Maintenance and repair •Business advisory	Painting, machinery repair, janitorial Management consulting, accounting	Frequently purchased on contract or retainer basis, often handled internally	Brand associations, product quality, service	Demand often inelastic if unique product; otherwise, wide range of prices possible through negotiation	Difficult to expand distribution; importance of location varies with amount of customer contact	Personal selling dominant for highly personalized service; referrals important; advertising more important as becomes less personal

more, and is characterized by more concentrated buying by more people. Industrial buying situations are categorized as straight rebuy, modified rebuy, and new task.

Certain kinds of industrial goods (e.g., raw materials and components) become a part of the finished product, whereas others (e.g., installations and supplies) become part of the maintenance, repair, and operating activities involved in getting products produced.

Buying behavior toward industrial products and the use made of these products largely determine marketing mix responses toward different product categories. For example, expensive installations, depreciated over time, typically require high-level expenditure authorization and participation by groups of buying influentials. To reach these influentials, emphasis is usually placed on personal selling and service in the marketing mix. With less expensive products purchased routinely in straight rebuy situations, emphasis is likely to be on price, especially with products that are hard to differentiate.

THE BURGEONING GLOBAL GROWTH OF SERVICES

Services are activities, benefits, or satisfactions offered for rent or sale that are essentially intangible and do not result in the ownership of anything. Services represent the fastest growing sector of world trade, accounting for about 30 percent of world trade in 1996 and, among industrialized nations, about 65 percent of trade with each other. As noted in Chapter 1, services play a paramount role among U.S. exports, with service trade surpluses helping to reduce our massive annual trade deficits by about one-third.

A major impetus for the burgeoning growth of the services sector has been the deregulation of service industries, beginning in the United States in the late 1960s. Since then, this movement toward deregulation of services by governments and service associations has spread throughout industrial nations, exposing them to free-market competitive forces. Major service industries affected include transportation, banking, telecommunications, and professional markets for the Merton MM, such as health care, law, and accounting. More competition has led to lower prices, which increase demand, new service entrants in global markets, and an accelerating search for new markets.

Other stimulants to the worldwide growth of service industries include advances in computer and telecommunication technology leading to faster transmission of information and resources and the horizontal integration of service-related industries into new growth industries, envisioned in the United States by the Telecommunications Act of 1996, designed to define and guide the effective integration of entertainment, cable TV, telecommunications, and Internet technologies.

CHARACTERISTICS OF SERVICES DEFINE MARKET PROBLEMS AND STRATEGIES

Services can be viewed from a number of perspectives that help to identify unique problems in marketing them and strategies to address these problems.

First, services can be viewed in terms of their relationship with more tangible products. Often, services augment and differentiate tangible products and vice versa. In the airline industry, for example, the consideration that secures the sale of airplanes to airlines could be the follow-up maintenance services offered; however, once the sale is secured, a number of other services (hotel reservations, car rentals, etc.) will be dependent on the dependable functioning of tangible airplanes.

Services can also compete with tangible products (e.g., leasing versus buying an automobile) or with other services (e.g., car rental services clamoring for airline traveler dollars).

Often, the key to competitive success in international markets is recognizing these relationships between intangible services and tangible products and how they are likely to change across borders (e.g., what services can be dropped, or added, to enhance the appeal of an offering in a given market?).

Marketing managers should also recognize the problems these relationships create in international markets. For instance, while a single export license is required for the sale of a tangible product (e.g., a turnkey production line or a fleet of vehicles) in a host country, such licenses are often required every time the home country seller services the product. This means that service contracts can be held hostage to political conditions in the host country.

SERVICES CLASSIFIED BY CUSTOMERS, CONTENT, AND CHARACTERISTICS

Services can also be viewed in terms of types of customers served, with service firms like Young and Rubicam (advertising) and Peat Marwick (accounting) serving the organizational market and service firms like Club Med, Thomas Cook, and Hilton Hotels serving the consumer market.

Still another way to classify services is in terms of the extent to which they combine tangible and intangible elements. For example, a visit to a doctor's office may have a 5 percent goods content—say, a stethoscope—and 95 percent nongoods—say, the doctor's diagnosis and your feeling of satisfaction that you're in good shape. A janitorial service, at the other extreme, might be 80 percent goods content (mops, pails, etc.) and only 20 percent nongoods (a clean workplace). Services with a relatively high goods content are often classified as equipment based, whereas less tangible, nongoods services are classified as people based.

From the perspective of the marketer interested in segmenting and entering international markets, perhaps the most productive way to classify and define services—especially people-based services offered by consultants, writers, teachers, accountants and other professionals—is in terms of attributes that differentiate services from more tangible products. Table 13-3 highlights these differences and how they influence marketing mixes.

To illustrate these attributes, consider some of the problems faced by a sports team in marketing its services. Because this service is perishable, it can't be kept in inventory; a rained-out game is usually lost income. Because this service is variable, benefits will vary from game to game, ranging from boring to highly exciting. Because this service is intangible, there is no way to guarantee specific benefits from attending a game (e.g., watching the New York Jets snatch defeat from the jaws of victory can be an acutely distressing experience). Labor intensity is another problem—especially when most of the laborers are getting six-figure incomes—making it difficult to cut costs and raise profits through economies of scale and learning curve efficiencies. Because services are more inseparable from their providers than tangible products, provider-client interaction is a special feature of services marketing, with athletes often expected to serve as role models for customers.

In addition to these differences, many professionals (e.g., doctors and lawyers) face legal and ethical constraints that frequently make them more vulnerable to penalties for self-promotion or malpractice.

These characteristics of services have a number of implications for global marketers. For example, the variability of services puts a strong emphasis on quality control—in medicine, the law, and other professions—to ensure more favorable outcomes. And the fact that services are difficult to separate from their providers means that they don't lend themselves to standardization strategies, although this human factor does provide opportunities to differentiate services.

Another sizable challenge in marketing services globally derives from their intangible variability, which means that they are often statistically invisible, with information regarding income generated, jobs created, and activities undertaken difficult or impossible to come by. This low profile maintained by services also makes them a relatively easy target for governmental regulations, often made in isolation by agencies unconcerned with broader policy concerns. Typically, these regulations take the form of tariff and nontariff entry barriers designed to protect local services in a manner that would be difficult to justify for more tangible products. As an admittedly extreme example, Taiwan mandates that accountants from other countries seeking accreditation pass an extensive CPA exam in Chinese.

Table 13–3. Services: Characteristics and Marketing Mix Attributes

Service Characteristics	As Compared to More Tangible Products	Examples	Product	Price	Place	Promotion
				Marketing Mix Attributes		
Intangibility	More difficult to taste, feel, see, or otherwise sample before using	Quality of a haircut, audit, or advertising campaign	Build, sustain quality image and track record; tangible symbols in brand names (Merrill Lynch's bull)	Strong track record, quality image can justify high price; some services are indirect pricing to avoid issue (e.g., commissions)	Tangible aspects of service environment stressed (inflight meals, magazines in dentist's office, etc.)	"Image" advertising, spokesperson testimonials, free trials, referrals, and personal selling important to document expected benefits
Inseparability	More difficult to separate from person or image of seller	Psychiatrists, doctors, lawyers	Brand name associations with seller image (H&R Block)	Highly personal service fees often negotiated (accountants, real estate brokers); Strong seller image; often commands high fees	Channel opportunities restricted for highly personal services, encouraging direct-run operations (Jacoby and Myers) or franchises (H&R Block, McDonalds)	Promotion focuses on quality of service personnel (Club Med associates, reliable airline pilots), often using service personnel as spokespersons (H&R Block, bank presidents)
Variability • in use	Number of users more likely to change from time to time	Resort seasons, rush hour train schedules	Often incorporate tangible equipment (e.g., automatic teller machines) to spread usage to off periods	Wide range of negotiated prices possible	Important that service have supplies when needed	Media schedules must conform to service use periods; promotion encourages off peak use
• in quality	Quality of use experience more likely to change from time to time	Boring baseball games, 2-hour flight delay	Work to achieve, maintain high quality levels; often modify to relate to new needs	Must often price higher in peak seasons to recoup off-peak costs	Location can enhance "quality" image (Saks Fifth Avenue)	Emphasizes quality experiences (an exciting world series)
Perishability	Must often be consumed while being produced; difficult to keep in inventory	Physical examination, television air time	Customize service to meet needs of customer at time of use (Burger King, hamburger)	Emphasis on a variety of pricing incentives (seasonal, cash, quantity discounts, etc.) to insure commitment to use	Service must be made efficiently accessible to customer when needed	Promotes special incentives to commit to service use (e.g., tangible rewards for buying airtime, magazine subscriptions)
Labor intensity	Services are generally more dependent on quality, ability of personnel; difficult to achieve economy of scale, learning curve benefits	Physical examination, ocean cruise, income tax preparation	Important to select, motivate, and train service personnel for high productivity	Tends to push up price for services, since labor is typically the highest cost component	Service must be located for convenient access by staff members	Service employees encouraged to play active role in selling service, are often used in promotion (e.g., Avon Lady, Lawn Doctor)
Legal, ethical barriers	Higher standards mandated and policed by service industry itself and/or government regulatory bodies	American Association of Advertising Agencies, Security and Exchange Commission, utility regulatory boards	High codes of ethical behavior, especially for personnel services (drug tests for police, review panels for doctors)	Concern for legislative response often important in determining prices (e.g., medical services); Some service prices (utilities) determined by regulatory bodies	Personalized merchandising services (door-to-door), direct mail, selling) frequently subject to fraud and subsequent legal constraints	In regulated services, tends to be defensive in nature, anticipating regulatory curbs (e.g., a politician's apology, a utilities' rate increase justification) advertising even considered unethical in some fields (law, physicians)

SEGMENTATION IMPLICATIONS

Categorizing products and services in terms of uses, characteristics, and buyer behavior is an excellent basis for segmenting markets and for determining marketing mix emphasis. For example, the marketing manager for a large insurance company can define market segments in terms of its "unsought" status: what age, income, and attitude characteristics do people have in common that make this product unsought? Similarly, market segment profiles can be derived from characteristics of people who perceive products as shopping, specialty, new task, straight rebuy, etc. A management consultant interested in introducing her expertise into international markets can tailor product, price, and promotional strategies to reflect the inseparability, labor intensity, and intangibility of her services. In devising segmentation and marketing mix strategies, marketers should be aware that the same product or service can be viewed differently by different customer groups. For example, a package of computer software sold to consumers might be perceived as a convenience good by members of the computer "hacker" segment and as a shopping good by a member of the new owner segment. In the industrial market, the same software might be used to activate a production line in a maintenance, repair, operating application, or, among professional people, be perceived as an administrative tool.

CATEGORIZING PRODUCTS IN INTERNATIONAL MARKETS

In addition to categorizing products in terms of characteristics, uses, and buyer behavior, Keegan[1] suggests the following categories for defining global products and services in terms of their marketability and marketing mix support calculated to ensure the success of product/market growth strategies.

- *Local products.* Products that are perceived as having potential only in a single market (e.g., certain types of clothing—saris and kilts—worn in specific countries).

- *Multinational products.* Products adapted to the perceived unique characteristics of national markets (e.g., electrical appliances designed to accommodate power facilities in different countries).

[1] Warren J. Keegan, *Global Marketing Management*, 6th ed. Englewood Cliffs, N.J.: Prentice Hall, 1994.

- *International products.* Products perceived as having potential for extension into a number of national markets (e.g., McDonald's fast food restaurant chain).

- *Global products.* International products that have achieved global status (e.g., world brands such as Marlboro cigarettes, Exxon oil, and Coca-Cola). In general, global products employ the same positioning and marketing mix strategies in all countries, with small modifications to meet local culture and competitive requirements.

GLOBAL PRODUCT BENEFITS

As products move from local to global status, benefits multiply. Sales volume increases to the point where expensive regional and national headquarters offices are justified. Economies of scale and learning curve savings accrue. The firm's products are able to maintain a single, unified brand image that helps introduce new products and generates sales, particularly among the increasing number of customers who travel across borders.

Additionally, global or international status creates opportunities for international leverage through comparative analysis.

- *International leverage* assumes that excellence and experience in one area of the global landscape—production, R&D, marketing— can be transferred to other areas.

- *Comparative analysis* assumes an experience record for a product in one or more markets and the ability to find market comparability in either the same or displaced time. For example, sales and profit growth of MM systems in Canada might be compared with sales and profit growth in the similar U.S. market to pinpoint areas where performance in one or the other country is markedly above or below the other and to examine why these discrepancies exist. Or, comparative analysis might be undertaken in the "displaced" Mexican market, which, it might be assumed, would achieve parity with the U.S. market in the forseeable future, with plans and projections based on this assumption.

STANDARDIZED VERSUS CUSTOMIZED PLANS

If an important task of global marketers is determining the most effective status for products in international markets—local, multinational, international, global—an important, related issue is the extent to which product or service offerings will have to be adapted to the nature and needs of the different markets they will be entering. Global brands like Coca-Cola, Honda, and Marlboro can employ a marketing mix that is essentially the same worldwide—a standardized plan with only minor changes to account for local differences in such areas as language and legal requirements. A product that lends itself to a standardized plan reaps many advantages as noted previously (e.g., centralized economies of scale and the benefits of comparative analysis).

Other products might require sizable changes in product design or other marketing mix elements to achieve success in international markets. These customized plans are usually costlier than standardized plans, although they do usually provide such benefits as faster responses to local competitive challenges and the development of managers with international marketing skills.

Forces like economic integration and the increased sophistication of communication technologies are moving markets toward greater unification, lending these markets to standardized marketing plans. For most products, however, standardized plans aren't feasible, as evidenced by a study of 174 consumer packaged goods products, which showed that only one in ten was exported without significant modification, with an average of 4.1 changes made in such areas as brand name, product features, packaging, labeling, and user instructions.[2]

As illustrated in Global Focus 13-1, failure to modify products/services to meet local market needs can have expensive consequences.

GLOBAL FOCUS 13-1

When Product Plans Go Awry

Two examples illustrate what happens when well-laid product plans fail to account for customers, competitors, cultures, and conditions in entry markets.

---

[2] John S. Hill and Richard R. Still, "Adapting Products to LDC Tastes," *Harvard Business Review,* Vol. 62 (March–April 1984), pp. 92–101.

- McDonald's early efforts to penetrate the European market failed when the company tried to apply standards and practices successful in North America. For example, North American standards of quality and uniformity—which meant importing products long distances or placing costly local orders—and the firm's emphasis on fast service forced McDonald's costs much higher than those of competitors like Blimpie's and Burger King. This competitive disadvantage was exacerbated by McDonald's decision to locate outlets in European suburbs. Unlike Americans, most Europeans live in cities and are much less mobile.

- During the April–June 1993 quarter—normally the second best of the year—the Euro-Disney theme park in France lost a disastrous $87 million, while stock values plunged 20 percent. The key reasons were misjudged economic trends (e.g., higher-than-expected interest rates made Disney's $3.7 billion of debt very expensive; the European recession hit recreation spending particularly hard) and misjudged cultural environments (e.g., Disney's Puritanical codes—stipulating, as examples, alcohol-free restaurants and undergarments women employees should use—were anathema to the insouciant French, who were also less willing than other nationals to wait on long lines or to change lunch hours to conform to American schedules). Interestingly, the same values resoundingly rejected in France were resoundingly successful in Disney Japan, where more visitors traipsed through the theme park in 5 years than traipsed through the original Disneyland theme park in 35 years.

REASONS FOR MODIFYING PRODUCTS

Key reasons for customizing offerings pertain to the nature and needs of customers, markets, countries, competitors, and the exporting company.

• *CUSTOMER CHARACTERISTICS AND NEEDS*

Degree of cultural grounding in an entry market can strongly influence the need to adapt a product. For example, in Muslim countries, which are strongly grounded in cultural taboos against alcohol and pork products, products containing these ingredients would obviously have to be adapted to conform to these taboos. In general, consumer nondurable products have the highest sensitivity to cultural tastes and constraints and are most likely to require adaptation. Consumer durables (e.g., cameras, home electronics products) are less sensitive to cultural grounding, and industrial products (e.g, steel, chemicals) and high-tech products (e.g., scientific equipment, medical equipment) least sensitive.[3]

In addition to cultural characteristics, customer physical characteristics can also mandate adaptive changes. For example, racial characteristics (skin pigmentation, height, etc.) mandate adaptation of products relating to these characteristics (e.g, skin care products and room furniture).

• *ECONOMIC DEVELOPMENT*

For reasons discussed in Chapter 6, the general stage and state of a country's economic development can mandate an adaptation strategy. For example, products might be packaged to conform to family size and income (e.g., 4- instead of 6-packs and family-sized food packages).

• *POLITICAL AND LEGAL CONSIDERATIONS*

For a variety of reasons covered in Chapter 7, countries erect tariff and nontariff barriers to certain imports that usually lead to product adaptation by exporters. For example, by simply changing the stated purpose of a wrench, one firm succeeded in relegating it to a much lower tariff classification. Sweden bans all aerosol sprays, Japan requires testing of all pharmaceuticals in their laboratories, and French law mandates that all product-related presentations (labels, instructions, promotion, etc.) be in the French language.

• *PRODUCT CHARACTERISTICS AND COMPONENTS*

Fayerweather[4] suggests five product characteristics useful as criteria defining the need for, and nature of, adaptation required to expand into additional markets: primary functional purpose, secondary functional purpose, durability and quality, method of operation, and maintenance. Following is how Merton marketing planners used these criteria to define adaptation needs of MM systems in countries where economic, political, and cultural environments would permit entry:

- *Primary functional purpose.* In its domestic market, the MM's primary purpose was to help educate professional people quickly, effectively, and economically, providing an interactive on-line learning format and access to vast data bases. Foreign markets that needed professional education programs represented potential for MM systems.

---

[3] S. Tamer Cavusgil and Shaoming Zou, "Marketing Strategy-Performance Relationship: An Investigation of the Empirical Link in Export Market Ventures," *Journal of Marketing*, Vol. 58 (January 1994), pp. 1–21.

[4] John Fayerweather, *International Business Management: A Conceptual Framework*. New York, McGraw-Hill, 1969.

- *Secondary functional purpose.* Each MM system and its associated software were also capable of performing computational and analytic tasks more typical of personal computer applications. To the extent that foreign markets had no need for professional education programs, they might have need for the benefits provided by these more traditional applications.

- *Durability and quality.* How could MM systems be expected to hold up in different foreign environments? Would servicing the systems be a problem and, if so, would service be available? If available, at what cost? (In high-pay countries, for example, the market for home appliances costing less than $40 is limited because it's too expensive to repair them.) Can Merton afford to improve product durability and quality to the point where service needs are not an issue? If so, will the product still remain competitive?

- *Maintenance.* If service was available at a competitive cost, was it of consistently high quality to accommodate the diverse, sophisticated maintenance needs of MM's users?

- *Method of operation.* Were technological conditions in the prospective entry country consistent with MM operations? For example, would it be possible to access the Internet? Were voltage and cycle requirements in the country consistent with MM operations?

• *COMPETITIVE CONDITIONS*

A company will often find—or create—a niche for itself in international markets by an adaptation strategy that differentiates its offering from those of competitors.

• *COMPANY CONSIDERATIONS*

Some firms mandate specific first-year ROI levels that an entry strategy must achieve, which can lead to product adaptation strategies to bring first-year costs in line with this profit objective.

PRODUCT/MARKET ADAPTATION STRATEGIES

The four product/market strategies depicted in Figure 13-2 for bringing product/service offerings into line with the criteria just discussed focus on the two dominant, most expensive elements of the marketing mix—the product and the communication campaign—and range from a standardized plan involving only small changes in product and promotion to a customized plan for radically changing both.

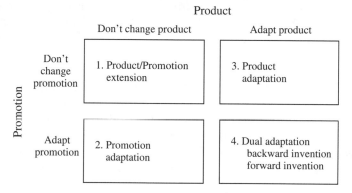

Figure 13–2. International Product/Promotion Strategies

• *PRODUCT-COMMUNICATIONS EXTENSION*

A product is marketed in a foreign market with the same product and promotional appeals used in the home market. Straight extension has been a success in some cases and a disaster in others. As examples, Kellogg cereals, Heineken beer, and Pepsi Cola are all sold in about the same form worldwide. But, Philip Morris couldn't sell U.S.-style blended cigarettes in many markets that prefer straight cigarettes; General Foods couldn't sell powdered Jell-O in the British market, which prefers a cake form; and Philips only sold its coffeemakers in Japan when it reduced their size to fit smaller Japanese kitchens.

• *PRODUCT EXTENSION, COMMUNICATIONS ADAPTATION*

The same product fills a need or serves a purpose that is different in different global markets. For example, American outboard motors are used for recreational purposes in the home market but for commercial fishing in the oriental market. Here, the communications campaign supporting the product, including basic appeals and media, is adapted to the differing nature and needs of the global market, incurring costs for revising communication programs to reflect local conditions.

• *PRODUCT ADAPTATION, COMMUNICATION EXTENSION*

Differing local-use conditions mandate changes in the product while the communication strategy remains essentially unchanged. Examples of this strategy, which is the most frequently used of all in global marketing, include IBM adapting its worldwide personal computer lines to meet local needs, which mandated 20 different keyboards in Europe alone, and Exxon reformulating its gas for different weather conditions in different countries. In both situations, the company communication strategy was essentially unchanged. For example, Exxon's "Put a Tiger in Your Tank" appeal is used universally.

• *DUAL ADAPTATION*

Both the product and the promotion strategy are adapted to local market needs. This strategy represents a combination of the preceding two strategies and is illustrated by Hallmark's greeting card strategy in Europe. There, people are used to writing individual messages on cards, rather than having the messages written for them as they are on cards sold in the United States. The result is different products with different communication appeals.

An extreme example of dual adaptation, product invention, can take the following two forms.

- *Backward invention*, typically used when introducing products in less developed parts of the world, involves simplifying the product back to an earlier stage of its development. For example, NCR sells large numbers of its reintroduced crank cash registers in the orient and Latin America.

- *Forward invention*, in which a firm designs new products to meet new needs in global markets. For example, Anton/Bauer, a small Connecticut company, developed a portable power system that addresses the problem of different power availabilities around the world, ranging from 50 to 230 volts and 50 to 60 cycles. Composed of batteries and chargers, the system "reads" the type of power plugged into and adjusts accordingly. Also, Procter & Gamble developed Ariel laundry detergent for the European market, where washload requirements (soaking time, water temperature, load size, etc.) differ from country to country.

Forward invention is generally considered to be the riskiest, costliest, and most time-consuming of all the product-market strategies, but it can pay off in the highest profits and, often, gain the firm worldwide recognition.

PRODUCT LIFE CYCLES HELP
PLAN STRATEGIES

In international markets, two versions of the Product Life-Cycle (PLC) model help plan marketing strategies appropriate to various product/ market situations, including identifying threats and opportunities, targeting markets, and formulating marketing mixes.

On the macro level, the international PLC model states that certain kinds of products (e.g., innovations like the Merton Mighty Mind, for which a need and market exist) go through a cycle consisting of introduction, growth, maturity, and decline stages. For market and cost reasons, the location of production of these products shifts internationally at different stages of the PLC. During the introductory stage, for example, production occurs only in the home country. Then, during subsequent stages, production moves to other developed countries and then to less-developed countries, still usually controlled by the original firm. Between the stage when the product is introduced and its decline, it faces increasing competition and becomes more price-sensitive and standardized. The company producing the product requires more capital to finance global ventures and, eventually, becomes a net importer.

Regardless of the stage of global development, the acceleratng pace of product introductions, abetted by the increasing ability of nations (like India, Israel, and the Philippines) with low production costs and pools of skilled workers to replicate products more quickly and cheaply, have shortened PLCs in global markets and made product introductions more expensive and risky. Previously, these introductions could be spread out over years; however, firms must now prepare for PLCs that can be measured in months or less.

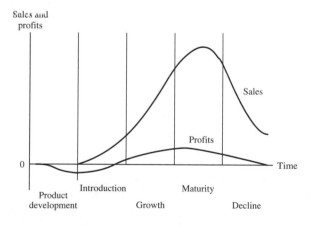

Figure 13–3. Sales and Profits over Stages of Product Life Cycle

THE PLC ANTICIPATES GROWTH STAGES

On the micro level, the PLC model can be applied to the experience, over time, of a product in a single market and interpreted in a manner similar to the interpretation of the international PLC. According to this interpretation, products successfully introduced into a competitive global or domestic market go through the same four stages—introduction, growth, maturity, and decline—with each stage posing threats and opportunities to which marketers must respond in order to maintain product profitability (Figure 13-3). Typical threats, opportunities, and responses characterizing each stage of the PLC are listed on Table 13-4.

Table 13–4. Threats, Opportunities, and Marketing Mix Responses Characterizing Each PLC Stage

Characteristics	Stage in Life Cycle			
	Introduction	Growth	Maturity	Decline
Marketing objective	Attract innovators and opinion leaders to a new product	Expand distribution and product line	Maintain diffential advantage	(a) Cut back (b) revive (c) terminate
Industry sales	Increasing	Rapidly increasing	Stable	Decreasing
Competition	None or small	Some	Many	Few
Industry profits	Negative	Increasing	Decreasing	Decreasing
Profit margins	Low	High	Decreasing	Decreasing
Customers	Innovators	Affluent mass market	mass market	Laggards
Product mix	One basic model	Expanding line	Full product line	Best sellers
Distribution	Depends on product	Expanding number of outlets	Expanding number of outlets	Decreasing number of outlets
Pricing	Depends on product	Greater range of prices	Full line of prices	Selected prices
Promotion	Informative	Persuasive	Competitive	Informative

PLC CHARACTERISTICS

Depending on a diversity of considerations—including kind and amount of competition, level of user benefit, marketing effort expended, and sophistication of the product's technology—PLC length can vary dramatically. For example, costly, complex technology kept color television in the introductory stage of the PLC for more than a decade. At the other extreme, a number of simple, inexpensive, aggressively marketed fad products, (e.g., pet rocks and Hoola Hoops) traversed all the stages of their cycles in fewer than 2 years. Market life cycles, which follow the same introduction-growth-maturity-decline stages that PLCs follow, is another important consideration. For example, depending on the stage of market development, a product can be in different life-cycle stages in different countries, suggesting different strategic responses in each.

In international markets, where initial investment required to introduce products is typically greater and payback is longer and riskier than in domestic markets, the message of the PLC is to generally avoid introducing products that will have short life-cycle curves (e.g., fad or fashion-oriented products, products that can't be differentiated from competitive products, or high-tech products with insufficient backup). This caution is reinforced by global trends that are substantially shortening product life cycles.

TYPICAL PLC STAGES

Following are descriptions of typical situations and responses during each PLC stage, assuming a product perceived as new succeeds in an entry market and transverses all the PLC stages. In entering the MM in selected international markets, Merton planners made these assumptions and used these descriptions to help understand the situation of the MM during any given PLC stage, anticipate what would happen during the next stage, and formulate strategies and tactics based on this information.

• *INTRODUCTION*

The main objective of this stage is to build sales for the product, frequently at the cost of profits. Although competiton is limited—or in the case of a major innovation, nonexistent—profit margins are low for the following reasons.

- The initial market isn't sufficiently large to generate sales volume and economies of scale required for profitable operations.

- Production and marketing costs, on a per-unit basis, are usually higher than they will be during subsequent stages, reflecting the high costs of gaining momentum.

Because costs are high, usually only one model of the product is sold during this stage. For a convenience item (e.g., a new magazine), distribution is extensive, through many dealers; for expensive shopping or specialty items (e.g., automobiles), it is usually selective or exclusive, through few dealers. Depending mainly on product type, the product may have a high status price or a low mass market price.

Promotion generally aims to make prospects aware of the product and inform them of its features and benefits. Product trial is encouraged through coupons, samples, or invitations to try the product.

• *GROWTH*

The main marketing objective during this stage is to expand distribution and range of product alternatives. Primary demand for the product class increases rapidly as more firms enter a highly attractive market with substantial untapped potential. Unit profits increase because members of an expanding market are willing to pay higher prices for the still-limited quantity of products available. To accommodate the needs of this fast-growing market, modified versions of the product are offered (e.g., MM's programs for additional professional groups). Additionally, distribution is expanded, price ranges are offered, and mass promotion becomes more persuasive, focusing on competitive features and benefits.

• *MATURITY*

This stage is characterized by intense competition, and sales stabilize as the market becomes saturated with firms eager to capitalize on still-sizable demand. The main marketing objective of the firm is to maintain its differential advantage and profits associated with this advantage, through more product models and features, lower prices, more service options, and more innovative promotion. As discounting becomes popular, total industry and unit prices begin to decline. As the most lucrative target markets become saturated, other, less attractive market segments become the focus of marketing efforts. A full product line is made available, sold through many outlets at different prices.

• *DECLINE*

Demand decreases during this stage because customers are fewer and other products are more attractive. Sellers now face three alternatives: (1) cut back on marketing programs, reducing the number of products marketed, distributors, and promotion used; (2) revive the product by repositioning, repackaging, or otherwise remarketing it; or (3) terminate the product. As industry sales decline, the product mix concentrates more on the best selling products, most productive distributors, and most effective pricing and promotion strategies.

NEW PRODUCTS: ANYTHING THAT'S NEW

From the perspective of the global marketer, a new product is anything perceived to be new, including a major or minor invention or innovation or a slight or major modification of an existing product. The product may be new to the market or just to the company that introduces it into the market.

When existing products known to the company are introduced into foreign markets, the key question facing the marketer concerns the extent to which the product's record in the existing market is relevant in the proposed new market. As discussed in Chapter 12, the answer usually hinges on the extent to which the new market resembles the existing market and the sophistication used in measuring the potential in this market.

In the U.S. domestic market, about 70 percent of new products brought to market are product modifications, 20 percent are minor innovations, and 10 percent are major innovations. In international markets, the most characteristic type of new product is an existing product already marketed by the company and introduced for the first time into a selected national market. The least common, and most risky, type of new product introduction is of a product that is new to the company and to the foreign market.

Regardless of how the product is categorized, many firms consider the continuing, systematic development of new products critical to growth and profitability in competitive domestic and global markets. These firms find new products an invaluable means of achieving a diversity of corporate objectives (e.g., matching competitors, completing a product line, meeting sales and profit objectives, and utilizing excess capacity). In international markets, new product introductions often also represent the best way to gain early access to the best target markets and distribution channels.

Other firms shun new product development, assuming, instead, a "follow the leader" posture in relation to new product pathfinder firms like Apple Computer, Microsoft, GE, 3M, and Gillette. Reasons cited for their reluctance include fragmented markets that produce lower sales and profits from smaller segments, a shortage of new product ideas resulting from a shortage of new technologies, shorter product-life spans to earn back investments, accelerating costs of new product development; and lack of capital to meet these costs.

Perhaps the main reason for reluctance to enter the new products sweepstakes pertains to the high odds against success. A recent study by the Conference Board of 700 firms showed that only one in seven new product concepts saw the commercial light of day and that one-third of these commercialized products never return a profit. The failure rate among industrial products is about 20 percent; between 15 and 20 percent for services, and 40 percent for consumer products.

ORGANIZING FOR NEW PRODUCT DEVELOPMENT

The four most common structures for developing new products include the following.

- A *brand manager* structure in which a single manager assumes responsibility for new product development, in addition to determining objectives, defining target markets, and devising marketing mix strategies for a single product or product line.

- A *new product committee*, which is composed of top managers from key functional areas who meet periodically to screen new product ideas and then return to their regular positions.

- *Venture teams*, which are composed of managers from different functional areas with authority to plan and carry out new product ventures, independent of other functional departments.

- A *new product department*, which is composed of specialists in all aspects of product development—research, finance, production, marketing—responsible for all stages of the new product development process, from idea generation to commercialization.

In a multiproduct, multicountry company, the enormous number of possible new products, combined with the huge number of information sources, suggests the latter organizational option: a full-time new product unit. According to one study,[5] there is a strong correlation between functionally organized firms with new product departments and the speed of introducing new products abroad: 40 percent of innovations from such firms went abroad in 2 years or less, compared with 6 percent of innovations that went abroad in functionally organized firms lacking such new product departments.

THE TREND TOWARD DECENTRALIZATION

Recently there has been a pronounced trend to supplement centrally directed new product development departments with foreign-based resources[6] to help multinational firms compete more effectively. As firms like Asea Brown Boveri and the Dutch electronics giant Philips have discovered, funding product development in worldwide business units rather than in centralized business laboratories offers a number of benefits, including greater awareness of and access to technological developments in local and global markets, faster technology transfer from parent to subsidiary, and the development of new products expressly for selected global markets.

---

[5] William Davidson and Richard Harrigan, "Key Decisions in International Marketing: Introducing New Products Abroad," *Columbia Journal of World Business* (Winter 1977).

[6] "In the Labs, the Fight to Spend Less, Get More," *Business Week* (June 28, 1993), pp. 102–104, and "For Best Results, Decentralize R&D," *Business Week* (June 28, 1993), p. 134.

NEW PRODUCT DEPARTMENT FUNCTIONS

Typically, new product departments carry out the following steps in the new product development process: (1) idea generation, (2) idea screening, (3) concept development and testing, (4) marketing strategy development, (5) business analysis, (6) product development, (7) test marketing, and (8) commercialization. Here is how the Merton new product department followed these steps in developing new products for the global market:

• *IDEA GENERATION*

This step in the process entails both sources of new ideas, and methods for generating these ideas.

- *Idea sources.* Sources can include customers, suppliers, competitors, salespeople, distributors, agents, subsidiary executives, home office executives, internal reports, and actual observation. Table 13-5 shows percentages of new product ideas from these sources in consumer and industrial markets. At Merton, information from these sources was systematically gathered and organized into the firm's MIS database (discussed in Chapter 4) and then channeled to relevant screening and decision centers. On occasion, an idea for a new product emerged when global scanning indicated sudden demand spurts for products in specific nations, indicating potential that could be transferred to other nations.

Table 13–5. Sources of New Product Ideas

Source	Industrial Products (%)	Consumer Products (%)	Total (%)
Research & development	24.3	13.9	20.8
Internal other than research and development	36.2	31.6	34.6
User suggestions, complaints	15.8	12.7	14.7
Formal research user needs	10.5	17.7	13.0
Analysis competitor products	27.0	38.0	30.7
Analysis published information	7.9	11.4	9.1
Suggestions from suppliers	12.5	3.8	9.5

Source: Leigh Lawton & David Parasuraman, "So You Want Your New Product Planning To Be Productive" *Business Horizons* (December 1980).

- *Idea generation methods*. Supplementing Merton's systematic procedures for gathering new product ideas were techniques for transforming these ideas into product concepts. Two of these techniques—product analysis and brainstorming—involved, first, systematically assessing a diversity of competitive personal computer systems to identify key features and benefits that produced market success. Then, during brainstorming sessions, department members were brought together to generate ideas in a free-wheeling environment in which criticism was discouraged and participants were encouraged to "piggyback" on the ideas of others. All ideas were recorded, with the realization that few, if any, would emerge from the next stage of the process.

• *IDEA SCREENING*

The purpose of this second step of the process was to reduce ideas generated during the first step to the few worth further consideration. In so doing, department members aimed to avoid "drop" errors, whereby a product with real potential gets dropped from consideration (e.g., both IBM and Kodak dropped the Xerox copy technology), and "go" errors, whereby a firm decides to go with a product that later fails (among history's biggest product flops are Ford's Edsel, Dupont's Corfam, Polaroid's Polavision, RCA's Videodisk, the SONY Betamax, IBM's PCjr, New Coke, and Nutrasweet's Simpless fat substitute).

Basic to Merton's screening process was a checklist, covering economic considerations (e.g., investment required and profit potential), market criteria (e.g., prospective competition, size of market potential, and availability of distribution channels), and product characteristics (e.g., its fit with existing product line and production capabilities and its anticipated product life). In addition to providing a quantitative index of success by giving weights to each criteria area and scores to each product concept in each attribute area, this checklist also pointed out areas where action could be taken to improve success chances. For example, if the product scored low in the area of promotable features, design changes could be undertaken to remedy this shortcoming.

After the new product concept emerging from this checklist analysis was written up on a standard form containing estimates regarding its market, competition, strengths and shortcomings, development costs, and profit return, it moved to the next stage of the process.

• *CONCEPT DEVELOPMENT AND TESTING*

This third step of the new product development process aimed toward further developing product ideas into product concepts, defined in terms meaningful to prospective consumers. The general approach was to develop the initial idea into alternate product concepts and to evaluate the relative attractiveness of each concept by presenting an elaborated version of each, with descriptive copy and illustrations, to consumer focus groups who responded to questions like: Does this product meet a real need? Does it offer significant benefits over competitive offerings? How would you improve it? What should it cost? What is the likelihood that you would buy it?

• *MARKETING STRATEGY DEVELOPMENT*

If the new product concept survived to this step, it had been developed and tested to the point where a marketing strategy could be formulated. The statement elaborating this strategy, which would be the model for the marketing plan formulated later if the product were to be commercialized, typically contains sections describing: (1) the product, the market for the product, and the competitive environment in which it will be launched; (2) the planned marketing mix strategy in support of the product launch; (3) long-range marketing mix strategies and sales/profit projections, and (4) proposed schedules and budgets.

• *BUSINESS ANALYSIS*

During this step in the new product development process, assumptions and projections of previous steps are exposed to the harsh light of economic analysis. Key questions asked include: What size investment will we require to launch and sustain this product? At what rate will sales, costs, and profits grow? Will anticipated return on investment be sufficient to justify this investment over other less risky alternatives? What will be the effect of the growth of this product on other products in our line? Tools and techniques used to address these questions included breakeven, cash flow, and return on investment analyses.

• *PRODUCT DEVELOPMENT*

During previous steps, the proposed new product had undergone a series of changes, from a word picture to "paper prototype" drawings to actual product mock-ups.

During this stage of the process, the Merton research and development department was charged with the job of developing prototypes of the product that would embody all the attributes of the final product and could be used to determine its commercial feasibility. The cost of this step exceeded the combined cost of the previous steps but produced prototypes that could be tested functionally, under laboratory conditions, to get feedback from prospective buying influences (e.g., professionals who would later be customers for models of MM systems). For example, could the product be improved? How? Were promotional claims believable and persuasive? Was price consistent with perceived value? How did this product compare with competitive offerings?

• *TEST MARKETING*

This step of the process involves introducing the new product offering into a real-life environment (e.g., two test market cities) and then measuring the relative impact of various marketing mix combinations under the experimental conditions described in Chapter 5. Typically, however, this step is omitted as excessively expensive and competitively risky. In testing Merton product concepts, test market studies were replaced by consumer panels that helped produce desired degrees of secrecy, reliability, and validity of research findings.

• *COMMERCIALIZATION*

This final step of the new product development process is invariably the most costly, involving outlays for full-scale production and marketing investments that can exceed $200 million in commercial markets. To improve the odds of successfully marketing a new product in a new country, Merton focused on four decision areas.

- *Where to launch the product*, with the decision based on a thorough analysis of environmental threats and opportunities and market compatability in the prospective entry market.

- *At whom to launch*, with the decision based on an understanding of the nature, needs, present size, and growth potential of prospective target markets.

- *When to launch*, with decisions based on an understanding of when target market needs would be greatest and competitive responses most manageable.

- *How to launch*, with decisions based on data showing how much to spend for the new product launch and how these funds should be allocated among the four components of the marketing mix.

All of these areas of concern were documented in a marketing plan that helped coordinate and control marketing efforts supporting the new product launch.

CHAPTER PERSPECTIVE

Understanding products and services in consumer and organizational markets is the basis for strategic planning decisions pertaining to how they should be priced, positioned, distributed and promoted in foreign markets. For example, the status of a product as "local," "international," "multinational" or "global" largely defines the degree to which marketing mix supports will be standardized or customized. The risk and cost of introducing new products into foreign markets can be mitigated through evaluative, analytical processes that follow the product from initial idea generation to final commercialization.

KNOW THE CONCEPTS

TERMS FOR STUDY

accessory equipment
augmented product
backward invention
brand manager
commercialization
comparative analysis
components
consumer products
convenience goods
customized plans
dual adaptation
forward invention
generic product
global products
industrial products
installations

international leverage
international products
local products
multinational products
new product development strategies
product adaptation strategies
product life cycle
products
psychic satisfactions
raw materials
services
shopping products
specialty goods
standardized plans
supplies
unsought goods

MATCHUP EXERCISES

1. Match up the product concept in the first column with the descriptor in the second column.

    1. nondurable

    a. the warranty accompanying Black & Decker drill presses

    2. augmented

    b. a drill press

    3. core

    c. the holes made by the drill press

    4. durable

    d. the paper clip attached to the product warranty

2. Match the product categories in the first column with the products in the second column.

    1. convenience

    a. you need a new refrigerator

    2. supplies

    b. what you use to sweep the factory floor and paint the walls

3. shopping
4. components

5. installations

c. the motor in the refrigerator
d. the escalator that takes you to the refrigerators
e. You buy a copy of *The National Enquirer* at the checkout counter

3. Match the stage of the new product development process listed in the first column with the descriptor listed in the second column

1. concept development and testing
2. idea generation
3. idea screening
4. business analysis

5. marketing strategy development

a. Let's brainstorm this.

b. That's a goofy idea!
c. Well then, how about this one?
d. With a good promotion push, it should sell.
e. It may sell, but no way will it generate enough profits.

4. Match the global product/communication strategy in the first column with the situation described in the second column.

1. product-communication extension

2. product extension, communication adaptation
3. product adaptation, communication extension

4. dual adaptation

a. American bicycles positioned for recreation in the United States and basic transportation in China
b. no additional R&D, manufacturing, or promotional expense
c. General Foods recognizes that the British drink coffee with milk and the French drink it black
d. gas formulations change, but not Exxon's "Tiger in Your Tank"

5. Match up the PLC stage in the first column with the situations summarized in the second column.

1. introduction

2. growth

3. maturity

4. decline

a. fewer competitors, outlets, sales
b. stable sales, lower margins, less competition
c. expanding lines, outlets, sales, price ranges
d. informative promotion, innovative customers, increasing sales

QUESTIONS FOR REVIEW AND DISCUSSION

1. How would you define Club Med and Windows 95 along core, actual, and augmented dimensions? Which dimension would be most important in positioning, promoting, and pricing each?

2. Anderson Consulting, the largest consulting firm in the world, generates more than 65 percent of its gross revenues from services abroad. In terms of characteristics of services that distinguish them from more tangible products, discuss problems you, as a partner in this firm, would face in opening an office in Japan.

3. Following up on question 2, assume that, after 2 years of operation, and unlike most other Anderson offices in oriental countries, Anderson's Japanese office still isn't generating a profit. Discuss how use might be made of international leverage and comparative analysis to address this problem.

4. The Ray-O-Vac Company, producer of batteries and other consumer goods for global markets, plans to announce the development of a new, more powerful battery for powering vehicles. In terms of Fayerweather's criteria, describe considerations that Ray-O-Vac marketers will have to account for in building this new battery into a high-leverage global product.

5. Discuss the nature and role of promotional expenditures at each stage of the product life cycle for a new line of high-resolution television sets that are only one-eighth of an inch thick and hang on the wall like a poster.

6. Could the eight stages of the new product development process be applied as effectively in generating, developing, and commercializing ideas for new services or, at the extreme end of the tangibility spectrum, new ideas?

ANSWERS

MATCHUP EXERCISES

1. 1d, 2a, 3c, 4b
2. 1e, 2b, 3a, 4c, 5d
3. 1c, 2a, 3b, 4e, 5d
4. 1b, 2a, 3d, 4c
5. 1d, 2c, 3b, 4a

QUESTIONS FOR REVIEW AND DISCUSSION

1. Along the core dimension, each would be defined in terms of problem-solving services or benefits offered. For example, and depending on the market segment attracted to each, Club Med's core dimension benefits might include finding a mate, acquiring a lovely tan, expanding cultural horizons, or just getting away from all that snow. Core benefits of Windows 95 might include professional advancement, more productive employment of time and money, or expanding social and learning experiences through access to the Internet. Actual product dimensions would define each in terms of quality level, features, styling, brand name, and packaging. In the case of Club Med, for example, these dimensions would cover aspects like the comfort of accommodations, reliability of tour guides, cost, and other components of the vacation package (side trips, etc.), while for Windows 95 they would encompass things like cost, ease of operation, associations of the Microsoft brand, and programs included in the software. The augmented dimension for both would include additional services and benefits, including money-back warrantees if not satisfied, lessons in the use of Windows 95, and a toll-free telephone number to call for additional information.

   While actual, core, and augmented product features would probably all be used to position, promote, and price the Club Med and Windows 95 offerings (e.g., promotion for Club Med would include information on prices, destinations, and accommodations), core benefits are what buyers are ultimately paying for. Hence, from the marketer's point of view, these benefits (the lovely tan, the adventures on the Internet) would probably be of most use.

2. As distinguished from products, services tend to be less tangible and more variable, perishable, and labor-intensive. They are also more likely to face legal and ethical barriers and be inseperable from the provider. The labor-intensive aspect of this consulting service suggests that it would be difficult, and expensive, to recruit the professionals required to staff this new office and that these costs would be difficult to reduce through economies of scale. Meanwhile, since your consulting services are perishable and can't be kept in inventory, there would be no way to recoup losses while the office was generating billings through expensive personal contact work with prospective clients, often involving taking engagements at discounted fees. And because of the variability of services and professional ethics involved in client relations, it would be impossible (and unethical) to promise prospective clients specific benefits, further diluting the persuasive impact of your new business presentations. Inseparability of your services from their providers probably means that your consul-

tants must spend a lot of nonbillable time developing personal relations with clients and prospects.

3. International leverage implies that a firm engaged in global marketing can transfer success factors from one country to another, including systems, strategies, services, and personnel. Comparative analysis is the process that facilitates this transfer. For example, other, profitable, Anderson offices similar in tenure, scope, objectives, and markets served might be compared to the Japanese office to identify success factors that might succeed in making the Japanese office profitable.

4. *Primary functional purpose:* Battery market potential would first be assessed in terms of primary applications for which they were developed and where in the world these applications existed. *Secondary functional purpose:* Additional, secondary applications for the batteries would be researched, with market potential figures upgraded in terms of where these applications existed. For example, although designed for vehicles, possibly the batteries could be used in power plants in developing countries with little access to centralized energy sources. *Durability and quality:* The batteries would be tested against conditions under which they would be used throughout the world, including arctic and tropical climates. *Maintenance* requirements for the batteries would be assessed against maintenance resources in prospective global entry markets. *Method of operation* analysis would aim to determine if conditions and facilities existed in prospective entry markets (e.g., for recharging the batteries) to maintain the batteries properly. Based on these analyses and the feasible modifications that could be made on the batteries consistent with uncovered needs, Ray-O-Vac marketers could begin marketing planning and product modification strategies to transform the new batteries into global products.

5. During the introductory stage of this product's life cycle, advertising and publicity would perform an essentially pioneering role, attempting to make innovator and early adopter groups aware of, and informed about, the new TV technology and building primary demand for the product's class. Sales promotion would also be stressed to encourage early trial, and personal selling would be used to get distributors interested. During the growth stage, with competition much more aggressive, the focus would be on building selective demand for the product itself, rather than for the product class; advertising and publicity continues to be important, but sales promotion is reduced because fewer incentives to buy the product class are required. During the maturity stage, when competition increases appreciably, sales promotion becomes important again in the promotion mix; firms that have achieved a leadership position engage in reminder advertising; others, highly aggressive persuasive advertising.

During the final, decline stage, reminder advertising continues to prevail; publicity and sales promotion is downgraded or eliminated; and salespeople give the product minimum attention.

6. The eight stages of the new product development process could be applied to new services or new ideas quite easily. To illustrate, envision a situation where a group of politicians meet to hammer out a platform for a candidate for high office (the "product" who will communicate the ideas in the platform). Ideas would be generated during a brainstorming session (balance the budget? introduce a flat tax? install a "pro-life" plank in the platform?) and then screened for consistency with larger party missions and goals. Next, they would be developed and tested among a sample of the electorate (probably using staff pollsters). Then, successful ideas would be transformed into a marketing strategy including media advertising, publicity, and speaking engagements; subjected to cost-benefit economic scrutiny during the business analysis stage, to determine if the expected additional votes resulting from this strategy are worth the additional tangible and intangible costs; and then further developed, test marketed (e.g., during local primary elections), and finally commercialized during introduction into the rough and tumble of the actual campaign.

14

INTERNATIONAL PRODUCT PLANNING II: PRODUCT DESIGN AND DEVELOPMENT STRATEGIES

OVERVIEW

Although product planning concepts are the same throughout the world, the complexity and diversity of environmental threats and opportunities in international markets make product planning considerably more challenging than in domestic markets. In both domestic and global markets, however, the goal is the same: developing products and marketing strategies that will meet customer needs and company objectives in such areas of concern as product design, branding, quality, service, packaging, and labeling.

PRODUCT PLANNING MEETS CUSTOMER NEEDS AND COMPANY GOALS

In Chapter 13, we began our discussion of the four elements of the marketing mix by defining categories and characteristics of products and services, and illustrating a systematic approach to create, evaluate, and commercialize new products in international markets.

In this chapter, we continue our discussion of the product component of the global marketing mix with an examination of planning considerations calculated to help achieve and maintain profitability in international markets. These considerations pertain to product design, branding, quality, service, packaging, labeling, lines, and mixes. We also examine the scope and impact of product counterfeiting on product planning and appropriate responses to different manifestations of this problem.

INTERNATIONAL PRODUCT PLANNING IN CONTEXT

Product planning in global markets does not take place in a vacuum. Most successful products reflect an understanding of how the product will be used, by whom, and in what kind of competitive, economic, technological, cultural, and political climate. Uninformed product planning, beginning with the basic design of the product, can doom an otherwise successful concept.

PRODUCT DESIGN: A CRUCIAL DECISION

Often the most crucial decisions affecting the success of products sold in global markets pertain to their design, particularly as these decisions relate to customer preferences, costs, and compatibility.

• CUSTOMER PREFERENCES

What customers want and expect in products has to be the main consideration in product design, ignored at the sellers' peril. Global Focus 14-1 illustrates product failures and successes tracing directly to design features based on these wants and expectations.

GLOBAL FOCUS 14-1

Learning from Product Design Successes and Failures

The following examples highlight the importance of designing products compatible with customer preferences, cost constraints, and competitive conditions in entry markets.

- Parking Solutions, a small family manufacturer of Redondo Beach, Ca., overcame competition from 17 Japanese manufacturers in selling its automobile parking lifts to Tech Corporation

---

of Hiroshima. A company spokesperson described the parking lifts of Japanese manufacturers as "overengineered and over-priced." The Japanese like the American lifts because they are simply designed, easy to operate, and less costly.

- Kryptonite Corporation of Canton, Mass., got a sales boost in its Asian market when it received the award for outstanding design and function of a bicycle lock by the Japanese Design and Promotion Organization.

- The Olivetti Company discovered that its modern, award winning, lightweight typewriter, enormously successful in Europe, couldn't compete against the heavy, bulky typewriters designed and sold in the United States. Olivetti was forced to adopt its typewriter design (on display in the Museum of Modern Art) to preferences of American consumers.

Source: *Business America*, World Trade Week 1993 Edition, Vol. 114, No. 9, U.S. Department of Commerce, Washington, DC, pp. 6–7.

• *COST*

The cost to make and market a product puts a floor under the price charged and can be the main determinant of the product's competitiveness and profitability in the global market. Key considerations, in addition to the cost of designing to suit customer preferences, include the cost of foreign labor and materials, if any, used in its production and the cost of hurdling tariff and nontariff barriers erected in the entry country.

• *COMPATIBILITY*

Products must be designed to be compatible with the environment in which they will be used. Different climates, different measurement systems (the United States is the only nonmetric country in the world), and different power and broadcast systems are but a few of the environmental constraints that can affect product design. Of particular importance to designers of American products are product standards mandated by individual countries and regional economic communities. For example, with the European Economic Area (EEA) agreement in force as of January 1994, design requirements must be met in order to sell many categories of products—including toys, construction products, pressure vessels, gas appliances, medical devices, telecommunications equipment and machinery—in 18 European countries. In addition to these national and supranational standards, Richard Robinson[1] suggests consideration of the following nine key environmental factors and product design changes deriving from each.

---

[1] Richard Robinson, *International Business Management*. Hinsdale, Il: Dryden Press, 1985.

Environmental Factor in entry country	Design Change
Low level of technical skills	Product simplification
High labor cost	Automation or manualization
Low literacy level	Remarking and simplification
Low income level	Quality and price change of product
High interest rates	Quality, price change (investment in high quality not financially desirable)
Low maintenance level	Change in tolerance, simplification
Climatic differences	Product Adaptation
Isolation (maintenance and repair difficult, expensive)	Product simplification, improved reliability
Different standards	Recalibration, resizing

These suggested changes focus primarily on design characteristics of the tangible product. A complete product planning effort would encompass aspects of the augmented product and the core product, including brand name, quality and service levels, packaging and labeling characteristics, and decisions pertaining to length and width of product lines and mixes.

PRODUCT BRANDS: DEFINITIONS AND DECISIONS

A brand is a name, term, sign, symbol, design, or combination thereof that identifies and helps to differentiate and control products and services of a single seller, such as Honda or Ford, or a group of sellers, such as the Direct Marketing Association. In international markets, the brand is one of the easiest aspects of the offering to standardize and may help standardize other products in the line and marketing mix elements (e.g., price, quality, promotion). Standardized products and brands do not necessarily go together; for example, it's possible to have a standardized brand name on a local product (e.g., a German beer brand brewed in the United States) or vice versa (e.g., an American appliance with a local brand name in a foreign country).

Brands can be local, national, regional or worldwide in scope. However, consistent with the general sluggishness of U.S. export efforts discussed in Chapter 1, few U.S. brands get beyond the national level. Indeed, with the exception of a few global brands (Coca-Cola, Levi's Jeans, etc.), the majority of U.S. brands achieve more than 80 percent of sales from the domestic market, with most of the rest coming from culturally similar markets.[2]

A brand name is that part of the brand that can be spoken (e.g., the Prudential Insurance Company). A brand mark is that part of the brand that can be recognized but is not utterable (e.g., the Prudential's Rock of Gibralter brand mark). A trademark is a brand name or mark that is given legal protection (e.g., the Xerox trademark can only be legally used by the Xerox Corporation). A copyright is legal protection given literary, musical, or artistic works so they can be published or sold only by the copyright holder.

BRAND SPONSORSHIP DECISIONS

Brand sponsorship options available to sellers include a manufacturer's brand, a private brand, or a generic brand. A manufacturer's, or national brand, is assigned by the manufacturer of the product (e.g., Hellman's mayonnaise). A private, or dealer, brand, is assigned by the wholesaler or retailer of a product, such as Ann Page brand mayonnaise (A&P). Generic brands are plainly marked with no identification. Dealers see generic brands as a way to increase profits by saving on advertising, packaging, and other costs associated with manufacturer and private brands.

Frequently, a seller opts for more than one branding strategy. For example, the Whirlpool Corporation manufactures products under its own brand name and under Sears' private brand name (Kenmore).

Competition for supermarket shelf space between manufacturer's brands and private brands is a fast growing trend in both domestic and international markets that is especially troubling to manufacturers because they must frequently make unwanted concessions to dealers.

BRANDING BENEFITS BUYERS, SELLERS, SOCIETY

Illustrative of how branding benefits buyers, sellers, and society at large is a situation that existed in the former Union of Soviet Socialist Republics (U.S.S.R.), a command economy that mandated centralized control of production and distribution, with few of the niceties of competitive free markets. Under this system, most color television sets for the (then) far-flung Soviet empire were produced in two huge factory complexes.

---

[2] Barry N. Rosen, J. J. Boddewyn, and Ernst A. Louis, "U.S. Brands Abroad: An Empirical Study of Global Branding," *International Marketing Review*, Vol. 6 (Spring 1989), pp. 7–19.

Unfortunately, the Soviet population quickly and painfully recognized that the output of one of the complexes was unfit for human consumption; practically everything that could go wrong with a color television set did, with the promptness of breakdowns contrasting sharply to the length of time required for repairs. Since there was no easy way to distinguish between the output of the two factories, the public response was to stop buying color television sets, throwing the industry into chaos.

Now contrast this situation with an analagous situation in competitive markets where companies brand their products. From the buyer's viewpoint, the brand name makes it easy to identify and shop for the brand that will meet the buyer's needs and standards. (It will also make it easier to shop for new products this branded manufacturer offers.) In that the seller has put its corporate reputation on the line with its brand name, it also helps ensure a consistent level of product quality. The strength of this brand name, and its associations of quality and unique product values, makes it easier for the seller to control product pricing and promotion. These associations can also help build a strong corporate image for all the seller's product lines, attracting a loyal, profitable group of target customers and facilitating the successful introduction of new products under the brand name. Branding also helps sellers segment markets; for example, the color TV manufacturer can offer different brands of TVs to attract different benefit-seeking segments.

Finally, branding benefits society at large. A successful branded product encourages other firms to improve on this success. Thus, branding stimulates competition, innovation, and continuing product improvement, in addition to making shopping more efficient and maintaining product quality. Indicative of the enormous psychological power of brands is a study of American consumer goods showing, on average, that the #1 brand in a category earns a 20 percent return, the #2 brand earns a 5 percent return, and the rest lose money.[3]

BRAND DECISIONS: NAMES, QUALITY LEVELS, AND SERVICE

Given the importance of branding, many firms implement formal procedures for arriving at brand decisions. At Merton, for example, branding decisions for international products were made in the new product department, usually with approval from senior management. These decisions pertained to brand name strategies, brand quality levels, and customer service levels associated with Merton brands.

---

[3] "The Year of the Brand," *Economist* (December 24, 1988), pp. 95–100.

BRAND NAME STRATEGIES

The following four brand name strategies were considered by department members in devising brand names for Merton products marketed globally, such as the Mighty Mind line of computer systems.

- *An individual brand name strategy*, with a brand name applied to each product in the line, and the company name deemphasized. An example is Procter & Gamble's product line (Tide, Cheer, Folger's, Crest). The advantages are that brands can be targeted to specific markets, failure of one brand doesn't endanger others, and more individual brands occupy more shelf space. On the other hand, a strong companywide image is often sacrificed, as are mass production and marketing economies.

- *Separate family names* for different categories of products. For example, Sears' has a family brand name for appliances (Kenmore) and another family brand name for tools (Craftsman). The advantages of separate family names are that it is easier to implement a brand extension strategy of launching new or modified products under a successful brand name, there is less expenditure on research to identify successful brand names, and there is less cost for promoting brand name recognition and preference.

- *A blanket family name for all products.* Examples include General Electric and Heinz 57 product lines. Generally the same benefits apply here as for the separate-family-names strategy.

- *A company brand name combined with an individual brand name.* Kellogg's Rice Krispies is an example. One advantage is that it is easier to launch new products under the company brand, while targeting markets under individual brand names.

Deciding which of these brand name strategies, or combinations thereof, to implement depends on product/market conditions in which products are introduced and commercialized. For example, if a firm's product mix lends itself to segmentation, an individual brand name strategy might be most appropriate. If a firm sells most of its products in a few markets, a blanket family name might be more appropriate. However, if a firm's product lines differ appreciably—such as Swift and Company's Premium brand hams and Vigoro fertilizer—a family brand name might not be able to stretch far enough, and a combination family/individual brand name strategy might be more appropriate.

Another important consideration in deciding on brand name strategies in international markets derives from stereotyped attitudes or "country of origin" effects toward foreign products that can help or hinder marketing efforts. One study, for example, showed the following quality scores assigned by Germans to their products and those of other countries: German, 54; British, 30; Dutch, 24; French, 16; Belgian, 8; Italian, 2. Among Italians, who were listed last in terms of German perceptions, assigned quality scores were: German, 37; Dutch, 25; Italian, 24; British, 10; French, −1. Another study showed that the "Made in U.S.A." label had lost ground appreciably in global perceptions to the "Made in Japan" label. National perceptions of the products of other nations should probably be taken into consideration when planning all aspects of the marketing mix strategy, particularly a brand name that advertises the product's derivation. In Germany, for example, the Maxwell House brand, along with its "great American coffee" slogan, proved to be a turnoff when it was found Germans have about as much respect for American coffee as they have for American beer. In another situation, a Brazilian manufacturer of sensitive oil drilling equipment overcame negative stereotypes of Brazilian products in Mexico by first exporting components of the equipment to Switzerland, where they were assembled and stamped "Made in Switzerland." Facing these negative stereotypes, a successful branding strategy often uses local names or well-known local brands to contribute to a national identity. Alternately, if the country's products are favorably perceived in an entry country—as is the case with many imported beers in the United States—the brand should probably reflect this fact ("Becks—The most popular beer in Germany").

CHOOSING EFFECTIVE BRAND NAMES

At Merton, the following five-step process was used to select effective brand names for new products introduced into the global marketplace.

• *ESTABLISH BRAND NAME CRITERIA*

Primary criteria against which prospective brand names were assessed included compatability with customer perceptions, the image desired for the product, and the product's marketing mix. In the case of the Merton Mighty Mind line, for example, planners wanted a name that suggested the high-tech nature of the product, and that would lend itself to product promotions. Beyond that, the brand name selected should be distinctive; suggest something about product features and benefits; be relatively easy to recognize, recall, and pronounce; and be applicable to other products added to the line. Of particular importance in the global market, the name should translate easily into the language of prospective foreign customers, without unanticipated negative connotations. (Examples of these embarrassing language blunders: Coke, in Chinese, translates to "bite the wax tadpole"; the Chevrolet Nova translates into Spanish as "it doesn't go"; Sunbeam's Mist Stick hair curling iron translates in German to "manure wand.")

- ## CREATE A LIST OF POTENTIAL BRAND NAMES

Primary sources include names of products already in the mix, the name a dealer gives the product under a private name policy, a name licensed from a firm that holds a trademark on it, or any of a variety of original names, including initials (IBM, CBS), invented names (Kleenex, Exxon), numbers (Century 21), mythological characters (Samsonite luggage), personal names (Ford), geographical names (Southwestern Bell), dictionary names (Whirlpool appliances), foreign names (Nestle), and word combinations (Head and Shoulders shampoo).

- ## SCREEN THE LIST TO SELECT THE MOST APPROPRIATE FOR FURTHER TESTING

Here, planners referred back to the original selection criteria.

- ## OBTAIN CONSUMER REACTIONS TO THE REMAINING NAMES

This step involved informal surveys and focus group interviews with Merton staff and prospective buyers of MM systems.

- ## CONDUCT A TRADEMARK SEARCH

A multinational firm must register trademarks in every country in which it markets its products, a process that can be time-consuming and expensive. In order to be legally protected, a trademark must adhere just to the product, its package, or its label; can't imply characteristics the product doesn't possess; and must not be confused with other trademarks. Once registered, a trademark gives the firm exclusive use of a "word, symbol, combination of letters or numbers, or other devices, such as distinctive packaging" for as long as the trademarked product is marketed. However, a brand name can become generic public property by becoming too popular, as happened to brand names like aspirin, linoleum, and nylon, and is threatening to happen to brand names like Xerox and Kleenex.

PRODUCT COUNTERFEITING THREATENS GLOBAL TRADE

Counterfeit products, defined as goods bearing an unauthorized representation of a trademark, patented invention, or copyrighted work, are reaching a magnitude where they seriously threaten to disrupt international trading patterns. Hardest hit are the products of innovative, fast-growing industries (computer software, pharmaceuticals, entertainment) and highly visible consumer goods brands (Polo, Gucci, Izod).[4] The fact that these

---

[4] Faye Rice, "How Copycats Steal Billions," *Fortune* (April 22, 1991), pp. 157–164.

tend to be major categories of U.S. exports helps explain the estimated $70 billion U.S. companies lose each year because of product counterfeiting and other infringement of intellectual property. (Worldwide, the International Chamber of Commerce, estimates the trade in counterfeit goods at 5 percent of total world trade.)

From the perspective of an American exporter, responses to product counterfeiting depend primarily on where the firm's products are being counterfeited and sold. Seventy-five percent of counterfeit goods are produced outside the United States, with China, Brazil, Korea, India, and Taiwan the major offenders. If these products are sold in the country of origin, infringement actions are usually brought under the laws of that country. In 1995, for example, an intellectual property agreement was reached with China, under threat of sanctions, to close down a number of factories in business only to counterfeit American products.

Products counterfeited abroad and sold in the United States should be stopped at the customs barrier, although lack of personnel and the increasingly high-tech character of counterfeit products makes enforcement difficult. Problems involving the 25 percent of counterfeit products that are either made in this country or imported and labeled here are best resolved through infringement actions brought in U.S. federal courts.

Although there is no such thing as an international patent, trademark, or copyright, some protection exists under such international treaties and agreements as the Paris Convention for the Protection of Industrial Property, the Patent Cooperation Treaty, the Berne Convention for the Protection of Literary and Artistic Works, and the Universal Copyright Convention, as well as regional patent and trademark offices.

GLOBAL USE PATTERNS DEFINE QUALITY LEVELS

Defined in terms of user perceptions and applicable to national, private, and generic brands, quality is the rated ability of the product to perform its functions through such objective and subjective attributes as durability, safety, reliability, appearance, ease of operation, and service.

In international markets, desired degree of product quality is invariably relative to use patterns and standards in the country where the product is marketed. For example, DuPont adopted ISO 9000 standards (a set of technical standards chosen by the European Union to encourage manufacturing and service organizations to implement sound quality procedures) after losing a big order to an ISO-certified British firm. Alternately, high quality by standards in developed countries may represent unnecessary cost in less-developed countries.

A strong emphasis on quality among consumers in North America is evidenced by strong demand for product quality in Japanese automobiles and electronics and in European automobiles, clothing, and food. A number of domestic companies are catering to this growing interest in quality, as illustrated by Ford's "Quality is Job #1" promotion campaign. In international markets, quality is also growing as a key criterion for product purchase, especially for products where quality differences are not easy to perceive (e.g., refrigerators or color TV sets). A study by the PIMS group (Profit Impact of Marketing Strategies), for example, concluded that companies that innovate and deliver quality achieve higher rates of return in both mature and stagnant markets. These companies also avoid the unprofitable trap of competing on the basis of commodity or undifferentiated items. Global Focus 14-2 highlights the importance of quality, and perceptions of quality, in achieving success in global markets.

GLOBAL FOCUS 14-2

How Customer Perceptions Define Quality

A 1991 survey by *Popular Mechanics* found that many U.S. car buyers say they would rather buy American than Japanese if the cars were similar. What happens when indeed the Japanese and American cars are not only similar but identical?

The Plymouth Lazer and the Mitsubishi Eclipse are identical sports coupes built by Diamondstar Motors (a 50-50 partnership between Chrysler and Mitsubishi). Whatever the nameplate, the car sold for $11,000 for a basic model, around $17,500 for a souped-up version, in 1991. Sales, however, were not the same. In 1990, Chrysler's 3,000 dealers sold 40,000 Lasers while Mitsubishi's 500 dealers sold 50,000 Eclipses. That astounding difference says a lot about the image problem facing American-made cars. "People perceive the Japanese car to be of better quality. It is a lot easier to sell than a Laser," says Ira Rosenberg, the owner of adjoining Plymouth and Mitsubishi dealerships in Crystal Lake, Illinois.

Source: John Harris, "Advantage, Mitsubishi," *Forbes* (March 18, 1991), p. 100.

This trend toward greater emphasis on quality in products is summarized in Figure 14-1, which shows that, while superior quality increases profitability only slightly over high quality, low quality hurts profits substantially, and profits increase appreciably between average and high quality levels. However, circumstances can change these conclusions. For example, if all competitors in an entry market deliver high quality, lowering quality to offer a lower price might be a quick path to profits.

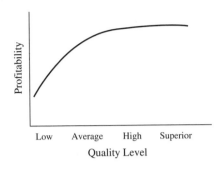

Figure 14–1. Relationship Between Quality Levels and Profitability

DETERMINING BRAND QUALITY

Sellers have three options available in deciding the level of quality to be built into their products: (1) continually upgrade quality; (2) maintain the existing level of quality; or (3) reduce quality, usually in response to rising costs or in the expectation of higher profits.

WEBER'S LAW HELPS DEFINE QUALITY LEVELS

In general, if quality is raised, sellers hope buyers will recognize the change; if quality is lowered, they hope buyers won't notice. A useful way to determine how much to raise, or lower, brand quality is to apply Weber's law, named after the nineteenth century German scientist Ernst Weber, who discovered that the just noticeable difference (jnd) of a stimuli was an amount relative to the size of the stimuli that precedes it. Weber's law maintains that K, or the jnd, is a constant that varies over the senses and can be determined as follows:

$$K = \Delta I / I$$

where ΔI equals the smallest increase in stimulus intensity that will be perceived as different from the existing intensity, and I equals the existing stimulus intensity.

For example, would it be worth the more expensive technology for Merton to improve the visual resolution of the Mighty Mind by 10 percent? Possibly, if focus group research indicated the average K of prospective buyers to be 8 percent, over which level they would notice a change in visual resolution.

On the other hand, if prospects' K—the level at which they would notice this change in visual resolution—was 11 percent, the change wouldn't be noticed and probably shouldn't be made. Weber's law is applicable in many other marketing situations, such as determining how much to raise or lower a price, or when people will notice changes in color or noise intensity in promotional campaigns.

OVERLOOKED SERVICE OPPORTUNITIES

Along with product quality, quality of customer service is assuming increased importance as a competitive tool, and many firms have established customer service departments to address customer needs and complaints. The importance of service in competitive international markets is highlighted by a recent survey of international users of heavy construction equipment, which showed that, next to the manufacturer's reputation, quick delivery of parts was the most important criterion for selecting a supplier.

This survey also revealed major customer complaints, all relating to the service function: orders are delayed, credit memo notices aren't sent, guarantees and warrantees aren't honored, returns and allowances aren't sufficient, after-sales service is ignored, and damaged parts aren't replaced.

GLOBAL FOCUS 14-3

The Increasing Importance of Service in Competitive Global Markets

The experience of 3 companies illustrates the importance of service as a key variable in competing effectively in international markets.

- The Hutchinson Technological Corporation, Hutchinson, Minnesota: According to Rick Penn, director of sales and marketing, "high quality service is as important as high quality products in meeting or exceeding customer requirements. "Toward this objective, Hutchinson, a manufacturer of computer and medical components, has implemented a "Service Plus" program to systematize employee and customer feedback and measure customer satisfaction. For example, results of a recent survey showed a rating of at least 82 percent in the areas of quality, frequency of contact, delivery and price. The firm also maintains a quality control laboratory in Asia to measure and test returned parts from Asian customers "on the spot."

- Royal Dental Manufacturing, Everett, Washington: According to Harold Tai, CEO, exports account for more than 20 percent of Royal Dental's total sales of dental chairs and doctor stools, sold through dealers mainly to customers in Eastern Europe, Russia, Saudi Arabia, China, and Korea. "We are doing particularly well in Poland," says Tai, "thanks to ongoing economic privatization efforts that have helped modernize dental care and generate demand for the latest in dental equipment." While U.S. dental technology, internationally recognized for quality standards, is a large part of the reason for Royal Dental's success, Tai gives equal credit to the firm's service program. "We maintain fast, efficient communication with our dealers and customers, through mail, fax, and U.S. Department of Commerce-sponsored shows in such countries as China, Pakistan, and India; additionally, our dealers worldwide send technicians to our factory for training in use of our equipment, so they can better serve dentists and health care professionals who purchase and operate our equipment."

- Paper Machinery Corporation, Milwaukee, Wisconsin: As the world's primary source of converting machinery for the production of paper products, Paper Machinery, in 1996, supplied approximately 40 percent of the worldwide export market for paper cup and container forming machines, with markets in China, Japan, Europe, and South America and major marketing efforts currently focused on East European Nations and the Commonwealth of Independent States. During the decade leading up to 1996, the 185-employee firm increased its gross earnings nearly fivefold. According to Donald Baumgartner, president, the key to the firm's continued profitable growth is service: "no customer in any of the 40 countries we serve is more than a local phone call away from a service call. We even routinely call on customers who don't call us just to make sure our machinery is working properly."

Source: *Business America*, U.S. Department of Commerce, June, 1994, pp. 30–33 and March, 1996, pp. 22–23.

FULFILLING CUSTOMER SERVICE NEEDS

Primary service decisions in both domestic and global markets pertain to (1) services included in the service mix and (2) level of service to offer. Both of these questions can be addressed by systematically analyzing customer needs, competitive offerings, and company resources. Merton, for example, conducted a survey that prioritized customer service needs with respect to MM systems, with good warranty coverage, prompt deliveries, and low service cost heading the list in one entry market. Survey findings also listed the following as least important service attributes in this market: convenient servicing locations, returns and allowances, and replacement guarantee.

Then, having identified the most and least important service attributes, Merton conducted surveys to determine (1) the level of service customer firms were presently receiving from firms competing with Merton and (2) the level of service Merton could afford to offer. Service mix and service level decisions were then based on data from these surveys. For example, although good warranty coverage was the most desired service attribute, none of Merton's competitors in this entry market offered the level desired by customers, so Merton designed a warranty slightly superior to that offered by its main competitor in this market.

Figure 14-2 shows the approach used by Merton to monitor its service mix. The vertical dimension ranks these attributes from extremely to slightly important, while the horizontal axis rates how effectively service needs of MM buyers were met. Note, for example, that the two most important service attributes—good warranty coverage and low service price—are positioned in Quadrant II, with its keep-up-good-work mandate. The third important attribute—prompt deliveries—is positioned in Quadrant I, where the mandate is to concentrate here. The three least important attributes are positioned in Quadrant III, but this didn't overly concern Merton planners since this was the Low Priority area.

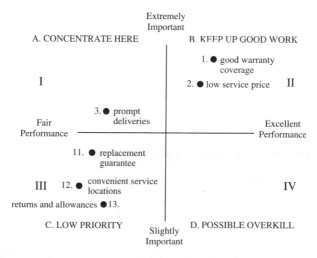

Figure 14–2. Approach for Measuring and Controlling Service Effectiveness

PRODUCT PACKAGING DECISIONS RESPOND TO ENVIRONMENTAL NEEDS

As with decisions relating to product branding, quality, and service, product packaging decisions can strongly influence customer responses to the product, and all marketing mix elements supporting the product.

In arriving at packaging decisions for MM systems and parts in international entry nations, Merton accounted for the following packaging objectives relating to Merton marketing objectives and conditions in these nations.

• *CONTAIN AND PROTECT THE PRODUCT*

The package in which a product is exported is usually composed of three separate packages: the immediate product container, called the primary package; the package containing the primary package, called the secondary package; and the package used to transport and store a number of secondary packages, called the shipping package. Materials available to contain and protect products include paperboard, plastic, metal, glass, styrofoam, and cellophane. (A major protective packaging innovation of the 1990s was asceptic containers for milk and fruit drinks. The Swedish Company Tetra Pak International converted 40 percent of milk sales in Western Europe to its asceptic packaging system, which keeps perishables fresh, without refrigeration, for 5 months.)

In deciding on materials to include in packages that would combine to maintain and protect MM systems that were shipped, unloaded, and stored in international markets, planners took into account extra handling, longer transportation needs, and protection against climate conditions (humidity, excess heat, etc.) that would otherwise adversely affect product shelf life.

With large shipments, containerization was used, whereby shipping packages containing MM systems were put in sturdy containers that were sealed until delivered, thereby reducing damage and pilferage. Pilferage was also discouraged by using only shipping codes on outside packaging whenever feasible.

• *ENCOURAGE PRODUCT USE*

Jumbo detergent packages and six-packs of soda are examples of package designs that encourage greater use of the product, as do packaging features that make it easier to use the product, such as boil-in bags, flip-top beer cans, and software packages for MM courses, which made it easy to file and retrieve them. In foreign markets, conditions peculiar to specific countries will often dictate package design, such as where lack of refrigeration or income suggest a quantity fewer than six per pack.

• *IDENTIFY AND PROMOTE THE PRODUCT*
Package design can facilitate communication on two levels:

- The *information level*, by identifying the brand and providing ingredients (or components) and directions, and

- the *promotional level*, by differentiating the product from competing products with a sales message highlighting features and benefits.

Key packaging decisions addressed by Merton planners in this area follow: Where should instructions appear on the package? What informational message and promotional "image" should the package convey? Will promotional inserts be needed? How can package aesthetics—size, color, and shape—be tailored to the promotional message?

As with any promotional message, color can play an important role in packaging to gain attention and help shape the product's image. For example, research indicates that African nations prefer bold colors, and that, in industrialized countries, silver is associated with luxury, black with quality, and white with generic products. Illustrative of the impact of color in promotion is the experience of Pepsi Cola in southeast Asia, where market share was lost because consumers associated Pepsi's light blue promotional color with death and mourning.

• *NEW PRODUCT PLANNING*
A package design can reinforce the image of the product as new (e.g., depicting a new cereal), or can be, in itself, what is "new" in the product, such as toothpaste pump dispensers or microwaveable containers for frozen dinners. Typical concerns pertaining to this objective include what size, color, shapes, and other visual and written messages will best communicate "newness"? Will a family packaging policy, with every package the same (e.g., Campbell Soup) make it difficult to implement this objective?

• *CHANNEL COOPERATION*
Package design can help address needs of wholesalers, retailers, and other channel members by making it easier for them to handle, store, and display products; mark prices and control inventory; and ensure reasonably long shelf life. Key questions in developing packages that take distributor needs into account follow: Are there traditional packaging practices expected by dealers? What are competitors' packaging practices? Will the distributor expect features (e.g., Universal Product and Optical Character Recognition Codes that allow electronic scanners to enter product/price information into a data base) that help to improve inventory control and customer service? Do company packages exhibit an adverse

environmental impact, or additional customer cost, that would not be acceptable in the entry country?

LABELING DECISIONS SUPPLEMENT PACKAGING DECISIONS

The main function of a label is to provide information about the packaged product, or about the seller of the product. The label itself may be printed as part of the package itself or on a tag affixed to the product.

Labeling decisions typically involve three kinds of labels:

- _Grade labels_ that announce product quality with letters (Grade A), numbers (#1), or conditions ("choice");

- _Informative labels_ that focus on the care, use, and preparation of the product ("This side up");

- _Descriptive labels_ that explain important characteristics or benefits ("23% more coffee").

In general, labeling decisions supplement packaging decisions in helping to encourage product use, promote communication, segment markets, and plan new products. Depending on the country, labels can also play an important role in responding to social and legal considerations. In the domestic market, for example, open dating indicates the expected shelf life of the product to avoid spoilage. Nutritional labels disclose amounts of nutrients, fat, sodium, and calories in processed foods. Unit pricing allows customers to compare values among competing brands by stating prices in terms of basic units, like ounces or pints.

In labeling products for export, it's important to observe the importer's language requirements, such as binguality requirements for Canada (French and English), Belgium (French and Flemish), and Finland (Finnish and Swedish).

PRODUCT LINE AND MIX STRATEGIES

A product line consists of related products with similar features, markets, and/or end-use applications. The Merton MM product line, for example, is composed of computers of various degrees of size and sophistication, with associated software tailored to the needs of different market segments. Taken together, all of Merton's product lines, including its lines of computer accessories marketed to organizational markets, constitute its product mix.

Product line decisions facing Merton planners in various countries included the following.

- *Product line length* decisions, pertaining to the number of products included in the line (generally, products are added as long as they contribute to profits and don't cannibalize sales and profits from existing products);

- *Product line stretching* decisions, pertaining to products added to an existing line to attract less profitable markets (downward stretch), more profitable markets (upward stretch), or both (two-way stretch);

- *Product line filling* decisions, focusing on plugging gaps in an existing line, usually to gain additional sales or profits, use excess capacity, or respond to competitive initiatives or dealer needs;

- *Product line featuring* decisions, pertaining to which products to feature in promotional campaigns.

Product mix decisions facing Merton planners in different markets included the following.

- *Mix width* decisions, pertaining to how many different lines Merton would market (as with product line length decisions, this decision is generally dependent on profitability of new lines, consistency with company mission, and danger of cannibalizing sales from other lines);

- *Mix consistency* decisions, pertaining to how closely related the firm's products are in terms of common end uses, distribution outlets, price ranges, and markets served. A consistent mix of product lines is particularly important in international markets, where such factors as high entry costs and limited communication and distribution channels, often limit profit opportunities. Mix consistency can offset these limitations by helping firms concentrate production and marketing efforts, achieve scale economies, and create strong brand images and relations with distributors.

Product life-cycle positions for Merton's product lines and mixes often suggested which of the preceding decisions was appropriate. For example, if products in the firm's mix were situated primarily in the highly competitive growth stage, line stretching and filling decisions might be indicated to meet these threats. Mix width and consistency decisions might also be made in response to competitive PLC environments, with products added or modified during growth periods and pruned and narrowed during periods of decline.

For individual products comprising the MM line, three strategies in particular were appropriate during later PLC stages, when competition became more intense, and markets and profits began to decline:

- *Repositioning strategies* involved use of advertising and promotion campaigns to create changed consumer perceptions of the product, as when Merton opted to change its blue chip image to accommodate its line of less expensive computer systems geared to the needs of less affluent target markets. The danger of such a strategy is the possibility of losing, or confusing, the firm's main market.

- *Product life extension strategies* entail one or more of the following tactical options: new uses for the product; new product features or benefits; new classes of customers for present product; increased product usage; and/or a changed marketing strategy. All these options came into play when Merton, late in the MM's life cycle in the domestic market, redesigned and repositioned this product to serve new groups of customers in global markets.

- *Product deletion strategies* involve removing products from the line when they are no longer profitable. They include (1) a continuation strategy of continuing to market the product until it must be dropped; (2) a milking strategy of cutting back marketing expenses to maintain profits during declining PLC stages; and (3) a concentrated strategy of aiming all marketing efforts at the strongest existing segment, and phasing out all others.

A danger in milking and concentration deletion strategies is that they will be applied prematurely, without regard to the impact on the rest of the line (or mix) and without fully considering possibilities in repositioning and product life extension strategies.

CHAPTER PERSPECTIVE

Basic product planning concepts are the same in domestic and international markets: Products must be designed, branded, packaged, and labeled and cost/benefit decisions must be made pertaining to levels of service and quality associated with the augmented product. Additionally, product line and mix strategies must be formulated to ensure that the needs of customers and distributors are profitably met. In the complex global market, however, a diversity of factors make these decisions, and strategies emerging from them, more critical and difficult.

KNOW THE CONCEPTS

TERMS FOR STUDY

blanket family name
brand
brand mark
company/individual brand name
copyright
country-of-origin effects
generic brands
individual brand names
labeling
manufacturer's brand
package aesthetics
packaging
private brand

product compatibility
product deletion strategy
product design
product life extension strategy
product line strategies
product mix strategies
product planning
quality
repositioning strategies
service mix
separate family names
trademark

MATCHUP EXERCISES

1. Match up the branding strategy in the first column with the descriptor in the second column.

1. manufacturer's brand

2. blanket family name

3. generic brands
4. family/individual brands

5. private brands

a. one name for two or more products
b. obtains most sales for most product categories
c. emphasize products, not names
d. names designated by distributors
e. Chrysler Dodge, Dodge Aries

2. Match the product attribute in the first column with the appropriate planning consideration in the second column.

1. branding

2. quality
3. service
4. packaging

a. Will greater product use be encouraged?
b. Individual, family, or both?
c. Increase level above the jnd?
d. Profits increase most between "average" and "high" levels.

3. Match up the product line/mix strategy in the first column with a key strategy objective in the second column.

1. product line length

a. plug gaps

2. product line stretching
3. product line filling
4. product mix consistency
5. product mix width

b. add related lines
c. attract new markets
d. add profitable products
e. add profitable lines

QUESTIONS FOR REVIEW AND DISCUSSION

1. By the year 2000, Campbell Soup wants half of company revenues to come from outside domestic markets, up from 30 percent in 1995, with Asia—and China in particular—targeted as the area with the greatest growth potential. In China, most of the competition will come from homemade soup. To counter this competition, Campbell plans to keep prices attractive, promote its products on convenience, and make extensive use of local ingredients in its soups (drawing the line, however, on dog and shark fin soups). How will the strength of Campbell's brand name, worldwide, help Campbell achieve its goal? How will it motivate Chinese buyers to select Campbell soups over alternatives? And how will it benefit the Chinese economy, as it moves haltingly toward a free-market model?

2. How would you categorize the brand names "Merton Mighty Mind" (for computers) and "Merton Moon Chip" (for chip circuits)? What alternative categories might have been selected? Why (or why not) is this category preferable? Why (or why not) does it meet criteria for an effective brand name?

3. Describe how Weber's law might have been employed with respect to all components of the marketing mix (product, price, place, promotion) for a service that purchases unsold space on airlines and ocean lines at sizable discounts and then sells them to the traveling public at a discount from the retail price that still permits the firm to make a profit. Travel agencies will receive a commission for selling the tickets, which will be promoted primarily in advertisements in travel sections of newspapers.

4. A study of Canadian buyers of industrial equipment ranked service elements in the following order of importance: (1) delivery reliability, (2) prompt quotations, (3) technical advice, (4) prompt discount credits, (5) after-sales service, (6) sales representation, (7) ease of contact, and (8) replacement guarantee. Given these priorities, what advice would you offer a distributor selling to Canadian buyers whose service level profile looks like this:

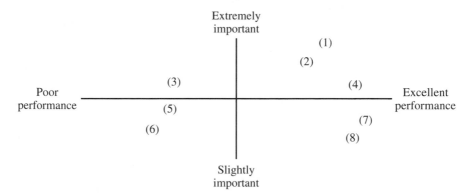

5. The Apple Computer company has seen virtually all its lines of computers and computer software counterfeited, with about 70 percent of faked merchandise made and marketed outside the United States, and 20 percent either manufactured in this country or imported into this country and labeled here. Suggest a strategy that Apple might use to effectively combat this unauthorized representation of their inventions, copyrights, and trademarks.

6. Discuss how and why the Merton Mighty Mind computer system, over the course of its life span, might use the following strategies: product line stretching, product mix consistency, and product life extension.

ANSWERS

MATCHUP EXERCISES

1. 1b, 2a, 3c, 4e, 5d
2. 1b, 2d, 3c, 4a
3. 1d, 2c, 3a, 4b, 5e

QUESTIONS FOR REVIEW AND DISCUSSION

1. Campbell's strong brand name, strongly promoted in global markets, will provide benefits for customers, the company, and the economy. For example, using the Chinese entry market as an illustrative example, prospective customers will benefit from a brand name, and its promotional-induced associations, that they can relate to their wants and needs and quickly identify when shopping. The Campbell Company will benefit in that they can focus their promotional efforts

on a single product name, thus achieving benefits of standardization, as well as benefits from being able to maintain price and production levels consistent with Campbell's strong, positive brand image. A well-promoted brand name will also help Campbell introduce dozens of new soups in this market under this name, knowing that prospective customers will bring to these new products the same positive associations they have for present Campbell products. And this desire to build a loyal customer base will serve as an incentive for Campbell to maintain high levels of product quality. Branding will also help Campbell segment its China market, with different branded product lines (e.g, Hungry Man, Ranchero) for different market segments. Finally, Campbell's branding strategy will benefit the Chinese economy to the extent that competitors are motivated to innovate in improving their products and marketing campaigns to emulate Campbell's success, as well as helping to improve shopping efficiency and maintain product quality.

2. The names "Merton Mighty Mind" and "Merton Moon Chip" illustrate the company-brand-name-combined-with-individual-brand-name category. Alternative categories that might have been selected include a blanket family name (Merton computers, Merton chip circuits) and separate family names (Mighty Mind computers, Moon Chip circuits). One advantage of the company-individual brand name combination is that new products can be launched under the company (Merton) brand, while markets can be targeted under the individual brand name. Also, unlike the situation with individual brand names, a strong, focused, companywide product image can be maintained. As to consistency with criteria for effective brand names, these brands seem to meet them: They suggest the high-tech nature of the products (the Moon chips were used on lunar space probes); suggest product benefits; are relatively easy to recognize, recall, and pronounce; and can be applied to other products added to each line.

3. *Product:* The routes chosen for travel discounts would have to be perceived as sufficiently attractive. *Place:* The discount offered travel agents would have to be sufficiently large to justify their administering the service. *Price:* The discount offered prospective customers would have to be perceived as sufficiently large to attract target market members. *Promotion:* The size of newspaper ads would have to be perceived as sufficiently large to attract the attention of prospective customers.

4. This service profile indicates that the firm's customers are not well served by the firm's outside sales force, with generally poor performance ratings for technical advice, after-sales service, and sales representation. Once the order is placed, however, customers are well served, with high ratings for reliability, prompt quotations, and

prompt discount credits. Indeed, customers might be too well served, perhaps to compensate for the lack of effective salespeople, since the two relatively unimportant attributes—ease of contact and replacement guarantee—are also highly regarded. According to this analysis, the firm should probably work harder on training its salesmen to do a more creative, conscientious job of selling its products, while perhaps achieving savings by cutting back on its guarantees.

5. For counterfeiting initiated in the United States, Apple has had considerable success through infringement actions brought in federal courts; for counterfeiting initiated outside the United States, but conducted in this country (e.g., imported fakes are assembled or marketed here), Apple supplements federal court infringement actions by cooperating with the Customs Bureau to stop smuggling of fakes into this country. In addressing the problem of fakes made and marketed overseas, Apple uses a full range of corrective options, including legislative action, bilateral and multilateral negotiations with and among offending countries, private actions taken with other companies in Apple's field, and individual actions (e.g., staged raids with local authorities or bringing offenders into the Apple family by converting them to legitimate licensees, thus giving them a profit stake in apprehending other offenders).

6. Product line stretching would be used, probably during growth and maturity life-cycle stages, to attract new market segments to the line of thin TV sets—downward stretch with cheaper models for less profitable markets, upward stretch for more profitable models, and two-way stretch for markets at both ends. Product mix consistency considerations would help ensure that new lines (e.g., a line of CD-ROMS) were consistent with the firm's product mix in terms of common end uses, distribution outlets, price ranges, markets served, and promotion programs to reach these markets. For example, if the firm has a standardized promotion program to reach many global markets, a new line added to the mix should probably also fit within this standardization. Product life extension strategies, employed during maturity and decline stages of the life cycle, would focus on new uses for the product (e.g., as a component in a modularized entertainment center), new product features or benefits, new classes of customers for the product, and increasing product usage.

15

PRICING IN INTERNATIONAL MARKETS I: ESTABLISHING OBJECTIVES AND POLICIES

OVERVIEW

Of all marketing mix elements, price is the most flexible and typically has the greatest direct impact on customer perceptions, sales, and profits. Setting productive prices, especially in competitive global markets, is a complex, challenging task, involving the establishment of realistic objectives, as well as policies, strategies, and tactics that will work to achieve these objectives. Considerations involved in the price planning process include accounting for the nature and behavior of costs, customers and competitors, as well as economic, legal, and political constraints on pricing peculiar to global entry markets.

PRICING OBJECTIVES DEFINE POLICIES AND STRATEGIES

In this chapter, we continue our examination of international marketing mix elements with a discussion of the price planning process whereby global marketers arrive at pricing objectives, policies, strategies, and tactics. An example involving Merton's planned entry of MM systems into a selected foreign country illustrates key relationships among these four concepts.

An objective of this entry might be to achieve a 20 percent share of this market within 2 years. This objective, in turn, might define a set of pricing policy guidelines indicating a penetration pricing strategy of pricing MM systems below competitive levels. This strategy, in turn, would entail a number of tactics such as raising or lowering prices in response to competitive initiatives.

In the domestic market, this process of devising and implementing pricing strategies to achieve profit objectives is complex enough, involving a sophisticated understanding of such variables as the behavior of costs, demand patterns of customers, and responses of competitors. Its complexity is magnified in global markets, where an array of economic, logistical, political, cultural, and legal considerations and constraints must be accounted for.

In examining these considerations and constraints, we begin with a discussion of the importance of price in terms of its impact on sales, profits, markets, and other marketing mix elements and then examine the first two stages of the price-planning process: establishing pricing objectives and policies through the systematic analysis of data on products, costs, markets, competitors, and other uncontrollables. In Chapter 16, we examine pricing strategies and tactics that emerge from these objectives and policies.

PRICES INFLUENCE SALES, PROFITS, AND MARKETING MIXES

To illustrate the critical role of prices in generating sales, profits, and marketing mix values, we will make some assumptions about the price of an MM system being introduced into a competitive foreign market and the consumers' responses to this product.

Assume, first, that Merton's costs to make and market each system are $900 but that it decides to price each at $2,000. Also assume that most prospective customers in this country perceive the combination of values comprising each system to be worth only $1,100, so sales are disappointing until Merton lowers its price closer to this $1,100 market price.

Now assume a different scenario. In an effort to penetrate this new market quickly, Merton prices the MM at a level equal to its actual costs—and below competitor's prices—at $900 per unit. The firm anticipates that this price will increase sales and generate economies of scale (i.e., lower procurement, production, and marketing costs associated with mass production economies and efficiencies) that will soon begin to generate big profits. At this lower price, however, prospective customers perceive MM systems to be cheap versions of competitive MM systems, subject to expensive breakdowns, so sales increases are again disappointing. Realizing its miscalculation, Merton planners raise the MM's price up toward the $1,100 price that customers perceive the units are worth and discover, to their delight, that sales and profits increase with each incremental increase.

This example illustrates a number of characteristics of the important, complex price component of the marketing mix. It is certainly the most flexible of marketing mix elements, subject to change on very short notice. It is also the only marketing mix element that produces revenues; the other elements represent costs. In the domestic market, price planning has been rated as the most important problem facing marketing executives,[1] due to a diversity of reasons also applicable in international markets, such as increased competition, rising costs, governmental interventions (taxes, tariffs, deregulation, etc.), and more resistant customers.

Beyond these general characteristics, this example illustrates the direct, specific influence price can have on consumer perceptions, sales revenues flowing from these perceptions, and profits flowing from sales revenues.

To illustrate the dramatic impact of prices on profits, consider one of the price increases Merton makes that doesn't also increase costs: from $1,000 to $1,100. Note that this 10 percent price increase (100/1000) levers a 100 percent increase in profits—from $100 to $200.

PRICES SUPPORT MARKETING MIX ELEMENTS

Since a product's price, which can refer to both monetary and nonmonetary exchanges of goods and services, helps position the product offering, communicate its tangible and intangible values, determine how and where it will be distributed, and even define its target markets, price planning is invariably done in conjunction with product, place, and promotion planning.

In the case of the MM, for example, special price incentives were offered to foreign distributors to encourage them to carry the MM line; quality differences between the Merton MM and competitive MM models were reflected in price differences; and selection of appeals and media for promoting MM systems reflected this price-quality relationship. Thus, just as price can enhance customer perceptions, sales, and profits, it can also enhance the effectiveness of marketing mix elements in achieving marketing goals.

This relationship among price, marketing objectives, and other marketing mix elements will become clearer as we examine the approach used by Merton planners to arrive at profitable price policies and strategies for the Merton product line in international markets.

---

[1] "Segmentation Strategies Create New Pressure Among Marketers," *Marketing News* (March 28, 1986), p. 1.

PRICING VIEWED AS A MARKETING FUNCTION

In general, firms interested in penetrating international markets are well advised to view pricing as a marketing, rather than an accounting, function. This marketing perception of pricing is typical of multiline, multinational firms serving consumer markets, where planners consider such things as demand patterns, costs, degree of price flexibility, discounts and allowances offered distributors, price changes over the course of a product's life cycle and legal considerations in determining price ranges. The context for these considerations is an informed understanding of global competitive environments—including target markets, competitors, and environmental constraints—designed to avoid failure to (1) relate prices to needs and perceptions of target market members; (2) properly integrate prices with other marketing mix elements; and/or (3) modify pricing policies and strategies to match changing competitive environments.

This isn't to say that a simple cost-plus accounting approach to price planning isn't ever appropriate. In some situations, cost is the only real consideration, with competition and customer response largely immaterial. For example, large public utilities set prices on a cost-plus basis to achieve targeted profit returns acceptable to regulatory boards.

ESTABLISHING GLOBAL PRICING OBJECTIVES, POLICIES, AND STRATEGIES

At Merton, however, pricing of its computer systems and components was invariably perceived as a marketing function in both domestic and global markets. Reflecting this perception, the following approach was used to establish pricing objectives, policies, and strategies.

• *ESTABLISH PRICING OBJECTIVES*

Typically, in global markets, pricing objectives are based on the following external and internal considerations.

- *External considerations.* How customers perceive the offering, costs involved in delivering the offering to customers, prices of competitive offerings, and foreign exchange rate pluses or minuses.

- *Internal considerations.* Company mission, and business objectives deriving from this mission (e.g., Merton's expensive, blue chip image), company resources (e.g., financial, marketing, manufacturing), and the nature of the product (e.g., easy to distinguish from competitive models).

Based on an assessment of these considerations, price planning in global markets typically sets out to achieve one or more of the following objectives.

TARGETED RETURNS

Targeted return objectives, used by both distributors and manufacturers, specify a percentage dollar return on either sales or investment. For example, retailers and wholesalers set a percentage markup on sales large enough to cover anticipated operating costs plus a desired profit. Targeted return on investment (ROI) pricing refers to the practice of pegging a price at a level that achieves a specified after-tax return on invested capital. Common ROI targets are typically between 10 and 30 percent after taxes, with lower returns usually set in response to competition and higher returns set when little competition is anticipated.

In larger multinational and global companies, a target return on investment objective simplifies measuring and controlling the performance of many divisions and departments, all of which use capital. It can also simplify the pricing process. Over time many firms learn that their investments have earned a certain average rate of return, which becomes the target rate desired for new product introductions. This emphasis on mandated profit return, however, can obscure other important factors affecting pricing decisions and is often cited as a reason for the lackluster performance of American firms against Pacific Rim companies willing to sacrifice short-term profits for larger long-run profits.

MARKET SHARE LEADERSHIP

Market share leadership goals usually forego initial profits for larger, long-range profits by pricing products below the market to achieve a strong market position. In this entrenched leadership position, firms benefit from mass market economies of scale, while competitors (Pepsi versus Coca-Cola or Goodrich versus Goodyear) are forced to play a more expensive game of catch-up. Leader firms are also better positioned to increase prices, later, to make up for early low prices.

PRODUCT QUALITY LEADERSHIP

Product quality leadership objectives typically require high introductory prices to connote product quality to target market members. Customer perceptions are a key consideration in achieving this objective. If the product's prestige image drops below its high price, sales and profits will also drop.

Other objectives that pricing strategies and tactics can help achieve include (1) helping to sell other products (e.g., a supermarket's low price for Perdue chickens attracts customers who pay higher prices for other products) and (2) simple survival (e.g., in the face of too much capacity or competition or too few customers, an airline's "Super Saver" ticket prices, while not profitable, at least ensure a sufficiently large number of passengers and dollars to cover fuel costs and flight personnel salaries.

• *UNDERSTAND DEMAND BEHAVIOR*

Basic to an understanding of pricing policies and strategies best calcu lated to achieve pricing objectives is an understanding of how consumers perceive products, as shown in demand curve behavior. If, for example, prospective customers perceived an MM system to be unique and necessary, then Merton price planners might adopt a strategy of pricing them well in excess of what it actually takes to make and market them. Alternately, if MM systems are perceived as no different from competitive makes, such a pricing strategy could kill the MM's competitive chances.

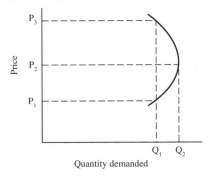

Figure 15-1. Demand Schedule for MM Systems

To illustrate the relationship between customer perceptions of product values and prices, assume the demand schedules shown in Figure 15-1 as depicting relationships between price and demand for MM systems. Note that the demand pattern for MM systems depicted in this schedule slopes upward from (P_1, Q_1), through (P_2, Q_2) to (P_3, Q_1). Thus, up to point (P_2, Q_2), demand for the MM actually increases, even though its price is also increasing. Even at point (P_3, Q_1), where price is three times as high as at point (P_1, Q_1), demand is still at least as strong as at this point. Inelastic demand schedules like this, where price changes have little effect on quantities demanded, characterize products that people want and that have few substitutes, for which buyers do not readily notice a higher price, or find such a price justified. A doctor's bill, for example, might fit these criteria. From the perspective of a price planner, such a desirable demand pattern suggests high profit potential through higher prices without declining sales. Products with many substitutes not perceived as necessities exhibit an elastic demand pattern whereby relatively small changes in price trigger large changes in demand. For example, in the competitive domestic market, a 10 percent increase in the MM's price triggered a 40 percent sales decline.

Another important variable in determining the price of a product is the amount of this product that a seller is willing or able to make available at different prices (i.e., the supply curve). For example, at low, unprofitable prices, Merton would probably make fewer MMs available than at high, profitable prices, although eventually a limit on the amount Merton could make available would be reached, regardless of price.

When a demand curve, like *DE* in Figure 15-2, is superimposed on a supply curve *AB*, an equilibrium point *F* is reached at which the quantity and price sellers are willing to offer equal the quantity and price buyers are willing to accept. This is the product's market price.

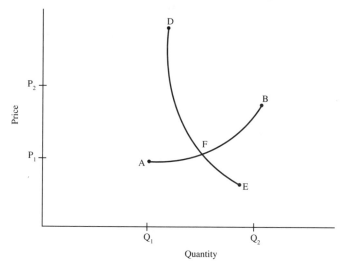

Figure 15–2. Equilibrium of Supply and Demand

• *UNDERSTAND COMPETITIVE PRICES*

Since all marketing-oriented pricing policies and strategies assume that product prices will be pegged above, below, or at competitive price levels, an understanding of competitive prices is a necessary step in the price-planning process.

In the case of a product like the MM, entering a foreign market where no competition exists, information on competitive prices must be deduced or envisioned. Surveys among prospective customers and focus group interviews can provide useful clues as to the worth consumers place on MM product/service values (as well as data on which to develop demand schedules described earlier in this chapter). Supplementing these surveys and interviews, Merton planners also used the substitute method, involving careful analyses of products similar to the product being introduced. For example, in one prospective entry market, average per-student cost of professional training was used as a surrogate for purchases of MM systems featuring professional training software.

• *UNDERSTAND COST BEHAVIOR*

Especially in international markets, where exporter costs tend to appreciate dramatically over their domestic counterparts, an effective cost accounting system is a must for identifying and applying all costs involved in making, marketing, and moving products into and through global channels. Without an understanding of the nature and extent of these costs, marketers can't determine the profit consequences of prices pegged at, above, or below competitive prices, nor can they identify ways to reduce or eliminate costs that put them at a competitive disadvantage.

In general, export-related costs fall into three categories:

- Costs of modifying the product offering for global markets;

- Costs for operating the export function (personnel, marketing research, shipping and insurance, overseas promotional costs, foreign communication costs, etc.);

- Entry costs (tariffs, taxes, commercial, political, and foreign exchange risks, etc.).

Table 15-1 illustrates the extent of price escalation that can occur in exporting a product that retails for $12 in the domestic market. Four different scenarios are offered, all including a CIF (cost + insurance + freight) and a 20 percent tariff on the CIF cost. Beyond this common cost, additional costs are added for each scenario for things like a value-added tax, an importer's margin, and various margins for distributors. Note that the least costly scenario increases the domestic retail price by 70 percent; the most costly increases it by 275 percent.

In addition to these export-related costs, firms planning global entry strategies must also account for the following kinds of costs involved in making and marketing products for domestic markets.

- *Fixed costs (FC)*, such as rent, taxes, and executive salaries, remain constant regardless of how many product units are produced.

Table 15–1. Export Price Escalation

International Marketing Channel Elements and Cost Factors	Domestic Wholesale-Retail Channel	Case 1 Same as Domestic with Direct Wholesale Import CIF/Tariff	Case 2 Same as Case 1 with Foreign Importer Added to Channel	Case 3 Same as Case 2 with VAT Added	Case 4 Same as Case 3 with Local Foreign Jobber Added to Channel
Manufacturer's net price	6.00	6.00	6.00	6.00	6.00
+Insurance and shipping cost (CIF)	—	2.50	2.50	2.50	2.50
=Landed cost (CIF value)	—	8.50	8.50	8.50	8.50
+Tariff (20% on CIF value)	—	1.70	1.70	1.70	1.70
=Importer's cost (CIF value + tariff)	—	10.20	10.20	10.20	10.20
+Importer's margin (25% on cost)	—	—	2.55	2.55	2.55
+VAT (16% on full cost plus margin)	—	—	—	2.04	2.04
=Wholesaler's cost (=importer's price)	6.00	10.20	12.75	14.79	14.79
+Wholesaler's margin (33⅓% on cost)	2.00	3.40	4.25	4.93	4.93
+VAT (16% on margin)	—	—	—	.79	.79
=Local foreign jobber's cost (=wholesale price)	—	—	—	—	20.51
+Jobber's margin (33⅓% on cost)	—	—	—	—	6.84
+VAT (16% on margin)	—	—	—	—	1.09
=Retailer's cost (= wholesale or jobber price)	8.00	13.60	17.00	20.51	28.44
+Retailer's margin (50% on cost)	4.00	6.80	8.50	10.26	14.22
+VAT (16% on margin)	—	—	—	1.64	2.28
=Retail price (what consumer pays)	12.00	20.40	25.50	32.41	44.94
Percentage price escalation over domestic	—	70%	113%	170%	275%
Percentage price escalation over Case 1	—	—	25%	59%	120%
Percentage price escalation over Case 2	—	—	—	27%	76%
Percentage price escalation over Case 3	—	—	—	—	39%

- *Average fixed costs (AFC)* are fixed costs divided by the number of units produced. The more MMs produced, the less the average fixed cost assigned to each MM. For example, if it costs $1,000,000 in fixed costs to set up production for the MM, and 10,000 units are produced, each would be allocated an average of $100 in fixed costs.

- *Variable cost (VC)* is a cost directly related to production; when production stops, so do these costs. Material costs or sales commissions are examples of variable costs, which can be controlled in the short run by simply changing the level of production.

- *Average variable cost (AVC)* is total variable cost divided by number of units produced. Usually high for the first few units produced, AVC decreases as production increases owing to various economies of scale. For example, after a time, production workers would learn to assemble more MMs per hour, and salespeople could sell more in a given day. Eventually, however, a point would be reached where AVC would begin to move up as existing facilities reached capacity and new facilities (e.g., a new factory) would be required.

- *Total cost (TC)* is the sum of total fixed and variable costs for a specific quantity produced.

- *Average total cost (ATC)* is total cost (TC) divided by number of units produced.

- *Marginal cost (MC)* is the cost of producing each additional unit and indicates the minimum extra revenue that should be generated by each additional unit. It is usually equal to the variable cost of producing the last unit.

The interrelationships among these costs is graphically displayed in Figure 15-3, which shows how each changes with changes in quantities produced. Note that all these costs drop over the quantity output range and then begin to rise at different quantity levels. Also note that marginal cost per unit begins to rise at a lower level of output than average variable cost, intersects AVC and ATC curves from below at their low points, and then rises rapidly. (The fact that AVC and ATC are averaged over many units keeps their rise gradual; marginal cost, the same as variable cost per unit, rises rapidly because it is assigned to a single unit.) For pricing purposes, the marginal cost per unit is the most important cost, since this is the extra cost revenues must cover. Thus, to optimize profits in manufacturing, the firm should produce that level of output where marginal cost is just less than or equal to marginal revenue (i.e., the revenue brought in by the last unit sold). All units produced up to this point have been profitable, and the accumulated profits represent the most the company can expect to make on the product.

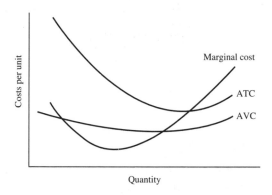

Figure 15–3. How Unit Costs Change as Quantity Increases

Figure 15-4 shows another important cost consideration for establishing prices over the product life cycle. Although cost curves trend upward in the short range, these curves trend downward over the long range, as production experience (the learning curve) and more efficient production equipment and methods lock into place.

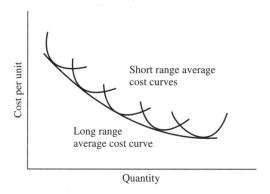

Figure 15–4. Long Range Cost Curves Curve Downward

BRINGING COSTS DOWN TO COMPETITIVE LEVELS

Especially in highly competitive international markets, where a diversity of internal and external influences affect demand, an understanding of the nature and behavior of costs associated with making and marketing products at different price and demand levels is important not only for establishing initial prices and modifying these prices over the product life cycle but also for identifying ways to bring costs in line with those of advantaged competitors. Here, for example, are some of the possibilities a global company might explore to reduce escalating costs for such factors as international transportation and distribution and global accounts demanding price concessions:

- Search the firm's international manufacturing system to identify potentially lower-cost sources of materials and methods;

- Audit the existing distribution system to identify less costly alternative intermediaries, or greater efficiencies and economies in physical distribution systems and procedures;

- Use other marketing mix elements. For example, design a simplified, but suitable, version of the product to sell at a competitive price, or modify the product offering to bring it in under a lower tariff classification (it's often possible to get a lower classification—called a duty drawback—by importing components and materials used in the manufacture of the exported product from the importing country). It might also be possible to develop a promotional campaign to persuade target market members that the higher price is justified in terms of benefits to them not otherwise available. (e.g., AT&T's campaign to convince prospective users that superior quality and service justify the higher rates they pay).

Global Focus 15-1 examines a cost-management technique, called target costing, that works back from the "ideal selling price" to systematically consider these and other cost-optimization options in the context of customer wants and company goals.

GLOBAL FOCUS 15-1

How Competitive Companies Price New Products

Over the past 15 years, company after company has learned that quality must be designed into products before they are manufactured—that it is expensive and misguided to inspect for quality after the product has left the production line. Today, the most competitive companies are applying the same logic to determine the price of new products. Before a company launches a product (or family of products), senior managers determine its ideal selling price, establish the feasibility of meeting that price, and then control costs to ensure that the price is met. They are using a management process called target costing.

Target costing drives a product development strategy that focuses the design team on the ultimate customer and on the real opportunity in the market. Leading Japanese electronics and vehicle manufacturers have used target costing to their advantage, and companies are now introducing it in the United States, Germany, and elsewhere. Its rigorous cost-management technique helps prevent senior managers from launching low-margin products that do not generate appropriate returns to the company, but its greater value lies in its ability to bring the challenge of the marketplace back through the chain of production to product designers. Target costing ensures that development teams will bring profitable products to market with the right level of quality and functionality and with appropriate prices for targeted customer segments. It is a discipline that harmonizes the labor of disparate participants in the development effort, from designers to manufacturing engineers to market researchers and suppliers.

The logic of target costing is simple. Looking at tomorrow's marketplace, the organization maps customer segments and targets the most attractive ones. It determines what level of quality and functionality will succeed within each segment, given a predetermined target price. The organization then designs the sourcing, production, and delivery processes that will enable it to achieve its desired profits at this target.

Source: Robin Cooper and W. Bruce Chew, "Control Tomorrow's Costs Through Today's Designs," *Harvard Business Review* (January–February 1996), pp. 88–98. One-time permission to reproduce granted by Harvard Business School Publications, 1997.

HOW POLITICAL/LEGAL CLIMATES AFFECT PRICING

In Chapter 6, we examined a diversity of government policies, statutes, and regulations that restrain or encourage foreign trade. As they relate to exporters, these initiatives have a direct impact on pricing in five areas: transfer pricing, monetary valuations, escrow requirements, dumping regulations, and pricing legislation.

• *TRANSFER PRICING*

Transfer pricing refers to the price a producer charges for goods shipped to a subsidiary. For example, should this price encompass only costs directly associated with making the product, or should other, indirect costs such as overhead and a profit margin be included? In the domestic market, a producer like Merton generally designs transfer pricing policies that motivate divisional managers to achieve divisional goals while contributing to overall company goals. For example, if Merton's transportation cost for transferring MMs to subsidiary A on the West Coast is twice what it is for East Coast subsidiary B, an adjustment will be made to make the actual transfer price paid by each comparable, and competitive, in each marketplace. Implicit in this arrangement is the assumption that each subsidiary, by being able to price the MMs competitively, will be motivated to sell sufficient quantitites to compensate for adjusting the transfer price.

In the global marketplace, however, a new set of considerations enters into transfer pricing formulas because of differential tax and tariff constraints. To illustrate, assume country A has a moderately high tariff, but a low tax rate on imports, while country B has a slightly lower tariff but an extremely high tax rate on imports. In this situation, it might profit an exporter to charge a lower transfer price to its country A affiliate, assuming that the high profits realized would be taxed at a much lower rate than in country B, where the high transfer price might eliminate any profits to be taxed. And profits realized in country A would more than offset the higher tariffs charged there.

This was the reasoning of Hoffman LaRoche, which charged its low-tax Italian subsidiary only $22 a kilo for librium, while charging its high-tax British subsidiary $925 per kilo, effectively eliminating any profits to be taxed. Hoffman LaRoche's experience illustrates one important reason why companies are generally trending away from this accounting game of balancing tax and tariff consequences in pegging transfer prices. The British government—which, like all governments, has the right to reallocate income and expenses—sued the company for back taxes and won. All industrialized countries now carefully review situations where transfer pricing seems based primarily on tax/tariff tradeoffs (Section 482 of the U.S. tax code is devoted in its entirety to the subject), and just the idea of the expense and bother entailed in defending this practice is sufficient to deter many companies. Global Focus 15-2 examines how governments are acting—and companies reacting—with respect to legal and legislative initiatives designed to curb transfer pricing abuses.

GLOBAL FOCUS 15-2

Penalizing Transfer Pricing Abuses: Actions and Reactions

The U.S. Internal Revenue Service has begun to look more closely at transfer pricing on sales of goods and services among subsidiaries or between subsidiaries and the parent company. It has filed claims against hundreds of companies in recent years, claiming that multinational companies too often manipulate intracompany pricing to minimize their worldwide tax bills. Experts calculate that foreign-based multinationals evade at least $20 billion in U.S. taxes. Other countries have also strengthened their review systems. Japan has created specific transfer pricing legislation that penalizes marketers for not providing information in time to meet deadlines set by the government. German tax authorities are carefully checking intra-company charges to deem their appropriateness.

In its biggest known victory, the IRS made its case that Japan's Toyota had been systematically overcharging its U.S. subsidiary for years on most of the cars, trucks, and parts sold in the United States. What would have been profits in the United States were now accrued in Japan. Toyota denied improprieties but agreed to a reported $1 billion settlement.

Increasing communication among tax authorities is having a dramatic effect and will continue to accelerate, especially with the trend toward shifting profits. Historically, transfer pricing from the point of view of a U.S. company meant the shifting of income out of the United States, but with the corporate tax rate at 34 percent, many U.S. multinationals must be prepared to justify transfer pricing on two or more fronts.

The entire tax equation has become more complicated because of changes in customs duties. In many countries, revenues from customs and indirect taxes are greater than revenue from corporate taxes. Authorities will jealously guard the income stream from customs taxes, and marketers could find gains on income taxes erased by losses on customs taxes.

Source: "Pricing Yourself into a Market," *Business Asia* (December 21, 1992), p. 1. © The Economist Intelligence Unit. Reproduced by permission of the Economist Intelligence Unit.

Another deterrent to transfer pricing abuses, fostered by economic communities, is the trend toward global equalization of tax rates and the realization that benefits of transfer pricing based on competitive market conditions usually offset benefits from playing tax/tariff games. An example of how such manipulations can distort normal marketing processes is the manager of a foreign affiliate who kept receiving big bonuses for extraordinary profit performance until his firm realized his profits were largely a by-product of the firm's policy of charging artificially low transfer prices into, and high transfer prices out of, this country.

• *CURRENCY VALUATIONS*

Currency valuations include both devaluation and revaluations of a country's currency. Devaluation involves reducing the value of a country's currency relative to currencies of other countries. For example, if the number of Japanese yen required to purchase an American dollar—and products financed by dollars—falls from 200 to 100, then that is the extent to which the dollar has been devalued in Japan. The effect of devaluation is the same as reducing prices of exported products by the amount of the devaluation, although prices in the home country aren't affected.

Another effect is to increase sales of devalued products in foreign countries and productivity, investment, and employment at home. The devaluing country's balance of payments is also usually improved, as the value of exports exceeds the value of imports. (The Chapter 9 discussion of the Mexican devaluation of the peso illustrates this process.)

Still another effect of devaluation is to increase the cost of products sold to the devaluing country, now priced in more expensive foreign currency. Indeed, to the extent that products exported from the devaluing country include foreign-made components, devalued prices will be increased. For example, American computers sold in Japan in the early 1990s, when the dollar was devalued versus the yen, were less of a price bargain if they contained more expensive Japanese microchips.

Revaluation is devaluation in reverse; instead of decreasing in value relative to the currencies of other countries, the value of a country's currency increases. Thus, exports become more expensive and less competitive, and the advantages of devaluation turn into disadvantages—sales and productivity decline, and the balance of payments tilts against the revaluing country.

Marketers on the wrong side of a currency valuation change (e.g., those who are competing in an importing country against the devalued products of an exporter, or in a foreign devaluing country with revalued prices) face difficult pricing decisions. If the marketed product has a strong, safe competitive position, it might be possible to pass the revalued price increase on to the customer. Otherwise, options include sourcing from the devaluing country (as the Honda automobile company did when, in 1993, in announced that 90 percent of its automobile parts would be manufactured in the United States), absorbing cost increases by reducing prices to meet devalued competition, and/or reducing marketing and operating costs.

Beginning in the mid-1980s, when the U.S. dollar began a long decline against many worldwide currencies, researchers got a good idea of how countries actually do respond on either side of the devaluation equation.

- U.S. exporters, whose products were now less expensive in importing countries, generally lowered foreign-currency-denominated prices to improve their competitive positions.

- Foreign manufacturers (such as Japan) have, on average, absorbed about half of the decline in the trading value of their currencies.

Other strategies employed by countries facing the competition of a devalued currency include (1) changing to markets where a better exchange ratio exists (e.g., Germany refocuses sales of Mercedes and BMWs from the United States to Japan); (2) pushing products that are generally immune to the competitive effects of devaluation (e.g., U.S. oil field service companies sell in the Middle and Far East regardless of currency value fluctuations); or (3) setting up manufacturing operations in the devaluing country (i.e., Honda in the United States).

To illustrate other strategies to protect companies against adverse exchange rate fluctuations, assume that the exchange rate is $1 = 2.10 German marks (DM) and that a German exporter to the United States agrees to accept $250,000, to be paid in 90 days, for a shipment of computer parts, valued at 525,000 DM ($250,000 × 2.10). However, in 90 days, the value of the dollar has dropped to 2 DM, meaning the German exporter loses 50,000 DM on the deal ($250,000 × 2).

One protective strategy the German exporter could have used would have been to quote prices in German currency, thereby ensuring receipt of the dollar equivilant of 525,000 DM at the end of 90 days. Because this tactic passes the risk of devaluation to the buyer, however, it isn't always possible. Some foreign governments insist on quotations in their own currencies, and many foreign buyers have the leverage to mandate these quotations.

Another protective strategy is for the exporter to insist on shorter terms when negotiating with countries with a history of shaky currencies. In this case, if the German seller had insisted on payment in 15 instead of 90 days, there would probably be less likelihood that the dollar would have devaluated by the amount it did.

Still another protective strategy for companies exporting to countries with fluttering exchange rates is through the forward exchange market whereby, for a premium, a bank guarantees that an exporter will be paid at an agreed upon exchange rate. In this example, regardless of the fluctuation of the dollar versus the German mark, the German exporter would be paid at the $1 = 2.10 DM exchange rate at the end of 90 days. Of course, if the value at that time was $1 = 2.20 DM, the exporter would swallow the loss.

• *ESCROW REQUIREMENTS*

Escrow requirements typically require exporters to tie up money that would otherwise be earning income as the price of doing business in a foreign country. Examples include the following.

- *Cash deposit requirements* mandating that an exporter has to tie up funds, equal to a percent of anticipated profits in an importing country, for a specified time period.

- *Profit transfer rules*, which restrict conditions under which profits may be transferred out of the country.

In both situations, transfer pricing manipulation can be a way of reducing deposit requirements or transferring profits out of the country.

• *DUMPING*

Dumping is defined by the U.S. Congress as "unfair price cutting having as its objective the injury, destruction, or prevention of the establishment of American industry" and includes price differentials resulting from sales of imports on the U.S. market at prices either below those of comparable domestic goods or below those in the producing country. Thus, for example, Japan could be penalized for dumping motorcycles in the United States if it could be proven that they cost consumers less here then they cost Japanese consumers or were priced lower than comparable American motorcycles. Sometimes, a "dumping" charge is the unintended result of a firm's attempt to manipulate transfer payments in its favor or respond to an unfavorable currency devaluation in a foreign market. More likely, a firm will dump products to achieve a larger, faster share of a foreign market or to remove excess inventory and maintain price stability in its home market.

What makes dumping difficult to prove is generating evidence, in the face of shifting currency valuations, that the product did, indeed, cost more in the home country or, in the face of an exporters' efforts to differentiate their products, that there is anything comparable in the importing country. Additionally, both price discrimination and injury must be proven. (The International Trade Commission did find the Japanese firms of Honda and Kawasaki guilty of dumping motorcyles on the U.S. marketplace and imposed a special 5-year tariff, between 1983 and 1988, that began at 45 percent.)

The GATT definition of dumping is less expansive, defining the practice as selling the product in a member importing country at a price less than the price at which it left the exporting country. "Comparable product" prices in the importing country aren't an issue.

Some dumping is continuous (e.g., government subsidized farm products sold on international markets for less than in the domestic market) and some is sporadic. Sporadic dumping tends to be more disruptive, since it is difficult to anticipate and plan for. Some firms, to avoid the penalties of dumping without sacrificing the benefits, make nonprice arrangements with affiliates and distributors as incentives to flood their markets (e.g., generous discounts or credit extension arrangements can have the same effect as a generous price reduction on the open market).

• *PRICING LEGISLATION*

Pricing legislation, which varies from country to country, generally encompasses laws and regulations in the following areas that influence prices to both ultimate and intermediate customers over the course of product life cycles.

PRICE CONTROLS

Price controls, either mandated by legislative processes or encouraged by legislated policies, are much more common in foreign than in domestic markets. Sometimes, surplus production of such raw materials as coffee, oil, tin, and rubber motivates these controls. Often, they are imposed in an effort to control a runaway inflation or redress a shortage of foreign exchange. And, frequently, they effectively result from combinations in restraint of trade between and among foreign manufacturers and wholesalers that are tolerated much more in foreign than in domestic markets. (In the domestic market, price fixing, in collusion with competitors, is illegal except when carried out under the supervision of a government agency, such as in regulated transportation industries.)

Recognizing the threat represented by these foreign combinations and cartels to American trade, Congress passed the Webb-Pomerane Act in 1918, which helps U.S. exporters compete with large European cartels by combining to share costs of export operations to reap common rewards. The Act exempts companies in these Webb-Pomerane associations from the normal strictures of antitrust legislation and enforcement. As of 1992, only 22 Webb-Pomerane associations actively existed, accounting for less than 2 percent of U.S. exports and casting doubt as to their general efficacy. A better strategy for contesting the effects of price controls is through petitioning regulatory authorities. Generally, arguments for relief from price controls demonstrate that the petitioning firm isn't achieving sufficient return on investment to justify continued investment and production.

PRICE DISCRIMINATION

Price discrimination, or offering different prices to buyers at the same trade level (e.g., all wholesalers of MMs in the same sales volume category) is illegal in the United States but not in many other countries. Thus, arrangements with channel members to gain competitive advantage through price incentives are often more feasible in these countries. (A universally legal form of price discrimination is discussed in Chapter 16.)

PRICE INCREASES

Price increases in the domestic market are generally unregulated except for public utilities, with companies free to raise prices at will. This isn't always the case in global markets, and firms should look for exceptions in planning pricing strategies.

Other areas of pricing legislation that companies should investigate in planning pricing strategies pertain to (1) resale price maintenance, or the requirement that dealers charge specified resale prices; (2) minimum pricing legislation, requiring that sellers not sell below cost in an intent to destroy competition; and (3) deceptive pricing legislation, which forbids, among other things, false claims that prices were reduced from former levels and unverified claims that a firm's price is lower than other prices in the trading area.

CHAPTER PERSPECTIVE

The price of a product influences how customers perceive it, how profitable it will be, and how it should be positioned, promoted, and distributed. The complex challenge of pegging the "best" prices for different segments of international markets entails formulating productive pricing objectives, policies and strategies, and implies a sophisticated understanding of how costs, customers, competitors and country legislatures behave.

KNOW THE CONCEPTS

TERMS FOR STUDY

cost behavior
cost categories
cost curves
currency valuations
demand schedule
devaluation
dumping
escrow requirements
exchange rates
forward exchange market
marginal cost
market price
market share leadership
price controls

price decreases
price discrimination
price escalation
price increases
price legislation
pricing failures
pricing objectives
pricing policies
product quality leadership
revaluation
supply/demand
target return objectives
transfer pricing

MATCHUP EXERCISES

1. Match up the price-related marketing objectives in the first column with the corporate actions in the second column.

1. market share leadership

2. survival

3. product quality leadership

a. During market doldrums, automobile dealers price below cost and offer large rebates.

b. Mercedes Benz, however, refuses to cut its price.

c. Anticipating economic doldrums during good times, appliance dealers stop discounting.

4. current profit maximization

d. Fuji achieves a strong market position by pricing its photographic equipment below the market price.

2. Match up the price-type in the first column with the quote in the second column.

1. market price

a. "If we can get $100 apiece for these cellular phones, we'll market half a million of them."

2. inelastic price

b. "I know he charges $300 an hour, but he's worth it."

3. transfer price

c. "We'll charge our Japanese subsidiary $40 a liter."

4. devalued price

d. "We'll give Wal-Mart a bigger discount than we give K-Mart because we need their business more."

5. discriminatory price

e. "Better stock up—French wine will never be this cheap again."

3. Match up the cost-type in the first column with the descriptor in the second column.

1. fixed costs

a. total cost divided by number of units sold

2. variable costs

b. what it costs to produce that last widget

3. average total cost

c. remains constant no matter how many units are produced

4. marginal cost

d. directly related to production and marketing

QUESTIONS FOR REVIEW AND DISCUSSION

1. Hewlett-Packard, a $16 billion company that produces technical products for business and dominates the high quality, high end of the hand calculator market, achieves competitive advantage in selected markets based on customer perceptions of unique, high value products worth their high price. Presently, Hewlett-Packard, with a work force of 15,000 in Asia and sales of $3 billion, is embarking on market growth strategies in Japan and Malaysia. Discuss the relationship between Hewlett-Packard's high quality/price image and the following aspects of its market growth strategy: (1) target market selection and (2) product/place/promotion elements of H-P's marketing mix.

2. Which of the following objectives would Hewlett-Packard be working

to achieve in implementing its Asian growth pricing policies and strategies: target return, market share leadership, product quality leadership, survival, helping to sell other products in the line?

3. Identify the following on the following graph depicting supply/ demand relationships defining the entry of Merton MM computer systems into a selected market: line *DE*, line *AB*, point *F*. What are the strategic implications of this information from the perspective of Merton's marketing manager?

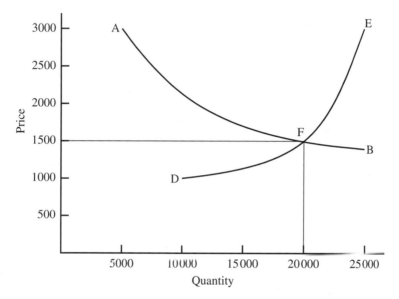

4. The following table shows price escalation generated in shipping 1,908 cases of assorted chemicals, weighing 35,000 pounds, from Kansas City to Encarnación, Paraguay. Note that the price of the shipment has more than doubled in transit. Discuss three ways in which the final retail price might be made more competitive.

Item			As A Percentage of F.O.B. Price
F.O.B. Kansas City		$10,090	100%
Freight to New Orleans	$ 110		
Freight to Encarnación, Paraguay	1,897		
Counselor invoices	21		
Forwarding fee	8		
Insurance ($19,000 value)	383		
Port charge	434		
Documentation	3		
Total shipping charges		2,856	28
C.I.F. value		$12,946	
Duty (20% on C.I.F. value)		2,584	26
Distributor markup (10%)		1,547	15
Dealer markup (25%)		4,289	43
Total retail price		$21,384	212%

5. Define the following costs involved in printing a newspaper.

- The cost of renting the printing plant;
- The cost of extra paper and dyes purchased to print an "extra" edition of the newspaper;
- The cost of producing the last newspaper, which includes the "extra" edition;
- The sum of all costs divided by the number of newspapers produced.

   Which of these costs defines the point at which additional copies produced will no longer produce a profit? How does price fit into this equation?

6. Motorola, the world's fourth largest semiconductor manufacturer, opened a multi-million-dollar chip manufacturing plant in Hong Kong, in expectation of supplying the entire $16 billion Pacific Rim market for semiconductors by the year 2000. Interpret the following long-range cost curve, in terms of what it depicts and how it will affect Motorola's pricing strategy for its semiconductors.

7. In selling its semiconductors to its Asian customers, would it be more desirable if the exchange rate of the U.S. dollar falls or rises against that of the oriental currency? What measures could Motorola take to protect itself against the less desirable situation?

ANSWERS

MATCHUP EXERCISES

1. 1d, 2a, 3b, 4c
2. 1a, 2b, 3c, 4e, 5d
3. 1c, 2d, 3a, 4b

QUESTIONS FOR REVIEW AND DISCUSSION

1. As it relates to target market selection, Hewlett-Packard's high price/ high quality strategy focuses marketing efforts on small selected markets whose members can afford H-P's unique, high value products. Target marketing at H-P also involves continual monitoring of market members to measure customer satisfaction (John Young, H-P's former CEO, notes that nine of ten customers who rank themselves highly satisfied purchase from H-P again, a highly profitable result in light of Young's estimates that it costs five times as much to gain as to keep a customer).

With respect to the relationship between H-P's high price and the other marketing mix elements, some effects follow. *Product:* Research and development, advanced product design, and "zero defects" quality control help H-P maintain a quality level perceived to justify its pricing strategy. For example, in its move to expand its Asian market, H-P, since 1991, has streamlined its manufacturing, project management, and design capabilities in Asia. *Place:* To a much lesser extent than is the case with lower-end price competitors, H-P's products are most likely to be sold directly to customers, rather than through mass market outlets. This personalized service is considered a part of the price customers are paying for H-P products. *Promotion:* Although H-P does not centralize advertising strategy or implementation—delegating most product-related advertising to overseas business units who are encouraged to be guided by local trends and cultures—all promotion campaigns are constrained by company-wide identification and design standards reflective of H-P's high quality/high price image.

2. The two most important objectives that H-P's pricing policies and strategies are designed to help achieve are (1) product quality leadership in selected markets, which the firm's maintained high price, with its quality associations, helps achieve, and (2) target profit return objectives, which are made easier to achieve through H-P's product quality leadership and the predictable willingness of brand-loyal H-P customers to buy H-P products at H-P's price.

3. Line *DE* on the graph is a supply curve that depicts the quantity of MM computer systems that Merton would be prepared to make available at different prices. For example, at the $3,000 price (point *E*), Merton would be willing to reorder its production priorities and resources among its various product lines to make 25,000 units available. (Note that this isn't many more then the 24,000 units Merton would be willing to make available at the profitable $2,500 price, at which level of production the firm begins to run out of capacity and resources to produce more units.) *AB* is a demand curve, indicating the number of MM systems customers would be willing to purchase at different price levels. At a $3,000 price (point *A*), Merton's research indicates that only 8,000 customers would buy Mighty Mind systems, for an overall sales volume of $24,000,000. Then, as the price gets lower, more customers purchase MM systems, with the number reaching 20,000 at the $1,500 price, for an overall sales volume of $30,000,000. The fact that sales volume increases as price is lowered— at least up to a point—indicates that demand for MMs in this particular market is elastic. In another market, where the MM is perceived as both unique and necessary, demand might exhibit an inelastic pattern, where sales volume increases as the MM's price increases. Point *F*, where supply and demand curves intersect, is called the equilibrium point, or market price, where what people will buy just equals what the seller is willing to offer. From a marketer's perspective, understanding supply/demand relationships is critically important in devising product, price, place, and promotion marketing mix strategies. For example, if supply/demand analyses showed Merton's marketing manager that the MM exhibited an inelastic demand curve, she

would price it high to optimize profit return and base positioning and promotion strategies on this high price/high quality image. In any event, she would avoid the mistake of pricing the MM too high for the market (point *E*) or too low (point *D*).

4. Three ways whereby the retail price of this shipment of assorted chemicals might be made more competitive at its destination include any or all of the following. (1) Begin with a lower price at F.O.B. Kansas City. This could be done if the seller uses a marginal pricing strategy—assuming fixed costs have already been captured in marketing these chemicals in the U.S. domestic market—and/or relinquishing a portion of desired profit in Paraguay in order to compete more effectively. (2) Source portions of this order (e.g., the containers for the chemicals or components in the chemical mix) from Paraguay, which might appreciably reduce the high duty on the chemicals. (3) Change to less costly distribution channels, if available.

5. Rental cost is a fixed cost; extra paper and dye, a variable cost; cost of producing the last newspaper, the marginal cost; sum of all costs divided by number of newspapers produced, average total cost. Marginal cost defines the point beyond which additional copies produced will no longer produce a profit; to recoup costs, revenues from this last newspaper produced must equal marginal cost. As long as marginal revenue (the additional sales volume produced by each additional newspaper run off) exceeds marginal cost (the cost of producing each additional newspaper), each newspaper produced will add to profits. Profits will be greatest where marginal cost and revenue are equal, when output equals the total profit on all newspapers produced to this point. The price to be charged for the newspaper can be induced by working back from desired profits, costs, and the planned newspaper run to reach this point.

6. The long-range cost curve depicted shows that, while short-range average cost curves, which make up the long-range costs, tend to decline and then increase, the long-range curve just declines. The short-range curves decline because learning curve efficiencies and economies of scale combine to push costs downward; they increase because a point is eventually reached where Motorola will incur new costs (e.g., to build additional production capacity) that exceed learning curve and scale savings. However, since each short-range cost curve is lower than its predecessor, the aggregate long-range cost curve trends downward, meaning that, in spite of temporary dislocations, Motorola can afford to lower its prices over time. Personal computers, video cameras, and videocasette recorders are but a few examples of products whose prices have decreased dramatically as costs decreased and competition increased.

7. Assuming its products for export were manufactured in the domestic market, it would be more beneficial for Motorola if the exchange rate of the U.S. dollar fell against that of foreign currencies. This would mean, for example, that German marks or Japanese yen could purchase more dollars and more products priced in dollars. For Motorola, this would mean it could afford to lower its prices below those of competitors in these countries, possibly achieving a competitive edge without sacrificing profits, because it would still be getting the same number of dollars. To protect itself from situations where the value of the dollar rises against foreign currencies, meaning it would have to lower its price to remain competitive, Motorola might use the services of the Forward Exchange Market to ensure payment in noninflated dollars or negotiate shorter payment terms so that currency revaluations could be anticipated and countered.

16

PRICING IN INTERNATIONAL MARKETS II: FORMULATING STRATEGIES AND TACTICS

OVERVIEW

Basic pricing strategies in international markets, from cost to demand based, reflect economic and competitive climates in which they are pegged. Supporting these basic strategies are price modification strategies that recognize differences among customers in such areas as functions performed, quantities purchased, and time of purchase and payment. In addition to setting prices, price planning involves determining terms of sale and payment and changing prices in response to competitive changes in global markets.

PRICING STRATEGIES HELP ACHIEVE MARKETING GOALS

In Chapter 15, we examined major considerations involved in arriving at productive, profit-oriented objectives and policies that help define pricing strategies and tactics calculated to help achieve them. We also examined characteristics of international markets pertaining to costs, customers, competitors, and legislation that make price planning a much more difficult, complex challenge than in domestic markets.

In this chapter, we examine a variety of price strategies employed to achieve diverse marketing goals in diverse international competitive climates. We begin with cost-based pricing strategies appropriate to monopolistic and oligopolistic markets and then move on to demand-based strategies appropriate to competitive free markets. Also examined are price modification strategies that support both cost- and demand-based strategies.

PRICING OPTIONS: COST- AND DEMAND-BASED

Companies that set prices in international markets have three strategic options:

- Set a uniform price everywhere, resulting in different profit returns in different countries with different costs;

- Set cost-based prices in different countries, using the same markup of its costs everywhere and pricing itself out of markets where costs are too high;

- Set demand-based prices in each country, deemphasizing cost differences among countries and generally charging what markets can afford.

Which option to choose—the first two cost-based, the third demand-based—is contingent on a variety of factors that combine to define the competitive environment in each market.

COST-BASED STRATEGIES: ROI, MARKUPS, AND BREAKEVENS

Cost-based pricing strategies, including cost-plus, markup and breakeven pricing, are most used by companies getting started in global markets, especially when facing little or no competition.

• *COST-PLUS PRICING*

Cost-plus pricing, the simplest method of cost-based pricing, merely adds a predetermined profit to costs. This strategy is largely used by monopolies with no competitors (e.g., power and light utilities) and products sufficiently unique or prestigious to dominate their market. For example, in determining the price for MM systems in such markets, Merton first estimated the number of systems it would be able to sell in a certain price range over a specified time period and then added total variable and fixed costs (TVC and TFC) to total desired profit. Price was then obtained by dividing this amount by the number of systems to be produced. Thus,

$$\text{Price} = \frac{\text{TFC + TVC + Projected Profit}}{\text{Units Produced}}$$

To illustrate, if sales of 5,000 units were projected for a given market and Merton desired a profit of $500,000, the price of each system, given the following total fixed and variable costs, would be

$$\frac{\$1,500,000 + \$3,000,000 + \$500,000}{5000} = \$1,000$$

Two problems exist with cost-plus pricing: First, it assumes that fixed and variable costs can be separated out and assigned to specific products, which often proves to be a problem. Second, it assumes that consumer demand patterns and competitive responses to prices are largely irrelevant, which doesn't always prove to be the case.

• *MARKUP PRICING*

Markup pricing, one form of cost-plus pricing, is used mainly by wholesalers and retailers, who often carry thousands of products and couldn't possibly analyze demand and competitive factors for each. A simple formula for determining product markup pegs the final price of the product equal to the purchase cost to the company divided by 1.0 minus the desired markup percentage. For example, assuming a retailer purchases a MM for $1,000 and desires a markup of 40 percent, then

$$\frac{\$1,000}{1-0.40} = \frac{\$1,000}{0.60} = \$1,666$$

The size of a distributor's markup depends on a variety of factors, including industry practices, manufacturers list price, inventory turnover desired, effort required to compete successfully, and other available discounts discussed later in this chapter. In general, distributors in industrialized foreign countries expect higher percentage markups than do domestic distributors, often to compensate for a comparative lack of aggressive selling and generally less efficient operations. Typically, distributors using markup pricing take consumer demand into account by dropping prices on products that don't sell at the desired markup.

• *BREAKEVEN-POINT PRICING*

Breakeven-point pricing considers both cost and market demand to identify the point at which the firm begins to get its money back on a product. In essence, this breakeven point is the point at which total revenues—units sold times price per unit—equals total fixed and variable costs.

Breakeven points can be computed in terms of units or sales dollars:

$$\text{Breakeven Point (units)} = \frac{\text{Total Fixed Costs}}{\text{Price–Variable Costs (per unit)}}$$

$$\text{Breakeven Point (sales dollars)} = \frac{\text{Total Fixed Costs}}{1 - \dfrac{\text{Variable Costs (per unit)}}{\text{Price}}}$$

For example, assume Merton plans to sell MM systems in a foreign market for $1,000, with $1,500,000 in fixed costs assigned to its production and $600 in variable costs assigned to each system sold. In units, the breakeven point would be 3,750 ($1,500,000 / $1,000–$600); in dollars, $3,750,000 ($1,500,000 / 1–($600/$1,000). Beyond this breakeven point, income generated represents profits. If Merton research indicates that it can easily exceed this point, it should launch the MM.

Breakeven analyses, while useful as a rough indicator of the relationship between costs, revenues, and prices, is subject to a number of limitations when used as the sole measure of these relationships. For example, it assumes fixed costs can be precisely assigned to specific products (when many shared fixed costs can't be) and that variable costs can be clearly identified (when many semivariable costs can't be). Also, many breakeven analyses assume that total cost lines continue to rise linearly when they are much more likely to assume erratic configurations due to things like experience curves and sudden rises in costs as capacity is reached and new facilities are required.

• *ROI PRICING*

Return on investment (ROI) pricing, also called targeted return pricing, measures total investment in a product—which, in the case of a new product like the first MM, includes sizable up-front costs in addition to current fixed and variable costs—and then sets a price that will earn a predetermined profit return on this investment. Targeted pricing is practiced mainly by capital-intensive firms, such as aircraft manufacturers and public utilities. The method for setting prices under ROI is

$$\text{Price} = \text{AVC} + \frac{\text{TFC}}{\text{PV}} + \frac{\text{ROI} \times \text{I}}{\text{PV}}$$

where AVC = average variable cost, TFC = total fixed cost, PV = planned volume, and I = investment.

For example, during the MM's growth period in a highly favorable foreign market, each system was priced at a level that would produce a 10 percent profit return on investment. Thus,

$$\$2,300 = \$600 + \frac{\$5,000,000}{3,000} + \frac{0.10\ (\$1,000,000)}{3,000}$$

Since the demand curve indicated that 3,000 MMs would be sold in one target market at the $2,300 price, this became the MM's price. Like other forms of cost-based pricing, an ROI pricing strategy assumes that planned sales volume will actually be achieved at the derived price. This assumption worked well for global firms like Kodak, IBM, and Toyota until the early 1990s, when economic and competitive pressures frequently made it impossible to price products to achieve ROI goals.

• *MARGINAL COST PRICING*

Marginal cost pricing disregards fixed costs for making and marketing products when pricing these products for global markets, assuming these costs have already been captured in the domestic market. Thus, the base price for each product is the marginal cost of producing and marketing it for export markets, a strategy that can go a long way to offset price escalation.

OLIGOPOLISTIC STRATEGIES: COPY CATS AND KINKED DEMAND

An oligopoly consists of a few firms—generally, but not necessarily, large ones—that account for most of an industry's sales. In the United States, oligopolistic industries produce automobiles, cigarettes, turbines, breakfast cereals, and refrigerators. In its early stage of growth in the U.S. market, the Merton MM, with a few other large competitors, also found itself in an oligopolistic market climate.

In foreign markets, U.S. firms can plan pricing strategies under oligopolistic conditions through Webb-Pomerane associations, discussed in Chapter 15, which exempt companies from U.S. antitrust legislation if they combine to compete with European and other foreign cartels.

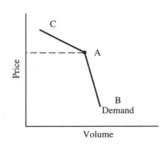

Figure 16–1. Oligopolistic Kinked Demand Curve

In this oligopolistic climate, a few sellers are highly sensitive to each other's marketing and pricing strategies, giving rise to the kinked demand curve shown in Figure 16-1. Note that all competitors are pricing their products at point *A* on this curve. The rationale for this copy-cat pricing strategy is that if one competitor lowers its price to point *B*, all the other competitors will follow, thus largely canceling out the advantage of the lowered price, with demand barely increasing. On the other hand, if one firm increases its price to point *C*, none of the other competitors will follow, and this firm will rapidly lose sales to its lower-priced competitors.

Note two characteristics of this oligopolistic pricing strategy. First, unlike monopolistic, cost-based strategies, it must also account for buyer and competitor behavior. Thus, although Merton used breakeven and ROI analyses to arrive at a kink price point, this point was now determined more by how buyers and competitors would respond than by predetermined profit goals. Second, unlike previous cost-based strategies, this oligopolistic strategy no longer aims to optimize profits but simply to satisfy what all competitors agree, at least implicitly, are reasonable profit goals.

DEMAND-BASED PRICE STRATEGIES: SKIM OR PENETRATE?

To this point, our focus has been on pricing strategies appropriate to environmental climates in which competitors are monopolistically nonexistant or oligopolistically cozy with each other. In the real world, however, firms don't typically enter or grow in such markets. Sooner or later, if the product is capable of attracting a market, it will also attract competitors. And competitors rise or fall based on their ability to relate to demand patterns in their markets.

Anticipating this demand-based competitive climate, Merton price planners usually faced two strategic options: penetrate or skim the market.

PENETRATION STRATEGY

A penetration strategy would suggest a low introductory price in this market, perhaps even lower than the cost of producing MMs. The objective of this low price would be to stimulate market growth by grabbing market share from existing or prospective competitors, as do the Japanese, Taiwanese, and Koreans in achieving dominant market positions all over the world. For example, Japan achieved dominance in the domestic Random Access Memory (RAM) market by selling its device, identical to the American device, for $10, or $8 less than the cheapest American price.

Achieving a dominant share of a target market usually produces long-term benefits that easily compensate for short-term profit losses. For one thing, it's difficult to knock leader companies off their top rung; companies like Coca-Cola, Lipton Tea, Goodyear Tires, Life Savers and Quaker Oats have all been leaders in global markets for more than 80 years. For another, a position of leadership usually ensures economies of scale in making and marketing products, which make it easier to generate profits and control prices—including raising prices—than playing catch-up with the competition.

In considering a penetration strategy, price planners should also recognize conditions under which such a strategy is most likely to succeed. Usually required is a large, expandable, price-sensitive target market, and the possibility of economies of scale, with per-unit production and distribution costs decreasing as sales increase. Additionally, the lower price should effectively discourage competition and, particularly in international markets, not invite charges of violating price legislation and regulations, such as for dumping or predatory pricing.

SKIMMING STRATEGY

Much safer, from a legal/political perspective, is a price skimming policy, with prices pegged high to lure the comparatively small target market more attracted to the quality, uniqueness, and usefulness of the MM than to its price. Then, after sales to this primary target market began to fall off, the MM's price would be lowered to attract members of the next target market down the line, and so on. A skimming price is appropriate if the product isn't attracting excessive competition, if a high price helps support a quality image, if there are a sufficiently large number of target market members willing to pay this price, and if a positive short-term return on investment is mandated. Other factors supporting a skimming pricing strategy include limited production facilities and the need to work weaknesses out of manufacturing/marketing processes.

HOLDING PRICING STRATEGY

A third demand-based pricing strategy, especially appropriate in compensating for unfavorable exchange rates in international markets, is a strategy of holding a company's share of market. In the early 1980s, for example, when the dollar appreciated against most other currencies, American companies based prices on the competitive situation in each market, and the ability of customers to pay, rather than on U.S. prices translated into foreign currencies at current exchange rates. As noted in Chapter 15, most companies facing depreciated currencies in competitive markets follow this strategy of relating prices to demand, to the extent that they absorb, on average, 50 percent of the effective resulting price increase.

PRICE DISCRIMINATION FAVORS DIFFERENT SEGMENTS

Discriminatory pricing, a demand-based strategy appropriate in both consumer and organizational markets, is defined as the legally sanctioned practice of selling a product at two or more prices that do not reflect a proportional difference in costs. Conditions favorable to discrimination include

- Different segments of the market (accountants, doctors, lawyers, etc.) must show different intensities of demand.

- One segment won't undersell the product to the segment paying a higher price.

- Cost required to police price discrimination doesn't exceed the extra revenues produced by discriminating.

- Price discrimination doesn't breed ill-will.

- Discrimination doesn't violate legal prescriptions (summarized in Chapter 15).

FORMS OF PRICE DISCRIMINATION

A familiar form of price discrimination is place discrimination, in which, for example, a customer at a football or soccer game pays more for a seat at midfield than in the end zone, although the cost of installing each seat is the same.

Other forms of discriminatory pricing, all implemented by Merton in foreign market entry strategies, included customer, time, and product price discrimination. Following are examples of each.

Customer discrimination was used when Merton charged professionals working for large firms less than self-employed professionals for MM systems—a strategy analagous to corporate discounts offered by airlines and car rental companies.

Time discrimination was used when Merton increased the price of MM systems during periods of peak demand, usually after the summer months, with vacations over and company training programs starting up again.

Product discrimination was used when Merton charged more for software training programs that were in high demand, even though the actual cost of producing and marketing all programs was essentially the same.

PROMOTIONAL PRICING ATTRACTS MARKET SEGMENTS

Merton's demand-based promotional pricing strategy for MM systems involved pricing them below list, or even below cost, in order to achieve larger sales or profit goals. For example, it was not unusual for MM's distributors to discount the price of MM customized software during special sales campaigns designed to increase sales of MM computers. The overall increase in sales and profits easily compensated for smaller profits on the software.

At the peak of its maturity stage in some foreign markets, as competition among computer system producers became intense and differences among the systems became more difficult to perceive, Merton also used cash rebates as an additional incentive for end users to purchase the systems and for distributors to push them. This incentive allowed Merton to retain its original price and the blue chip image associated with this price.

EXPECTED PROFIT STRATEGIES CONTROL BIDDING

Another demand-based strategy employed by Merton in the organizational market was expected profit pricing. Table 16-1 shows how this approach, used mainly in response to requests for bids by large prospective customers, worked in a sealed bid Merton submitted to a large accounting firm for an order of 1,000 MM systems.

Table 16–1. Highest Expected Value Determines Selected Bid

Company Bid	Company Profit	Estimated Success Probability	Expected Profit
$ 600,000	$ 20,000	.70	$14,000
800,000	220,000	.30	66,000
1,000,000	420,000	.05	21,000
1,200,000	620,000	.01	6,200

At the time this bid was made, Merton had managed to reduce its costs for making and marketing each MM system to $580. Thus, if it were to charge $600 for each MM, for a total bid price of $600,000, it would make a total profit of $20,000. At this low bid price, collective management wisdom and past experience indictated that Merton had a 70 percent chance of getting the order, so the expected profit from this $600,000 bid was $14,000 (0.70 × $20,000). Other expected values of bids of $800, $1000 and $1200 per MM, following the same approach, indicated that a bid of $800,000, with a 30 percent chance of succeeding, generated the highest expected profit—$66,000—so that was Merton's bid.

PRODUCT LINE PRICING STRATEGIES

Unless a product is introduced as a discrete entity in itself, pricing considerations and concerns are usually dictated by perceptions of products as components of larger product mixes and product lines. For example, the Merton MM line of computers and associated software was part of a mix of electronic products and components for consumer and organizational markets. In this broader context, three demand-based strategies were used to help achieve marketing objectives: price lining, optional pricing, and captive pricing.

PRICE LINING

When Merton introduced a more sophisticated MM system to its existing product line, many of the analyses required to peg a price for this product had already been made in pricing other MMs in the line. For example, price planners already knew what profit margin the new product would be expected to generate and what kind of product image it should reflect.

Pricing the new MM in this product line context, the planners' main concern focused on cost differences between this model and others in the line, prices that competing firms charged for similar MM models, and assessments of the new model by prospective customers. Also guiding their planning were considerations pertaining to establishing price differentials among products within the line of MMs. They realized, for example, that price points should be spaced far enough apart so that customers would perceive functional and quality differences among different models; otherwise, customers would simply buy the lowest priced model. They also realized that prices should be spaced farther apart at higher levels, where consumer demand becomes more inelastic. Thus the deluxe MM model at the top of the line was priced at $400 more than the next most expensive MM, which was priced only $300 above the lowest priced unit.

From the viewpoint of Merton and its distributors, price lining offered a number of benefits. An assortment of MM models could be offered to attract many market segments, and members of these segments could be encouraged to trade up, thus increasing sales and profits. Also, a broad product line, with models throughout the price range, is a strong deterrent to competitors.

OPTIONAL PRICING

Under an optional pricing strategy, companies face the problem with major products of which components and accessories to offer as options and which to offer as standards. For example, an auto manufacturer can attract customers with a stripped-down model at a very attractive price and then sell-up to more attractive, option-loaded models. This was General Motors' normal pricing strategy until the early 1980s when, in response to Japanese automakers, it included in its sticker price many useful items previously sold only as options.

In international markets, optional pricing decisions can also offer practical legal benefits. For example, by including as part of an automobile accessory a tool that had previously been sold separately, the manufacturer bypassed the relatively high tariff on that tool and acquired immunity from antidumping regulations by making the product no longer comparable to competing goods in the target market.

CAPTIVE PRICING

Under a captive pricing strategy, firms produce products that must be used with the main product and that influence the price of both products and overall profitability. A camera manufacturer, for example, might set a low price for cameras, and a higher-than-market price for the film used with the camera, thus making up with film profits what is lost in camera profits. This strategy proved effective for Merton when, in highly competitive, price-sensitive markets, it could lower prices on its MM models while concurrently increasing prices on customized software to take up some of the profit slack.

PRICE MODIFICATION STRATEGIES: TERMS OF SALE AND PAYMENT

Whether a firm adopts a cost- or demand-based strategy, an important additional component will be price modification strategies that define conditions under which ownership will pass from seller to buyer—terms of sale—and under which payment will be made from buyer to seller—terms of payment. Terms of sale and payment can vary in degree of their attractiveness to buyer and seller and represent a modification of quoted prices that affect, favorably or unfavorably, the profitability of transactions for either party. To the extent that they favor the buyer, they represent potent competitive tools for persuading market intermediaries to carry products and end users or consumers to buy them. The examples in Global Focus 16-1 highlight the importance of relating terms of sale and payment to customer needs and accounting for the effects of these terms on profitability.

GLOBAL FOCUS 16-1

Different Companies, Different Price Strategies

The complexity of export pricing, and its impact on profits, is illustrated by different approaches to price modification taken by different companies.

- Baughman, a division of Fuqua Industries, manufactures steel grain storage silos and related equipment and has traditionally exported approximately 30 percent of its sales. Baughman's products are of high quality, and pricing has not often been an active element of the marketing mix. The firm's export sales terms consist of an irrevocable confirmed letter of credit in U.S. dollars with no provisions for fluctuating exchange rates. Export and domestic prices are identical before exporting costs are added. However, Baughman will make concessions to this policy to secure strategically important sales.

- Ray-O-Vac, a producer of batteries and other consumer goods, has been exporting successfully since the 1950s. Exports account for 20 percent of total business, and major markets include Europe, the Far East, and Japan. These markets are entered through wholly owned subsidiaries that are treated as cost or profit centers. Competitive pressures demand flexible pricing, and discounts are often granted to gain market share. Branch managers may adjust prices on a day-to-day basis to counter exchange rate fluctuations.

- During a 4-year period, Hart-Carter International exported $12 million worth of agricultural machinery to more than 90 countries without a single default. The firm's policy with respect to new customers is to use a credit form of payment, whereby the firm presents proof of shipment to a U.S. bank in which the foreign customer has established credit, receiving payment the day goods are shipped. Later, as the firm gains experience with new customers, they reduce credit requirements, even placing many

> on an open account basis. Almost without exception, these open accounts pay within 30 days
>
> - Richard Winter, owner of Schummel Novelty Products of Englewood, Colo., offers this caution for exporters: "In international financing, be careful to prepare letters of credit properly. Once you do so, there is hardly any risk, but when they are improperly prepared, you hear horror stories." Even with his background in law and accounting, Winter still has all his firm's letters of credit checked by a banker and the president of Schummel's freight forwarding company.
>
> Source: "Stories of Exporting Success," *Business America* (October 1993 and June 1994).

TERMS OF SALE

The terms of sale, discussed next, include (1) terms, called Intercoms, that define degrees of responsibility assumed by buyers and sellers in transporting goods from point of origin to final destination and (2) trade discounts and allowances available to buyers under certain conditions advantageous to the seller (e.g., buying in quantities or paying bills on time).

• *INCOTERMS*

Incoterms are internationally accepted standard definitions for terms of sale by the International Chamber of Commerce (ICC) that went into effect in 1990. The most common of these terms used in global marketing are defined next. They indicate the point from which ownership of exported goods passes from buyer to seller, ranging from ex works with most risk and cost assumed by the buyer, to delivered duty paid, where this obligation is assumed by the seller.

- *Ex-works (EXW)* means that charges for transporting the goods are assumed by the buyer at the point from which the order originates (e.g., the mine, factory, warehouse).

- *Free carrier (FCA)* means that the seller is responsible for loading goods into the means of transportation at a designated inland shipping point; the buyer is responsible for all subsequent risks and expenses.

- *Free alongside ship (FAS)* means that the exporter assumes charges for delivering the goods alongside a vessel at the port, including unloading and wharfage. Loading, ocean transportation, and insurance are left to the buyer.

- *Free on board (FOB)* means that the seller's price covers all expenses up to and including delivery of goods on an overseas vessel provided by or for the buyer.

- *Cost and freight (CFR)* means that the seller's price includes the cost of transportation to a named overseas port of import. The cost of insurance and the choice of insurer are left to the buyer. With a CIF provision in a quote, the seller's price includes all cost, insurance, and freight to the point of debarkation from a vessel or aircraft.

- *Delivered duty paid (DDP)* means that the seller delivers the goods, with import duties paid, right to the buyer's facility. With delivered duty unpaid, destination customs duty and taxes are paid by the buyer.

Note that these arrangements between sellers and individual buyers are made with the understanding that different market conditions will mandate different incoterm responsibilites. Often, however, sellers find it in their economic interest to mandate a single arrangement for all customers regardless of location. Here the options include the following.

- A *uniform delivered pricing strategy (UDP)* allows the firm to charge the same freight rate to all customers regardless of their location. This rate would be sufficiently high to cover the seller's shipping costs but sufficiently low to allow individual dealers to compete effectively on price.

- *Basing point pricing* takes into account the location of a firm's most lucrative domestic and foreign markets and places a "basing point" at the center of each area, which becomes a low rate zone. For example, if France represented the market with the largest potential in Europe for Merton products, Paris might become the base point for lowest freight rates, which would increase from that point to areas of lesser potential.

- Under *freight absorption pricing*, Merton would absorb all, or most, of the freight cost to buyers. This strategy is typically employed as the strongest geographic pricing incentive for distributors to take on a product, but can create an unacceptable profit drain to the seller.

Increasingly, sellers are moving toward freight absorption terms, usually on a CFR or DDP basis, as being in their best economic interest. As a sales tool, such a strategy allows the seller to offer foreign buyers an easily understood delivered cost and cuts down on expensive administrative procedures for buyers. Such a strategy also offers opportunities for sellers to negotiate volume discounts on purchases of transportation services and maintain control of product quality and service, ensuring arrival to the buyer in good condition.

• *TRADE DISCOUNTS*

Following are price modifications, in the form of discounts and allowances, to a seller's basic price designed to reward customers for certain favorable responses, such as volume purchases and buying off-season.

- *Functional discounts*, also called trade discounts, are offered by manufacturers to trade channel members in return for performing distribution functions discussed in Chapter 18.

- *Quantity discounts* are offered to customers who purchase merchandise in larger than normal quantities.

- *Cash discounts* are price reductions offered to customers as an incentive to pay bills on time. For example, a discount of 2/10, net 20, means that payment is due within 20 days, but the buyer can deduct 2 percent from the bill if it is paid within 10 days.

- *Allowances* are reductions from the list price covering periodic or unanticipated contingencies such as a special promotion or the failure of the product to sell. For example, recognizing early distributor perceptions that MM systems might not sell in certain global markets, Merton offered unusually generous return allowances to distributors: a full refund on their purchase price, less 10 percent to cover shipping and handling charges. Promotional allowances were also extremely generous, with Merton contributing $2 for every $1 contributed by a distributor.

TERMS OF PAYMENT

In global markets, payments usually flow from buyer to seller along a spectrum of arrangements—from cash in advance to consignment—that become progressively less beneficial from the seller's perspective and more beneficial to the buyer. Considerations involved in deciding which arrangement best meets the needs of both seller and buyer include the customer's credit rating, industry practices, the amount of payment, the relative strength of buyer and seller, and the seller's capacity for financing global transactions.

Following are characteristics and relative benefits of each approach.

• *CASH DEPOSITS IN ADVANCE*

Exporter requests payment in cash, in whole or part, in advance of shipment. This approach is typically used when exchange restrictions in destination country, or doubtful customer creditworthiness, render payments slow or speculative. Volume of international trade handled this way is small.

• *EXPORT LETTER OF CREDIT*

If irrevocable and confirmed by a bank in the exporting country, the export letter of credit (LOC) affords the exporter the best protection next to cash in advance in obtaining payment. The LOC eliminates the possibility of cancellation of the order before payment, protects the exporter from exchange restrictions in the destination country, and ensures payment on presentation of such shipping documents as a full set of bills of lading in negotiable form, parcel post receipts, and consular invoices. LOCs can be revolving or nonrevolving, can help ensure financing, and give importer "float."

• *DOLLAR (OR FOREIGN CURRENCY) DRAFTS*

Usually drawn on a bank for immediate payment or for acceptance 30, 60, or 90 days after sight or date, and accompanied by shipping documents to the bank holding the draft, this form of finance also offers protection against currency restrictions and customer credit risk. With either sight or time draft, buyer can extend the credit period by avoiding receipt of goods.

• *OPEN ACCOUNT*

No written evidence of debt or any guarantee of payment exists with this type of credit. It is common in trade among European Union countries and in other situations where exchange controls are minimal and exporters have good relations with creditworthy customers or are selling to branches or subsidiaries. A major objection to open account sales in international trade is the possibility of litigation with no written confirmation of debt; usually, bad debts are easier to avoid than rectify.

• *CONSIGNMENT SALES*

In countries with free ports or free trade zones, consigned merchandise can often be placed under bonded warehouse control in the name of a foreign bank, with partial lots released against regular payment terms when sales are generated. The merchandise is not cleared through customs until the sale has been completed. Like open account sales, no tangible obligation is created, leading to potential legal complications.

PRICE CHANGE STRATEGIES: WHEN AND HOW

Whether perceived as a discrete entity, or as part of larger product mixes or lines, a product that successfully competes in global markets must have its price changed sooner or later. For example, it will have to be lowered to meet competitive challenges or raised to reflect favorable supply/demand conditions in the marketplace.

• *CUTTING PRICES*

Typical reasons for cutting a price generally prevailed during the late maturity and decline stages of MM systems in most markets; falling market share had produced excess capacity and the need to generate sales to remove this excess. Another key reason for cutting prices was illustrated by price reductions of MM models during Merton's introductory stage in competitive markets—a drive to achieve a position of market leadership, with the economies of scale associated with this position.

• *RAISING PRICES*

As noted in Chapter 15, a relatively small price increase can lever dramatic profit increases, assuming demand doesn't decrease appreciably as a consequence of this increase. Although price increases are almost always more difficult to implement than price decreases, they can often be justified for the following reasons.

- *Unexpectedly high demand for the product* justifies increasing a price perceived as too low.

- *Cost inflation* forces all manufacturers in a field to raise prices more or less simultaneously.

- *Unbundling of services* often provides a justification for increasing the price of individual services. For example, the tax division of a large accounting firm might unbundle financial planning services, which are easier to "value price" in terms of customer perceptions than are routine tax compliance activities, which are billed at a lower hourly rate.

- *Discounts, allowances, rebates and other price adjustment arrangements* can justify increases in the product's price.

- *Use of escalator clauses*, with built-in contractual assurances that an agreed-upon profit will be realized, often permits price increases in negotiating government contracts.

ANTICIPATING REACTIONS TO PRICE CHANGES

Planners should anticipate potentially adverse responses to a product price change by customers and competitors and should help ensure that they are favorable. For example, when Merton raised the price of MM systems in certain foreign markets, the firm sent out promotional messages stressing that this increase was evidence of the MM's quality and value and that, as such, it might soon be unobtainable even at the new, higher price. Similarly, when Merton lowered the price of MMs during competitive and maturity stages, promotion addressed possible perceptions that the product was about to be replaced by a later version, or that the price would come down even further if customers just waited it out.

CHAPTER PERSPECTIVE

Basic pricing strategies, designed to follow pricing policies in achieving marketing objectives, reflect the economic/competitive climate in which they are pegged, from purely cost-based strategies in monopolistic markets to demand-based strategies in competitive climates. For example, over the course of a product's life cycle in a selected foreign market, a company might begin with cost-based breakeven and ROI pricing strategies, then, as demand and competition grow, adopt skimming, penetration, and eventually holding pricing strategies. Supplementing these basic strategies would be a number of tactically oriented price modification strategies, governing terms of sale and payment, designed to attract customers and intermediaries while achieving profit goals. A key price planning decision throughout the product life cycle is when and how to raise or lower prices.

KNOW THE CONCEPTS

TERMS FOR STUDY

basing point pricing
breakeven point pricing
captive pricing
CIF
competitive pricing strategies

consignment selling
cost-plus pricing
expected profit pricing
freight absorption pricing
freight forwarders

incoterms
kinked demand
letter of credit
markup pricing
oligopolistic pricing
open account
optional pricing
penetration price

price change strategies
price discrimination
price lining
promotional pricing
ROI pricing
skimming price
targeted return pricing
terms of payment
terms of sale

marginal cost pricing

MATCHUP EXERCISES

1. Match up the cost-based pricing strategy in the first column with the descriptor in the second column.

1. breakeven
2. a 40 percent markup
3. cost-plus price
4. ROI

5. oligopolistic price

a. purchase cost/0.60
b. total revenues = total costs
c. price at the kink
d. price that earns a predetermined profit
e. (costs + projected profit)/ projected sales

2. Match up the demand-based prices in the first column with the descriptors in the second column.

1. promotional pricing

2. captive pricing

3. penetration pricing

4. price discrimination

5. expected profit pricing

a. Merton Mighty Mind computers will be discounted by 20 percent.
b. But the cost of training and development software used with MMs will be increased by 10 percent.
c. Of course, senior citizens will be given the usual 10 percent discount.
d. We need a large, expandable, price-sensitive market and probable economies of scale.
e. We estimate we have a 50 percent chance of getting the order if it's priced at $800,000.

3. Match up the price modification terms in the first column with the descriptors in the second column.

1. ex-works

a. no written evidence of debt

2. DDP

3. open account

4. UDP

5. 2/10 net EOM

b. firm charges same rate for all customers

c. most risk and cost assumed by buyer

d. most risk and cost assumed by seller

e. must pay by the end of the month

QUESTIONS FOR REVIEW AND DISCUSSION

1. In terms of conditions favoring either a penetration or a skimming price strategy, discuss the pricing strategy most appropriate for (1) an eminent Harvard professor retained to help eastern European governments establish free-market economic policies and programs, and (2) McDonald's aggressive push into the French market in the late 1980s, primarily because France was the only major country where McDonald's lagged behind Burger King.

2. HCR, a woman-owned firm based in Rochester, N.Y., was recently awarded a contract to conduct a 1-year-long feasibility study on health care in the Republic of Tatarstan, Russia. Assume that, in preparing your proposal for conducting this study, you anticipated the following costs in U.S. dollars: professional amenities (renting and furnishing an office, hiring secretarial help, etc.), $36,000; 150 billable hours a month, at $50 an hour; $10 an hour profit. Using the cost-plus formula, determine the hourly fee you listed in your proposal.

3. Viracom, W.S.A. of Owatonna, Minn., a maker of tempered, heat-strengthened, laminated, insulated, coated and security glass, set its sights on exporting in 1987. Since then, it has seen its export department increase from one to ten people, with 70 percent of exports going to Pacific Rim countries. A typical Asian Viracom service facility requires $20,000 in specialized equipment and two installation specialists paid at the U.S. equivalent of $15 an hour, with customers charged $25 an hour for their services. Using the breakeven formula, determine the number of hours it will take to breakeven on Viracom's investment in this equipment and in these specialists.

4. Discuss how foreign competition in differentiated oligopolistic markets (autos, cameras, cereals, etc.) can change the situation from that depicted in diagram A to that depicted in diagram B.

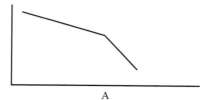
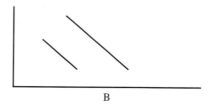

A
B

5. In terms of conditions that favor price discrimination, why would it be difficult to implement such a policy during a Bruce Springsteen concert tour?

6. Describe how Foremost-McKesson, a large international drug wholesaler, might use discounts and allowances to enhance its profitability and that of its retailer customers (mainly pharmacists and drug stores).

7. Given the following data, which bid should the company make?

Company Bid ($)	Company Profit ($)	Estimated Success Probability
5,000	1,000	.80
10,000	2,200	.40
20,000	3,500	.20

ANSWERS

MATCHUP EXERCISES

1. 1b, 2d, 3e, 4d, 5c

2. 1a, 2b, 3d, 4c, 5e

3. 1c, 2d, 3a, 4b, 5e

QUESTIONS FOR REVIEW AND DISCUSSION

1. For the American consultant, conditions favor a skimming strategy; there is little chance that a high price will generate excessive competition, since the consultant's credentials and knowledge are unique. Also, there is a large market, comprising, potentially, Russia and all the satellite nations that had been a part of the ex-Soviet Union. Additionally, a high price will reinforce the aura of preeminence so important to the trust and confidence of the consultant's clients. McDonald's, on the other hand, would employ a penetration pricing strategy. It achieves large economies of scale through the high volume brought on by low prices, thanks to its production line food preparation methods. If it increases its price, it will not be able to attract volume from Burger King and other fast food French restaurant chains in an expanding, price-sensitive market.

2.   Price = $\dfrac{\text{Total Fixed Costs + Total Variable Costs + Projected Profit}}{\text{Units Produced}}$

$\dfrac{\$36,000 + \$90,000 \ (1800 \ \text{hours} \times \$50) + \$18,000}{1800 \ \text{hours} \ (12 \times 150 \ \text{per month})}$ = \$80 per hour

3. Breakeven Point (units) = $\dfrac{\text{Total Fixed Costs}}{\text{Price} - \text{Variable Costs (per unit)}}$

$\dfrac{\$20,000}{\$25-\$15}$ = 2,000 hours

4. Diagram A depicts the kink point where a few large firms that dominate an oligopolistic industry tacitly agree to set prices. If a competitor prices below this point, the other competitors will follow, thus eliminating the competitive benefit of a lowered price, with demand barely increasing. And if one firm increases its price, none of the others will follow, so the firm will rapidly lose its sales to its few lower-priced competitors. However, aggressive competiton from offshore firms (e.g., Japanese auto manufacturers competing in the United States) can transform this oligopolistic environment to one of monopolistic competition, where kink points are replaced by demand curves, and successful firms push their curves to the right as customer preferences are based on nonprice features.

5. Of the four forms of price discrimination, the most likely form practiced at a Bruce Springsteen concert would be place discrimination, with locations close to the performer costing considerably more than those further away. Time discrimination probably wouldn't be practiced, since the concert would be given at only one time in each city visited. Customer discrimination probably wouldn't be practiced except, perhaps, for attendees selected by Mr. Springsteen, since attendees would be mostly from the same market segment (e.g., few senior citizens or children). Also, product discrimination probably wouldn't apply, since Mr. Springsteen doesn't come in different models. Ticket scalping could also make price discrimination difficult, to the extent that it violates three conditions required for effective discrimination (i.e., one group shouldn't be encouraged to sell lower priced tickets at higher prices to other groups, the seller shouldn't incur excessive costs in policing price discrimination, and discrimination shouldn't generate ill-will, which large-scale scalping does).

6. Foremost-McKesson could help improve the profitability of its retailer customers through a series of discounts and allowances to improve

sales and reduce costs. For example, promotional allowances would help retailers finance sales programs to improve revenues, while retailer costs would be reduced through functional discounts for performing such activities as stocking and delivering merchandise, cash discounts for paying bills on time, and quantity discounts for buying and stocking in larger, more economical quantities.

7. The company should put in a bid of $10,000, which produces the largest expected profit ($2,200 $\times$ .40 = $880).

17

INTERNATIONAL PROMOTION PLANNING

OVERVIEW

The promotion element of the marketing mix, which is composed of two-way communication designed to inform, remind, or persuade, combines with other marketing mix elements to create more efficient marketing processes and mutually satisfactory exchanges. Planning promotional campaigns in international markets entails, initially, establishing objectives based on an assessment of marketing communication opportunities and the need to modify the marketing mix elements. Then, direct and indirect elements of the promotion mix—advertising, publicity, sales promotion, and personal selling—are combined so as to optimize the effectiveness of each, and the final promotion plan is documented with budgets and timetables. Promotion planning in international markets must account for a diversity of circumstances and challenges not encountered in domestic markets, including limited information; diverse legal, cultural, and economic constraints; and national, expatriate, and cosmopolitan personnel with conflicting needs, values, and attitudes.

PROMOTION MIX ELEMENTS INFORM, PERSUADE, OR REMIND

This chapter deals with the promotion mix, a component of the marketing mix that involves communication with customers and prospects to inform, persuade, or remind them about a company's goods, services, image, or impact on society.

Promotion mix elements encompass indirect advertising, sales promotion, word-of-mouth, and publicity/public relations communications that support direct personal selling communication, as when a Merton salesperson attempts to persuade a prospect to purchase a Mighty Mind computer system.

Of all the marketing mix elements, promotion planning in global markets is most likely to be constrained by political, economic, and cultural influences. It also presents the greatest problems in recruiting, selecting, motivating, and compensating personnel to plan and carry out promotional campaigns.

WHAT PROMOTIONAL PEOPLE DO

Promotional campaigns can be directed toward consumers or businesses; may be commercial or noncommercial; may be product or nonproduct oriented; and may encompass local, regional, national, or international markets.

The task of the international marketing manager is to blend and focus indirect and direct elements of the promotion mix so that they reinforce each other and the other marketing mix elements. A product or service that is designed, priced, and distributed to meet the needs of clearly defined target customers is only as successful as the promotional support it receives.

In this chapter, we examine the impact of global environmental influences on promotion planning, offering an approach for planning and implementing successful global indirect and direct promotion programs in international markets. We also examine problems and approaches involved in managing and motivating sales personnel in global environments.

ADVERTISING AROUND THE WORLD

Led by Japan, worldwide advertising expenditures—the largest component of the indirect promotion mix—have increased, on average, more than 10 percent per annum over the past decade. In 1995, total annual worldwide advertising expenditures, outside the United States, was more than $140 billion. Leading global advertisers were Unilever, Procter & Gamble, Nissan, and Nestle. The United States, with global advertising expenditures in excess of $100 billion, spent more than three times as much on advertising as Japan, the United Kingdom, Germany, Canada, and France combined. Although worldwide per-capita advertising expenditures average $55, U.S. per-capita expenditures are over $500, and many countries (including Switzerland, Finland, Norway, Canada, and Australia) average over $200 per capita. The lowest per-capita expenditures are in Africa and Asia.

The quality of international advertising is generally very high; advertising agencies are as good as those in the United States, and preeminent in some media, such as cinema and poster advertising.

A MODEL OF THE COMMUNICATION PROCESS

Figure 17-1 incorporates the main features common among recent models of the communication process and illustrates the stages through which a message passes as it flows from the sender, or source, to the receiver, or audience.

Before we can send a letter to a friend, for example, our mental images have to be converted into a form that will be understood by our friend and that can be transmitted, via words or other symbols, so we write them down, or encode them. The Merton Company combined printed copy with color illustrations to create an image that target market members would hopefully understand and respond to.

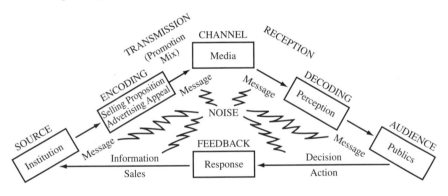

Figure 17–1. The Marketing Communications Process

The next stage, transmitting the message through a media channel, requires that we affix postage and mail our letter. Merton's messages, including information on the company name and image and differential advantages of MM systems, were transmitted through various media, including direct mail, newspapers, and magazines.

At the other end of the channel, our friend receives and opens the mail. In Merton's communications, the audience for its promotional messages usually consisted of members of its target market. It is obvious, but important, to recognize that the audience at the receiving end must be able to decode the message from the form in which it was received. Encoding and decoding depend on a common frame of reference.

Because communication requires effort, expense, and time, most messages are sent with the expectation of some kind of response, or feedback. From your friend, this response might be an answer to your letter or no answer. From the audience for Merton's message, it might be to buy or not to buy an MM system, or perhaps to develop a more favorable attitude toward Merton and its line of products, with the likelihood of purchase some time in the future.

Every stage of the communication process is vulnerable to interference from noise, which can be internal or external. Internal noise might be distracting thoughts. External noise usually occurs in physical forms such as electrical interference in a television or radio transmission. It is all other messages distractingly clamoring for attention, such as the many advertisements that surround Merton print advertisements.

For global marketers, this model helps them understand the dynamics of the marketing communications process and how it differs as applied in domestic and international markets, where members of culturally different target markets respond to promotional messages transmitted through different media and surrounded by levels and layers of noise unheard in domestic markets.

PLANNING PRODUCTIVE PROMOTION PROGRAMS

An effective promotion program in the global marketplace generally has three outcomes:

- The promotional message reaches the intended audience;

- The message is understood by this audience;

- The message stimulates recipients to take a desired action (e.g., buy, try, or distribute the product).

The following eight-step approach is designed to achieve these outcomes: (1) assess marketing communication opportunities; (2) determine degree of standardization/adaptation; (3) analyze marketing communication resources; (4) establish objectives; (5) determine promotion mix; (6) develop promotional appeal; (7) develop promotion budget; and (8) determine campaign effectiveness.

STEP 1: ASSESS MARKETING COMMUNICATION OPPORTUNITIES

This first step of the promotion planning process involves an understanding of the nature and needs of target markets, the environments that shape these needs, and what company and product attributes can most profitably be communicated to these markets. In addition to potential buyers of the company's products, this audience could include current users, deciders, and influencers among individuals, groups, or publics. For example, Merton planners would profile target markets in terms of uses and benefits expected from MM systems and economic and cultural characteristics that would help determine effective promotional appeals.

STEP 2: DETERMINE DEGREE OF STANDARDIZATION/ADAPTATION REQUIRED

A standardized promotional campaign conveys essentially the same message, by essentially the same means, in all markets. For example, Exxon's message of power, conveyed by the "Tiger in Your Tank" slogan, is applied globally. As compared to a campaign that is modified to the nature and needs of each country, a standardized campaign usually generates considerable savings through centralization. Fewer agencies, domestic or foreign, need be used, and there is less expense, effort, and duplication in such areas as copy, artwork, media, and research. Standardized campaigns are also easier to control—allowing comparisons of similar creative executions in different venues—and offer more opportunities for creative leverage as the effect of promotional innovations can be measured from similar bases. Additionally, standardized campaigns benefit from the overlap of readership, listeners, and viewers in contiguous countries (e.g., the magazine *Paris Match* has readers in Belgium, Switzerland, Luxembourg, Germany, Italy, and Holland). Another argument favoring standardized campaigns is the notion that differences between attitudes and needs of people in different countries are diminishing, and they are more likely to respond to a single campaign. Studies of the feasibility and applicability of standardized campaigns seem generally agreed on the following conclusions.

- Certain products, by their very nature, have universal appeal that lends itself to standardized promotion campaigns (e.g., Swiss watches, Italian designer clothes, Scotch whiskey, and frequently purchased, low cost mass marketed items like cigarettes and colas).

- Buyer motivation patterns are the key determinant of when a standardized campaign is feasible. If people buy similar products for different reasons, the campaign should be modified; if they react similarly to the same promotional stimuli, the campaign should probably be standardized.

- Promotion campaigns directed toward business markets are generally easier to standardize than campaigns directed toward consumer markets, since buyer motives, products, and product uses tend to be more uniform.

Laws that restrict the amount spent on advertising, media used, product advertised, and type of copy and illustrations acceptable represent another constraint on standardized promotion campaigns in many countries. For example, in Germany, use of comparative terminology ("We're the best!") is illegal; in Italy, it's illegal to use many common words like "deodorant" and "perspiration"; in Kuwait, only 32 minutes a day is allocated for TV commercials; in Britain, the Monopolies Commission forbids advertising that might help to create a monopoly (prompting the commission to throw certain P&G commercials off the air); in Austria, taxes on the media (radio, television, cinema) in different states range from 10 to 30 percent of billing. In other countries, many items can't be promoted in the media, including candy, dancing, cigarettes, alcohol, chocolate, airlines, indecent words, and contests.

Given these considerations and constraints, most multinational firms with products that lend themselves to standardization adopt a pattern standardization approach that allows some degree of campaign modification to meet local conditions. Typically, these firms develop a prototype promotional campaign at headquarters, which is delivered to foreign subsidiaries who are given considerable leeway to adapt the creative expression to local conditions.

STEP 3: ANALYZE MARKETING COMMUNICATION RESOURCES

At this point in the promotion planning process, sufficient information about markets, products, and environments will have been generated to arrive at decisions as to what resources will be required to launch and maintain a promotional campaign. In general, promotion campaigns in foreign markets—especially in competitive environments and during early stages of the campaign—are more expensive than those in domestic markets, often leading to decisions to scale back initial plans by focusing on one or two key markets. For example, European liquor marketers concentrate promotional efforts in the United States and Britain, where volume consumption is greatest.

STEP 4: ESTABLISH OBJECTIVES

Unlike marketing objectives, which typically pertain to quantified measures like sales, profits, or share of market, most promotional objectives are stated in terms of long or short term behaviors by people exposed to promotional communication.

For example, the MM, introduced by Merton into a foreign country, might have a succession of such behavioral objectives assigned to its supportive promotion over the course of its life cycle. Initially, a key objective might be to make people aware of the product; then, when awareness is achieved, comprehension of product benefits might be the promotional objective (brand acceptance), followed by conviction (brand preference), desire (brand insistence), and action (brand trial or purchase). Satisfaction after purchase might be the final objective.

Whatever promotional objective or objectives are projected for a campaign, they should be clearly stated, measurable, and appropriate to the stage of market development. For example, a clearly stated action objective to "increase sales by 15 percent next year" would hardly be realistic if most prospective customers were not even aware of the product.

STEP 5: DETERMINE PROMOTION MIX

This step involves allocating resources among sales promotion, advertising, publicity, and personal selling. In the domestic market, key considerations in allocation decisions include characteristics of each promotional tool; the nature and life-cycle stage of the product being promoted, and planned distribution strategies. Figure 17-2 shows the relative importance of promotion tools in consumer and industrial markets, which tends to also apply in developed areas of the global market.

• *CHARACTERISTICS OF PROMOTION MIX COMPONENTS*

Here is how promotion mix allocation decisions were made for the MM, given the following characteristics of promotion mix components:

SALES PROMOTION

Sales promotion includes short-term, one-time incentives to distributors or customers designed to reinforce other components of the promotion and marketing mixes and stimulate sales (e.g., coupons, contests, samples, games, trade shows).

Trade shows, in particular, offer marketers many more opportunities to achieve promotional goals in foreign than in domestic markets, with more than 8,000 shows held worldwide each year, transacting more than $25 billion in business.[1] In Europe, for example, trade shows and fairs have been a tradition for almost 1000 years, and individual European distributors and manufacturers attend, on average, more than nine a year.

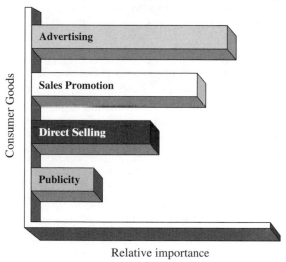

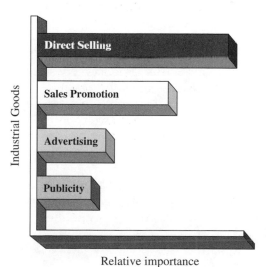

Figure 17–2. Relative Importance of Promotion Tools in Consumer Versus Industrial Markets

---

[1] Echo Montgomery Garrett, "Trade Shows," *World Trade* (December 1993), pp. 88–89).

For Merton, advantages of participating in trade shows as a means to penetrate global markets successfully included introducing, demonstrating, and promoting MM systems; finding intermediaries to help make and market these products (e.g., distributors, bankers, investors, government officials); sizing up the competition in prospective target markets; and generating feedback on marketing effectiveness. To help realize these benefits, Merton set specific goals (e.g., number of sales leads or prospective distributors), and implemented follow-up procedures.

Possibly the largest drawback of trade show participation is the cost, although this can be mitigated by attending expositions where tickets are sold to offset exhibitor costs, or by sharing expenses with distributors, representatives, or even competitors.

Another way to mitigate trade show costs is to participate in events sponsored by the U.S. Department of Commerce or exhibit at U.S. trade centers or export development offices. Global Focus 17-1 shows how one company, with assistance from the Department of Commerce, builds its entire international marketing program around overseas trade shows.

GLOBAL FOCUS 17-1

Overseas Trade Shows Enhance Direct Selling

Dugal Corporation of Miami, Florida, has built its international marketing program around overseas trade shows. The small family-owned company exports all its products, consisting of a complete line of European-style fashion jewelry.

David Poniman, executive vice president, and his wife, Joanna, president and chief designer of the jewelry, go to 20 trade shows a year in Europe, southeast Asia, the Middle East, and South and Central America. They spend only one week of each month, on average, in their Miami headquarters.

David Poniman explained, "We arrange to attend two or more trade shows in a region during a foreign trip to make the best use of our time and to keep our costs down. While there, we visit with distributors with whom we had previously established a business relationship. We always arrive in a city a day or two before a trade show and stay a day or two afterward."

The U.S. Export Assistance Center in Miami, operated by the U.S. Department of Commerce and other federal agencies, helps the Ponimans make even more efficient use of their time. The center alerts commercial officers in U.S. embassies by electronic mail that they are coming so they can receive a briefing and advice on any problems they may face in the country. Poniman considers U.S. sponsorship of exhibits at trade shows valuable because it lends prestige to an exhibition and commands greater attention from business people in the host country.

Trade shows tie in well with Dugal's way of doing business, which is direct selling—the firm has no sales agents. The Ponimans meet distributors face-to-face and make deals on the spot. "Customers appreciate not having to rely on pictures," Poniman said. "They can see the jewelry and feel it and decide on that basis whether they like it."

The personal contact gives Joanna Poniman an opportunity to observe the reactions of customers in different countries to the jewelry so that she can modify it to suit their tastes.

Source: *Business America*, Vol. 115, No. 6 (June 1994), p. 10.

ADVERTISING

Advertising is short- or long-term nonpersonal communication by an identified sponsor through diverse media. Its objectives include to inform (new products, new product uses), to persuade (buy the product, change brands, request more information), and/or to remind (of product's existence, where to buy it). Major advertising media are characterized as print (newspapers, magazines) or electronic (television, radio). Business and trade journals, the main media used by international marketers, can be global, regional, or country-specific in scope, and horizontal (catering to functions across industries, such as purchasing or industrial distribution) or vertical (catering to a single industry like chemical engineering) in content. Some journals, such as *Business Week* and *The Wall Street Journal* are standard sources worldwide. Information on print media circulation and rates is available from the Standard Rate and Data Service (SR&D), which publishes a complete list of international publications as well as circulation audit information similar to that generated for the U.S. market. For areas not covered by SR&D, publishers and local representatives can provide this information.

Another popular advertising medium among firms entering global markets is direct marketing, primarily direct mail and catalog marketing. Direct mail, which includes letters, ads, samples and foldouts sent to prospects on mailing lists, permits high target-market selectivity, can be personalized, is flexible, and allows easy measurement of results. While cost-per-thousand-people-reached (CPM) is higher than with magazines or electronic media, people reached are usually better prospects. As better mailing lists and more reliable postal services emerge in areas like Asia, Latin America, and the Middle East, use of direct mail grows apace.

CATALOG MARKETING

Catalog marketing involves mailing catalogs to a select list of customers, or making them available in stores, in order to make the seller's name known, generate requests for information, stimulate orders, and serve as reminders between orders. Advantages and disadvantages are basically the same as for direct mail. Among the global companies that use catalog marketing as a key element of their promotion mixes are Avon, L.L. Bean, and Walt Disney, which send out millions of catalogs worldwide promoting everything from pantyhose to videotapes. Catalogs are particularly effective in promoting organizational and high-tech products requiring the service of specialists.

PUBLICITY

Publicity is short-term nonpaid, nonpersonal communication about products and people in print or electronic media. Because it is presented in an editorial format, readers tend to perceive it as more believable than advertising. Significant opportunities for publicity involve portraying global firms as good citizens in host countries, in introducing new products, and in anticipating and countering criticism.

PERSONAL SELLING

Personal selling involves face-to-face sales presentations among exporters, intermediaries, customers, and prospects. It can generate long- and short-term personal relationships that add persuasive conviction to sales presentations that relate products and services to buyer needs. Roles assumed by salespeople include order takers, such as a retail store salesperson or a salesperson calling on a supermarket manager; missionary salespeople called on mainly to find, qualify, and educate actual or potential users; technical salespeople who function as consultants to client companies; and creative salespeople of tangible or intangible products who create demand by influencing prospects to buy. Frequently, salespeople performing various roles will team up to generate and maintain demand. For example, a missionary salesperson might locate and qualify a prospect for a large order of Merton computer systems, following which a creative salesperson will team up with a technical salesperson to close this sale. Subsequent orders for additional Merton products might be handled by inside order taker salespeople. In addition to teaming up with one another, salespeople will team up with other elements of the promotion mix, such as advertising, to generate inquiries, and with sales promotion, to provide additional incentives to buy. Although personal selling is generally the most effective promotional tool available to global marketers, it is also the most expensive, with an average sales call cost varying between $300 and $1,200, depending on industry and product or service sold.

• HOW MERTON MELDS PROMOTION MIX ELEMENTS

During the introductory stage of the MMs life cycle in a typical global entry market, advertising in professional journals was designed to create product awareness among prospective users, and publicity was used to help transform this awareness into comprehension and conviction.

Advertising and publicity were also placed in journals sent to prospective distributors to encourage them to handle the line, supplemented with special presentations at trade shows (where, for example, Merton retained a hospitality room and promoted its presence via a direct mail campaign for selected buyer and distributor prospects).

Merton's initial emphasis on lining up distributors for MM systems was consistent with its push distribution strategy, designed to push MM systems through channels. The promotion campaign aimed at prospective users was a pull distribution strategy, designed to build consumer demand so that they would ask distributors for the product.

As awareness, comprehension, and conviction objectives were achieved among distributors and prospective MM buyers and the MM entered the growth stage of its product life cycle, proportionately more resources were allocated to the "personal selling" promotion mix element, with the efforts of salespeople now made more efficient and productive by the awareness, comprehension, conviction, and word-of-mouth promotion engendered by advertising and publicity campaigns. Further enhancing personal selling efforts, and the effectiveness of other promotion- and marketing-mix elements, were sales promotion tools. Examples of these tools included contests to encourage greater productivity among distributors, MM displays at trade shows, and catalogs that MM sales representatives left with prospective buyers.

In devising promotion mixes for the global market, Merton faced an additional concern not generally faced in its domestic market: the lack of available media. Even when markets are similar in demographic characteristics, media situations can vary dramatically. For example, television advertising barely exists in the Nordic countries; in other countries, there is a dearth of print media—magazines and newspapers—serving target markets. In others, too many publications serve too many market segments to get effective coverage.

Another consideration constraining media choices is cost. For example, advertising agency compensation arrangements and media prices differ dramatically from country to country, with one study showing a range of from $1.58 in Belgium to $5.91 in Italy to reach 1000 readers.

Still another constraint on media allocations needed to create productive promotion mixes is coverage. Given media limitations, it's often practically impossible to reach certain target markets, or, if they can be reached, it's often prohibitively expensive. How effectively are media reaching target markets? It's frequently impossible to find out. Most industrialized countries have organizations like the Audit Bureau of Circulation (ABC) to audit print media circulation, but often their findings are inaccurate and unreliable.

Even if circulation can be measured, there is generally a dearth of demographic and psychographic marketing data (age, income, attitudes, preferences, etc.) on consumers to flesh out these figures.

STEP 6: DEVELOP THE PROMOTIONAL MESSAGE

Focus in this area is on the basic message, or appeal, of the promotional campaign and the creative execution of this appeal in art, copy, photographs, video, film, sales presentations, and other promotional materials. In domestic promotional campaigns, appeal and execution usually work together. For example, the macho appeal of Levi Straus jeans is executed using Western cowboy models, music, and themes in its promotion. In countries without a common "old West" heritage, however, this execution of the appeal won't have nearly the impact as in the domestic market. In Japan, where Levi's Western execution barely budged market share, brand awareness, and ad recall figures, the campaign was changed to capitalize on the Japanese fascination with American movie stars, who endorsed Levi's jeans. Brand awareness soared to 75 percent and advertising awareness to 65 percent.[2]

The experience of Levi Straus illustrates some of the problems in transferring domestic appeals and executions to foreign markets. Different languages and perceptual frameworks among foreign customers cause different interpretations of promotional messages, as illustrated by these examples:[3]

- Coors beer's message—"Get Loose With Coors"—did not fare too well in Japan, where it translated to "Get the runs with Coors."

- In Latin countries, The Chevrolet Nova (renamed the Caribe) translated into "No Go"; Ford's Fiera into "ugly old woman"; and Evitol shampoo into "dandruff contraceptive."

- The color white denotes purity in Europe, death in Asia.

- Coca-Cola's "Coke adds life" theme in Japanese translates to "Coke brings your ancestors back from the dead."

Other problems in translating appeals to foreign countries derive from the sheer diversity of languages (in Israel, 50 different languages are spoken), which represents nightmare problems for translators; high illiteracy

---

[2] Richard Arroyo, "Levi Conquers Japan with Hero Worship," *Advertising Age* (December 13, 1982), p. 24.
[3] Marty Westerman, "Death of the Frito Bandito," *American Demographics* (March 1989), pp. 28–32.

rates that put a premium on visual promotional communication; and culture/subculture differences (in Hong Kong, there are ten distinct patterns of eating breakfast among youth, the elderly, urban and suburban residents) that must be accounted for in tailoring appeals to local needs and perceptions. Even the nature of advertising copy can pose problems in translating basic appeals, with the abstract, terse writing characterizing American advertising difficult to translate into other foreign grammars.

Given these problems, it's not surprising that a survey of 50 experienced advertising executives concluded that only strong buying appeals (e.g., "top quality", "low price") can be transferred more than 50 percent of the time to foreign markets and that creative executions of these appeals translate effectively less than 25 percent of the time. Interestingly, most of these same executives also agree that, despite these difficulties, it's worth the effort to work toward globalization of promotion and products because of cost savings, control, and creative leverage benefits. For example, Pepsico uses four basic commercials, worldwide, to communicate product appeals, with each foreign appeal a modification of the basic setting of people having fun at a party or on the beach to reflect music preferences, racial characteristics, and the general physical environment of North America, South America, Europe, Africa, and Asia.

Consistent with this trend toward globalization has been a dramatic increase in global advertising agencies that interpret promotion and marketing mix elements in terms of tastes, needs, and attitudes in global markets.

STEP 7: DEVELOP THE PROMOTION BUDGET

Once decisions as to promotion campaign standardization and implementation have been made, a total promotion budget can be prepared. In international markets, this involves determining worldwide costs, and cost breakdowns per country and among promotion mix elements. Typical considerations for allocating dollars among these entities are affordability, percent of sales, and competitive parity, which all assume that external influences (i.e., how much is available, how much was sold, how much do competitors spend) dictate promotional allocations. While these approaches are all applicable in certain situations in domestic markets and can be used as a check in almost any market situation, the most effective approach in the global marketplace is typically the objective-and-task approach, which first determines what must be done to achieve promotional objectives and then estimates what this will cost.

STEP 8: DETERMINE CAMPAIGN EFFECTIVENESS

After marketing communication tasks have been assigned, which may involve assigning tasks to foreign intermediaries or other exporters for cooperative promotion efforts, the promotion plan is formalized in a written document including a situation analysis, copy platform, and timetables for the effective integration of promotion mix elements with other elements of the marketing mix. Also included in this plan are the means for measuring its effectiveness once it is implemented, in terms of how actual performance measures up to planned objectives. This typically involves asking the target audience whether they recognize or recall specific advertising messages, what points they recall, how they felt about the message, and previous and current attitudes toward the company and product. Also included would be behavioral measures of audience response, such as how many people bought the product, liked it, and talked about it to others.

MANAGING PROMOTION PERSONNEL ABROAD

In this section, we examine the nature and scope of personnel problems associated with managing people involved in promotional activities in international markets. (Chapter 8 focuses on issues and approaches involved in recruiting, selecting, training, motivating, and compensating personnel in international markets.)

The globalization of business and the intense competition it engenders also engender intense competition for people to develop markets effectively. In general, people engaged in promotional activities in international markets can be viewed from three perspectives useful in understanding and addressing their needs: functional perspective (what they do), status perspective (who does it), and tenure perspective (how long they do it).

The largest—sometimes the only—group of promotional people representing a home country in a host country is usually the sales force. If a company's presence in a foreign market is large enough, it will support this sales force with people responsible for such promotional functions as advertising, distribution, customer service, and product management. Middle managers responsible for these functions, operating either from the home or host country, typically report to a marketing manager.

GLOBAL PERSONNEL STATUS

In terms of status, all these direct and indirect promotional people and their managers fall into one of three major categories.

• *EXPATRIATE PERSONNEL*

These citizens of the home country working in host countries are usually employed in top and middle management positions and in sales positions requiring specialized technical or applications knowledge. Advantages of assigning home country personnel to a foreign country include their proven effectiveness, better training and knowledge of company products and policies, and prestige added to sales presentations (e.g., English or German expatriates explaining features of their luxury autos).

Disadvantages include higher costs for maintaining expatriate, as compared to local, personnel; the frequent unwillingness of home company employees, who perceive uprooted families and short-circuited career paths, to live abroad; and high cultural/legal barriers that discourage expatriates. Global Focus 17-2 examines changing attitudes in American companies toward sending people abroad and steps being taken by progressive firms to address problems implicit in these expatriate assignments. That most U.S. firms are not effectively handling expatriate assignments vis-à-vis foreign counterpart companies is indicated by a survey undertaken by the Conference Board[4] among 152 companies—two-thirds based in the United States and the rest in Europe and Asia. Among the survey findings: only 38 percent of American respondents guarantee expatriates a position on their return, as compared with 74 percent of European companies; 77 percent of American expatriates surveyed return to jobs with less responsibility than the positions they held abroad, up to half of them within 3 years of their return.

GLOBAL FOCUS 17-2

Managing Expatriate Careers

Much is said about the strategic and competitive necessity of an effective global workforce. Yet even today, American companies are terribly behind when it comes to handling international assignments. Tales abound, from horror stories of not being properly prepared to go abroad to returning home and finding little has changed.

---

[4] Judith Dobrznski, "A Study Sees a Down Side to Going Overseas as an Executive," *The New York Times* (August 16, 1996), p. D2.

There are signs, however, that attitudes toward international assignments may be changing among companies. International assignments are moving to the forefront of management and organizational dynamics. Companies are realizing that well-managed foreign assignments are a key element in developing global corporate competencies. Such assignments are linked with executive and leadership development to create an experienced and effective global workforce. Once regarded as a surefire way for employees to earn a lot of money but fall short of the top slot, international asignments are gradually regarded as logical and required steps in career paths.

One major problem is the fact that very few companies take full advantage of their repatriated employees' knowledge. Finding ways to integrate and refine the information gained abroad by employees and to infuse that knowledge into operations will be a worthwhile challenge for U.S. businesses.

Changing attitudes toward foreign assignments must begin at the top. An important element is to include globalization issues in senior management performance evaluations, complete with specific goals. At Armstrong World Industries, Inc., for example, three group vice presidents are each responsible for a portion of the company's international business as well as for managing global executive teams that meet three or four times a year to discuss strategies and exchange competencies.

Senior executives who remain at home in the domestic market cannot end up driving the corporation. Expatriate professionals agree that top executives must have at least one formal international assignment, for 3 to 5 years, during their careers. A high percentage of the top 200 people at Ford Motor Company have had a foreign assignment or are foreign nationals working in another country. "It is not unusual to be at a meeting in Dearborn and find seven or eight participants from other countries; we value people if they have served abroad; we do it almost routinely," explained W.R. Gromer, director of executive development at Ford.

As those who make the corporate policies gain more international exposure, it is hoped that the benefits returning expatriates can bring to the company will be realized. These benefits include the expertise gained from the necessity of becoming familiar with all aspects of the job. An expatriate is often on his or her own—more so than an American in a comparable position in a U.S. division who can count on others nearby for expertise. The expatriate often comes back with knowledge of trade rules and regulations, business practices, joint venture methodology, as well as fluency in the language and customs of the host country.

Source: Barbara Ettore, "A Brave New World: Managing International Careers," *Management Review* (April 1993), pp. 10–15. Reprinted by permission from *Management Review* © 1993. American Management Association, New York. All rights reserved.

• *FOREIGN NATIONALS*

Working at home for a foreign company, foreign nationals are distinctly in favor among exporting companies. One study estimated that the proportion of executive, technical, and sales positions held by foreign nationals in overseas markets increased from 16 percent in 1972 to over 65 percent in 1990. The key reasons for this increase are that host country personnel require less salary and expense than expatriates and transcend cultural and legal barriers. Legal barriers include a desire to mitigate foreign corporate domination, increase the proportion of locals in exported jobs, control foreign competition with local industry, and increase foreign investment in local economies. They include limits on the time a job can be filled by an expatriate and work permits that restrict positions for expatriates to jobs that can't be filled by locals.

• *COSMOPOLITAN PERSONNEL*

Usually found at the managerial level, cosmopolitan personnel are expatriates from country A working in countries B or C for a company headquartered in country D. At one time, for example, the Burroughs Corporation's Swiss company was run by a Dane, its French company by a Swiss, its Danish company by a German, and its German company by an Englishman. Such arrangements reflect the growing internationalization of business and the notion that personnel skills and motivations are not the exclusive property of one country.

GLOBAL PERSONNEL TENURE

In terms of amount of time spent in specific foreign positions, tenure periods range from temporary troubleshooters to permanent expatriates and host country personnel. Temporary troubleshooters are generally start-up teams transferrable to any location where new operations are being started or existing operations need help. For example, General Motors maintains a permanent staff of 300 HOSP (Home Office Status Personnel) expatriates who are shuffled around the world to cope with market entry or growth problems.

CHAPTER PERSPECTIVE

Planning promotional programs in global markets involves integrating and interpreting promotion mix elements—including advertising, sales promotion, publicity, and personal selling—in terms of diverse needs, perceptions, and environmental constraints. Key decision areas include setting objectives, standardizing campaigns, creatively translating promotional appeals in different cultures, allocating resources to countries and mix elements, and managing home and host country promotional personnel.

KNOW THE CONCEPTS

TERMS FOR STUDY

advertising
advertising appeal
Audit Bureau of Circulation (ABC)
awareness
business/trade journals
catalogs
conviction
cosmopolitan
decoding
direct mail
direct promotion
electronic media
encoding
expatriate
indirect promotion

mailing lists
marketing communication
medium
message
personal selling
print media
promotion budget
promotion mix
publicity
public relations
sales promotion
telemarketing
trade fairs
trade missions

MATCHUP EXERCISES

1. Match up the communication process component listed in the second column with the activity listed in the first column, which involves Kellogg's advertising campaign promoting Rice Krispies in Japan.

1. Instead of "snap, crackle, pop," which the Japanese find hard to pronounce, the Rice Krispies critters are scripted to say "patchy, pitchy, putchy."

   a. media

2. Research indicates that, just as in the United States, Japanese homemakers are the primary target market for the Rice Krispies advertising campaign.

   b. audience

3. The Rice Krispies critters are portrayed primarily in family magazines read by target market members.

   c. feedback

4. Post campaign research indicates that   d. encoding
the Rice Krispies campaign was primarily
instrumental in increasing sales above
planned expectations.

2. In 1996, the Tupperware Corporation conducted more than 13 million Tupperware parties in more than 100 foreign countries. From just one of these parties, match up the selling activity in the second column with the behavioral outcome it is calculated to produce in the first column.

1. awareness

    a. Tupperware sales representative explains product features and benefits to party participants.

2. comprehension

    b. Sales representative demonstrates how product features and benefits make product superior to alternate means of storing food.

3. conviction

    c. Party participants receive invitations to Tupperware party, including incentives to attend.

4. desire

    d. Sales representative shows how product features and benefits can solve storage problems facing participants, saving money, improving nutrition, and making them more appreciated by family members.

5. action

    e. Sales representative concentrates on using the peer pressure of the group to get all participants to commit to a purchase of Tupperware products.

3. Match up the promotion mix component in the first column with the second column descriptor.

1. advertising

    a. nonpaid, nonpersonal presentations

2. publicity

    b. most important in marketing industrial goods; less important in marketing consumer goods

3. sales promotion

    c. short-term incentives to buy or distribute product

4. direct selling

d. most important in marketing consumer goods; less important in marketing industrial goods

4. Match up the approach for preparing a promotion budget in the first column with the descriptor comments in the second column.

1. affordable

a. "Sales dictate ad expenditures, not vice versa."

2. percent of sales

b. "We'll spend what we've got left over after we've covered our other costs."

3. competitive parity

c. "Here's what we'll have to do, and here's what it will cost."

4. objective and task

d. "The way to keep up is to spend what they spend."

QUESTIONS FOR REVIEW AND DISCUSSION

1. Judith Sans of Atlanta, Georgia, began marketing her natural cosmetics and skin care products overseas in 1985 when she joined a trade mission to the Far East to meet representatives of foreign businesses. Her firm now sells in more than 20 countries, with exports accounting for more than 50 percent of total sales volume in 1995. Promotion for Ms. Sans product line is strongly associated with healthy, natural life-styles, including proper dietary and exercise regimens. What advertising, publicity, and sales promotion tools might she combine to market a new natural skin care addition to her product line?

2. Referring to the Judith Sans effort in question 1, discuss problems she might face in getting her promotional message before members of a target market in a country that is less developed than the domestic market.

3. Track through each of the stages of the marketing communications model as it might be applied in introducing a new Merton MM laptop computer.

4. When the Xerox Corporation introduced its new line of copiers (Models 1020, 1035, 1045, and 1075) for different segments of the global business market, its promotion campaign combined local and international media to carry a creative theme built around a symbol chosen to convey the endurance of the product line: the marathon (e.g., "Finally, there's a copier that's as rugged as it is compact. Introducing the Xerox 1020 Marathon copier...."). Speculate on considerations in the first five steps of the campaign planning process that might have produced this campaign.

5. Referring to step 5 of the promotion planning process, present a rationale for using expatriate staff members to sell the new Marathon copiers in the European market. Assume that your audience is leaning toward the use of foreign nationals for this purpose.

ANSWERS

MATCHUP EXERCISES

1. 1d, 2b, 3a, 4c
2. 1c, 2a, 3b, 4d, 5e
3. 1d, 2a, 3c, 4b
4. 1b, 2a, 3d, 4c

QUESIONS FOR REVIEW AND DISCUSSION

1. The market for natural products—including organically grown fruits and vegetables, drinks, and body care products—is substantial and growing worldwide. Use your imagination to add to the following list:

Advertising: ads in health magazines, commercials on radio programs about healthy life-styles; mailings to cosmeticians on leased mailing lists; mailings to health publication subscriber lists.

Sales promotion: samples or trial sizes in counter displays; booths at trade fairs; cents-off coupons.

Publicity: press kits to newspapers and radio stations explaining features and benefits of the new product.

2. Problems faced by Sans in getting her healthy life-style message before members of her target market would probably begin with identification of this target market and definition of market needs as they relate to this product. Strong cultural differences and lack of demographic and socioeconomic data to help interpret these differences might make market analysis a daunting job. And even when these target markets are identified and defined, Sans will probably face equally daunting problems in reaching them, given the less-developed state of available media. For example, will timely mailing lists be available, directed toward markets (e.g., cosmeticians) she hopes to influence? Will electronic (radio, television) and print (newspapers, magazines) media be available targeted to user or distributor target markets? If so, will these media be affordable, in terms of CPM criteria? And even if affordable media are available, will there be any reliable way to measure their relative efficacy in reaching markets and achieving promotion goals?

3. With the customer-user in mind, and based on survey research identifying the nature and needs of various target markets, Merton's advertising department should:

- Translate the new product's features into customer-perceived benefits (e.g., enough memory to support popular spreadsheet programs, high resolution monochrome monitor for less eyestrain, will run all available software) and then encode the most important or unique benefit into the advertising appeal ("The FULL-MEMORY computer that lets you do serious work anywhere.")

- Transmit this message through selected media representing the communications channel (e.g., computer magazines). When the message is received it must be decoded. Therefore, along with the jargon of the computer buff, the advertiser should provide a translation, in everyday language, to help broaden the market for the new computer to include serious computer novices. Its content will be perceived by each member of the audience in terms of that member's unique life experience, attitudes, wants, and needs.

Throughout the process, noise can be expected (e.g., other ads and editorial matter competing for the reader's attention), but its negative effects can be minimized by an attention-getting layout; compelling, carefully worded copy; and repetition.

The success of the communication can be estimated from the amount of feedback in terms of desired response like dealer inquiries, user inquiries, and sales.

4. The first step of the campaign planning process—assessing marketing communication opportunities—would involve Xerox planners in an analysis of the nature and needs of different target markets—defined geographically, demographically, and behavioristically (e.g., product specifiers or users in small businesses in Germany or Spain). This analysis would also examine how products in the Marathon line would best meet these needs as well as explore the cultural, economic, and political conditions in each market that would influence the campaign.

The second step in the planning process—determining the degree of standardization/adaptation needed—would rely on data derived from the first step to make any necessary modifications in the planned campaign. Thus, while the Marathon theme will characterize all campaigns in all markets, cultural, legal, and language differences among countries might mandate some changes in individual cases, such as constraints against boastful or comparative advertising, or words that might be offensive in certain countries.

The third step—analyzing marketing communication resources—would involve Xerox planners in cost-benefit analyses to determine projected costs of the campaign, and the probable return on campaign expenditures. For example, research into different media costs in different markets might indicate that existing resources won't be able to cover a broad-based global campaign, leading to a decision to "roll out" the campaign, starting with the most potentially profitable markets.

The fourth step—establish objectives—will be implemented using data already developed on the nature and needs of markets, and resource constraints in reaching these markets. Since promotional objectives focus on desired behaviors, ranging from awareness to action, the main emphasis here will be on measuring and pitching presentations toward perceptual states in each market (e.g., in markets where prospective buyers or influencers are aware of, and favorably disposed toward, Xerox products, presentations might focus more on achieving conviction and desire behaviors).

The fifth step—determining the promotion mix—will focus on allocation of resources among advertising, publicity, sales promotion, and direct selling elements of the marketing mix, now and in the future. For example, during the first stage of the Marathon introduction, emphasis might be on sales promotion (especially trade shows and demonstrations) and publicity (writeups in business and technical journals to generate awareness and comprehension). Then, advertising and direct marketing might be emphasized as part of push strategies to persuade distributors to handle the line and pull strategies to persuade end-users to specify Xerox Marathon products. Also emphasized would be sales promotion in the form of catalogs, price lists, demonstration models, and other incentives for distributors and buyers to buy the copiers. Direct selling might now be emphasized to capitalize on all the good spade work done by earlier promotion efforts to generate leads and get prospective buyers in a state where they desire the product and are ready to act by trying or buying it.

5. Your argument might begin by summarizing arguments for the opposition: Foreign nationals would certainly transcend cultural and legal barriers facing expatriate salespeople and would probably cost much less to maintain in terms of direct costs (salary, benefits, moving expenses, etc.) and indirect costs (turnover, cultural acclimation, etc.). However, given the price of the new line of Xerox copiers, the extra costs for maintaining an expatriate salesforce would be a very small percentage of the total volume that could be generated if the product line achieves its sales goals. And given the variety and technological sophistication of the new line, only well-trained expatriate sales-people, who actively participated in its design and development, could properly present the line to prospective customers and ensure that sales goals were achieved. Furthermore, as a global company, Xerox must provide this kind of expatriate training to its future man-agers if it is to compete in international markets successfully.

18

INTERNATIONAL DISTRIBUTION PLANNING I: DISTRIBUTION CHANNEL STRATEGY

OVERVIEW

Distribution is generally the most globally differentiated and least understood of all marketing mix components; it is also the component least susceptible to change and most likely to block a successful entry strategy. Especially in the international marketplace, where channels lengthen and materials handling problems multiply, efficient channel and global logistics strategies can help offset high costs and level the competitive playing field. Designing cost-effective, total-systems distribution strategies in global markets begins with an understanding of available channel structures, flows, functions, values, and costs as they relate to customer needs and company objectives and resources.

DISTRIBUTION PLANNING MOVES GOODS THROUGH CHANNELS

The fourth or place component of the marketing mix entails distribution planning designed to implement marketing plans by getting the right product or service to the right place, in the right form, at the right price, to the right customers, at the right time. It is also, frequently, the component that has the most direct, decisive influence on other marketing mix components. For example, Merton's selection of a channel (e.g., agents or brokers) to introduce its MM systems into a new foreign market will help determine the MM's price (which must account for distribution costs discussed in Chapter 15), its promotion program (which will involve supporting distributor promotion efforts and working with distributor salespeople), and the product itself (which must be attractive and profitable to the distributor and fit into his or her existing product line).

Distribution planning involves systematic analysis and decision making pertaining to the movement of materials and final goods from producers to consumers. These decisions encompass channel selection and control, as well as the four elements of the physical distribution process: transportation, warehousing, inventory management, and order processing.

Key goals of the distribution planning process include integrating the elements of the physical distribution process with each other, with selected channels, and with the product/price/promotion elements of the marketing mix.

In this chapter, we focus on the first stage of the distribution planning process in global entry markets: designing, finding, and managing distribution channel systems that best meet a diversity of selection criteria such as customer needs, product characteristics, and company resources and objectives. We begin with an overview of the types of channels available, the functions they perform, the flows they facilitate, the decisions they make, the costs they incur, and the benefits they provide for exporters. Then we examine considerations and criteria involved in designing and managing efficient channel systems. In Chapter 19, we examine global logistics considerations controlling the flow of products into, through, and out of channels between maker and customer.

CHANNEL FUNCTIONS ENHANCE MARKETING COST-EFFECTIVENESS

Distribution channels are defined as individuals and organizations, also called intermediaries, that help get materials and finished products from producers to consumers. Worldwide, they are among the most varied of all marketing mix elements, the least understood and controlled by marketing management, and the most likely to block a company's entry into global markets. Channels can vary in length (number of intermediaries used), depending on the functions the manufacturer needs to have performed and the feasibility of delegating these functions to others.

At one extreme the manufacturer assumes all distribution functions, including contacting customers, matching products to customer needs, promoting products, physically distributing the products, and financing sales. At the other extreme, practically all these functions are delegated to various kinds of distributors, including wholesalers, retailers, agents, and brokers.

In Merton's domestic market, for example, stocking distributors provide a number of functions that combine to make marketing MM systems a lot more efficient and less expensive than were Merton salespeople to sell

MM systems directly to customers. For one thing, these distributors are better equipped than a single company would be to locate and contact the tens of thousands of prospective MM customers and match MM systems to their needs. In addition to saving Merton the expense of hiring and managing a huge salesforce, these distributors also provide a diversity of other useful functions: They promote Merton products on the local level, assume risks of financing the purchase of MM systems by extending credit to their customers, feed back useful research to Merton planners on changing needs and product applications in their territories, and assume a large part of the cost of storing and moving MM systems out to customer premises. From the all-important perspective of the customer, these functions combine to get the right products to them at the right time, from the right place, in the right form.

In the global marketplace, exporters like Merton might have no choice but to assume most, or all, distribution functions; in underdeveloped countries, for example, channels similar to those in domestic markets usually don't exist. If they do exist in more developed countries, channel management might not be willing to distribute the exporter's product unless strongly motivated. Even if an exporter can get distribution for a product line in a developed foreign market, the likelihood is that delegated functions—particularly selling, promotion, and matching functions—will not be performed as effectively as in domestic distribution channels. The examples of successful export strategies in Global Focus 18-1 illustrate how U.S. firms managed to achieve distribution in foreign markets in the face of these limitations.

GLOBAL FOCUS 18-1

Direct and Indirect Selling: Exporters Go Both Ways

There are two basic distribution approaches in exporting: direct and indirect selling.

In direct selling, the U.S. firm deals with foreign importers and is usually responsible for shipping the products overseas. However, direct selling may include using the services of foreign sales representatives or agents. In the indirect method, the U.S. firm relies on another firm that acts as a sales intermediary and normally assumes responsibility for marketing and shipping the products overseas. The decision to market products directly or indirectly should be made on the basis of a number of key considerations, including the size of the firm, the nature of its products, previous export experience, and business conditions in the selected overseas markets.

The following export success stories show the application of these considerations.

- Second Chance Body Armor, Inc., of Central Lake, Michigan, sells its specialized line of bullet-resistant vests to foreign countries through a network of native experts in police and military work who help the 45-employee firm secure contracts with official agencies in their countries.

- Gamble Brothers of Louisville, Ky., obtained an agent in the United Kingdom who found a strong demand for the firm's wood kitchen cabinet components. From that point, sales blossomed in Ireland, Spain, the Benelux countries, and Greece.

- Hallmark Sales Corporation of Houston, Texas, a wholesale exporter of industrial equipment and supplies, hired employees fluent in Spanish to keep in direct contact with customers from offices the firm set up in Mexico and Argentina.

- SAS Institute Inc. of Cary, N.C., maintains a network of wholly owned subsidiaries in Canada, Europe, and the Asia/Pacific region. This strategy allows the company to adapt its products to particular markets effectively because the subsidiaries are staffed almost exclusively with nationals with an understanding of local culture and business practices.

- H.F. Henderson Industries of West Caldwell, N.J., chooses to sell its automatic weighing machines directly to foreign customers rather than through overseas agents or distributors. For that reason, the firm emphasizes travel and a willingness to adapt to language and cultural differences. Henry Henderson, Jr., president, has made seven trips to China, where he has socialized with the Chinese and learned their ways of doing business. He has also traveled to Australia, South Korea, Hong Kong, France, Russia, Switzerland, Austria, Hungary, Italy, Finland, and Brazil, among other countries.

- The Ohmart Corporation of Cincinnati, Ohio, took the opposite tack of building a strong organization of international sales representatives. The 130-employee manufacturer of industrial process measurement and control systems has chosen, as representatives, experienced engineers capable of presenting technical data to customers' technical staffs.

Source: *Business America*, World Trade Week 1993 Edition, Vol. 114, No. 9 (1993), pp. 4–5.

CHANNEL NETWORKS IN CONSUMER AND INDUSTRIAL MARKETS

In planning distribution networks for the MM line in both domestic and global markets, Merton planners first had to decide what external distribution channels, if any, to use. Then, if it was decided to use external intermediaries, subsequent decisions had to be made regarding types of channel intermediaries to use (e.g., retailers or wholesalers) and elements of physical distribution needed to ensure that Merton products moved efficiently and profitably to customers. (Chapter 19 examines global logistics considerations that address physical distribution processes.)

Figure 18-1 illustrates channels commonly used to distribute consumer and industrial products.

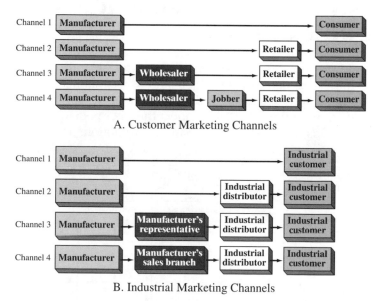

Figure 18–1. Consumer and Industrial Marketing Channels

• *CONSUMER PRODUCTS*

Figure 18-1a shows the main channels of distribution for consumer products. Channel 1 consists of a manufacturer selling directly to consumers, as when Fuller Brush or Avon sells products door-to-door or L.L. Bean sells through direct catalog sales. Channel 2 contains one distribution level, as when large retailers like Sears, IKEA, and Wal-Mart sell cameras, furniture, and other products they buy directly from manufacturers. Channel 3 contains two distribution levels, as when small manufacturers of food, drugs, and other products sell to wholesalers, who then sell to retailers, who then sell to consumers. Channel 4 contains three distribution levels, as when jobbers in the meat-packing industry buy from wholesalers and sell to smaller retailers, who sell to consumers.

• *INDUSTRIAL PRODUCTS*

Figure 18-1b shows the main channels for distributing industrial products. A manufacturer can use its own salesforce to sell directly to industrial customers (Channel 1), or to sell to industrial distributors who sell to industrial customers (Channel 2), or to use manufacturer's representatives or its own sales branches to sell to industrial distributors, who sell to industrial customers (Channels 3 and 4).

CHANNEL FLOWS INFLUENCE CHANNEL CHOICE

From the perspective of a marketing planner assessing channel options in domestic and global markets, an understanding of channel flows is a good starting point for weighing costs and benefits of each option. As illustrated in Figure 18-2, these flows, which connect the intermediaries in a channel, encompass goods, ownership, information, promotion, and payment.

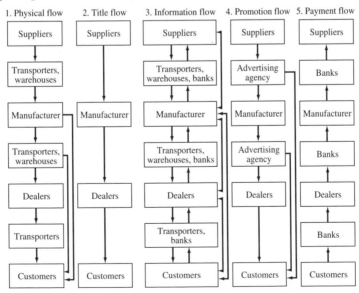

Figure 18–2. Marketing Flows Emphasize Complexity of Channels

Here is how Merton planners envisioned that these flows would affect the distribution of MM systems and choice of channel strategies in diverse markets.

- *Physical flow.* Suppliers ship parts to Merton, which are then assembled into Merton systems distributed through various intermediaries further down the line.

- *Title flow.* Merton buys parts and then assembles and sells MM systems; thus, the ownership passes from suppliers to Merton, then to dealers, and finally to the consumer. Sometimes Merton assumes the risk of resale by offering merchandise on consignment, delaying payment from the dealer—and passage of ownership—until the product is sold.

- *Information flow.* If products are to succeed, each link on the chain must adjust according to information provided by other channel members.

- *Promotion flow.* Merton receives promotional materials from suppliers for parts it needs and then promotes its products and services to dealers that carry and promote MM systems and components to prospective customers.

- *Payment flow.* This is a backward flow, where money passes from customer to intermediary to Merton to Merton's suppliers to pay for goods delivered, using payment methods discussed in Chapter 16 (open account, consignment, letters of credit, etc.).

Note that the more cluttered a channel is with intermediaries, the more complex, costly, and risky these flows become. For example, products can get lost, stolen, or damaged with long physical flows; cash flows can get dammed with long payment flows, and communications can get distorted and delayed with long information and promotion flows. Assessing the relative value of a channel then becomes a matter of balancing the cost of these flows against the value of functions distributors can perform for sellers.

RETAILERS AND WHOLESALERS IN GLOBAL MARKETS

More than 90 percent of all goods sold in developed countries move through wholesale and/or retail channels, so it behooves marketers formulating a channel strategy to understand characteristics, costs, and benefits of each, and how they can be linked to achieve various marketing objectives.

In the next section, we describe types of retailers and wholesalers as they exist in the United States and in most developed countries. In countries where they don't exist, exporters face the challenge of either creating their own channels or using alternate channels, as illustrated earlier in Global Focus 18-1. This next section also examines approaches for identifying and working effectively with retailers, wholesalers, and other global intermediaries.

RETAILERS DEFINED BY OWNERSHIP

By ownership, retailers are classified as either independents or chains. A retail chain, characterized by common ownership of multiple units, engages in centralized purchasing and decision making and is able to serve a large, dispersed market because of specialization, standardization, and elaborate control systems. Although accounting for a relatively small proportion of outlets in developed countries, retail chains are responsible for more than half of total retail store sales.

RETAILERS DEFINED BY SERVICES AND FACILITIES

To stay in business, retailers must offer location, price, service, convenience, and product assortment features while keeping costs down. The features each stresses will determine the nature of the retail operation.

Following are predominant types of store and nonstore retailers, and the mix of features each employs to implement its marketing strategy.

STORE RETAILERS

• *CONVENIENCE STORE*
Convenience stores provide convenience in the form of long hours and locations close to residential areas. They are food oriented and cater to emergency purchases. Thus, prices are higher, selection is limited, and the stores are basically self-service. 7-Eleven is an example of this kind of retailer in the domestic market.

• *SPECIALTY STORES*
Specialty stores focus on product depth rather than width. For example,

Blockbuster Video outlets carry a narrow product line (videotapes) and a depth of film categories and titles. Typical product lines carried include apparel, gourmet foods, appliances, toys, electronics, and sportswear. Salespeople are generally knowledgeable, and prices are relatively high. Hours and location must be convenient enough to draw some impulse shoppers, but depth of product offerings provides the main draw.

• *DEPARTMENT STORES*
Department stores are organized into separate departments for purposes of buying, promotion, service, and control. They feature a high degree of product assortment including fashion apparel, furniture, home furnishings, and appliances. Because they must serve large numbers of customers to turn over their large inventory, department stores are centrally located and offer convenient hours. Pricing varies according to store image.

• *FULL-LINE DISCOUNT STORES*
Full-line discount stores, like K-Mart and Wal-Mart, are department stores with low prices, relatively broad merchandise assortments, brand name products, low-rent locations, wide-aisles, self-service, many merchandise displays, and less emphasis on credit sales.

• *CATALOG SHOWROOMS*
Catalog showrooms offer deep discounts on high-ticket, brand name products, and even less service than discount stores offer. Customers must often wait in line to examine, or pick up, merchandise selected from catalogs. Credit and return policies are limited, location is often inconvenient, and facilities are spare.

• *SUPERMARKETS*
Supermarkets are relatively large, low margin, low price, high volume, self-service operations with convenient locations and hours, and a wide selection of groceries, meat, fish, prepared foods, household products, and produce.

• *SUPERSTORES*
Superstores combine the food and product assortment of supermarkets with that of department, or sometimes specialty, stores. Products carried include garden supplies, TVs, clothing, wine, boutique items, books, banking and dry cleaning services, bakery products, household appliances, and a full line of supermarket items. They typically occupy about twice the 15,000 to 20,000 square feet of supermarkets and generate more than twice the $6 million of average annual supermarket sales.

• *COMBINATION STORES*
Combination stores combine food/grocery and general merchandise

sales in one facility, with general merchandise providing 30 to 40 percent of overall sales. Combination stores go further than superstores in appealing to one-stop shopping, typically occupying between 50,000 and 200,000 square feet. Size and customer volume allow these retailers to operate more efficiently, increasing impulse purchases and size of average transaction (often selling products in bulk quantities). Prices are often discounted, generally reasonable, for low profit food items and higher profit general merchandise.

A hypermarket is a variant on the combination store that integrates a supermarket and a discount department store and occupies at least 60,000 square feet. Europe has about 2,500 hypermarkets; the United States has about 1,500.

Other forms of low-price store retailing showing appreciable recent growth include limited-line and warehouse food stores, off-price chains, discount drug stores, factory outlet stores, and flea markets. All are characterized by few customer services, low prices, and plain store fixtures.

NONSTORE RETAILERS

• *SERVICE BUSINESSES*

Service businesses, like movie theaters, banks, taxi companies, hospitals, and health clubs provide a product that is a service.

• *VENDING MACHINES*

Vending machines use coin or card-operated machinery to dispense goods and services, such as soda, food, cigarettes, automatic teller machines, video games, and airline life insurance. Advantages include around-the-clock sales and no need for sales personnel. Disadvantages include risks of pilferage, damage, and high maintanance costs.

• *DIRECT MARKETING*

Direct marketing includes mail order catalogs, direct response advertising, direct mail, telemarketing, and television shopping, as discussed in Chapter 17. A recent innovation being promoted by Service 800 SA in Europe and AT&T in the United States, called international telemarketing, is a quasi toll-free service that facilitates contacts among sellers, customers, and prospects in 42 countries. Main uses include customer inquiries, order placement, service calls, and office-to-office data transmission.

TYPES OF WHOLESALERS

There are three principal types of wholesalers: merchant wholesalers, agents/brokers, and manufacturer wholesalers.

MERCHANT WHOLESALERS

Merchant wholesalers are independently owned operations that buy and take possession of goods for future resale. They represent the largest group of wholesalers, accounting for more than 50 percent of sales in developed markets. This group is further divided into full-service and limited-service wholesalers.

• *FULL-SERVICE WHOLESALERS*

Full-service wholesalers buy merchandise, maintain inventory; provide trade credit; store and deliver merchandise; offer research, management, and promotional assistance; and service customers with sales personnel. This model is common in the pharmaceutical, grocery, and hardware industries. General merchandise (fill-in) wholesalers carry a wide assortment of products (e.g., hardware, apparel, and drugs) for retailers, but don't offer much depth within any product line. Specialty merchandise (limited line) wholesalers carry an extensive assortment within a limited product range (e.g., health and frozen foods) and offer a broad range of functions. Rack jobbers set up displays on racks or shelves and sell their merchandise—usually heavily advertised, branded products (e.g., health and beauty aids, stationery, toys)—on consignment. Franchise wholesalers service independent retailer affiliates, such as hardware and auto parts suppliers, who use a standardized storefront design, business format, name, and purchase system. Industrial distributors sell to producers rather than retailers. They may carry a broad range of merchandise (e.g., ball bearings, power tools, and motors), a general line, or a specialty line. They perform a full range of wholesaler services, including inventory, credit, and delivery, for their customers.

• *LIMITED-SERVICE WHOLESALERS*

Limited-service wholesalers do not provide the full range of functions provided by full-service wholesalers. A drop shipper, for example, takes an order, finds a company to fill it, takes title to merchandise, but does not maintain inventory. Cash-and-carry wholesalers provide no credit, delivery, merchandising, or promotional assistance; have no sales force; and don't aid in marketing research or planning. They are important for "fill-in" items, (e.g., auto parts) or perishable goods (e.g., fruit) have low prices, and offer immediate product availability. Truck wholesalers carry semiperishable merchandise (e.g., bread or milk) and simultaneously sell and deliver along a regular sales route. Mail-order wholesalers maintain no sales force, relying on catalogs to get attention for their products, which retailers may order and receive by mail.

BROKERS AND AGENTS

Brokers and agents work for commissions or fees, provide trained sales forces, and help manufacturers expand sales. This form of wholesaling does not involve ownership of goods and limits the amount of service offered. Brokers are employed as needed to bring buyers and sellers to terms. Though paid by the seller, they are useful to both because of their knowledge of market conditions and their ability to negotiate. Agents are permanent, independent salespeople who represent either the buyer or the seller. They may represent more than one manufacturer, which removes the need to invest in a salesforce. There are several different kinds of agents.

• *MANUFACTURERS' AGENTS*
Manufacturers' agents represent two or more firms carrying complementary, noncompeting items. By selling many different products, these agents make it economically feasible to cover geographically scattered markets. Small manufacturers may have only one product represented by agents, which gets wider exposure by being grouped with others. Manufacturers' agents work on commission, do not offer credit, carry limited inventory, and have little to say about pricing and promotion.

• *SELLING AGENTS*
Selling agents, although also independent, handle a manufactuer's entire product line. This, too, saves the manufacturer from maintaining a sales force. The selling agent negotiates terms of pricing, delivery, and credit, and may perform other wholesaler functions except ownership of goods. Selling agents are prevalent among small manufacturers.

• *PURCHASING AGENTS*
Purchasing agents work for the buyer, choosing and often warehousing and shipping suitable merchandise to the retail outlets served.

• *COMMISSION MERCHANTS*
Commission merchants are common in agriculture. They take goods on consignment, sell them, and keep a portion of the proceeds as a commission.

MANUFACTURER WHOLESALERS

Manufacturer wholesalers are owned and operated by manufacturers with sales volume that justifies such an investment. These operations consist of sales branches that warehouse and sell goods and sales offices that are limited to arranging for merchandise distribution.

RETAILER AND WHOLESALER MARKETING DECISIONS

Understanding marketing decisions made by retailers and wholesalers in such areas as target market selection and product, place, price, and promotion strategies can help exporters tailor marketing mix programs that will attract and maintain productive distribution relations.

• *TARGET MARKET SELECTION*

For both wholesalers and retailers, all decisions regarding products, distribution, price, and promotion follow this initial decision. Both attempt to narrow prospective markets to the most profitable segments. Using such demographic data as age, income, and geographic location of profitable prospect groups, retailers tailor product offerings, prices, store location, and store atmosphere to attract these groups.

Wholesalers use retailer characteristics to identify profitable target markets. Will they serve large or small retailers? Variety stores or specialty stores? Those in need of quick delivery? Backup service? Financing? Answers determine the nature of wholesale operations.

• *PRODUCT ASSORTMENT AND SERVICE*

Some of the questions addressed by retailers in deciding on product assortments follow. Should a wide variety of products be stocked, or only a few lines, with a depth of products within each? Should high quality or lower priced goods be emphasized? Additionally, intangibles such as service and the atmosphere in which products are presented are considered. Customers buying high quality merchandise expect high quality service and a posh store atmosphere.

Wholesalers are usually expected to carry a large assortment of products to meet retailers' immediate needs. Since wholesalers generally pay for the goods they stock, however, carrying a large inventory is expensive, and the tendency is to pare lines down to the most profitable products, without losing retail customers. Retailers' desire for services such as credit and delivery must also be considered in attempting to find a balance between serving customers and maintaining profitability.

• *PLACE*

A number of options are open to retailers in selecting a location. An isolated location may be fine for a discount store or catalog showroom, where price advantages will impel customers to go out of their way to shop.

Specialty stores and service businesses may choose to locate in an unplanned central business district, with its heavy foot traffic. In neighborhood or regional shopping centers (shopping malls), a planned mix of stores benefits all retailers.

Wholesalers mimic low-end retailers in their choice of location. For them, a functional building in a low rent, low tax neighborhood is ideal. Key considerations include proximity to manufacturers, retailers, or major connecting highways. Money spent on improving facilities is usually directed at increasing efficiency, such as by computerizing or automating warehouses.

• *PRICE*

For retailers, price decisions depend on product decisions. A high quality product line will require higher prices; a strategy that rests on quick turnover of stock points to lower pricing. High overhead resulting from liberal customer services and "atmosphere" will raise prices. Still, the key to profitability is intelligent buying, with an understanding of the price that can reasonably be charged for the goods. Retailers often employ creative pricing policies, where underpriced items draw customers who then buy more profitable products. Or products are overpriced initially because a percentage of stock will sell at that price, with markdowns made later.

Wholesalers, like retailers, operate under a "buy low, sell high" law of profitability. However, if wholesalers can find appropriate merchandise at low prices, the price break will usually be passed on to retailers to encourage volume buying or to attract new customers.

• *PROMOTION*

Retailers vary greatly in the types and degree of promotion they use to attract customers. A funeral home would never advertise that its prices were "insane," and an out-of-the-way discount store would never rely on word-of-mouth advertising. As with all other marketing decisions, target market determines promotional strategy.

Because image counts less, and because they perform a straightforward service, wholesalers advertise little. Some wholesalers do employ sales forces, however, and find it wise to promote themselves to retailers in other ways.

VMS STRUCTURES AID CHANNEL COOPERATION

Manufacturers, wholesalers, retailers, and other channel intermediaries interact in many ways to get the distribution job done. But each member is dissimilar from the others, with its own immediate interests uppermost. Although each channel member benefits individually when the whole system works well, competitive pressures often prevent individual members from behaving to benefit the group. For example, dealers might pressure suppliers for pricing arrangments that eliminate profits for other channel members, or suppliers might do the same to dealers.

Vertical marketing systems (VMSs) are arrangements among channel members that help mitigate these pressures and ensure cooperation. In these arrangements, the producer, wholesaler, and retailer function as a unified system, reducing conflict to a minimum. There are various types of VMSs:

• *CORPORATE VMS*

A corporate VMS combines successive stages of production and distribution under single ownership. For example, Sears, a retailer, has equity in many manufacturers that supply its products, while Sherwin Williams, a manufacturer, owns more than 2,000 retail outlets.

• *CONTRACTUAL VMS*

A contractual VMS comprises independent channel members that join together for mutual benefit. In the producer-wholesaler-retailer model, there are three possible combinations.

- *Producer-wholesaler.* This may take the form of a franchise operation, where the manufacturer licenses the wholesaler to distribute the product. Coca-Cola, for example, licenses bottlers worldwide to process its syrup concentrates into soda, which is then sold to independent retailers.

- *Producer-retailer.* This arrangement also usually consists of a franchising operation, where the producer gives the retailer the right to sell its products in return for the retailer's meeting producer-imposed conditions. The automobile industry, with its system of dealerships, is an example of this type of VMS. Service industries, too, often use this approach. For example, restaurant and motel chains are often made up of individually licensed and owned retail operations.

- *Retailer-wholesaler.* These systems are split into those controlled by the retailer and those controlled by the wholesaler. In wholesaler-sponsored voluntary chains, independent retailers are encouraged to band together to order large quanitties from the wholesaler, who passes on price advantages otherwise available only to large chains. The producer and wholesaler benefit from larger orders, and the retailer benefits from lower prices. Retailer-controlled systems are called cooperatives, in which retailers join together to create their own wholesaling operation. Co-op members buy from the jointly owned wholesaler and share in the profits it generates.

• ADMINISTERED VMS

An administered VMS is based on the size and power of one of the channel members. IBM, for example, can command greater cooperation and support from resellers through its potent market presence.

VMS ALTERNATIVES: HORIZONTAL AND MULTICHANNEL SYSTEMS

Horizontal marketing systems encourage cooperation among channel members through combinations of companies on the same channel level. By working together either temporarily or permanently, companies can combine capital, production capabiliites, or marketing resources to achieve more than any company working alone. Two examples follow.

- H&R Block and Hyatt Legal Services formed a joint venture in which Hyatt gains market penetration for its legal clinics by renting space and office facilities in H&R Block's tax preparation offices. Block benefits from renting its facilities, which would otherwise have a highly seasonal pattern.

- A number of savings banks locate office facilities and automated teller machines in supermarkets to gain quick market entry at low cost. The supermarkets benefit by offering in-store banking convenience to customers.

Multichannel marketing systems achieve cooperation and increased sales by setting up two or more marketing channels to reach one or more market segments. For example, McDonald's sells through a network of independent franchisees but owns a third of its outlets.

DISTRIBUTION SYSTEMS IN GLOBAL MARKETS

Some forms of distribution systems in global markets present challenges to exporters that are usually difficult to surmount. For example, Japanese *kieretsu* systems link importers, producers, distributors, and retailers, either through banks or trading companies, into distribution systems that combine features of vertical, horizontal, and multichannel systems. Frequently these systems—perhaps best illustrated by the Mitsubishi *kieretsu* that includes 150 companies with a total capitalization of 15 percent of the Tokyo stock exchange—create barriers to the successful penetration of an entry market by foreign "outsiders." Similar barriers are created by monopoly distribution systems characterizing many of the command economies of former communist bloc countries and some developed countries (e.g., the distribution of alcoholic spirits in Sweden and Finland).

FACILITATING INTERMEDIARIES

One way for a firm—especially smaller firms without experience or expertise in penetrating global markets—to address costly problems in exporting products to foreign markets is to retain the services of an export management company (EMC) or an export trading company (ETC). EMCs are usually small domestic firms that serve either as agents or distributors for several exporting firms. The marketing services they perform for their clients depend mainly on whether they function as agents or distributors. As agents, the EMCs earn commissions, don't handle or take title to goods, and operate under formal or informal contracts that specify exclusivity agreements, price arrangements, promotional payments, and sales quotas. As distributors, EMCs purchase and take title to products from client companies, provide a fuller range of marketing services, and assume the trading risk.

An export trading company (ETC), based on a concept originated by European trading houses in the seventeenth century and brought to fruition in Japan in the twentieth century (where, in 1996, nine trading companies acted as intermediaries for about half of Japan's exports and two-thirds of its imports), received a strong growth impetus in the United States with passage in 1982 of the Export Trading Company Act. Under this act, a wide variety of structures were permitted for ETCs to help them match the Japanese *kieretsu* model. For example, antitrust regulations were relaxed to permit competing companies to form joint ventures, and banks were permitted to participate in ETCs to allow better access to capital and easier receipt of title to goods. Today, modern ETCs perform a diversity of functions for exporting and importing clients, including assistance in (1) selecting competent distributors; (2) arranging for financing, insurance, and export documentation for trade transactions; (3) developing marketing plans; (4) fostering research and development; (5) establishing personal contact with foreign buyers; (6) handling countertrade requirements; (7) evaluating credit risks of foreign buyers; (8) handling promotion at foreign shows; (9) arranging for foreign packaging and marking; and (10) preparing training programs, advertising, and promotion for use in foreign markets.

DESIGNING CHANNEL SYSTEMS IN INTERNATIONAL MARKETS

Channel design decisions pertain to kinds of intermediaries that make up channel systems and how these intermediaries are linked to connect producers and customers in the most efficient and effective manner. In international markets, however, distribution system intermediaries and linkages that might be assumed in domestic markets aren't necessarily available or otherwise feasible, so the marketer, perforce, must settle for the possible.

In general, exporters face two decisions in designing distribution systems to serve global markets. The first decision pertains to which of three basic distribution systems the exporter will employ:

- *Indirect exporting*, which involves dealing with another U.S.-based firm, such as an EMC or ETC, that serves as a sales intermediary, saving the exporter the cost of setting up its own channels.

- *Direct exporting*, which involves either selling directly to foreign customers or through local representatives that sell directly to customers.

- *Integrated distribution*, which involves an investment in foreign intermediaries to sell products in one or more global markets.

The second decision confronts exporters that decide on a strategy of integrated distribution. Specifically, should intermediaries selected be distributors or agents? As already noted, distributors are usually organized along product lines, purchase and take title to goods, provide a complete marketing service, and are more independent than agents who operate on a commission basis and don't usually physically handle the goods.

Consideration of the following interactive factors will help marketers relate channel opportunities in global markets to company objectives and resources in designing new channel systems or modifying existing systems.

• *COMPANY OBJECTIVES*

Particularly in areas of desired market share and profit return, company objectives can have a strong influence on the nature and design of channel systems. For example, a strong competitive presence needed to quickly develop market share in a territory might indicate a distribution system including joint ventures and strongly motivated stocking distributors.

• *CUSTOMER CHARACTERISTICS*

Understanding the nature and scope of target markets, and the needs and behavior of target market members, is a logical starting point for identifying distributors to serve these markets. Start with a broad view of relevant demographic factors and then focus on specifics that will help identify and profile desired distributors.

For example, how does your prospective foreign target market compare with known domestic markets in terms of such criteria as age, income, and education level? What are product information needs of market members? How price sensitive are they? How important are quality and service values? What are the buying habits of target market members; how do they usually purchase the product or service marketed, and from whom? How do they respond to different selling approaches? If feasible, actually interview prospective customers (including distributors, who are also customers).

In general, the larger a target market, the greater the need for distributors, regardless of the stage of a country's market development. If market size is in the millions, retail distribution and direct marketing channels for consumer products are usually required; if the market is characterized by many low volume retailers, wholesalers are almost certainly needed to service them.

• *PRODUCT CHARACTERISTICS*

Frequently, product characteristics are the single most important consideration in identifying worthwhile global channels. Some key concerns follow. How standardized is the product? (Will distributors have to customize it to meet customer needs?) Is it an expensive product? (Products with a high unit price, such as MM systems, are often sold through shorter, more direct channels, because selling price is a small percentage of total price, and such products usually require specialized selling expertise.) How perishable is the product? (Perishable products usually require fewer, and more specialized, channel members to get them to market quickly.) How bulky is the product? (Bulky products call for channel arrangements that minimize shipping distances.)

• *THE COMPETITIVE CLIMATE*

Exporters entering highly competitive entry markets face the problem of differentiating their product or service to attract both end customers and distributors. A potent brand name or attractive, patented feature or significant price advantage are possibilities. However, even this might not be enough to attract distributors who, worldwide, usually aren't interested in taking on new or untested products; they want to represent products for which demand has already been created. Even if the distributor does agree to represent the product, it doesn't guarantee that the distributor will exert the sales effort to increase demand.

Facing a highly competitive market and low distributor motivation to take on, or push, a product line, exporters have two options.

- Provide additional incentives for distributors to take on and push the line (e.g., payments for performance, guaranteed gross margins, or subsidizing the cost of promotional programs in support of the product).

- Bypass outside intermediaries to set up their own distribution channels, with the future option of signing up distributors when the product, by its share of market growth, has proven itself.

• *CHANNEL CHARACTERISTICS*

Channel structures and functions in international markets might differ from those in domestic markets in ways that could affect channel selection and design. For example, in global markets, retailers and wholesalers generally expect more financial and sales support from their suppliers and are more likely to demand full acceptance of returns.

Another key variable is the coverage offered by existing channels. Specifically, are channels available to cover target market territories? And will they supply the kind of coverage desired (e.g., intensive, selective, or exclusive)?

• *LEGAL/POLITICAL REALITIES*

Channel design decisions usually culminate in legal commitments with outside distributors (wholesalers, agents, brokers, etc.) that can be extremely difficult to change or terminate. In many countries in Europe and Latin America, laws and regulations governing channel relationships tend to be much harsher than U.S. laws with respect to agency/principal relations, often viewing termination of an agent as a matter of national concern rather than as a private matter among individuals. Exacerbating these contractual problems is the fact that, in many foreign and legal jurisdictions, sales agent and distributor are not defined, legally, as they are in the United States. In the United States, a distributor is an independent business that represents a number of competing companies; abroad, many distributors not only stock for the local market but represent a single manufacturer, functioning as both distributor and exclusive sales representative. Not carrying competing products, this distributor will expect exclusivity and many other contractual prerequisites not normally expected by U.S. distributors.

Also, in such jurisdictions, agents are given the power of attorney, meaning that they can legally bind principals to contract and expose them to legal and economic risk. In some Latin American countries, the economc risk for canceling a contract can equal five times annual gross profits, plus the value of the agent's investment, plus many additional payments. Often, these indemnities increase with the time the contract is in force and include compensation for the increased value of the market created.

In some countries, channel design decisions can also be shaped by legislation requiring that foreign firms be represented only by distributors that are 100 percent locally owned, or, in a few cases, legislation that totally prohibits the use of dealers in order to protect consumers from abuses attributed to them.

• *FINANCIAL IMPLICATIONS*

Three areas of financial concern to exporters engaged in establishing or modifying distribution channels in international markets follow.

- *Capital requirements* to set up a desired channel system, covering such accounts as beginning inventories, preferential loans, construction, staffing, and training costs.

- *Continuing costs* for maintaining channels once established, which are a function of a number of factors, including stage of the life cycle of the product and distributor relationship, the relative power of the principal vis-à-vis intermediaries, and functions (selling, materials handling, etc.) performed by each.

- *Risk*, which is also a function of many factors, including the stability of a market's currency, the strength of the relationship among principal and intermediaries, and the extent to which they share risk in contractual relationships.

FINDING DISTRIBUTORS IN INTERNATIONAL MARKETS

Before embarking on a search for distributors to help market products or services in established or entry global markets, the principal should first gather information covering the considerations already discussed and pertaining to how threats and opportunities in distribution climates can best be shaped to match the principal's goals and resources. This information will help define components of effective distribution systems and negotiate these systems into being.

For informed principals, there are so many domestic and foreign private and government sources of information on available distributors that the biggest initial problem is often where to start. One excellent starting point is the Trade Promotion Coordinating Committee (1-800-872-8723), an interagency group that has the task of developing and coordinating U.S. export programs. This committee directs inquirers to sources of up-to-date information on types and names of distributors in prospective entry markets and arranges contacts with those of particular interest. Two services of the U.S. Commerce Department—the Agent/Distributor Service and the World Traders Data Report—locate and profile foreign firms interested in export proposals submitted by U.S. firms.

Private sources of information on distribution availabilities in global markets include country and regional business directories that are published worldwide or domestic lists, which categorize distributors by country and line of business and can be ordered from Dun & Bradstreet, Reuben H. Donnelly, McGraw-Hill, Kelly's Directory, and Johnson Publishing. Principals can also solicit information from facilitating agencies (e.g., banks, advertising agencies, and shipping lines) or take a more direct role and solicit information and applicants at major trade fairs.

MANAGING CHANNELS IN INTERNATIONAL MARKETS

Finding and selecting distributors in international markets and motivating them to team up to profitably market products or services is only the beginning of a complex, dynamic partnership that must be effectively managed to produce mutual long-term benefits. For this partnership to work in the face of cultural, logistical, operational and legal constraints in global markets, effective two-way communication among the partners is key in order to effectively convey goals, implement marketing plans, and resolve conflicts. As illustrated in Global Focus 18-2, this partnership among sellers and distributors in global markets can be the basis of a successful global maketing strategy.

GLOBAL FOCUS 18-2

Distributors as Strategic Business Partners

"We treat our worldwide distributors as customers and also as strategic business partners," said Peter J. Rogers, Jr., Director of Marketing Systems for MICROS Systems, Inc., of Beltsville, Md. The 450-employee firm makes point-of-sale systems, a modern form of cash register, for hotels, restaurants, cruise ships, casinos, theme parks, and stadiums.

"Our market niche is the hospitality business—hospitality knows no national boundaries," Rogers said. "We have incorporated the concept of hospitality into the way we operate, which means we are very much customer-focused."

He continued, "Our philosophy of pleasing our customers is fundamental to our success in exporting, as well as in domestic sales, and it applies not only to our distributors but to end users of our equipment. We place a high value on the teamwork approach. Before we pick distributors or hire employees, we make it clear that the company's goal is to serve customers. Our distributors are strategic partners in the sense that they are a key piece of our business strategy, of giving our customers assurance that they have strong backup in sales and marketing, technical assistance, and software programming and development."

MICROS Systems, which was established in 1977, has developed its export program over the past 15 years. It has 50 international distributors and six overseas subsidiaries—two in the United Kingdom and one each in France, Germany, Switzerland, and Spain. It has an office in Frankfurt, Germany, to support its operations in Europe, the Middle East and Africa, and an office in Singapore to support operations in Asia and the Pacific Rim. Today, MICROS Systems exports 28 percent of its products.

To give the best service in foreign countries, MICROS Systems has a policy of hiring nationals for its support operations. Rogers explained, "Because they understand the culture, we think they are best able to help us grow in their countries."

Typically, MICROS Systems sells its equipment to distributors, who add value by modifying the equipment for local conditions, such as installing the data base in a foreign language. The distributor may then sell the equipment to a hotel, which has access to an effective locally based sales and service staff, which in turn is backed up by MICROS Systems corporate headquarters.

Source: "Stories of Exporting Success," *Busines America*, Vol. 115, No. 6 (June 1994), p. 8.

GOOD DISTRIBUTOR AGREEMENTS FACILITATE GOOD COMMUNICATIONS

Approaches for implementing productive, two-way communication include distributor advisory councils and personal visits among the partner firms. Invariably, however, these initiatives are no better than the basic agreements between the principal and intermediaries on which they are based. In general, these agreements should cover a specific time period (usually 1 or 2 years), with a trial period of between 3 and 6 months for new distributors. Other areas covered include products covered, geographic boundaries, other distribution methods allowed, methods of payment (including terms of sale), currencies used, functions and responsibilities of intermediaries, credit and shipment terms and procedures, information each partner is entitled to, and means of communicating this information.

Beyond these specific content considerations, here are some general guidelines for preparing productive, protective distributor agreements.

- Be specific in defining performance. For example, use phrases like "Agent agrees to sell a minimum of ten MM systems every quarter."

- Be specific in defining consequences of nonperformance. For example, "Agent will transfer to principal all legitimate property, including trademarks, patents, company name, and lists of customers and contacts."

- Be specific as to what law will govern contract disputes. If feasible, specify U.S. common law, rather than the harsher code law characterizing many other world jurisdictions.

- Be specific as to what forum will adjudicate disputes. Almost invariably, from the principal's perspective, arbitration or conciliation are preferable to civil law courts.

- Finally, be specific as to the language in which contract clauses will be interpreted. Even if written in the language of the agent or distributor, consider interpreting the contract in the language of the principal.

CHAPTER PERSPECTIVE

The distribution planning process entails designing channels and physical distribution systems for moving products from manufacturers to ultimate consumers or users efficiently and economically. For exporters, longer channels, more complex channel flows, and problems in attracting distributors and setting up physical distribution systems can create costly roadblocks to successful market entry. Total costs and total systems approaches for integrating all elements of the distribution process help level the competitive playing field.

KNOW THE CONCEPTS

TERMS FOR STUDY

administrative VMS
agent
broker
channel flows
channel functions
channel management
channels
direct exporting
distribution planning
export management company
Export Trading Act
export trading company
horizontal marketing system

indirect exporting
integrated distribution
intermediaries
merchant wholesalers
multichannel marketing system
nonstore retailer
retailer
retailing functions
store retailer
vertical marketing system
wholesaler
wholesaler function

MATCHUP EXERCISES

1. Match up the number of levels in the distribution channel described in the first column with the activity described in the second column.

1. zero level
2. one level
3. two level

4. three level

a. a Tupperware party
b. Ikea holds a furniture sale
c. wholesalers sell beef to jobbers, who sell to small retailers
d. Mattel sells toys to wholesalers, who sell to retailers

2. Match up the distributor category in the first column with the second column descriptor.

1. selling agents
2. manufacturers agents

3. nonstore retailer

4. store retailer

a. 7-Eleven
b. market manufacturer's entire output
c. represent two or more firms making complementary product lines
d. the Bijou motion picture theater

3. Match up the concern in the second column with the decision area in the first column.

1. target market selection	a. how wide? how deep?
2. location	b. fast turnover, or quality image?
3. product assortment	c. customer wants and needs
4. price	d. proximity to customers and transportation
5. promotion	e. upscale, downscale, midscale?

4. Match up the descriptor in the second column with the channel flow in the first column.

1. payment	a. sales trends by product line
2. information	b. the only backwards flow
3. promotion	c. done by suppliers, dealers, and producers
4. ownership	d. consignment delays

5. Match up the forms of channel integration in the first column with the distributors in the second column.

1. contractual VMS	a. Sears obtains 50 percent of goods it sells from companies it partly or wholly owns.
2. corporate VMS	b. Ford licenses independent dealers to sell its cars.
3. administered VMS	c. Pillsbury and Kraft foods cooperate to advertise and sell products to retailers.
4. HMS	d. Campbell Soup's size and power command cooperation from retailers.

QUESTIONS FOR REVIEW AND DISCUSSION

1. Distinguish between intermediaries and facilitating agencies in terms of the basic role of each in moving products from producer to consumer. Why are decisions pertaining to the proper melding of intermediaries and facilitating agencies in channels important in devising and implementing marketing plans?

2. In 1996, overseas sales, resulting from more than 14 million Tupperware parties in more than 100 foreign countries, generated 85 percent of the Tupperware Corporation's $1.40 billion in total revenues. In terms of key considerations involved in deciding number of channel levels, why do you suppose Tupperware management chose a zero-level channel in preference to multilevel channels? (Note: Your

answer should also apply to other global zero-level channel users like Avon Home Products and Electrolux vacuum cleaners.)

3. In the 1970s, about 200 distributors handled about half of all pharmaceutical products distributed worldwide, with manufacturers distributing the rest directly. By the early 1990s, fewer than 125 distributors handled 65 percent, with McKesson far and away the largest distributor. Explain, in terms of channel flows, how this trend toward larger wholesalers and less direct distribution might have come about.

4. Describe what kinds of channel structures (vertical, horizontal, multichannel) are implicit in the following product/market situation. Sherwin Williams, the world's largest paint producer, distributes paint through more than 1,700 company-owned and independent paint stores, mass merchandisers, wholesale distributors, and, for some industrial products, direct selling.

5. In terms of functions performed by distributors, discuss reasons why IBM sold its company-owned product centers and opted to distribute its products only through independent channel members and sales personnel.

ANSWERS

MATCHUP EXERCISES

1. 1a, 2b, 3d, 4c
2. 1b, 2c, 3d, 4a
3. 1c, 2d, 3a, 4b, 5e
4. 1b, 2a, 3c, 4d
5. 1b, 2a, 3d, 4c

QUESTIONS FOR REVIEW AND DISCUSSION

1. Facilitating agencies, such as advertising agencies, banks, and transportation companies, assist in the performance of distribution functions but neither take title to goods nor negotiate purchases or sales; some intermediaries, such as brokers and sales agents, search for customers and may negotiate on behalf of the producer, but do not take title to the goods. Other intermediaries, such as wholesalers and retailers, buy, take title to, and resell the merchandise. The manner in which intermediaries and facilitating agencies are melded in designing

distribution channels is among the most crucial decisions facing management in that it intimately affects all other marketing decisions. For example, pricing depends on kinds of distributors used and costs entailed in moving products through channels, and advertising and selling decisions depend on training and motivation needed by distributors. The critical ability to reach and efficiently serve target markets is invariably a function of channel strategies.

2. Tupperware's decision to employ a zero-level channel was justified in terms of organizational goals and resources and the fact that the nature of the firm's products and markets lent themselves to this approach. For example, the firm manufactures a broad diversity of products, all of which lend themselves to demonstrations in a direct selling format (i.e., door to door, office to office, home sales parties). Also, because there is such a large market for Tupperware products—practically every household worldwide—the company can capitalize on economies of scale that are usually generated by multilevel channels. Given these conditions, Tupperware management, which has the resources to recruit, train, and manage an international salesforce, decided that its return on its investment in this salesforce, which included discounts and commissions it would otherwise have to pay distributors, made the zero-channel option the best "opportunity cost" of all channel alternatives. An additional benefit was the degree of control a zero-level channel gives Tupperware. The firm can hire, train, motivate, and compensate salespeople to their specifications and know that they will sell only Tupperware products.

3. Just as mass marketing can create manufacturing economies of scale for producers, it can create distribution economies of scale for wholesalers, which tend to foster centralization and more efficient flows among channel intermediaries. For example, McKesson, in performing the information flow, provides suppliers with tailor-made reports showing detailed sales, inventory, and marketing research data, including best-shelf placement for pharmaceutical products and major illnesses and allergies requiring medical and pharmaceutical attention. Using this information and its sizable resources, McKesson is also better positioned to promote and sell its suppliers' products (promotion flow) and to make sure proper assortments and quantities of pharmaceutical products are stocked and transported throughout the channel (physical distribution). With all these distributional values available, plus the steady predictable sales volume and risk reduction that results when distributors take title to and pay for merchandise (title and payment flows), it is probably understandable that the trend is away from direct selling in the pharmaceutical field.

4. Sherwin Williams' company-owned outlets would be an example of a corporate vertical marketing system. When paired with independent paint stores, it is an example of multichannel distribution. It is also an example of horizontal integration to the extent that Sherwin Williams purchased other paint companies and now uses their channels in addition to its own.

5. A distribution network with a broad range of electronic product lines supplementing the IBM line and serving a broad diversity of consumer and organizational target markets (e.g., the Computerland and Prodigy networks) would have a larger base of prospective customers to contact and a broader base of products to match to the needs of these prospects. Additionally, this deeper product/market base would provide the foundation for more useful marketing research feedback and a more productive response to promotional efforts supporting IBM's product line. Finally, this independent distribution network would be better able to move IBM's products to customers, since this is their essential business, just as making electronic business machines is IBM's essential business. Another plus is that IBM is now sharing much of the financial risk with distributors (e.g., the risk of no-pay customers or another PCjr. debacle).

19

INTERNATIONAL DISTRIBUTION PLANNING II: GLOBAL LOGISTICS

OVERVIEW

Global logistics entails the coordination and control of materials management and physical distribution functions—including packaging, transportation, storage, order processing, and inventory management—which combine to move products between producers and customers in international markets. Guiding this effort are total systems and total cost concepts that view logistics functions as a single integrated entity, with decisions in one functional area, such as transportation, affecting decisions in all other functional areas to keep overall logistics costs as low as possible and consistent with customer needs, competitive offerings, and company objectives. Dramatic differences between domestic and international markets in materials management and physical distribution challenges can generate equally dramatic cost-benefit outcomes when the global logistics function is properly managed.

GLOBAL LOGISTICS: GETTING PRODUCTS TO CUSTOMERS

Concurrently with distribution planning efforts to design channel systems consistent with customer needs, competitive climates, and company resources, marketing planners are also focusing on global logistics issues involved in moving goods into and through these channels. These logistics issues often represent the largest deterrent to successful global marketing programs, especially when markets entered are highly competitive and channel availabilities are limited.

The global logistics function melds together a variety of activities—including packaging, transportation, storage, inventory control, and order processing—to coordinate and control two subfunctions: materials management, which focuses on the timely arrival of raw materials, parts, and supplies into and through the exporting firm, and physical distribution, which focuses on the movement of the firm's finished products to its customers.

The importance of global logistics in marketing planning can be measured by a number of costly concerns: higher transportation and storage costs brought on by longer distances traveled via diverse transportation modes; more intermediaries involved in logistics processes, including freight forwarders, customs agents and brokers, and banks; transactions among these intermediaries in different currencies and exchange rates; diverse border-crossing regulations and customs inspections protocols; humidity, pilferage, and breakage problems; differing freight rates and packaging/labeling requirements; inadequate docking and materials handling facilities in many markets; and red tape involved in acquiring marine insurance, licenses, and other documents required by exporting and importing nations.

Another measure of the importance of global logistics is the growing appreciation for the "team" concept among producers, suppliers, customers, and other channel members in the areas of performance, quality, and timing. Manifestations of this jointness of purpose include just-in-time (JIT) inventory systems, which reduce inventory carrying costs by ordering more frequently and in lower quantities; quick response (QR) inventory systems, under which suppliers and distributors cooperate to reduce retail inventory while providing a merchandise supply that more closely addresses buying patterns of consumers, and early supplier involvement (ESI) for better planning and product movement. Properly implemented, these strategic logistical tools can create competitive advantages and savings in an area where large savings are still possible, given that logistics costs typically comprise between 15 and 30 percent of the total landed cost of an international order.

TOTAL SYSTEMS AND TOTAL COSTS DEFINE GLOBAL LOGISTICS GOALS

Two interrelated concepts combine to help guide logistics planners: total systems and total costs.

• *TOTAL SYSTEMS*

The total systems concept views materials management and physical distribution functions—including packaging, order processing, inventory control, warehousing, and transportation—as an integrated whole, instead of as a group of discrete entities. Under total systems, decisions in one area influence decisions in other areas. For example, a warehouse location decision will influence the selection of transportation methods and the amount of inventory stocked by retailers served by the warehouse.

• *TOTAL COST*

The total cost approach to logistical management offers a means of integrating materials management and physical distribution functions, using statistical and mathematical techniques, so as to provide a set of alternatives that optimize cost-profit relationships in the entire logistical system. This doesn't mean that costs in each area (warehousing, transportation, order processing, etc.) are necessarily low but that overall logistical costs are as low as possible consistent with customer needs, company objectives, and competitive offerings. For example, the Armour Pharmaceutical company determined that high air freight costs to serve its global market lowered inventory carrying and warehousing costs and, by increasing average order size, lowered order processing costs. The sum of these costs was the lowest of all alternatives examined, each of which entailed lower transportation costs. (In international markets, these costs are figured after taxes, to account for the influence of different tax policies.)

Implicit in both total systems and total cost concepts is the notion of trade-offs within and among logistical functions. For example, within the inventory management function, as more money is spent to place orders, less money is spent to carry ordered goods in inventory. Among functions, as more money is spent for proper packaging, less money is spent for transportation, storage, order processing, and overall logistics costs. Global Focus 19-1 vividly explicates the implications of these tradeoffs among logistics functions in terms of system efficiency, company savings, and customer satisfaction.

GLOBAL FOCUS 19-1

Making Global Connections at Caterpillar

Imagine the following scenario. A part of a Caterpillar machine operating at a copper mine in Chile begins to deteriorate. A district center that continuously monitors the health of all the Caterpillar machines in its area by remotely reading the sensors on each machine automatically spots a problem in the making and sends an electronic alert to the local dealer's field technician through his portable computer. The message tells him the identity and location of the machine and sends his computer the data that sparked the alert and its diagnosis. Then, with the aid of the computer, the technician validates the diagnosis and determines the service or repair required, the cost of labor and parts, and the risk of not performing the work.

The technician's computer also tells him exactly which parts and tools he will need to make the repair. Then, with a touch of a key, the technician ties into Caterpillar's worldwide information system, which links dealers, Caterpillar's parts-distribution facilities, Cat's and its suppliers' factories, and large customers' inventory systems. He instantly determines the best sources of the parts and the times when each source can deliver them to the dealer's drop-off point.

Next, the technician sends a proposal to the customer by computer or phone, and the customer tells him the best time to carry out the repair. With a few more keystrokes, the technician orders the parts. The electronic order instantly goes to the factories or warehouses that can supply the parts on time. At the factories and warehouses, the message triggers the printing of an order ticket and perhaps automatically sets into motion an automated crane that retrieves the parts from a storage rack. Soon the parts are on their way to the dealer's pick-up site.

Within hours of the initial alert, the technician is repairing the machine. An interactive manual on his computer guides him, providing him with the latest best-practice procedures for carrying out the repair. When the repair is completed, the technician closes the work order, prints out an invoice, collects by credit card, and electronically updates the machine's history. That information is added to Caterpillar's data bases, which helps the company spot any common problems that a particular model might have and thereby continually improve its machines' designs.

This global information system is a critical part of Caterpillar's drive to expand its industry-leading position by minimizing the downtime and cost of operating and servicing its machines. The system promises to help Caterpillar and its dealers do an even better job of heading off major machine failures. For example, it will help a dealer spot and repair a transmission before it has been ruined and needs to be totally replaced.

Another obvious advantage is that by treating their inventories as one, Caterpillar and its suppliers, dealers, and customers will be able to slash their combined inventories significantly. Even bigger savings could flow from reductions in the time that technicians require to diagnose and repair machines. "The amount of time that will be saved is probably in the range of 20 to 30 percent," said James Baldwin, vice president of the Parts and Service Support Division. "When you consider that field service workers are billed out at $20 to $50 an hour, that's a significant savings."

Source: Donald Fites, "Make Your Dealers Your Partners," *Harvard Business Review* (March–April 1996), p. 88. One-time permission to reproduce granted by Harvard Business School Publications, 1997.

PLANNING COST-EFFICIENT LOGISTICS SYSTEMS IN GLOBAL MARKETS

To illustrate how logistics planning can design and coordinate materials management and physical distribution systems that achieve benefits of total cost and total systems concepts, we will first examine what each of the following functions entails, how and when each is used, and beneficial trade-offs within each in global markets: packaging, transportation, storage, order processing, and inventory management. We then examine trade-offs among these functions that improve cost-effectiveness.

• *PACKAGING*

Packaging in international markets is strongly influenced by a passage in the U.S. Carriage of Goods by Sea Act that states: "Neither the carrier nor the ship shall be responsible for loss or damage arising from insufficiency of packing." A related consideration, illustrated in Figure 19-1, relates to stress hazards facing products in global markets; breakage from these hazards, combined with pilferage and theft losses, actually exceed losses caused by fire, sinkings, and collision of vessels.[1]

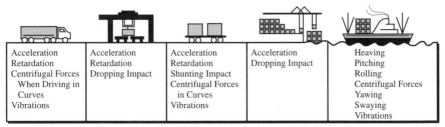

| Acceleration Retardation Centrifugal Forces When Driving in Curves Vibrations | Acceleration Retardation Dropping Impact | Acceleration Retardation Shunting Impact Centrifugal Forces in Curves Vibrations | Acceleration Dropping Impact | Heaving Pitching Rolling Centrifugal Forces Yawing Swaying Vibrations |

Note: Each transportation mode exerts a different set of stresses and strains on containerized cargoes. The most commonly overlooked are those associated with ocean transport.

Source: Reprinted with permission from *Handling and Shipping Management,* September 1980 issue, p. 47; David Greenfield, "Perfect Packing for Export." Copyright © 1980, Penton Publishing, Cleveland, OH.

Figure 19–1. Stresses in Intermodal Movement

To help ensure that these hazards are avoided and that merchandise arrives at ultimate destinations in safe, maintainable, and presentable condition, logistics planners should design product packaging to account for diverse threats and opportunities, including climate changes, nature and quality of port and inland transportation facilities, weight (especially when freight rates or duties are based on it), and special packaging instructions mandated by the importing country or company.

---

[1] Charles A. Taft, *Management of Physical Distribution and Transportation,* 7th ed. Homewood, Ill: Irwin, 1984, p. 324.

One solution to packaging problems in global markets is intermodal containers—large metal boxes that fit on trucks, ships, railroad cars and airplanes, and offer safety from pilferage and damage.

• *TRANSPORTATION*

Transportation costs—including tangible carrier costs and less tangible costs involved in pricing products, delivery performance, condition of shipped goods, and customer satisfaction—are usually the highest of all functional logistics costs. In global markets, firms assess the relative merits of the following transportation modes, two of which—air and water— are not extensively used in domestic markets.

AIR SHIPPING

Although the fastest growing of all transportation modes—with volume almost tripling between 1980 and 1996—total volume of airfreight in relation to total shipment volume in global markets is small: only 1 percent of volume and 20 percent of value. It is the most expensive of all transportation modes. Use of air transport may remove the need for extra warehouses because of its ability to span long distances quickly. High value, high density, perishable, and emergency goods dominate air shipments. Air shipments are also used when a firm is testing, or beginning operations, in a new country or is aggressively expanding operations in an existing market. Among the factors making air transport an attractive alternative are better ground facilities, containerization, and the ability to transport bulky cargoes on jumbo planes.

RAILROADS

The most popular worldwide transportation mode, railroads specialize in transporting large, heavy shipments over long distances. For shipments of a carload or more, they are comparatively inexpensive and provide good speed and reliability. Rail service is a good choice for shipments of lumber, coal, and agricultural products. Three recent trends have improved transporting capabilities of railroads: new shipping techniques and equipment to handle special categories of goods, more operating flexibility due to deregulation, and mergers to improve efficiency. In Japan, France, Germany, and other advanced countries, "bullet" trains are making railroads competitive with airlines.

WATER

Transport by ships and barges is second only to railroads as the most popular mode of transportation worldwide. It is relatively inexpensive but slow and less reliable due to its dependence on the weather. Because ships can go only where there is water, delivery areas are limited. Waterways in the domestic market are used mainly to transport low value, high bulk items, such as coal, grain, and cement.

In international markets, a number of ocean shipping options are available, including (1) liner service, which carries cargo and passengers on established, scheduled routes; (2) bulk service, which provides contractual services for individual voyages or for long time periods; and (3) tramp service, which is available for irregular routes and scheduled only on demand. Ocean carrier services can also be categorized by type of cargo carried, including (1) break-bulk cargo vessels, useful for oversized and unusual cargoes; (2) container ships that carry standardized containers to facilitate loading, unloading, and intermodal transfers; (3) roll-on-roll-off (RORO) vessels that ferry loaded trucks to their destinations; and (4) lighter aboard ship (LASH) vessels that ferry loaded barges to destinations, where they can operate on inland waterways. As with other modes of transportation, costs for water transportation can often be reduced through leverage achieved when the exporter joins an association of shippers.

TRUCKS

Because they can go almost anywhere, while trains follow the rails, ships the waterways, and airplanes air routes, trucks are the transportation of choice when flexibility is at a premium. Truck transportation is also fast and dependable, but because they are limited by their size to smaller cargoes, they are not as economical as rail or water.

PIPELINES

The Alaska Pipeline is perhaps the best known example of this kind of transportation, transporting more than 2 billion cubic feet of natural gas per day to the continental United States. There are no stops or alternate routes on pipelines, and only fluid products (gases, liquids or semi-liquids) can be transported. Once in place, however, pipelines provide cheap, reliable transportation.

In selecting from the preceding transportation modes those that would be most appropriate for transporting Merton products through channels to global customers, Merton planners had to balance three considerations: transit time, reliability, and cost.

- *Transit time* is often the major consideration in global transport decisions, in that faster, more frequent deliveries can lever dramatic savings in inventory size, need for overseas depots, and capital availability. Faster deliveries can also generate a competitive advantage when just-in-time inventory policies are an issue. Time is invariably the main consideration in shipping perishable and emergency products. Fast transportation in international markets, however, is expensive and subject to analysis to determine if it is justified by prospective savings.

- *Reliability*, as with transit time, can generate savings and competitive benefits. For example, if Merton distributors in Japan know that ordered merchandise will arrive on the day expected, they can maintain lower, cheaper safety stocks in inventory and be able to competitively fulfill customer needs.

- *Cost* is generally highest, on a per-item basis, for shipping products via airfreight, with ocean transport next. However, even high per-item costs can vary with a number of variables in global markets, such as favorable exchange rates, supply-demand patterns, and the monopoly power of individual carriers. Viewed in a broad logistical context, even extremely high transport costs can be justified for a number of reasons, as when savings exceed these costs, or customers will pay for fast service, or the product itself (e.g., diamonds) can absorb high transport costs.

COORDINATING TRANSPORTATION

Because a single shipment through channels to a foreign customer will probably involve a combination of transportation modes, Merton planners used international freight forwarders, specialized firms that act as agents for international marketers. In consolidating shipments and moving cargoes to overseas destinations, freight forwarders advise marketers on shipping documentation and packing costs, prepare necessary documents, and book necessary space aboard carriers. Freight forwarders offer economies of scale, since carload rates are much lower than less-than-carload rates. They also provide traffic management services, such as selecting the most reasonable transportation modes.

• *STORAGE*

Types of storage facilities available in the domestic market include private warehouses, already in business to serve target markets; space rented in public warehouses; or company-owned warehousing facilities.

Consistent with the total systems concept, Merton planners were attracted to distribution centers, designed to move goods rather than just store them as is done in storage warehouses. These large, highly automated and computerized centers receive goods, take orders, control inventory, and deliver filled orders to customers quickly and efficiently.

Basic storage issues facing global logistics planners pertain to which type, or types, of stocking locations to use and where they should be located. The approach for addressing these issues involves an analysis of markets, products, and competitive climates to measure costs versus benefits of maintaining storage facilities. For example, in a highly competitive market, where product applications such as production line components mandate reliably fast deliveries, distribution centers able to process and deliver orders rapidly might be a competitive necessity. Other, less critical products might be stocked at fewer, less localized public warehouses around the world. Unfortunately, availability of storage facilities abroad, and quality standards of those that exist, might not meet the needs of exporting firms, confronting planners with the problem of long-term, large-scale investment in such facilities and the need to justify this investment in terms of the profit potential of the market.

Strategies for reducing the cost of locating storage facilities abroad include capitalizing on differentials in factor endowments and using foreign trade zones.

Factor endowment differentials, such as costs for labor and capital, often exist between adjoining countries to the advantage of locating storage and distribution facilities. For example, the maquiladora program between the United States and Mexico permits firms to carry out labor-intensive operations in Mexico while sourcing raw materials and components from the United States, free of Mexican tariffs. Semifinished or assembled products are then shipped to the U.S. market and assessed only for the foreign labor component.

Foreign trade zones are special areas, outside the customs territory of the country in which they are located, that can be used for warehousing, packaging, inspecting, labeling, exhibiting, assembling, fabricating, or transshipping without the burden of duties.[2] Trade zones are located at major ports of entry and inland locations near major production facilities and provide exporting firms like Merton with benefits that easily offset any increased factor costs. For example, an exporting firm setting up operations in one of China's special economic trade zones receives substantial tax incentives, pays low taxes and prices for land and labor, and achieves "made in" status for products assembled in these zones.

• ORDER PROCESSING

Merton's challenge here was to get customer orders, which begin the physical distribution function, processed and filled quickly and accurately. Typically, when a customer order is received, order processing involves (1) determining customer credit standing and product availability; (2) issuing a shipping order and invoice, copies of which are sent to the customer and various departments; (3) noting the decrease in inventory; and (4) ordering new stock, when needed. If the quantity ordered isn't in stock, it is back ordered.

In integrating Merton order processing systems with systems of wholesalers in its distribution channels, Merton subsidized, where necessary, computerized systems initiated by electronic point of sale (EPOS)

---

[2] Patriya S. Tansuhaj and George Jackson, "Foreign Trade Zones: A Comparative Analysis of Users and Non-Users," *Journal of Business Logistics*, Vol. 10 (1989), pp. 15–30.

terminals. Resembling cash registers and connected to centralized EPOS terminals in distribution centers, the EPOS system recorded each sale and automatically sent an order to the distributor when inventory fell below levels determined through inventory control procedures.

In planning this integrated order processing system—which, in turn, was integrated with other elements of materials management and physical distribution systems—planners were quite cognizant of the trade-off between cost (EPOS was quite expensive) and the value of order processing timeliness and accuracy to customers.

• *INVENTORY MANAGEMENT*

Three key inventory management formulas define quantities of goods that should be maintained in inventory, when these quantities should be replenished, and how much should be ordered when they are replenished: the reorder point formula, the economic order quantity (EOQ) formula, and the average inventory formula. We assume, initially, that these formulas are being applied in Merton's domestic market by a distributor that is ordering MM systems from a Merton assembly plant for distribution to retailers of computer systems. Then we examine how conditions in global markets influencing transportation, storage, order processing, and packaging functions also influence these formulas. For example, longer distances traveled by products moving through channels and frequent lack of facilities for the efficient warehousing of goods and processing of orders affect inventory management. Finally, we examine how total cost and total systems concepts can mitigate adverse aspects of these conditions.

BALANCING COSTS AGAINST CUSTOMERS

All three formulas begin with the notion that Merton, ideally, would like to respond 100 percent to customer demand for MM systems by filling every order placed. They realize, however, that items in stock incur a diversity of carrying costs—including insurance, interest, warehouse utilities, obsolescence, and damage—so carrying enough inventory to fill all orders would incur excessive costs. On the other hand, carrying insufficient levels of stock could decrease sales and profits as customers switch to other sellers who can fill orders more reliably. The challenge, then, is to balance costs and potential profits.

• *THE REORDER POINT FORMULA*

The first formula for achieving this balance between costs and profits— the reorder point formula—ensures that there will be sufficient merchandise in inventory to fill customer orders often enough to keep them satisfied. Here is how this formula was applied by Merton's domestic distributor to ensure that customer orders are filled 90 percent of the time:

Order Lead Time		Usage Rate		Safety Stock		Reorder Point
6 days	×	2 MMs per day	+	5 MMs	=	17 MMs

Note that, after a distributor places an order for MM systems, it will take an expected 6 days (order lead time) for the order to arrive. During this period, the distributor will sell, on average, 2 MMs each day. To account for the odd day when the distributor sells more than 2 MMs (say, 6), a safety stock of 5 MMs is kept as a backup. Thus, when the inventory level gets down to 17 MMs (the reorder point), an order should be put in for a sufficient quantity of MM systems to take care of customer needs while waiting for the order to arrive.

• *THE EOQ FORMULA*

The EOQ formula shows the quantity of stock to reorder when the reorder point (e.g., 17MMs) is reached. As quantities ordered increase, economies of scale lower the cost of ordering each individual item. For example, one purchase order, costing $20 to process, can be used to order one or one thousand MMs; obviously, if 1,000 are ordered for inventory, ordering costs per unit ordered will be quite low. However, each item ordered incurs carrying costs (as already noted) so if 1,000 MMs were ordered, these costs would far exceed ordering cost savings.

The economic order quantity formula shows the trade-off point (i.e., the quantity ordered) at which ordering and carrying costs are equal (Figure 19-2). This also happens to be the lowest total cost for ordering the item:

$$EOQ = \frac{2 \, SO}{iP}$$

where S = annual quantity sold in units, O = cost of placing an order, i = carrying cost as a percent of selling price, and P = price per unit.

For example, assume the following figures for the domestic distributor of MM systems: S is 500, O is $20, i is 20 percent, and P (the price of each MM) is $2,000. Plugging these figures into the EOQ formula produces a figure of 7. In other words, the distributor should reorder 7 MMs each time the reorder point of 17 MMs (determined by the first formula) is reached. Since annual quantity sold is 500, 71 orders will be placed over the course of the year.

• *THE AVERAGE INVENTORY FORMULA*

The third formula employed by Merton distributors used data from the first two formulas to determine average inventory size (i.e., the average amount of MM systems in inventory at any given time). This formula is

$$AI = \frac{OQ}{2 + ss}$$

Average inventory AI is the amount of inventory ordered each time OQ (from the EOQ formula) divided by 2 and added to the safety stock ss (also used in the reorder point formula). Thus, assuming the Merton distributor maintains a safety stock of 5, average inventory would be rounded off 8 (7/2 + 5). Average inventory is especially useful as a basis of comparison with inventory management results of other competitors. For example, an excessively high average inventory figure might suggest that the distributor's carrying costs are too high.

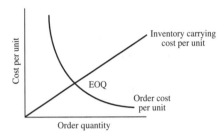

Figure 19–2. EOQ Is Point at Which Ordering and Carrying Costs Intersect

LOGISTICS FUNCTIONS AFFECT INVENTORY IN GLOBAL MARKETS

To examine how conditions in global markets affect these three inventory management formulas—and, by extension, quantities and costs of inventory maintained—assume the following changes in the numbers plugged into the formulas as a result of Merton attempting to penetrate the Indonesian market. These numbers, which might apply to a single distributor in Indonesia, are probably conservative (e.g., lead time could easily grow to more than 50 days).

• *REORDER POINT FORMULA*

1. Order lead time has been extended from 6 to 24 days because of longer distances, more channel intermediaries and facilitators to deal with, administrative and customs delays, and materials handling and physical distribution delays (special packing for transit, poor inland transit, etc.).

2. Sales still average two MM systems per day; however:

3. Safety stock requirements double, from 5 MM systems to 10 systems, largely due to (1) inconsistency of deliveries due to transport of shipments among different transportation modes, and (2) less predictable sales patterns in a new global market as compared to the domestic market.

Given these changes, the reorder point now changes from 17 to 58 MM systems; that is, when inventory reaches the level of 58 MM systems, more inventory will be ordered (i.e., 24 days × 2 MM systems sold each day + 10 MMs in the safety stock).

EOQ FORMULA

1. Annual quantity sold S is still 500 units.
2. Cost of placing an order O increases from $20 to $40, mainly due to additional paperwork and red tape involved in dealing with more intermediaries and facilitators, over longer distances, to place and expedite orders.
3. The price of each MM system P increases from $2,000 in the domestic market to $3,000 in this new foreign market, primarily to cover additional logistical costs involved in transporting the MM systems to Indonesia, and start-up marketing costs involved in aggressively entering this new market.
4. Inventory carrying cost as a percent of the $3,000 selling price remains at 20 percent.

Although the numbers plugged into the EOQ formula as applied in the Indonesian market have changed appreciably, the actual economic quantity of MM systems to order when the reorder point (58) is reached increases only from 7 to 8. Size of average inventory in Indochina, however, now increases from 8 MM systems to 14 systems, along with an increase in the costs of carrying this inventory.

INVENTORY AS AN INFLATION HEDGE

Beyond the formulas that help determine inventory size, reorder points, and quantities to reorder, another consideration affecting inventory policy in global markets pertains to currency exchange fluctuations. For example, in situations where a host country's currency is about to be devalued, increasing inventory will reduce the exporter's exposure to devaluation losses that would result from holding cash. Similarly, large inventories can provide a hedge against high inflation rates in that, unlike cash, its price can be increased in tandem with inflation rates. In such circumstances, the exporter must assess the trade-off costs of maintaining larger inventories versus the exchange rate savings from hedging against inflation or devaluation.

TRADE-OFFS AMONG LOGISTICS FUNCTIONS OPTIMIZE COSTS

Viewing these logistical functions from a total systems/cost perspective, Merton planners can implement a number of trade-offs to reduce overall logistics costs in serving the Indonesian market while making the entire logistics system work more efficiently. For example, setting up sourcing and production facilities in Indochina, while potentially expensive, might be cost-effective when compared to costs incurred in transporting MM systems from the U.S. mainland. Other trade-offs might involve altering transportation modes, improving order transmittal procedures (e.g., direct computer-order entry), and locating storage faciliites in low cost locations.

MANAGING THE LOGISTICS FUNCTION

Two general options are available to exporters in managing the logistics function: Do it yourself, or let someone else do it for you. If the first option is selected, two other possibilities present themselves.

Under a centralized framework, both local and headquarters management would report to a single person at headquarters with authority for coordinating and controlling logistics activities. This framework, which helps achieve cohesion, fast decision making, and economies of scale, is especially effective when the objective is rapid growth in global markets. A potential drawback is the ill will that can arise when local managers are appraised and rewarded on the basis of performance they do not control.

Under a decentralized framework, subsidiaries are perceived as profit centers, with managers given authority and responsibility to develop and implement marketing plans and programs. This framework works best when the firm serves many diverse global markets. Among the advantages of this model are better training and satisfaction of local managers and the ability to adopt to local conditions. However, some benefits of centralization are lost, such as coordinating diverse marketing plans and achieving quantity transportation discounts.

CONTRACT LOGISTICS USES SPECIALISTS

A growing preference among global firms, adopted by about one-third of the Fortune 500 companies, is contract logistics, whereby logistical management is contracted out to third-party logistics providers with specialized logistics experience and expertise. Services offered by these providers range widely, from purely consultive services based on proprietary systems and data bases, through subcontracting out portions of the logistical task, to use of their own assets to perform a complete logistics service. A key benefit of contracting out the logistics function to full-service providers in foreign markets is the ability to take advantage of an in-place network of channels and facilities able to start up and maintain materials management and physical distribution activities in unfamiliar markets. Global Focus 19-2 highlights dramatic benefits that can derive from such a full-service contractual arrangement.

GLOBAL FOCUS 19-2

How BLS Simplified NSC's Delivery Problem

Today, information moves around the world in a blink of an eye, and semiconductors are instrumental in making this happen. Increasingly, producers of semiconductors recognize that their product itself needs to move from producer to consumer nearly as fast.

One company that attempts to do just that is National Semiconductor Corporation (NSC) located in California. The firm realized that, in order to allow greater speed of delivery, its global supply network needed an overhaul. The old logistical network of decentralized control was a tangle of unnecessary interchanges, propped up by 44 different international freight forwarders and 18 different air carriers. "The complexity of it all wasn't allowing consistent service," commented Kevin Phillips, NSC director of worldwide logistics.

National Semiconductor wanted to change its 5- to 18-day delivery time and offer a 2-day delivery guarantee. The key factor in the strategy was the recruitment of a third-party logistics firm to provide valuable expertise as well as needed infrastructure. NSC turned to Federal Express's Business Logistics Services (BLS) as a partner. Phillips explained, "Our company competes on technology; we cannot compete on logistics; Federal's core competency is delivery; it can do what we can't. BLS was able to provide National Semiconductor with a formidable logistics network by granting access to 420 aircraft, 1869 worldwide facilities, more than 100,000 computer terminals; 31,000 surface vehicles; and an infrastructure with more than 90,000 employees. Phillips views NSC's partnership with Federal as "using the experts who spend billions on logistics."

Source: "Macro Logistics for Microprocessors," *Distribution* (April 1993), pp. 66–72. Permission granted by *Distribution*, the U.K.'s leading logistics magazine.

CHAPTER PERSPECTIVE

This chapter examines the logistical function in international markets, encompassing such materials management and physical distribution functions as packaging, transportation, storage, order processing and inventory control. Particularly in global markets, with longer transportation routes and more intermediaries to deal with, the high cost of logistical activities is usually the single largest deterrent to successful market entry. Guided by total systems and total cost concepts, logistics managers help transform these high costs into sizable savings by treating discrete logistics functions as components of a single system, with trade-offs within and among them to generate optimal efficiences at minimal cost. This chapter also examined situations in which centralized, decentralized, or third-party approaches for managing the logistics function were appropriate.

KNOW THE CONCEPTS

TERMS FOR STUDY

bulk service
cargo carrier
Carriage of Goods by Sea Act
carriers
contract logistics
economic order quantity (EOQ)
electronic data interchange (EDI)
electronic point of sale (EPOS)
factor endowment differentials
foreign trade zones
intermodal containers
inventory management
just in time (JIT)

logistics management
materials management
order cycle
order processing
packaging
physical distribution
reorder point
storage
total costs
total systems
trade-offs
tramp service
transportation modes

MATCHUP EXERCISES

1. Match up the first-column concept with the second-column descriptor.

1. global logistics

2. materials management

a. timely arrival of goods into and through the firm

b. movement of finished parts to customers

3. physical distribution

c. flow of products into, through, and out of international companies

4. logistics management

d. coordinates materials management and physical distribution

2. Match up the concepts in the second column with the logistics functions in the first column.

1. packaging
2. order processing
3. inventory management
4. transportation
5. storage

a. EPOS
b. RORO
c. EOQ
d. Carriage of Goods by Sea Act
e. foreign trade zones

3. Match up the inventory management concept in the first column with the descriptor in the second column.

1. the inventory level that triggers another order
2. the amount ordered when this level is reached
3. the time it takes between when the order is placed and the ordered goods arrive
4. making sure inventory arrives at precisely the time it is needed

a. EOQ
b. RP
c. order cycle
d. JIT

QUESTIONS FOR REVIEW AND DISCUSSION

1. Differences between distribution systems in the United States and Russia are striking. For example, in the United States in 1996, 40 percent of all shipments were delivered under quick response JIT conditions, with distribution costs representing about 10 percent of sales. In Russia, however, quick response is often no response, and costs of this sluggish distribution are about 300 percent higher than they are in the United States. In terms of logistical concepts, discuss reasons for this cost-effectiveness disparity.

2. One logistical system that does work well in Russia is that comprising McDonald's enterprise. From a joint venture agreement signed in 1988 (the largest ever between a food company and the then Soviet Union), this enterprise, by 1993, was the largest McDonald's restaurant in the world—employing over 1,000 people and serving 50,000 people daily—a 10,000 square-meter food production and distribution center. Located in the Moscow suburb of Solntsevo, the distribution center supplied the restaurant located in the center of Moscow and was itself supplied by farmers throughout Russia who had contracted to provide quality food supplies, including beef, onions, fruit, lettuce, pickles, milk, flour, butter, and a variety of potatoes needed to make McDonald's famous french fries. At full capacity, the meat line produces 10,000 patties per hour, and the bakery line, over 14,000 buns per hour. Storage space at the center holds 3,000 tons of potatoes, and the pie line produces 5,000 pies per hour. As with restaurants in the McDonald's chain built in Russia after 1993, the original Moscow restaurant accepted only rubles.

In terms of the McDonald's enterprise, define the following concepts: physical distribution, materials management, logistics management, total systems, total cost.

3. Which mode of transportation would you judge to be most appropriate for the following products and why:

- Kegs of beer for a fraternity party

- The late Jacqueline Kennedy's personal effects, auctioned off in New York

- Oil from Saudi Arabia to the United States

4. Here are three inventory management problems for the same company and product. The first involves reorder points, the second economic order quantities, and the third average inventory size:

- *Reorder point.* Assuming a distributor of consumer electronics products sells an average of five computer modems a day, desires a safety stock of 20 modems, and realizes that it will require an average of 20 days for an order of modems to arrive from the manufacturer, how many modems will remain in inventory when an order is placed?

- *Economic order quantity.* Assume that the annual demand for modems is 1,000 units, the ordering cost per unit is $25, and the inventory carrying costs are 25 percent of the $100 selling price of each modem. What is the amount to be ordered when the already determined reorder point is reached? How many orders would be placed in a year?

- *Average inventory size.* Given these facts and figures, what is this firm's average inventory of modems?

ANSWERS

MATCHUP EXERCISES

1. 1c, 2a, 3b, 4d
2. 1d, 2a, 3c, 4b, 5e
3. 1b, 2a, 3c, 4d

QUESTIONS FOR REVIEW AND DISCUSSION

1. The root cause of this disparity traces largely to 70 years of centralized command economy stress on productivity, while the means for
distributing this output (e.g., advertising agencies, banks, wholesale
and retail outlets) were generally perceived as lecherous, unproductive middlemen. As a result, distribution in Russia is primitive at best,
with poor supply lines and use of warehouse space, insufficient distribution and service centers, inadequate transportation facilities, and
archaic inventory management systems. What was generally ignored
in Marxist central planning is the value of the place/time/possession
utilities created by an efficient logistics system. Thus, for example, if
you purchase a digital watch battery in a supermarket you get the
proper battery, in a convenient location, when you need it, for a reasonable price. In creating these utilities, the distribution system also
performs a number of functions, often better than they could be performed by the producer, such as finding customers, matching products to customer needs, grading and storing products, financing purchases, and developing first-hand marketing information. Actually, an
efficient distribution system with a diversity of channels and intermediaries usually reduces the price we pay for products, as evidenced
by a comparison of prices for similar products in economies with
strong, mature logistical systems and those with weak, archaic
systems.

2. Physical distribution encompasses the broad range of functions
involved in the efficient delivery of foods from Russian farmers to the
production/distribution center, and from the center to the restaurant,
including packaging, transportation, order processing, inventory management, and storage. Materials management encompasses systems,
procedures, and controls to ensure that these functions work together
efficiently in moving raw materials (potatoes, lettuce) and finished
goods (Big Macs) to designated places, at designated times, in proper
condition. Logistics management entails the initial planning of phys-

ical distribution and materials management systems and activities, following total systems and total cost concepts. The total systems concept would view all physical distribution functions as a single integrated entity, with decisions in any one area affecting decisions in all other areas. For example, the decision to transport raw materials from the farms to the processing center and from the processing center to the McDonald's restaurant, in the fastest, most expensive way possible, consistent with JIT mandates, might dramatically improve the functioning of order processing, storage, and inventory management functions. The related total cost concept identifies a set of alternatives that optimize the cost-benefit relationships. For example, in the example just given (i.e., large investments in transportation and state-of-the-art order processing and inventory managment functions), total benefits in terms of zero-wastage of products and rapid preparation, presentation, and purchase of menu items might easily justify this expense.

3. Kegs of beer. by truck, because they require flexibility in delivery and are traveling a short distance

Jackie O's effects. by air, because they are high in value and low in bulk

Oil. by pipeline and water transport, because it isn't solid and must move a long distance

4. Reorder point:

Order Lead Time		Usage Rate		Safety Stock		Reorder Point
20	×	5	+	20	=	120

Economic order quantity:

$$EOQ = \frac{2(1,000)\ (25)}{(0.25)\ (100)} = 500 = 22$$

Average Inventory = OQ/2 + ss = 22.5 + 20 = 43

INDEX